Translated Nation

Translated Nation
Rewriting the Dakhóta Oyáte

Christopher Pexa

 University of Minnesota Press
Minneapolis
London

An earlier version of chapter 1 was published as "Transgressive Adoptions: Dakota Prisoners' Resistances to State Domination Following the 1862 U.S.–Dakota War," *Wicazō Ša Review* 30, no. 1 (2015): 29–56. Portions of chapter 2 were published as "More Than Talking Animals: Charles Alexander Eastman's Animal Peoples and Their Kinship Critiques of United States Colonialism," *PMLA* 131, no. 3 (2016): 652–67; and "Citizen Kin: Charles Eastman's Reworking of U.S. Citizenship," *SAIL* 29, no. 3 (2017): 1–28.

Copyright 2019 by the Regents of the University of Minnesota

All rights reserved. No part of this publication may be reproduced, stored in a retrieval system, or transmitted, in any form or by any means, electronic, mechanical, photocopying, recording, or otherwise, without the prior written permission of the publisher.

Published by the University of Minnesota Press
111 Third Avenue South, Suite 290
Minneapolis, MN 55401-2520
http://www.upress.umn.edu

Printed in the United States of America on acid-free paper

The University of Minnesota is an equal-opportunity educator and employer.

27 26 25 24 23 22 21 20 19   10 9 8 7 6 5 4 3 2 1

Library of Congress Cataloging-in-Publication Data
Names: Pexa, Christopher, author.
Title: Translated nation : rewriting the Dakhóta Oyáte / Christopher Pexa.
Description: Minneapolis : University of Minnesota Press, [2019] | Includes bibliographical references and index. |
Identifiers: LCCN 2018039742 (print) | ISBN 978-1-5179-0070-0 (hc) | ISBN 978-1-5179-0071-7 (pb)
Subjects: LCSH: Dakota Indians—Historiography. | Dakota Indians—History—19th century. | Dakota Indians—Government relations—History—19th century. | Dakota Indians—Intellectual life | Dakota Indians—Interviews. | BISAC: HISTORY / Native American. | LITERARY CRITICISM / Native American. | SOCIAL SCIENCE / Ethnic Studies / Native American Studies.
Classification: LCC E99.D1 P49 2019 (print) | DDC 978.004/975243—dc23
LC record available at https://lccn.loc.gov/2018039742

For my parents, Donna and Dennis

Contents

Preface	ix
Note on Language and Orthography	xiv
Introduction: Ambivalence and the Unheroic Decolonizer	1
1. Transgressive Adoptions	33
First Interlude: Grace Lambert, Personal Interview, Fort Totten, Spirit Lake Nation, August 10, 1998	61
2. (Il)legible, (Il)liberal Subjects: Charles Alexander Eastman's Poetics of Withholding	89
Second Interlude: Interview with Grace Lambert, Taté Tópa Dakhóta Wóunspe (Four Winds Dakota Teaching) Program, March 10, 1993	137
3. Territoriality, Ethics, and Travel in the Black Elk Transcripts	147
4. Peoplehood Proclaimed: Publicizing Dakhóta Women in Ella Cara Deloria's *Waterlily*	183
Third Interlude: Interview with Lillian Chase, Taté Tópa Dakhóta Wóunspe Program, Fort Totten, Spirit Lake Nation, February 26, 1993	221
Conclusion: Gathering the People	235
Acknowledgments	243
Appendix: Dakhóta Pronunciation Guide	247
Notes	249
Index	289

Preface

In Cannon Ball, North Dakota, during the summer and fall of 2016, in order to protect Íŋyaŋ Wakȟáŋǧapi Wakpá (River That Makes the Sacred Stones), or the Missouri River, from incursion and spoliation by the Dakota Access Pipeline, the #NoDAPL movement was born—or rather, it reemerged as the latest face of a centuries-long struggle against colonization of territories historically occupied by the Očhéti Šakówiŋ Oyáte, or People of the Seven Council Fires. The Oyáte are the confederacy of allied bands comprising the eastern Dakhóta-speaking Sisíthuŋwaŋ (Sisseton, or Dwellers of the Fishing Grounds), Bdewákhaŋthuŋwaŋ (Mdewakanton, or Dwellers of Spirit Lake), Waȟpéthuŋwaŋ (Wahpeton, or Leaf-Dwellers), and Waȟpékhute (Wahpekute, or Leaf Shooters) bands, the middle Nakhóta-speaking Iháŋkthuŋwaŋ (Yankton, or Dwellers at the End) and Iháŋkthuŋwaŋna (Yanktonai, or Little Dwellers at the End), and the western Lakȟótiyapi speakers, the Thítȟuŋwaŋ (Teton, or Prairie Dwellers). #NoDAPL and the camps at Cannon Ball were founded as nonviolent and prayerful acts to protect the water. And while the Oyáte have long occupied these lands, its reemergence in such an internationally visible and powerful way is remarkable. As founder of the Sacred Stone Camp, LaDonna Brave Bull Allard observed, "This is the first [physical] gathering of the Očhéti Šakówiŋ (Sioux tribes) since the Battle of the Greasy Grass (Battle of Little Bighorn) 140 years ago."[1] Although the water protectors' camps at Cannon Ball were eventually evacuated and bulldozed by the Bureau of Indian Affairs, the movement lives on in the chorus of Mní Wichóni (water is life or water is alive)—a phrase that has accrued broadly ecological meanings in addition to ones specifically grounded in Dakhóta/Lakȟóta/Nakhóta[2] sovereignty and ways of knowing.

We live in a time of Indigenous resurgence where, as Leanne Simpson (Michi Saagiig Nishnaabeg) declares, we are moving "ourselves beyond resistance and survival, to flourishment of our nations through the rebuilding of our own political and intellectual traditions."[3] The

FIGURE 1. Grandmas (from left to right) Lydia, Lillian, Grace, and Rachel Langer Young (with unidentified man in middle and child on right) in Fort Totten, North Dakota, circa 1940. Photographer unknown.

making of decolonial space at Standing Rock was a meaningful moment of resurgence for Dakhóta Oyáte and other Indigenous allies. But it was one whose global visibility and appeal the settler-state responded to with radically increased surveillance, militarized police force, and violence. Part of that violence was representational and involved state disinformation campaigns, as with the Morton County police department's allegation that water protectors were engaged in "an ongoing riot" on November 20, 2016, as they attempted to hold their position on the Backwater Bridge just outside the Očhéti Šakówiŋ camp.[4] How and to what effect settler regimes represent resurgent indigeneity as both eminently knowable and aberrant, and

PREFACE — xi

the strategies of Indigenous mobilization and resurgence these characterizations give rise to, are in large part what this book is about.

Between the Battle of Greasy Grass and the water protectors at Cannon Ball is a kind of long pause, a drawing in of breath. It is in the duration of this pause that *Translated Nation* enters. It interrogates how Dakhóta intellectuals used and revised liberal frameworks of belonging, including notions of citizenship, property holding, and territory, both to conceal from settler view and to reclaim for Dakhóta communities core relational philosophies based in the thióśpaye, or Dakhóta extended family. I begin with the 1862 U.S.–Dakhóta War's assault on Dakhóta peoplehood, and I end not with the 1934 Indian Reorganization Act, which sought to devolve some measure of self-determination back to tribes, but with oral histories of Dakhóta elders given in the 1990s. While this is a work of Indigenous literary criticism that foregrounds questions of representation, it also rearticulates community history and presence by centering Dakhóta archives past and present. As both of these things, it has been strongly shaped by critical methods and approaches from literary Indigenous studies. The kinds of questions I ask here include the following: What acts of Indigenous relinking to the past appear in the guise of complicity, or of acceding to assimilation's demands? How do notions of decolonization based in resistance privilege what's active and explicit rather than what's understated and covert? What forms of decolonial freedom come into view when we look beyond assimilation and resistance? How has the assimilation era often been misconstrued as a period of vacantness rather than one that laid the discursive and conceptual ground for contemporary Indigenous politics based in resurgent peoplehood?

Translated Nation offers an interrogation of settler-colonial regimes of legibility that sought to make assimilation-era Indigenous people legible as subjects of the settler-state, and of how Dakhóta intellectuals both used and defused these modes of control to rewrite and remake the Oyáte in literary forms. Reading written and oral materials—letters from Dakhóta prisoners, interviews by Nicholas Black Elk (Oglála), autobiographies, political tracts, and children's books by Charles Alexander Eastman (Waȟpéthuŋwaŋ), pageants and novels by Ella Cara Deloria (Iháŋkthuŋwaŋ), as well as contemporary oral histories of elders from the Mní Wakȟáŋ Oyáte (Spirit Lake Nation, or People)—I argue that it is in the most colonially complicitous poses where we find Dakhóta staking out representational territory for other

Dakhóta and doing the future-oriented work of remaking the people by reinvigorating the people's ethics.

This is a tribally specific, even a Dakhóta-centric, study, but its readings of Dakhóta texts will, I hope, provide some analogies for how other tribal peoples not only survived settler-colonists' attempts to eradicate and replace them but also laid groundwork for their own resurgences. I use Dakhóta terms when possible, and I play the role of translator in substituting key terms in Dakhóta when their English equivalents hold (or withhold) crucial relational meanings. These substitutions have allowed me not only to teach my readers something about the wide range of ways in which Dakhóta concepts and meanings informed the work of the intellectuals I examine but also to leverage linguistic translation in our present moment as a mode of cultural reclamation. For Dakhóta language students (like myself), I hope that placing literary texts in conversation with the rich meanings and nuances of certain Dakhóta words and concepts will be useful.

Another of the book's aims is to further develop an Indigenous peoplehood framework. Daniel Heath Justice (Cherokee) defines Indigenous "peoplehood" as being a matter of participating in the "relational reality of the tribal nation."[5] I reframe here Justice's notion of "relational reality" in relation to Dakhóta authors' performances within, and citations of, historical, oral-historical, literary, and ethnographic genres. Specifically, I explore how modern forms of Dakhóta relationality cite cosmological contexts in which peoplehood is a shared existential and political condition for various classes of beings, including humans, animals, and other-than-human persons such as spirits, rocks, and lightning. As an alternative to settler-colonial views of land as property or space abstracted away from interpersonal, everyday relations, land emerges from these Dakhóta texts as a sociopolitical location. Its political actors include these human and other-than-human persons, and through their mutual dialogue, the land becomes a common place, first in the sense of being a trope of Dakhóta historical presence in long-occupied homelands, and second as a place held in common among Dakhóta persons through which the ethical norms of peoplehood may be exercised.

Translated Nation explores what a concept of decolonial translation, considered as a tool for withholding knowledge and for creating opacities, could mean for how we think about Indigenous life and community rebuilding during moments when survival appears perhaps least likely, and ambivalences most disabling. As a critical intervention, decolonial translation describes how the upholding of settler-colonial logics of representation, of "playing Indian" in a bad or retrograde sense, in fact created space for Dakhóta intellectuals to cite, in ways that were illegible to settler audiences, Dakhóta ethical norms as a means of linking back to and reconstructing a peoplehood based in ethics of the thióšpaye. Translation shows up as intertextual proliferation and is a resurgent rather than resistive textual practice. This exploration entails a shift in how we imagine lived experiences of indigeneity during the federal policy era of allotment and assimilation, when Indigenous individuals' forms of self-publicity were often demonized as "savagely" authentic on the one hand or Christian, genteel, and harmless on the other—an either/or that has also crucially opened space for reclamations of gender identities that had been criminalized by the state.

This book invokes but ultimately goes beyond a standard periodization. To tell the story of the Oyáte's remaking only by focusing on the years between, say, the 1862 war and the 1934 Indian Reorganization Act would unduly privilege the settler-state's sense of time. In fact this book begins in the near present with Dakhóta women, some of whose voices run through its chapters. It began especially with my unćidaŋ, my maternal grandmother, Rachel Charboneau (née Langer Young), and in the conversations I overheard among adults and relatives who would gather around her kitchen table in her white and salmon, state-of-the-art Marlette mobile home in Rapid City. There were stories of young lovers frozen to death in the back of a hearse, scandalous stories of living lovers, weird stories about the relations between ghosts and humans, horror stories of the Grey Nuns' boarding school, and long-ago stories of talking animals, rocks, lightning, and other powerful nonhuman persons. They drew me in as a listener again and again, populating my childhood dreams and going to work on me still even as a much older person, leading me to ask my unčí and her sister, my grandma, Grace Lambert, about some of these stories and about how they could be devout Catholics yet relish telling me about how the Wakíŋyaŋ (Thunder Beings) once blasted a missionary's giant wooden cross from the top of Crow Hill. From that kind of contradiction, some of the main lines of this book began to take shape.

Note on Language and Orthography

Throughout this book, I write the Dakhóta language using the Standard Dakhóta Orthography. In cases where the original text uses another writing system, as with Clifford Canku and Michael Simons's translations of prisoners' letters, with the missionary Stephen Riggs's letters, and in Wazíyatawiŋ's *Remember This,* I retain spellings and orthographies from the original texts. The pronunciation guide at the end of the book is adapted from teaching materials used at a 2017 Dakhóta language camp in Bloomington, Minnesota.

Introduction

Ambivalence and the Unheroic Decolonizer

This book develops an approach to reading literary accounts of Dakhóta[1] life and agency during the allotment and assimilation era, when pressures from American settler society threatened the existence of Dakhóta and other Indigenous peoples through legal, military, religious, and other means. The allotment and assimilation era is typically regarded to coincide with the opening of the Carlisle Indian School in 1879 and with Congress's passage of the Wheeler–Howard Act, or the Indian Reorganization Act, in 1934.[2] I ask how Dakhóta people during this period took American settler-colonial demands to become productive, property-owning, Christian, and presumptively heterosexual U.S. subjects, then translated, or critically reframed, these into terms and uses consistent with Dakhóta ethics, gender understandings, and social practices. A kind of cultural camouflage allowed Dakhóta people to navigate the exterminatory violence of the so-called Indian wars of the mid- to late nineteenth century by creating accounts of Dakhóta life that played up its innocuousness, transparency, and availability to the settler society. They did so in part by virtue of being written in the colonizer's language and by using settler-colonial venues and literary genres: Ella Cara Deloria wrote a romance novel, ethnographies, and pageants, while Nicholas Black Elk performed mock ceremonies for white tourists, and Charles Alexander Eastman helped white children to "play Indian" by working with Ernest Thompson Seton and the Boy Scouts of America. Too often these intellectuals have been regarded as accommodationist at worst, or hopelessly ambivalent at best. But these were not the actions of sellouts engaged in translating Dakhóta life without pause for whites; nor were their ambivalences disabling. Instead these were translations done with pause; they were cultural performances that refused to disclose the ethical and political heart of the people who refused to assent to settler-colonial choices as presented yet also indulged in photo ops, both figurative and actual, for the settler society.

1

Some of the earliest literary representations of the Oyáte written by a Dakhóta author were Eastman's autobiographical sketches of "the wild life" before reservations, published in 1893–94 in *St. Nicholas: An Illustrated Magazine for Young Folks*. Given the exterminatory violence of the so-called Indian wars, these depictions were maybe understandably benign, playing up images of Indigenous backwardness, vanishing, and wildness.[3] Such images frequently appeared in more politicized settings, too. When Eastman joined Sherman Coolidge, Laura Cornelius Kellogg, Carlos Montezuma, Arthur Parker, and others to form the Society of American Indians (SAI) in Columbus, Ohio, in October 1911, they couched their purpose in notions of racial uplift for Indians, with the 1911 constitution including as its first article the goal "to promote and co-operate with all efforts looking to the advancement of the Indian in enlightenment which leave him free as a man to develop according to the natural laws of social evolution."[4]

These framings, based in an assimilation–resistance binary, continue to inform critical views of Indigenous life and agency during the assimilation era. For instance, Robert Warrior (Osage) cites "the blinding progressivistic optimism" of Eastman and other SAI members as evidence of their generation's inheriting "the integrationist legacy of post–Wounded Knee existence."[5] On the flip side of Warrior's reading, Siobhan Senier finds that "American Indian writers, especially under the threat of assimilation, explored a wide range of resistance strategies" to settler individualism, especially by invoking what she calls (following Jace Weaver's coinage) Indigenous "communitism."[6] Mediating somewhat between these critical views is one like Philip Deloria's (Yankton Dakhóta), which notes how the members of the SAI were and continue to be followed by "the shadow of assimilation," having been involved in "church, ethnography, museums, the colonial bureaucracy."[7] Despite acknowledging this "shadow," Deloria admits he can't hold back his admiration for someone like Eastman, calling him "such an extraordinary figure" that it would be difficult to look him in the face if he were to step out of the past and walk into the room right now.[8] Of these critical responses to assimilation-era writers, I find Deloria's to be maybe the most humanely insightful. My sense is that part of what made Eastman—like the other intellectuals examined in this book—so extraordinary was a deep love for his Dakhóta people but also how he negotiated what Kiara Vigil calls "an American cultural repertoire" of Indigenous authenticity, vanishing, and primitivism to embody and voice that love as a way of continuing the Oyáte into the future.[9]

While my reading of these future-oriented writings and performances is indebted to these and other scholars' work on assimilation-era Native authors and intellectuals, my focus here is more Dakhóta-centric than theirs. I highlight the tribally specific linguistic and epistemological grounds for Dakhóta intellectuals' uses of popular literary and performance genres to criticize settler-colonial society and, crucially, to remake Dakhóta peoplehood in ways that were largely unintelligible to white audiences except as nostalgic invocations of tradition. I read the emergence of this peoplehood, and its grounding in what I call thióšpaye ethics, across a range of texts and archives, including letters from Dakhóta prisoners, interviews by Nicholas Black Elk (known as Black Elk or Heȟáka Sápa), autobiographies, political tracts, and children's books by Ohíye s'a (Wins Often, or Charles Alexander Eastman), pageants and novels by Aŋpétu Wašté Wíŋ (Beautiful Day Woman, or Ella Cara Deloria), and contemporary oral histories of elders from the Mní Wakhán Oyáte (Spirit Lake Nation). These texts and archives reveal how Dakhóta intellectuals negotiated their own self-publicity in the wake of the U.S.–Dakhóta War, playing to liberal regimes of legibility while honoring and remaking tribal ties. Rather than focusing on the disabling aspects of ambivalence or multiple identifications, I draw out how Dakhóta intellectuals have used multiplicity, a representational shiftiness, to remain part of their own social frameworks while negotiating the possibilities and violences of what up to that point had been settler framings, ideologies, and social forms.[10]

As neither resistance writers nor fighters, Eastman's and other Dakhóta intellectuals' works form, for those in the know, a complex citational web of Dakhóta philosophy. To be in the know is to be aware of at least some portion of this web's basis in the thióšpaye, which means literally "camp circle" but which also suggests the Dakhóta extended family or band. As Ella Cara Deloria describes it in her popular ethnography *Speaking of Indians* (1944), the thióšpaye was at the heart of a Dakhóta sense of being civilized, where "to be civilized was to keep the rules imposed by kinship for achieving civility, good manners, and a sense of responsibility toward every individual dealt with."[11] Thióšpaye conceptualizations of virtue as existing in and deriving from relations of mutual responsibility shaped how assimilation-era Dakhóta authors imagined their place within their own communities, as well as how they wrote themselves as ambivalent yet autonomous, amiable but trenchant critics of the U.S. settler-state.

These citations of thióšpaye philosophy are the work of the unheroic decolonizer who sustains the life of the people, but whose heroism cannot be celebrated properly in his or her own time. After all, to pronounce the people (as a people, an Oyáte, and not a pan-Indian "race") as alive, rather than as already on their way out of the world, would have been a structural impossibility within settler fantasies of Indian vanishing. This sustaining work is still going on today, but in the open, heard in the voices and actions of living relatives, in the singing of a Custer scalping song to Minnesota tourists who listen uncomprehendingly with big smiles. As Leslie Marmon Silko describes in the closing pages of *Ceremony*, when faced with what has been withheld, one must have "the ear for the story" in order to discern the signal from the noise, to recognize the sources of meaning and vitality that can sustain the people: "In the west and in the south too, the clouds with round heavy bellies had gathered for the dawn. . . . The ear for the story and the eye for the pattern were theirs; the feeling was theirs; we came out of this land and we are hers."[12] This book tracks some of those sources, those givers of life for the Oyáte, beneath and within the clacking of rosaries, the tallying of blood quantum, and the pushing of the plow.

Rather than accommodating settler-colonial audiences, engagements and entanglements with settler society allowed the Dakhóta intellectuals I examine here to create embodied and literary forms of pageantry, or self-conscious publicity, to play up—as a ruse—Indian harmlessness, consumability, and vanishing. They did so as they remade the Oyáte in literary and performative ways. A rusing accommodation is partly what allowed for the covert resurgence I read in and as their citations of thióšpaye philosophy. Such rusing also crucially encoded (for other Dakhóta) the ethical basis for a resurgent peoplehood in view of settler audiences, whose comprehension of citational practices these intellectuals arguably did not solicit or want.

Citizens' Dress

Although it is a story of remaking and resurgence that I want to tell, that story begins in the rupture of the Oyáte because of settler-colonial violence and genocide. It was winter of 1862, Boxing Day, in the settlement of Mankato, Minnesota. On a scaffold erected for the occasion, thirty-eight hooded figures stood side by side, their bodies lining the square perimeter. A *New York Times* account from 1862 detailed "the ingenious manner" in which it was constructed, such that the condemned would drop simultaneously by virtue of a complex pulley system.[13] The same reporter described the crowd of "three to five thousand" gathered to witness the execution, with the street being so full that the "house tops were literally crowded" in order "to view the tragic scene."[14] This civilian audience was separated from the condemned by a sizable force of cavalry and infantrymen who might otherwise "take possession of the remaining prisoners and inflict summary punishment upon them." Once they were marched to the scaffold, the condemned Dakhóta were placed "round the platform," each "under the fatal noose," and were hooded. The rest of the writer's description wrangles with the men's last moments:

> All things being ready, the first tap was given, when the poor wretches made such frantic efforts to grasp each other's hands, that it was agony to behold them. Each one shouted out his name, that his comrades might know he was there. The second tap resounded on the air. The vast multitude were breathless with the awful surroundings of this solemn occasion. Again the doleful tap breaks on the stillness of the scene. Click! goes the sharp ax, and the descending platform leaves the bodies of thirty-eight human beings dangling in the air. The greater part died instantly; some few struggled violently, and one of the ropes broke, and sent its burden with a heavy, dull crash, to the platform beneath. A new rope was procured, and the body again swung up to its place. It was an awful sight to behold. Thirty-eight human beings suspended in the air, on the bank of the beautiful Minnesota; above, the smiling, clear, blue sky; beneath and around, the silent thousands, hushed to a deathly silence by the chilling scene before them, while the bayonets bristling in the sunlight added to the importance of the occasion.[15]

For those settlers in attendance, this moment's allure lay in its spectacle of avenging those who had been killed in the brief war waged by Thaóyate Dúta (His Scarlet People, aka Little Crow) and the Dakhóta warriors loyal to him.

That war, fought over the course of only six weeks in the autumn before the hangings, began over conditions of mass starvation among

Dakhóta that were created by delayed delivery of treaty annuities during the summer of 1862. But a deeper cause of the war and starvation was the removal of Dakhóta to a narrow, ten-mile strip along the south shore of the Minnesota River as a result of two land-cession treaties made in 1858.[16] Effectively exiled from homelands in Minnesota, and unable to subsist within this drastically diminished territory, eastern Dakhótas were forced to depend on government annuities, as promised by the United States in its earlier treaties signed at Traverse des Sioux in 1851. Historian Clifford Canku (Sisseton Wahpeton Dakhóta) gives the following account of the war's origins:

> So that impetus of taking away the land, the abundance of resources and so on was the main goal. . . . And that was the impetus of why they [Dakota] resisted. They didn't want to go to war. But what would you do if you were promised thousands and thousands of dollars if you moved onto a small portion of land, and the United States said we'll feed you, we'll give you implements so that you could be farmers, we'll do this, and we'll do that, and we'll do this. But when you did move onto those small pockets of land, you were starving. Your children were starving. Your women and your grandfathers and grandmothers, they were all starving. But what were they to do? So in this instance of Little Crow, they were pushed into a corner where they were either going to starve or resist.[17]

Canku describes here how Dakhóta people, despite having been promised land and farming tools from the 1851 treaty's "general agricultural improvement and civilization fund,"[18] found themselves cut off from traditional subsistence hunting and fishing (the Indian agent rejected missionary requests for ammunition, as this was seen as contrary to the civilizing mission), isolated from other relatives, and without promised tools and seeds, unable to grow sufficient food to survive.[19]

The *Times* reporter recalled "one little Hungarian boy" who had "lost his father and mother at the hands of the savages, and he shouted aloud 'Hurrah, hurrah!'" at the hanged men.[20] As the narration here merges the death of the warriors with the death of savagery itself, so the spectacle also sought to give proof of the inherent criminality of the Dakhóta warrior's body, enacting a fantasized ending not only to the Dakhóta "uprising" but also to a Dakhóta warrior masculinity.

INTRODUCTION 7

This settler-colonial fantasy denied the complex position of many Dakhóta who had lived with Presbyterian missionaries for some thirty years. That many of the condemned were converts and nominal, if not also formal, Minnesota citizens is noted by the *Times* special correspondent: "Nearly all these Indians were painted up in war style, and were hung in their blankets. The half-breeds wore citizens' dress."[21] Here the reference to "citizens' dress" recognizes how many Dakhóta, "half-breed" or not, had adopted aspects of settler society or "the customs and habits of civilization." In addition, we learn that "those professing to be Christianized sang 'I'm on the iron road to the spirit land,' while the 'bucks' sang a war song."[22] The *Times* account registers how some Dakhóta, like those who had been members of the Christianized Dakhóta community called the Hazelwood Republic (1854–62), were Minnesota citizens, as the Minnesota constitution had granted citizenship to white U.S. citizens and white immigrants but also to Indian people according to logics of blood and language: its third category granted citizenship to those possessing blood but not English, or "persons of mixed white and Indian blood, who have adopted the customs and habits of civilization." Its fourth category was for Dakhóta-only speakers, who constituted a majority at the time: "Persons of Indian blood residing in this State who have adopted the language customs and habits of civilization, after an examination by any District Court of the State, . . . and shall be pronounced by said court capable of enjoying the rights of citizenship within the State."[23] Dakhóta people have always occupied multiple spaces and identities, of course, and Hazelwood's example suggests how any perceived contradiction lay in policing access to settler citizenship based on one's proximity to whiteness.

Really, the *Times* article's last remark shows how the execution, even while staging a kind of colonial certitude about Indigenous others, was complicated by the prisoners' own blurring of relationships between heteropatriarchal Christianity and queer savagery, fort and blanket, colonizer and colonized. The hangings at Mankato drew out, in other words, the close interweavings of gender, criminality, and colonization in the courtroom, on the gallows, and in the years afterward, as a representational regime that sanctioned certain forms of Dakhóta life while barring others. In the trials preceding the execution, the testimony of one of the condemned men, "O-ta-kle, or Godfrey, a colored man connected with the Sioux tribe of Indians,"[24] described a similarly ambivalent position that many Dakhóta found themselves in at the outbreak of war. While mowing hay on the morning of August 19, 1862, when Dakhóta attacked the settler town of New Ulm, Minnesota, Joseph Godfrey, a "mulatto" farmer who was married to a Dakhóta woman, heard about the outbreak of war. After returning to his uncle's house to tell his wife the news, she warned him that if they did not try to get away from their farm, they "would be killed with the white people."[25] His uncle added that they "would be killed if we went toward the white folks; that we would only be safe to go on and join the Indians."[26] Heeding his uncle's warnings, Godfrey removed his metaphorical (and maybe actual) trousers and "put on the breech-clout."[27] Although he fought alongside the Dakhóta, Godfrey was praised by the military tribunal that was formed immediately after the war as "an instrument of justice" for his extensive testimony in more than fifty trials against other Dakhóta, who gave him the name Óta kté (Kills Many)—not for his battlefield prowess but for these courtroom betrayals. In spite of this use by the court, Godfrey was sentenced to death for having participated in the fighting, was subsequently spared by Abraham Lincoln along with 264 other condemned Dakhóta, and then was ultimately pardoned in 1866.[28]

Such ambivalences marked the difficult position not only of the condemned "half-breeds," of course, but that of many Dakhóta before and since the war, many of whom refused to fight against whites because they were related to them by marriage. As John Peacock explains, "Some Dakota families, indeed some Dakota individuals within their own minds, were (and continue to be) split between allegiances to full-blood relatives versus to the whites they married and with whom they had mixed-blood children."[29] Mixed or multiple allegiances were not new to the 1862 war either; rather, they had a long and significant history because intermarriage with non-Dakhóta was a common way for Dakhóta people to make alliances for peace and trade with other groups.[30]

If Godfrey's example and that of the "half-breeds" wearing "citizens' dress" suggest how Dakhóta people performed colonially legible selves even as they pursued agendas for and maintained loyalties to tribal relatives and communities, then ambivalence as an analytic may allow for reconsidering those complexities of self and community, person and people, under an assimilationist regime. Accordingly, I draw out forms of agency and community remaking that are illegible to the settler-state by asking what social forms and sympathies were not lost or capitulated but rather only deferred or driven underground

INTRODUCTION   9

in their translation from buckskin to balloon sleeves, from war song to praise song. I explore how Dakhóta responses to grievous conditions may be thought of as decolonial translations that were less acts of resistance than they were nuanced and covert acts of endurance, relinkings to the past, and resurgent movings toward the future. The works I discuss here are love letters to Dakhóta descendants not yet born; their safeguarding of a Dakhóta philosophy within complex citational practices was a way of helping to ensure that their children's children would someday be able to receive those letters and make themselves stronger through the reading of them.

Translation

The question of how Dakhóta peoplehood and kinship discourses are political negotiations structured in relation to a settler-state is a historical, and in this book a literary, one. It is also one of translation in a linguistic sense and is strongly informed by ways of being, doing, and knowing held in the Dakhóta language. Even though the authors I examine here wrote and published almost exclusively in English, they drew heavily on Dakhóta concepts, genres, and framings that are unique to the Dakhóta language. In foregrounding their citational practices, especially as these relate to notions of family, relatedness, and belonging, I share Dakhóta scholar and activist Wazíyatawiŋ's sense that for those raised in a Dakhóta-speaking family, "kinship terms . . . open doors to an entirely new set of values and move stated ideals about kinship from mere rhetoric in an intellectual argument to one based solidly in language and worldview."[31] I grew up addressing my relatives in such terms. I grew up hearing my unčí (maternal grandmother) talking with her sisters on the phone in Dakhóta. After her older sisters passed away and we visited the reservation less often, she spoke her mother tongue less frequently and so began, word by word, to lose the language. Still, she would teach me words and phrases, which I took with me into adulthood learning of the Dakhóta language. In writing this book, I have found that simple glosses or English-language equivalents for certain Dakhóta terms are inadequate for capturing the breadth and depth of their meanings, and in order to clarify these, I have consulted with community members and fluent Dakhóta speakers when possible or when necessary. I have also relied on intertextual analysis to capture both more complex and older contexts and meanings of certain key concepts like wakȟáŋ, which appears throughout this book but which I read most closely in my first chapter. The result is a mix of literary criticism, fieldwork, ethnohistory, and language activism.

However, what I have called ambivalence or unheroic decolonization is a political situation of brokerage and negotiation, and thus of translation in more than just a linguistic sense. This book's title on the one hand refers to settler-colonial framings of Indigenous peoples as domestic dependent nations. Other Indigenous studies scholars have used translation as a figure for settler-colonial processes of converting or transforming Indigenous lands and persons into property and heteronormatively gendered subjects. Eric Cheyfitz observes how translation, as an imperial and, one might say, racialized monologue, constitutes hierarchies of the literal versus the metaphoric, with the former being the proper/propertied domain of the empire and the latter being the appropriable stuff of the colonized.[32] In a similar vein, Mark Rifkin explains U.S. colonization during the allotment and assimilation era through translations or transpositions of Indigenous people's nonheteronormative sexualities and extended kinship networks into a heterosexual gender binary and nuclear family.[33] In this sense, it is the tribal nation that the settler translates into legible forms.

Following Scott Lyons (Anishinaabe and Dakhóta), I argue that to call Indigenous peoples "nations" is a relatively recent phenomenon that was inaugurated during the treaty-making era of U.S. Indian policy. As Lyons notes, treaties established Indigenous peoples as nations, ushering them into a colonial modernity as they did so. My sense, however, is that the vision of becoming modern implied within the term "nationhood" overshadows other practices of relinking to and rearticulating the past as an epistemological project for building Indigenous peoplehood in the present. In other words, to hitch our wagon to nationhood's modern star potentially obscures other ways of thinking about community, belonging, and sovereignty that are not based in the nation form and in the binds of state recognition within which tribal peoples are often caught. In this sense, as a corrective to an Indigenous nationalist paradigm,[34] my title references Dakhóta forms of community rebuilding, which were sometimes critiques of the settler-state and involved linking back to and rearticulating older forms of relation based in the thióśpaye and the Oyáte, but that were also in important ways entangled with the settler-state. These countertranslations' performance decoupled tribal peoplehood from tribal nationalism, tying the nation form most often to the settler-colonial state and to capitalistic exploitation of Indigenous lands, bodies, and lives. In this sense, it is the settler-colonial U.S. nation that is translated, its violence and exploitation of Indigenous people reflected back to itself and its settler citizens.

I make this claim about relinking to the past in full awareness of debates within Native American and Indigenous studies over reclamation as a problematically essentialist project that potentially creates or perpetuates gender-exclusionary practices through opportunistic (and often ahistorical) construals of tradition that are modeled more on settler constructions of sex and gender than on Indigenous ones.[35] Scholars like Elizabeth Povinelli and Audra Simpson (Kahnawake Mohawk) have criticized Indigenous essentialist claims for not always furthering the sovereignty of our communities, in part because they operate within settler-colonial parameters in which ethnographic or community-based knowledge is leveraged against Indigenous people in juridical contexts such as courtrooms, where proving ongoing connections to so-called tradition may be decisive in deciding land claims and other matters.[36] Simpson notes how the concept of radical indigenism, which appeared in the early 2000s and which aimed to reclaim Indigenous epistemologies as a decolonial practice, was "neither radical nor indigenous but rather, in the name of 'tradition,' structuring yet another expectation of a culturally 'pure' indigenous subject."[37] These representations, Simpson adds, do nothing to "contribute to our sovereignty" because they only further reify the "deeply simplified, atrophied representations" that Indigenous peoples "have been mired within anthropologically."[38] That is, by positing tradition as a source of present-day Indigenous knowledge creation, Simpson accuses cultural essentialists of walking into ethnographic entrapment as unwitting accomplices rather than liberators.

The Dakhóta relatives and ancestors I engage with here were neither purists nor anthropological sellouts. Rather, the texts they left us demonstrate how ambivalence, as cultural brokerage, necessarily involves decisions about what is said, to whom, and how much, or what Simpson sums up as "an ethnographic calculus of what you need to know and what I refuse to write."[39] To revise Simpson's notion of ethnographic refusal, we might say that the Dakhóta citational practices I track here are both endlessly proliferating and obscuring of the people, and thus always refusing totalizing forms of representation aimed at making the people intelligible, knowable, and thus more vulnerable to control by the settler-state. Irony and the perennial tease underwrite the two main and interrelated forms of translational practice: withholding and proliferation. By withholding I mean a representational means of both satisfying settler desires for Indigenous transparency (and availability for co-optation and control) while preserving certain key opacities; it is less explicit than refusal. In the context of translation theory, Lawrence Venuti has described a similar dynamic through what he terms a regime of fluency. He argues that what is usually judged to be a good translation is marked above all by a sense of fluency, where "the absence of any linguistic or stylistic peculiarities makes it seem transparent . . .—the appearance, in other words, that the translation is not in fact a translation, but the 'original.'"[40] By contrast, "bad" translations are marked by a lack of fluency that owes in part to using archaic words, unusual syntax, and standard rather than colloquial language, which produce the effect of seeming—well, translated. Bad translations alienate readers from authors, and their clunky prose creates distance from, rather than immediacy to, an original. Venuti adds that fluent translation tends toward domestication, as it involves "the forcible replacement of the linguistic and cultural differences of the foreign text with a text that is intelligible to the translating-language reader. These differences can never be entirely removed, but they necessarily undergo a reduction and exclusion of possibilities."[41] A translation that preserves these differences, or even highlights them, would thus be a corrective to the dominant regime of fluent translation.

A similar translational dynamic exists among assimilation-era Dakhóta intellectuals, who, whether seeking rights or Indian citizenship, whether performing for white tourists or writing a romance novel, were confronted with settler expectations that they make their Indianness transparently, immediately accessible. There was a demand, in other words, for the literary equivalent to what Philip Deloria calls, in the context of the Indian arts and crafts movement, a consumable authenticity.[42] Dakhóta intellectuals played to these demands, facilitating a view of Dakhóta "culture" as highly transparent and appropriable. However, even in situations where that transparency would seem most troubling—as for example with Eastman's how-to guide for Boy Scouts and Camp Fire Girls, *Indian Scout Talks* (1914)—important countertranslational moves wind up preserving Dakhóta difference and density. Or rather, these remain present but obscured through a proliferation of intertexts—from references to Dakhóta genres of oral tradition and history, to narrations of everyday activities, to a poetics of the Dakhóta language. These intertexts await readers who enter their weblike relations on and off the page. They await cocreators of the Oyáte. A notion of translational withholdings and proliferations thus allows for thinking translation beyond a model of communication. It instead asks how it can describe knowledge production and community formation in situations where translation crystallizes difference rather than sameness, and where it produces noise instead of signal.[43]

This view of translation resonates with other recent work by Indigenous studies scholars, especially Chris Andersen's (Métis) proposition that "Indigenous communities are epistemologically *dense* (rather than just *different*)," with part of this density coming from engaging with "terms like ethnicity, race, nation, or post-modernism" because these too "*are part of what makes us Indigenous*."[44] As I read Andersen here, Indigenous density comes from its (sometimes coerced, sometimes chosen) relationships to settler-states as well as to our own communities' and scholars' critical vocabularies, emphasizing the play of language in and between texts that reveals the continual emergence of new indigeneities. In this spirit of proliferating meanings, I take on the task of the translator, populating the texts I read in this book with meanings drawn from intertexts of various kinds, but especially from oral histories and ethnographies. Attending to the play of language in and between texts, I look out for/construct the emergence of new/old Dakhóta identities. Oral histories—the stories of grandmas who have gone to the next world, and the echoes of their teasing—are vital intertexts and are part of this unfolding dialogue. Vivifying and still heard, they exist not only in the digital archives of the Mni Wakháŋ Oyáte but in the continuation of their stories from mouth to ear, in dreams, in the living fear of lightning.

There is a strong basis in the Dakhóta language, too, for privileging performance over essence, citation over tradition; in Dakhóta linguistic ontologies is the sense of translation as a kind of linguistic performativity that founds newness in (potentially) transgressive relation to tradition. As Wazíyatawiŋ contends, the Dakhóta language has no equivalent to the English word "sorry."[45] Thus, she writes, with "no way to apologize for bad deeds or words . . . it is understood that as a Dakhóta, it is important to think carefully before acting or speaking so that there is no need for an apology."[46] Rather than limiting or foreclosing interpersonal relation, the inability to withdraw language from the arena of the social helps ensure that the individual will not be regarded as the autonomous guarantor of the integrity of what is spoken. Language shares and proliferates rather than hoards. One should proceed with care.

Rewriting the People, Centering the Oyáte

Another aim of this book is to position Indigenous peoplehood as a resurgent political discourse not only within our present but also within the assimilation era as well as its ethnocidal and genocidal demands, which would seem most antithetical to it.[47] I am interested in capturing some of the historical difficulty, debate, and complexities of representing the people, the Oyáte, first under conditions of exile and diaspora and later under an anthropological regime that only allowed for the people to exist as an exotic, appropriable, and ever-vanishing remnant. Something like Indigenous peoplehood, as lived experience, thought, and action, has arguably been around forever. But representing it, and especially as a site of decolonial struggle, is a relatively recent and momentous practice. Scott Lyons traces the development of peoplehood as a critical term in Indigenous studies back to anthropologist Edward Spicer's 1962 ethnography of "the Indians of the Southwest," *Cycles of Conquest*, noting how for Spicer, "land, spiritual life, and language use constituted a cultural foundation for identity that distinguished Native peoples from other ethnic groups." In his brief genealogy of peoplehood, Lyons also includes Robert Thomas's essay, "The Tap-Roots of Peoplehood" (1990), an essay by Tom Holm (Creek Cherokee), Diane Pearson, and Ben Chavis (Lumbee), "Peoplehood: A Model for American Indian Sovereignty in Education" (2003), and Taiaiake Alfred's (Kahnawake Mohawk) and Jeff Corntassel's (Cherokee) article, "Being Indigenous: Resurgences against Contemporary Colonialism" (2005). In each case, Lyons observes, these authors nominate certain aspects of Indigenous life as defining of "the people," whether "land, religion, language, sacred history, ceremonial cycle, and so on."[48] What troubles Lyons about this nominational work is that whatever defines the people may function, as any orthodoxy does, to exclude or marginalize members or citizens of tribal communities. In short, even though Indigenous peoplehood may be useful as a way of making political claims within and against settler-states—a fact that Lyons admits in the context of the United Nations especially—Lyons rejects the "problematic peoplehood paradigm" for its conservative tendencies toward cultural purity models and for creating enforcers of that purity, or "culture cops."

His proposed alternative is what he calls a "nation-people" or "realist nationalism," which recognizes that Indigenous peoples have since the late eighteenth century and the moment of making treaties with the settler-state been involved in a translational process of "modernizing the *ethnie*," where "the *ethnie* is primarily culturally defined," into the form of the nation, defined more by the "intersubjective recognition of membership, duties, rights, and responsibilities against the backdrop of a mass public culture and common economy."[49] In this translation from *ethnie* to nation, Lyons asserts, the *ethnie*'s "old cultural memories have to be publicized: depicted, displayed, and shared."[50] Nationalists, he concludes, "must always wear their cultures on their sleeves."[51]

But the nation form is, as Lyons points out repeatedly, a hallmark of modernity. Even in his reformulation of it in terms of tribal nation-peoples, the nation continues both to advance and hinder Indigenous resurgence—and hinder in the first and most damaging instance in the U.S. Supreme Court's infantilizing of Indigenous peoples as "domestic dependent nations." However, the specter of nationalist exclusions and violence also haunts criticisms of relinking to and reconstructing tribal pasts as retrograde in a bad (because essentializing) way. As an alternative, I propose that peoplehood, not nationhood, was the preferred term for Indigenous collectivity used by Dakhóta intellectuals in the assimilation era, with the "nation" tying instead most frequently to the United States and what Eastman ironically called its version of "civilization." Another problem I have with Lyons's model is hermeneutic and has to do with his sense that "old cultural memories have to be publicized." In response, I offer that some sleeves, like hearts or cultures, are notoriously difficult to read. Again, this is not to assert the existence of some sort of radical privacy or hidden essence. Instead, the publicizing of "old cultural memories" is a historically specific, nuanced process of representation. Often the performance of indigeneities—whether in print, clothing, ceremony, or spectacle— involves what is withheld as much as what is "depicted, displayed, and shared." Maybe this is just another way of expressing that I am more interested in representation and performance—what Lyons calls doing—than in essences, or being. In what follows, I try to understand Dakhóta peoplehood in genealogical and translational terms, with the aim of tracking how it has been deployed as a concept both to make political claims on the settler-state and also (crucially) to avoid and evade state scrutiny. In doing so I follow Homi Bhabha's sense that peoplehood emerges through "a process of political articulation and political negotiation across a whole range of contradictory social sites."[52] Analysis of these negotiations—always difficult, messy, and usually mediated by settler terms—forms the bulk of this book.

Of Teasing, Ethics, and the Everyday

Thinking about Indigenous life during the assimilation era in terms of either liberatory resistance or disabling ambivalence is problematic because both views require a monolithic model of reception rather than allowing or accounting for a continuum of diverse hearings and mishearings. But it also relies problematically on a narrative of subversion as the reinscription of norms, a narrative that Saba Mahmood has identified with liberal progressive politics.[53] Instead, I suggest that faced with ethnographic entrapment, co-optation, and physical violence (my relatives more than once ended up with a bar of lye soap in their mouths for speaking Dakhóta), the unheroic decolonizer teases in reply, and in teasing breathes some life back into their families and communities. The image on this book's cover, a work of ledger art by Dwayne Wilcox (Oglála Lakȟóta) entitled "Must Be Her First Powwow," captures the spirit of whispered evaluation that I find at the heart of the literary remaking of the Oyáte under forced assimilation policies: those intimate gestures camouflaged within a spectacle that would otherwise seem to be all about reinforcing white power. Others have likewise privileged the tease. Gerald Vizenor (Anishinaabe) tells us to look for signs of Indigenous vitality in the eyes and hands of photographic subjects who, in the ethnographic portraiture of Edward Curtis, were forced into "fugitive poses" on their way to presumed disappearance.[54] Thomas Biolsi describes this kind of hidden vibrancy when he recounts how, in an 1885 census of Rosebud Agency members, there were "some remarkable English translations of Lakota names. Peppered throughout the census, in between such names as 'Black Elk,' 'Walking Bull,' and 'Dull Knife' were names such as 'Bad Cunt,' 'Dirty Prick,' and 'Shit Head' (Rosebud Agency 1885)."[55] The names were adopted by people who had already been counted in the census in order to inflate their numbers and so receive more rations, as relatives at Pine Ridge had done. Biolsi adds, "From the point of view of the colonial administrators, all the Lakota looked alike—they had no individual identities in any practical administrative sense—and the OIA [Office of Indian Affairs] had no idea how many Lakota there were. If colonialism is about making the colonized 'legible,' 'readable,' and 'available to political and economic calculation,' the Lakota were yet to be colonized."[56] My contribution to this literature of the unseen, to a bibliography of the tease, is not only to show the specificities of Dakhóta remaking and resurgence but also to move these citational practices into our decolonizing present. Like the intellectuals it examines, *Translated Nation* enters the contradiction that U.S. settler-colonialism brought into being, finding room there to tease, ruse, breathe, and be Dakhóta within its strictures.

The engine of this rusing was (and remains) the ongoing threat of exterminatory violence by settler-colonists. One must keep one's difference close to the chest. Settler-colonial regimes of making Indigenous people into intelligible subjects of the state, as Elizabeth Povinelli has observed, show up as the demand and "struggle to inhabit the tensions and torsions of competing incitements to *be* and to *identify* differentially."[57] Within such demands, liberal tolerance toward indigeneity appears within a limited range, "inflected by the conditional (as long as they are not repugnant; that is, as long as they are not, at heart, not-us and as long as real economic resources are not at stake)."[58] I share Povinelli's sense that liberal tolerance and recognition politics are premised on a coercive logic that difference, if it is to be allowed, should not be too radical (the "not-us") or run counter to colonialist, capitalistic interests. This is essentially the model of permissible indigeneity we see within U.S. Indian reorganization policy during the 1930s, when Congress recognized tribal self-determination only in cases where institutions of governance conformed to "tradition." Povinelli adds how the "competing incitements" of late liberalism create incommensurable obligations for Indigenous persons, who are simultaneously called on to "be themselves" (that is, authentically "traditional") and not to be themselves (when those traditions are repugnant), and that this incommensurability or radical ambivalence can register as a kind of "panic" or tornness.[59] Because Dakhóta people, as a people, embodied what the settler-colonial state sought to exterminate (Minnesota governor Alexander Ramsey declared in 1862 that "the Sioux Indians of Minnesota must be exterminated or driven forever beyond the borders of the State"),[60] occupying a form of maximally repugnant difference from settler society, representations of the Oyáte had to be coded or ciphered, whispered behind hands to evade settler view and violence. One must keep one's difference, like a knife, close to the chest.

Throughout this book, I use the term "ethics" as something distinct from morality, which I find, as Colin Dayan has argued, "always depends on a communal surround of privilege that draws its power from the constructions that ordain right and wrong."[61] I share her sense that ethics need not mean something so "abstract" and potentially "coercive," but has instead to do with forms of relationality that extend kinship beyond the human to include one's locale and its other-than-human inhabitants. As she writes, "To be ethical, in this sense, is to know how to locate oneself in relation to what one does not know, a world adamantly not one's own. Whereas morality is an experience of non-relation, ethics demands the discomfort of utter relatedness even if it is distasteful or unsettling."[62] Likewise, by "ethics" here I do not mean a list of prescriptions or propositions; instead, I mean what precedes or makes propositionality possible: an anarchic, nonhierarchical responsibility born from long-standing relationships with place. The literary depictions of ethics I examine here link back to ideas and practices of radical decolonial relationality rather than invoke a prescriptive list of thou-shalts and thou-shalt-nots. Although there are surely prescriptions for how to be a good person in Dakhóta philosophy (Ella Cara Deloria documented many thióśpaye norms in her ethnographies), this book tracks Dakhóta ethics through story and other representations of anarchic responsibility that cluster around notions of personhood, sufficiency, and gift giving or generosity. These concepts only take on lived meaning in the context of Dakhóta communities. I examine in chapter 2 the ways in which translational withholding occurs through depictions of thióśpaye ethics and forms of relation that have little or no meaning apart from the regulatory communities and lands that both gave rise to and enforce those ethics.

Part of my aim in foregrounding the ethical as a site of ever-proliferating meaning is to delink indigeneity from essence but also to delink Indigenous celebrity with the presumption of hermeneutic closure. That is, I want to mess with the knownness of folks like Black Elk and Eastman, and instead of imagining that their stories and destinies are somehow already decided, or settling on their lives and writing as standing in for Dakhóta culture itself—whether that culture is reckoned as race (Eastman), spirituality (Black Elk), or ethnographic data (Deloria)—I want to open up space for critical reexamination and refusal. Yet I also hope to retain something of their representative reputations, their status as delegates of the Oyáte, in order to unpack the representational bind they found themselves in where, even as they voiced criticisms of the United States, that criticism was often framed within a liberal individualist cult of the author as the voicing of personal complaint or moralizing rather than as Dakhóta persons voicing a collective ethicopolitics.

In response to a similar dismissal in Islamic studies of the ethical as politics, Saba Mahmood argues for increased critical attention to what she calls positive ethics, or ethics that are "founded upon particular forms of discursive practice, instantiated through specific sets of procedures, techniques, and exercises, through which highly specific ethical-moral subjects come to be formed."[63] This alternative conception of ethics as performed rather than abstract, as moving from exteriority (bodily practices) to interiority (the self), contrasts with dominant notions of ethics as compartmentalized from the political and as belonging solely to a private rather than public sphere. Mahmood's work has been especially helpful in helping me think about the role of bodily performance in the making and remaking of Dakhóta persons and communities, and about instances where thióšpaye philosophy and ethics appear in lived rather than propositional forms, as practices of everyday life rather than as moral formulas. In their accounts of these quotidian practices, Dakhóta authors present images of Dakhóta life that can be playacted but never fully embodied outside of living Dakhóta communities. Although they appear to be giving material for "playing Indian," they are not indigenizing America but rather reindigenizing Dakhóta persons and thióšpayes.

The gendered aspects of a Dakhóta peoplehood discourse provide another key to how I develop my reading of thióšpaye ethics. For instance, I begin with the 1862 U.S.–Dakhóta War and its criminalizing of a Dakhóta warrior masculinity, then discuss in chapter 2, on Eastman, how the heteronormativity enshrined in U.S. allotment policy played a key role in how Dakhóta people negotiated their publicity. Both Black Elk's and Deloria's reclamations of warrior and storyteller/historian masculinities and femininities, respectively, form the basis for chapters 3 and 4. Throughout, I draw inspiration from the work of Indigenous feminist theorists who have observed how settler-colonialism and decolonization are not thinkable apart from gender and sexual violence. Beth Piatote, Dian Million, Mark Rifkin, Ann Stoler, and others observe how gender violence was foundational to the barring of Indigenous forms of relationality, sexuality, and belonging.[64] Piatote examines how residential and allotment schools restructured Indigenous economies, forms of labor, and gender roles. Similarly, Rifkin argues that gender violence, as U.S. allotment policy's naturalization of conjugal domesticity and private property ownership, should be viewed "as an organized effort to make heterosexuality compulsory as a key part of breaking of indigenous land holdings" and assimilating of detribalizing Indigenous peoples.[65] These Indigenous feminist theorists highlight how intimate spaces like the gendered body, the near family, and the extended family are crucial battlegrounds for both colonial violence and decolonial struggle.

A gender analytic has allowed me to focus instead on intracommunal dynamics, or what Jeff Corntassel and Mick Scow call "everyday acts of resurgence."[66] In doing so, I draw on works outside Native American and Indigenous studies by Lauren Berlant and Saba Mahmood that call for viewing representations of and by the oppressed in other terms. Berlant has declared the need for "better ways to talk about activity oriented toward the reproduction of ordinary life," noting that sovereign agency under a regime of biopower is different from sovereign agency under a regime of sovereignty, by which she suggests that agency within an increasingly managed system of life, in which certain populations pose a threat to the reproduction of "the good life of a society," can no longer be thought only in relation "to a melodrama of the care of the monadic self."[67] Instead, she argues, "we need to think about agency and personhood not only in normative terms but also as activity exercised within spaces of ordinariness that does not always or even usually follow the literalizing logic of visible effectuality, bourgeois dramatics, and lifelong accumulation or fashioning."[68] Berlant's critical interest is in persons (neoliberal subjects) who are not sovereign and who occupy a temporality of "getting by," whose lives demonstrate "a kind of interruptive agency that aspires to detach from a condition or to diminish being meaningful."[69] Her reorienting of agency away from sovereign (settler) subjects is, however ironically, useful for thinking about Indigenous points of view during the assimilation era because it is precisely the "melodrama of the care of the monadic self" that assimilation, especially in the guise of citizenship, sought to impose on Indigenous people. The monadic self underwrote allotment policy's recognition of the "civilized" bourgeois individual as being close enough to the unnamed universal white subject of law to count as a U.S. citizen. Also useful is Berlant's emphasis on an agency oriented toward diminishing meaningfulness, because it is in the downplayed (in the ruse of accommodating the settler) where the Oyáte could be nurtured and regrown. The unheroic decolonizer finds freedom in the space of the willfully misheard. Misprision is the decolonizer's best tool and alibi.

Critical Relationality: Dakhóta Lands, Waters, and Skies

Such (mis)translational work is one rung on the ladder of tribal sovereignty, which not only exists in the constitution-based form of tribal government created by the 1934 Indian Reorganization Act but also endures in the ethical norms of the thióšpaye. If, as Beth Piatote argues, assimilation policies targeting the elimination of "the Indian family home and relations" were themselves "Indian wars," then recovering the extensive and intensive meanings of "family" and "relations" is an essential part of tribal projects of resurgence and renewal.[70] I enlarge Piatote's insightful reading of the "intimate domestic" or "Indian home and family" to consider relatives of other, and other-than-human, kinds.[71] My readings of work by Dakhóta intellectuals center the ways in which the thióšpaye's reach goes beyond the nuclear family and the human world to embrace nonhuman relatives as well. We are always involved in relations of care or neglect with our relatives in the land, water, and skies, and we forget these at the cost of losing touch with our most basic sources of belonging. It is ultimately to Dakhóta territory—Dakhóta thámakhočhe ektá—that these intellectuals return us, as well as to forms of caretaking that make and remake the Oyáte.

Accordingly, I foreground three main ways in which thióšpaye ethics, as critical relationality, work as a flexible matrix for thinking Dakhóta survival, remakings, and change: (1) as a temporality for linking to the past and moving toward the future, (2) as a mode of place making, and (3) as expressing an ontological relationship to ancestral lands and their human and other-than-human occupants. In doing so, I build on Glen Coulthard's notion of a "grounded normativity," or the understanding of land as "a way of knowing, of experiencing and relating to the world and with others" that can "guide forms of resistance against other rationalizations of the world that threaten to erase or destroy our senses of place."[72] Where Coulthard focuses on forms of Indigenous critique and anticolonial resistance mobilized by relational senses of place, I draw out how Dakhóta forms of land tenure were represented in literary forms to do intratribal work of regeneration that were not directly about resistance. I also name specific aspects of relationality—not to pin these down or identify some pure version of Dakhóta tradition but instead to show how Eastman, Black Elk, and Deloria were engaged in the negotiation and reconstruction of tradition as a decolonizing activity for present and future generations.

I owe much to the work of Kim TallBear, who draws on her experience of growing up within a thióšpaye to theorize forms of what she calls caretaking as central to an "indigenous critical relationality."[73] She describes this relationality and its role in building a stronger thióšpaye as "relating and exchanging power and reciprocity ... with both living relations and those whose bodies we come from and whose bodies will come in part from us," adding that in thinking about bodies, she is thinking "of both the human and other-than-human bodies with whom we are co-constituted."[74] As TallBear implies, these relations unsettle colonial hierarchies of various kinds, including ones of gender and sex binaries, but also ones constructed along lines of the human/nonhuman/less than human and animacy/inanimacy. Following her and others' use of the term "other-than-human persons,"[75] I show how Dakhóta intellectuals invoked and evoked a wide array of other-than-human beings to reconstruct more egalitarian relations than what settler liberalism claimed to bestow through citizenship, and so imaginatively reanimated, repopulated, and reoccupied homelands that settler-colonial law had converted into lifeless property.

"Critical relationality" as a term stands to reorient us toward Dakhóta ways of thinking about place and its occupants, but also about time. I describe, for instance, how critical relationality performs a temporality of the pause, where pausing notates a deliberate suspension of activity, as was observed formally during treaty negotiations, but also in many other contexts, such as traditional forms of storytelling observed during the winter months.[76] More than these sorts of literal pauses, though, a temporality of pausing may also be an ethic of sufficiency, most pointedly in relation to capitalistic accumulation, of economic sufficiency. The premium that the Dakhóta have placed on limiting hunting and fishing in order to maintain good relations with animal others appears in my reading of Eastman's story of a young Dakhóta girl's relationship with a raccoon, "Wechah the Provider." There, the raccoon, Wechah, persuades the girl, Wasula, to limit her trapping to a specific season and quantity of animals. This deliberate suspension disturbs a capitalist logic of accumulation that Eastman

INTRODUCTION   23

elsewhere criticizes by recalling the words of Sitting Bull after the illegal gold rush on Ȟé Sápa (Black Mountains, or the Black Hills in South Dakota): "We have now to deal with another people small and feeble when our forefathers first met with them, but now great and overbearing. Strangely enough, they have a mind to till the soil, and the love of possessions is a disease in them."[77] Linking back to historical subsistence practices, Eastman's tale asserts possible thióšpaye interventions in extractive, overconsumptive capitalistic relationships with home places, suggesting the viability of forms of emplaced living in which power is transactionally negotiated between human and other-than-human beings. Whatever else we may say of Eastman's tale (and in writing and sharing portions of this book I have come across diverse and even hostile reactions to it and to his other stories—that it is an idealization, that it is Disney-fied or saccharine, that it could not possibly be political), it is not only a prescription for good Dakhóta behavior but also an evocative criticism of settler-colonial bad behavior.

Another brief example—one that is important for contextualizing the prisoners' letters I will examine in chapter 1—may help to illustrate the kinds of horizontal and decolonial relationships that thióšpaye ethics fosters. One of the most consequential locations for Dakhóta relational ethics has been treaties, with one of the most damaging treaties for eastern Dakhóta bands being the 1851 Treaty of Traverse des Sioux, which resulted in the loss of all but a strip of land along the Minnesota River. I want to briefly narrate it here not only for its importance in leading to the 1862 U.S.–Dakhóta War but also for its depiction of a politics of care that I link to thióšpaye ethics and the reconstruction of the Oyáte. In midsummer 1851, faced with a wave of settlers pouring into the new territory of Minnesota, and saddled with trader debts and depleted numbers of game animals, leaders of the Sisíthuŋwaŋ and Waȟpéthuŋwaŋ bands met with the U.S. commissioner of Indian affairs, Luke Lea, and the Minnesota territorial governor, Alexander Ramsey, to negotiate a treaty at Traverse des Sioux, near what is now called St. Peter. From a Dakhóta perspective, the negotiations centered around the failure of the United States to live up to its promises made in an earlier treaty. The treaty at Traverse des Sioux was the fourth in a line of treaties dating back to 1805, when army lieutenant Zebulon Pike brokered the purchase of an island at the confluence of the Minnesota and Mississippi rivers, at the place of origin where eastern Dakhóta people emerged, called Bdóte. The next took place at Prairie du Chien in 1825; it purported to be a peacekeeping mission by the United States in response to ongoing wars between the Dakhóta and their allies, and among the Anishinaabe, Sac and Fox, and Ioway peoples. A Detroit newspaper reported that the object was "not to obtain cessions from the Indians, but solely for the purpose of forming a treaty, to establish the boundaries, and insure tranquility between the Sioux" and their rivals. True to these purposes, William Clark negotiated the fixed delineation of Indigenous boundaries while demanding that the tribes recognize the "controlling power" of the United States.[78]

The first article of the Traverse des Sioux treaty makes a founding gesture of an accord based in equality. In English, the opening reads: "It is stipulated and solemnly agreed that the peace and friendship now so happily existing between the United States and the aforesaid bands of Indians, shall be perpetual." Here the convention invocation of a Kantian perpetual peace and friendship assumes a certain comprehensibility for everyone implicated in its gesture of accord. As the opening article of a political agreement, the words potentiate the actions to come: the "ceding" (a problematic term to translate into Dakhóta because cession presumes a concept of possession and alienable property) of a vast territory to the United States. However, the Dakhóta version, translated from English and written by Presbyterian missionary Stephen R. Riggs, inflects the notions of "peace" and "friendship" in culturally specific ways that are distinctly different from their English equivalents: "Isantanka Oyate qa Dakota Warpetonwan qa Sisitonwan ewicakiyapi kin hena okiciciyapi qa odakonkiciyap kin ohinniyan detanhan cantekickiyzapi kta e nakaha awicakehan wakiconzap qa yuxtanpi."[79] Gwen Westerman and Bruce White's translation into English reads, "The people of the United States and the Wahpeton and Sisseton Dakota people, those named, help each other and are allied with each other, earlier this day they purposefully resolved and concluded forever from this time to hold each other's hearts."[80] The phrase "to hold each other's hearts" (cantekickiyzapi) might have seemed to non-Dakhótas a florid metaphor for alliance—and certainly could also be translated in similar terms to the Christian command to "love one another." But this holding of the heart arguably references forms of relation that predated missions, and that replace an imagining of peace and friendship as the absence of conflict with an ethic of care. As Waziyatawin notes, even to think in the language is an activity of the heart, as the verb *čaŋtéyuza* means "to think, form an opinion."[81] She adds, "From a Dakota perspective, *thinking with our heart* encompasses the ethical considerations that must be at the forefront of any endeavor."[82]

One way of thinking with the heart is through engaging with others as relatives. Dakhóta people have long been adopters, enlarging thióšpayes and the Oyáte through various mechanisms like the huŋkádowaŋpi (literally "adoptee" and "singing," referring to what is an adoption ceremony) and later through laws like the 1978 Indian Child and Welfare Act, which sought to keep Indigenous children with Indigenous families of federally recognized tribes. Ella Cara Deloria's transcription of one Oglála informant's account describes how the huŋká's ceremonial adoptions confer obligations on both the adoptee and the new family members. In front of all the members of the thióšpaye, as well as "the four winds, the Above and the earth," who are "invoked to bless and witness the act," there is a founding of the "good":

> Because the family have thus made themselves good, all in a day
> shall they throw off all evil, and from that time forth, they shall
> live honored lives, shall take pity and show kindness towards other
> people, and shall assume all the obligations of good acts and quali-
> ties whereby all Dakotas render themselves worthy. And it shall
> be that they are hereby manifesting their intention to live according
> to the best as Dakotas understand it.[83]

After this mutual beholding—which involves the participation not only of the humans present but also of other-than-human persons, the four winds (wazíyata, or northward; wiyóhiŋyaŋpata, "where the sun arrives to spread daylight," or eastward; itókaǧa, or southward; and wiyóȟpeyata, "where the sun goes down," or westward), "high above" (waŋkáta), and "earth" (makhá)—the "candidates" (adoptees) "render horses to the ones who act as ceremonial father and mother to them." Deloria notes that at the end of each verse, or address to the directional powers, "the people said 'Wahini!' in unison, meaning thereby, 'So be it!' or," as Deloria adds in her own handwriting at the bottom of the page, "Amen."[84] The significance of horses, as both a gift to the new parents and as the vehicle by which the ceremony is performed (a horsehair wand is waved over the adoptees), is something I return to in chapter 3 as part of discussion of Dakhóta concepts of power and the ethical imperative to share power. In Deloria's account, a giveaway finalizes the making of a relative: "The especial meaning between the candidates and their ceremonial parents is that they shall be related thereafter as actual blood relations, as long as they live." Thinking back to the language of the Traverse des Sioux treaty, another founding of relation, the speech act performed by the treaty—"to hold one another's heart"—has the affective and enduring richness of the huŋká commitment, implying forms of caretaking based in anarchic responsibility exercised between the people of the United States and the Oyáte. These linkages suggest a shorthand or maxim similar to what Kenneth Morrison has described in connection to Algonkian concepts of personhood: namely, positive others who are powerful and who are of good heart, as they contribute to the solidarity and survival of the people, while negative, powerful others withhold.[85] It is perhaps no accident that the contemporary Dakhóta word for whites, wašíču, which among some thióšpaye referred to a "familiar spirit,"[86] has come to mean in popular usage "the fat takers."

On Interludes and Intellectuals

My late uŋčí, Rachel Charboneau, embodied many seemingly contradictory selves over the course of her long and rich life—Dakhóta woman, mission school truant, bootlegger, and, late in life, Catholic convert, to name just a few. But her lived experience was not that of a contradiction, however much she entered into that contradiction unwillingly as a child in boarding school. Rather, her story suggests how she negotiated multiple ways of belonging while maintaining a strong sense, especially through speaking the Dakhóta language, of being a Dakhóta woman. In her home in Rapid City, and in her sister's homes on the Spirit Lake Nation, I grew up at the feet of Dakhóta intellectuals, listening to stories about battles between the Uŋktehi (a water being) and Wakíŋyaŋ (a thunder being), who gave Mní Wakháŋ its name. There were jokes about young lovers who froze to death in the back of their Buick while making out, and who, when they were driven away by the ambulance driver, looked in the rearview mirror to be slow-dancing, her arms encircling his shoulders. There were boarding school recollections of pranks, truant officers, and abuses. Often, almost always, their stories mixed the old and new. Uŋčíwaye (maternal grandma) Grace Lambert, who liked to tease her sister, Rose, would modify what in Dakhóta are called eháŋna woyákapi, where *eháŋna* suggests "long ago" and *woyákapi* "a telling." These are the kinds of stories that anthropologists have often dismissed (as well as fetishized) as myths. In uŋčí Grace's stories, motorcycles show up alongside "crazy buffaloes," drunk old men speak with the voice of Tȟuŋkášida (literally "grandfather," but also used by Christian Dakhótas for God) at a place where Dakhóta people would traditionally pray. And so on. And on.

As I drafted chapters for this book, I found that much of my reading of these assimilation-era intellectuals is tangled up with what I had grown up hearing from my relatives—their laughter, imagination, and ethical sense. To limit my focus to the assimilation era would have unfortunately reified settler senses of time and reality. Like peoplehood, I have found that Dakhóta philosophy emerges continually—though at times fugitively—over time and from many sources, both human and otherwise. In order to give a sense of this emergence, and to bring out the book's through lines crystallizing around issues of place, relating, generosity, and caretaking, I have interwoven between the numbered chapters oral histories from Dakhóta elders of the Mni Wakȟáŋ Oyáte. I should emphasize that although this is a work of literary criticism, one way I have tried to exercise care as a Dakhóta scholar is by framing the readings I do here as a kind of lengthy marginalia not only to the words and works of Black Elk, Deloria, and Eastman but also to my own close relatives' histories and stories. Indeed, much of this book comprises stories narrated by them in sections I have labeled Interludes. I've named them such to give the sense of an almost musical pausing in a longer production, a pause suggesting various forms of relief from settler-colonial capitalism's obsessions with ideals of accumulation and historical progress on the one hand and Indigenous failures to embody those ideals on the other. They are appropriately called Interludes because they do not try to represent the entire history of the Dakhóta people but rather only provide glimpses of that whole. As Wazíyatawiŋ writes about the stories she recorded of her uŋkáŋna (maternal grandfather), Eli Taylor, the stories represent "a portion of one person's memory that helps to create the long story of our people."[87]

I gathered some of these histories personally, and one of them appears here as the First Interlude. Others I encountered through video recordings dating back to the early 1990s, when the Dakhóta Wóunspe (Dakota language teaching) program recorded and translated fluent speakers for cultural preservation and language instruction. Some of the tapes held the voices and images of my grandmothers, Lillian

Chase and Grace Lambert, while others recorded other Mni Wakȟáŋ elders responding to the interviewer, Eugene Hale, whose questions focus for the most part on place-names and eháŋna woyákapi. While the original language in the First Interlude was almost entirely English or wašíčuiya, the Second and Third Interludes were given almost wholly in dakhótaiya. Because of limited space, I have chosen to present just the wašíčuiya translation of these, by Eugene Hale, rather than giving versions in both languages, but I have indicated the Dakhóta original where I have found a wašíču word to be problematic. Conversely, I have annotated Dakhóta words that might be unfamiliar to most readers, or that appear in other texts and contexts throughout this book.

These Interludes hold stories about the war waged by Dakhóta akíčhita, or warriors, on Minnesotan settlers, of the death of my great-great-grandmother by lightning, of reservation locales vivified by spirits, other-than-human persons, and colorful humans too. While I cannot assign any exact percentage to it, the parts of this book that are family and extended family history loom largest in my mind. The power that Leslie Marmon Silko attributes to "family stories" among Pueblo people gives shape and sustenance beyond the individual storyteller and her family, so these "stories are always bringing us together, keeping this whole together, keeping this clan together."[88] Because of this power not only to bring together but also to give some critical distance and perspective to "wonderful stories" and "negative stories" alike, I think it only right to call our grandmothers intellectuals no less than, say, a trained anthropologist like Ella Cara Deloria.[89] As elders, they are our historians, our critics, and our language keepers, and for all these reasons, they hold an equal status to those who in academic settings would be termed intellectuals. At the same time, I want to acknowledge the difficulties that might arise from introducing an archive of tribal elders' interviews into a secular academic setting. Maybe most frustratingly, from my perspective and that of other Dakhóta scholars, academic and tribal scholars frequently work at loggerheads. As Wazíyatawiŋ observes about the "differing goals of academic and tribal historians," the premium placed on creating scholarship that "provides some revealing perspective, slant, or model that has not been articulated the same way previously and which allows the intended audience to view that topic in a new way" may present "a special dilemma" for Dakhóta scholars and historians, whose "first and primary responsibility . . . has always been to 'tell it straight.'"[90] In other words, interpretive newness and critical intervention are less important than, if not antithetical to, the responsibility of preserving and transmitting the perspectives and knowledge that have been entrusted to us.

As will become evident, those perspectives and knowledge are often just as much about loss as they are about recovery. In the closing words of the Third Interlude, my grandma Lillian recalls how the Spirit Lake reservation looked and felt in the early years of the twentieth century. Gesturing toward different towns that marked the different shores of what was once called Devils Lake by settlers, she wistfully notes that "this whole lake used to be ours at one time" before angrily adding, "They claim the lake now, those white people. They don't have any business." As Audra Simpson argues when addressing what it means to be a tribe member, narratives of citizenship "embed *desire* in ways that speak between the gulfs of the past and the present. . . . This desire is made from the intimacy, the knowledge, and the messiness of everyday life, and from the bonds of affection and disaffection that tie people into communities and communities into nations."[91] This book's Interludes thus make room for those desires—those through lines of everyday intimacy—to speak.

Chapter Map

The chapters are arranged in roughly chronological order and follow the emergence of peoplehood as a decolonizing discourse in the wake of the 1862 U.S.–Dakhóta War, imprisonments, and hangings. Interweaving these chapters and illustrating the unfolding of a thióšpaye philosophy over time are Interludes, which comprise the transcribed oral histories of my grandmothers from the late 1990s. Chapter 1 reads the religious, legal, and political contexts of the U.S.–Dakhóta War and its resulting concentration camps through missionary documents and letters written in the camps by Dakhóta prisoners. The war constituted a historical rupture for Dakhóta, effectively barring the existence of a unified Oyáte through a campaign of ethnic cleansing, removal, and concentration on reservations in Santee, Nebraska, Sisseton and what used to be called Devils Lake (Mni Wakháŋ), North Dakota, and reserves in Manitoba and Saskatchewan. My aim in this chapter is to examine and assess how prisoners' conversions to

Christianity engaged in a politics of withholding that allowed them to maintain crucial ethical ties to relatives while at the same time appearing to be dutiful converts and, at least potentially, good citizens of the United States. Co-opted by neither God nor liberal individualism, they adopted and adapted aspects of settler-colonial culture, filtering these through thióšpaye understandings as a way of helping the Oyáte to endure.

Chapter 2 examines a number of Charles Alexander Eastman's writings, especially his works for children, focusing on how they depict forms of relational citizenship based in an anticapitalistic ethic of sufficiency. By centering the Dakhóta oral-historical genre of hithúŋkaŋkaŋpi (long-ago stories) and Dakhóta peoplehood more broadly, this chapter proposes an alternative view of Eastman as citing Dakhóta thióšpaye philosophy both to reassert the Oyáte as a vital touchstone for present-day meanings of Indian citizenship and to critique the enduring conditions of U.S. settler-colonialism—a critique that became much more pointed in Eastman's later, better-known autobiography, *From the Deep Woods to Civilization* (1916). By viewing Eastman's stories about talking animals in *Red Hunters and the Animal People* (1904), which was largely viewed by Eastman's critical contemporaries as a politically innocuous analog to Rudyard Kipling's *Jungle Book* (1893), we may more clearly see his innovative translations of Dakhóta politics into narratives that simultaneously sentimentally appealed to and challenged U.S. settler society. These challenges came specifically in relation to Dakhóta conceptions of peoplehood and power.

Chapter 3 examines the transcripts of interviews with Nicholas Black Elk, an Oglála wičhášа wakháŋ[92] (holy man or ritual specialist) and Catholic catechist whose life story was famously transcribed as an as-told-to autobiography by John Neihardt in *Black Elk Speaks* (1932). Through close readings of Raymond DeMallie's edition of the Black Elk transcripts, *The Sixth Grandfather*, I examine Black Elk's account of the vision that he experienced as a nine-year-old boy, focusing on its ethical landscape as a Lakȟóta articulation of belonging and place making that challenged statist notions of territoriality—notions that sought to link an already limited (because juridically construed) Lakȟóta sovereignty to a reduced land base. I further develop how Black Elk linked a Lakȟóta critical relationality to theories and practices of gift giving and generosity. I focus especially on how these forms of critical relationality show up in his mock ceremonial performances for tourists, demonstrating how these reclaimed and reimagined Lakȟóta warrior masculinity as a means of decolonizing gender.

In chapter 4, I read Ella Cara Deloria's novel, *Waterlily*, for its idealizations of nonnuclear family gender roles, specifically women's role in transmitting ethical norms of the thióšpaye. Deloria's novel was written shortly after passage of the 1934 Indian Reorganization Act (IRA), in the early years of the 1940s, and yet there have been few critical readings of it in the context of the IRA or the Dawes Act, or of how its depictions of gender respond to these two key moments in federal Indian law. This chapter builds on Mark Rifkin's analysis of how allotment's conjugal couple and nuclear family continued despite the IRA's commitment to returning tribes to traditional forms of governance and social organization, with *Waterlily* depicting thióšpaye forms of social life as overflowing heteronormative framings but also to an extent upholding those framings in what Rifkin calls taking the "bribe of straightness."[93] My reading supplements Rifkin's by focusing on how *Waterlily* is a tribally centered and utopian representation of Dakhóta gender roles within the thióšpaye that asserts crucial differences from allotment's gender and sex ideologies, placing these differences, especially around Dakhóta femininity, as crucial means for continuing the Oyáte into the future. In keeping with my term of translation, I highlight how Deloria's gender reclamations appear within the genre of the heterosexual romance novel, which she uses as a way of ciphering from settler view her community-oriented task of disaggregating the compulsory monogamous heterosexuality that held over from allotment policy.

My hope throughout these chapters is that by putting into fluid but sometimes tense conversation a multiplicity of voices from diverse archives—written and oral, past and present, Dakhóta and non-Dakhóta—we may see how they form a dialogue about not only survival but also covert resurgence in the face of state violences that were both overwhelming but also, in their attack on the thióšpaye and Dakhóta families, insidiously pervasive. The story that emerges among and between these voices highlights the nuanced internal politics among the assimilation-era Dakhóta themselves. Such a story stands to move against views of Indigenous peoples as homogenous entities; more important, it shows that intratribal relationships—especially ethical norms shared, disputed, and reworked among relatives—perform tribal sovereignty in ways that are often illegible within the presumptive sovereignty of the settler-colonial state.

1 Transgressive Adoptions

The best way to civilize Indians is to imprison them.
—Major George Bradley

Survival Unthought and Unintelligible

Michel Trouillot describes the "erasure and banalization" that characterize historiography of the Haitian revolution, observing how the tropes of modern history writing are identical in form to figures of discourse in the late eighteenth century. He persuasively argues that these historiographical tropes take two forms: on the one hand, "some narratives cancel what happened through direct erasure of facts or their relevance"; on the other hand, some "narratives sweeten the horror or banalize the uniqueness of a situation by focusing on details."[1] The combined effect of these tropes or formulas is "a powerful silencing" of nondominant narratives, one that renders them, and questions about them, "unthinkable." An analogous erasure surrounds the aftermath of the U.S.–Dakhóta War between United States and Minnesota militia and Dakhóta warriors reluctantly led by the Bdewákhaŋthuŋwaŋ chief, Little Crow. The war constituted a historical rupture for Dakhóta, effectively barring the existence of a unified Oyáte through a campaign of ethnic cleansing, removal, and concentration on reservations including Santee, Nebraska, Crow Creek, Sisseton, and what used to be called Devils Lake (Bdé Wakháŋ or Mní Wakháŋ) in Dakota Territory, as well as reserves in Manitoba and Saskatchewan. Yet the war is itself a little-known event in the history of U.S. colonization, despite Minnesotan settlers at the time having called it a second Civil War, and despite contemporary Dakhóta people's sense of it having been a genocidal campaign of ethnic cleansing.[2]

In this chapter I address and redress that silencing by centering Dakhóta archives. These are both contemporary, as with interviews and oral histories, and historical, as with the letters written by Dakhóta prisoners in the concentration camps established after the war. Another of my aims here is to frame the war as an act of settler-colonial translation that, as my epigraph states, sought to civilize Indians by imprisoning them. Converting to Christianity and learning how to read and write were two important ways of translating someone into a settler-colonial subject intelligible to the missionaries who served at the camps. More important for my purposes, the power relations between some 1700 Dakhóta prisoners held at Fort Snelling and their white captors were complicated by countertranslational moves in which Dakhóta people adopted and reinvested settler-colonial vocabularies with their own ethical meanings. Rather than being signs of submission, religious conversion and literacy were repurposed as instruments of survival, or what James C. Scott calls "weapons of the weak." Unlike Scott, though, I argue that the invisibility or illegibility of these transgressive adoptions stems from a translational withholding that was less an act of resistance than it was a rekindling of Dakhóta ethics and peoplehood that the camps sought to wipe out. As I discussed in my introduction, these imprisoned ancestors negotiated their hypervisibility with an unheroic form of self-publicity, deferring to settler-colonial authority and only demurring beneath the sign of acquiescence. However, as I will show, their humble, often heartbreaking letters to relatives are the first move in a century and a half of resurgent rewriting of the Oyáte.

Another aim of this chapter is to highlight the ongoing violence of whitewashing the genocide through which the state of Minnesota was founded. Dakhóta activist and scholar Wazíyatawiŋ argues that the sesquicentennial anniversary of the state's founding is an opportunity to confront that violence, arguing, "Dakota people paid a terrible price so that white Minnesotans could claim this beautiful and bountiful land."[3] To recall the human costs of the war for Dakhóta people is thus to conjure what has been previously unthinkable within settler society: the recognition of moral obligations involved in commemorating a Minnesota statehood born from an ethnic-cleansing campaign. This genocide began in response to Dakhóta warriors' killing of five whites in Acton, Minnesota, on August 17, 1862, and included a campaign of ethnic cleansing that was spurred by the infamous call of Governor Alexander Ramsey in a special session of the Minnesota legislature convened on September 9, 1862, for "the Sioux Indians of Minnesota" to be "exterminated or driven forever beyond the borders of the state."[4] As Wazíyatawiŋ notes, what followed from Ramsey's pronouncement reads as a clear indictment of the genocidal campaign waged by the settler-state: "The hangings, the concentration camps and forced imprisonments, the forced gender segregation, the punitive campaigns into Dakota Territory to hunt down and terrorize those trying to flee, the bounties on Dakhóta scalps—all are examples of how Ramsey's plan was successfully implemented."[5] This campaign culminated in the punitive expeditions of General Alfred Sully and General Henry Sibley into western Minnesota and Dakota Territory, to which some 5,000 eastern Dakhóta, fearing punishment for their involvement in the war, which most of them did not engage in, fled from the thousands of amassed army troops and local militias.[6]

Years ago, in 1998, my grandma, Grace Lambert, talked about the war when I interviewed her at her home in Fort Totten, North Dakota. I had been asking elders who were my relatives about different locations on the reservation. That afternoon, I stopped at her house with my mother, Donna Pexa (Charboneau), and my uŋčí, Rachel Charboneau (Langer Young). Grace called the 1862 war an uprising, although I learned much later that it issued from a formal declaration of war by a soldier's lodge of Little Crow's band. In her account, she highlighted conditions of starvation among the Dakhóta, whose treaty rations had been withheld by traders. She also described divisions among Dakhóta who had intermarried with whites and how many mixed families were forced into an impossible choice of taking sides. But her account began in Acton, Minnesota:

> He said that these two boys, you know, they were Indian boys, they were going along in this little town here, somewhere in there was the building where the rations was kept for the village, you know, and the Indian village is over here somewhere, and it's all woods around Fort Snelling. And these two teenage boys, they're about thirteen, fourteen years old, one of them belonged to one of the chiefs, you know there's always a chief for all the, several, there's several fires, you remember?[7] Even the Oglalas have that too. Sicangu and Spotted Tail and all them, you remember? Well, them over here too, they have that, and so they have these chiefs. Anyway, there must have been a couple of chiefs in that camp maybe, 'cause these camps weren't all together, because there's too many of them. Somewhere there's another camp, and somewhere there's another area. Well, anyway, these two, one of these kids belonged to the chief, that was the chief's son, and they were going and here, they went in a chicken coop, they found an egg in there, you know, and they took it, you know, they came out and, right

now, the farmer that owned the chickens and that place was his farm, why, he was watching out for them kids and when they got in sight I suppose, right away, he was watching them, and he came outside and he was standing with his shotgun set on the porch, on his little porch, to see what them kids were going to do. Soon they came out with the egg, and the other kid said, "I dare you to break it," and the crazy kid, I guess he just dropped it so it broke, and he just shot him. And they said that's what started that war. So this kid, the other kid, here he took off and ran, but the other one was shot, he got killed right there, you know, that was a shotgun. And the kid who got back to the camp and he told them that the boy was dead, you know, that guy shot him. So that's how come the uprising came up. All the warriors got together and they went into the town and boy, they destroyed everything, cleaned that place just flat. That's how come they call it the massacre. And that was close to Fort Snelling, so right now somebody ran over to Fort Snelling and told them, so the soldiers start coming and that's when the Indians broke camp and they ran each, every direction. Some ran towards the river, and some ran towards the open, this way. There was no towns and all these places, they weren't there then. Some went right into Canada. That's how come they have Sioux Valley, that's one of those places. And that's when the party that was running through the open area was Lily's grandmother, my sister Lily said her grandma was seventeen years old at that time. And her sister had these two kids, but she had been living with a white man. But see, when these Indians were starving to death, well, already they were kind of in an uproar. They were undecided about what they should do, but they were telling their people that all these people that were married to white men, they were going to kill them, you know, the men and their children, but they were going to let the women live. They were planning on that already then.

Grace's story of the dropped egg speeds from the encounter in Acton to the white armed response and the Dakhóta flight from Minnesota. That egg is often given as the reason for the start of attacks on white settlements. But another reason appears in a related story where the farmer, Andrew Myrick (actually a local trader and store owner), was found dead with grass stuffed in his mouth—presumably an ironic reply to his saying "let them eat grass or their own dung" rather than giving Dakhóta people credit to buy food from him. Whether grass or eggs, these accounts give evidence for the conditions of mass starvation that existed among the Dakhóta because of withheld annuity payments. As Dean Blue (Phežútazi Ok'ápi, or Upper Sioux, Dakhóta) observes in his oral account of the war, "It's true that some young bucks [Dakhóta warriors] did kill some settlers. But the point is, they were hungry, they were starving because they were not allowed to go off the reservation to hunt," and because the U.S. government "withheld annuities; not just one year, not just two years, but three years—no annuities."[8]

Such depictions of settler treaty breaking and carceral reservation conditions are important correctives for what has been until recently a condition of settler-colonial amnesia surrounding the 1862 war. Even since the conflict's sesquicentennial anniversary in 2012, few scholars have explored how Dakhóta experienced and resisted state power in the concentration camps[9] that were created shortly after the battle of Wood Lake on September 23, 1862, and the surrender of Dakhóta at Camp Release[10] a few days later, on September 26. There are notable exceptions to this narrative absence[11] and this chapter contributes to that small but important body of work by reading an understudied archive of Dakhóta voices that appears in prisoners' letters. My purpose here is not to engage in a polemic against the ongoing conditions of settler-colonialism in the United States, although such an approach is certainly warranted. Instead, I want to open up space for dialogue in a different way than Wazíyatawiŋ does, but I think from no less critical a perspective. I find her sense that relationship is something that comes with "a responsibility that relays a culture, an identity, and a sense of belonging"[12] to be an important point of entry for engaging how Dakhóta people in the aftermath of the war found in thióšpaye (literally "camp circle" but meaning extended family as lived through relationships within and among tribal bands) philosophy and in living relatives the crucial resources for remaking a coherent sense of peoplehood after having been targeted for extermination by Minnesota settlers.

Iháŋkthuŋwaŋ (Yankton) anthropologist and author Ella Cara Deloria placed the thióšpaye at the core or Dakhóta peoplehood, writing in *Speaking of Indians* that

> the ultimate aim of Dakota life, stripped of accessories, was quite simple: One must obey kinship rules; one must be a good relative. No Dakota who has participated in that life will dispute that. In the last analysis every other consideration was secondary—property,

personal ambition, glory, good times, life itself. Without that aim
and the constant struggle to attain it, the people would no longer be
Dakotas in truth. They would no longer even be human.[13]

As Deloria observes, "kinship rules" form an ethical system that strad-
dles the epistemological ("one must obey kinship rules") and the ontological (being Dakhóta). As a shorthand, I use the term "thióšpaye
ethics" here and throughout this book as a way to unpack various
meanings of being a good relative. The ethical norms of the thióšpaye
are the complex core set of moral truths that bound Dakhóta people
to one another, as kin, in mutual obligations of respect, giving, and
power sharing.

In the Dakhóta concentration camps, ties among relatives were
explicitly targeted through the punitive means that Wazíyatawiŋ
names as well as through religious conversions to Christianity that
were based in a logic of cultural incommensurability. Stephen Return
Riggs, quoting the journal of his colleague and early Presbyterian missionary among the Dakhóta, Gideon Pond, tells the story of zealous
new converts in the concentration camp at Mankato, Minnesota. As a
prologue to the rest of this chapter, it is worth quoting at length:

> There are over three hundred Indians in prison, the most of whom
> are in chains. There is a degree of religious interest manifested
> by them, which is incredible. They huddle themselves together
> every morning and evening in the prison, and read the Scriptures,
> sing hymns, confess one to another, exhort one another, and pray
> together. They say that their whole lives have been wicked—that
> they have adhered to the superstitions of their ancestors until they
> have reduced themselves to their present state of wretchedness
> and ruin. They declare that they have left it all, and will leave all
> forever; that they do and will embrace the religion of Jesus Christ,
> and adhere to it as long as they live; and that this is their only
> hope, both in this world and in the next. They say that before
> they came to this state of mind—this determination—their hearts
> failed them with fear, and but now they have much mental ease
> and comfort.[14]

Pond visited the Mankato camp for less than four full days. Perhaps
not surprisingly, the camps seemed to him an ideal crucible for making Christians of heathens and liberal individuals of tribally attached

savages. The combined force of these ideologies was imagined, as my epigraph to this chapter ominously suggests, as the instrument for the civilizational conversion of people whose only crime was in being Dakhóta.

However, when prisoners undertook to learn reading and writing in order to communicate with their Dakhóta relations, often also addressing their white tutors as "brother" and "my relative," fault lines appear within Pond's and Bradley's either/or assessments. It is within these fault lines that I read space for countertranslations that take a humble but powerful form: as the continuity of a thióšpaye ethics and epistemology. I am not trying to deny the obvious: the Dakhóta lost their homelands and became subjects of the state. However, I find ample reasons to explore the nature of that subjection, including the diverse experiences of the prisoners as recorded in their letters and as evidenced in the variety of loyalties—often conflicted, never simple— held in relation to other Dakhóta relatives, to mixed-blood relatives, and to whites. In exploring Dakhóta subjection from the inside, if you will, I am not interested in reading the severely constrained position that prisoners found themselves in as a moment of positive cultural change. What follows is not an argument for hybridity or syncretism as the best, or even a particularly good, way of understanding how people were forced to adapt traditional lifeways and values to the pressures of state domination. Syncretism, of course, potentially reproduces liberal ideals of cultural inclusivism, as well as teleologies of social progress and national belonging (i.e., the "melting pot" or assimilationist ideal). Latent in "bridging" metaphors of cultural change is a masking of settler-colonial violence and a denial of Indigenous sovereignty.[15]

Instead, my analysis privileges the Dakhóta language, drawing inspiration from Dipesh Chakrabarty's analysis of the concept of *adda*, a Bengali form of sociality as well as of organizing time and space, whose illegibility to British outsiders made it a means for cultural and political resistance to colonization.[16] This is not an essentialist argument for cultural or linguistic purity or fixity but rather an "appeal to models of cross-cultural and cross-categorical translations that do not take a universal middle term for granted."[17] I am interested in the extent to which thióšpaye ethics remained largely unchanged through practices of selective adoption and translation of social forms in the camps. What fell out of, or was strategically withheld from, the linguistic and cultural translations that occurred in the camps? How were acts of cultural and linguistic translation also acts of transgression and border crossing, fugitive acts of raiding the settler-colonists' camps in order to make the lives of one's relatives more livable?

By focusing on the slippages between English and Dakhóta languages, languages that mediated the mass conversions of prisoners, we may see more clearly the transgressive adoptions of white culture by those prisoners. In my reading of the camps, transgression appears under the guise of compliance or assimilation (converting to Christianity, learning to write and read, practicing vocational trades), where the adoption of forms of whiteness did not mean relinquishing Dakhóta values but instead merely afforded some of whiteness's privileges (i.e., literacy training, communication with distant relatives, greater freedom of movement within the prison, and the chance of reduced or commuted sentences). More than the simple gaining of prison privileges, though, these transgressions also importantly cleared space for forms of solidarity that were unintelligible to settlers. By writing letters to family imprisoned elsewhere, some imprisoned Dakhóta were able to maintain, and even extend the reach of, thióšpaye epistemologies and so reclaim an important basis for remembering, decolonizing, and remaking a wounded peoplehood.

A Cautionary Note on Missionaries

Drawing out the texture of resistances that play out mainly for audiences in the know requires a view toward long-circulating Dakhóta ethical discourses. Accordingly, in what follows I draw on three main kinds of texts. First are the letters written by Dakhóta prisoners, fifty of which were recently transcribed and translated by Clifford Canku and Michael Simon as *The Dakota Prisoner of War Letters: Dakota Kaskapi Okicize Wowapi* (2013). These letters constitute an important archive for Dakhóta responses to colonization and offer a singular depiction of the material and ideological pressures faced by Dakhóta in Camp Kearney, adjacent to Camp McClellan in Davenport, Iowa. The translated letters have further value in how they may be read for evidence of the endurance of thióšpaye understandings and practices, which should be read for their political and philosophical implications. I explore this endurance in the second portion of the chapter, after I provide the basic historical backdrop for the camps and their various modes of state domination.

In addition to the Dakhóta voices that appear in these letters, I also include observations of the camps that appear in missionary documents. These include letters written by Stephen Riggs and Thomas Williamson from the camps and letters and notebooks from Dakhóta missions preceding the formation of the camps. I also cite ethnographic sources like James R. Walker's *Lakota Belief and Ritual* (1991), which details Dakhóta/Lakȟóta cosmology through interviews gathered between 1894 and 1916. By placing the words of prisoners in dialogue with these other sources, I hope to draw out the extent to which imprisoned Dakhóta translated and adapted state and religious rhetorics to suit their own purposes.

I acknowledge that seeking out resistance through readings of non-Dakhóta sources—particularly missionary ones—might seem misguided, given the textual fact of missionary authorship and the structural fact of Christianity's complicity in the violence of settler-colonialism. After all, Christianity furnished first the theological notion of "Discovery" and later assimilationist rhetorics through which white claims to civilizational superiority justified what George Tinker calls the "cultural genocide" of Indigenous peoples.[18] Yet despite the colonizers' hopes, colonialism did not unfold as a monologue but rather in interactional or relational ways. My readings of missionaries begin from the assumption that they provide ample opportunities for finding Indigenous voice and agency between the "authoritative" lines penned by missionaries. To rephrase Trouillot's remarks about the erasure of historical experience, if the unthinkable is going to become thinkable, then we must read for voice and agency in conditions where they were not only suppressed but also where they may seem to have been most fully erased.

Thióšpaye Betrayed: Placing the Camps in Historical Perspective

On his first visit to Fort Snelling in November, General Henry Hastings Sibley, leader of the Minnesota militia during the 1862 U.S.–Dakhóta War, described the camp as a "dismal fenced enclosure," even before deaths from starvation, exposure, and epidemic—including measles, diphtheria, and typhoid—would run riot in the coldest months of early 1863, killing more than a hundred Dakhóta. State authorities would call those imprisoned at Fort Snelling "captives," as they were not charged with committing war crimes during the military campaign of the previous six weeks. The remaining Dakhóta, 417 in all, who had surrendered to General Sibley's forces and were bound for sentencing and execution, were marched to Camp Lincoln, near Mankato. There 393 Dakhóta warriors were tried by a five-man military tribunal, where the average hearing lasted no more than ten minutes. At first the tribunal sought the death penalty only in cases of rape, which according to white accounts were numerous. After finding only two cases worthy of hanging, though, the tribune expanded its criteria to include killing of any kind, and treated even the killing of state and federal militia members as acts of insurrection.

This sudden suspension of what Carol Chomsky calls "a consistent de facto recognition that the members of an Indian tribe should be treated as legitimate belligerents in wartime"[19] reveals the retributive purpose of the tribunals, or what David Martínez (Akimel O'odham) asserts was "a settler population that saw itself above the Constitution and beyond any regard for human rights."[20] Chomsky adds, "Although the fighting men from Indian nations sometimes suffered retaliation for their actions in war, never before or after the United States–Dakota War were they condemned by any form of legal process for violence associated with warfare."[21] A total of 391 Dakhóta were then sentenced to death, but President Abraham Lincoln, afraid that so many executions would be perceived as its own kind of massacre, reduced the total number of condemned to thirty-eight. (Two other Dakhóta men, Little Six and Medicine Bottle, would be hanged at Fort Snelling on November 11, 1865.) The hanging, held the day after Christmas in 1862, remains the largest mass execution ever performed in the United States.[22]

Part of the camps' lack of visibility within existing theoretical frameworks for reading resurgence lies in an evasive legal nomenclature. While in the camp at Fort Snelling, Dakhóta were subject to an extralegal status, being neither prisoners of war nor criminals. Rather, they were merely "in captivity," as the captions of military photographer Benjamin F. Upton note.[23] In effect, the 1,700 prisoners endured a kind of civil death. Dakhóta were not U.S. citizens; nor were they members of what Americans considered a "foreign nation"; nor were the Dakhóta warriors considered to be members of a legitimate army. They were suffering the further consequences of their ambiguous "domestic dependent nation" status. Within this indeterminate legal identity, they were not seen or seeable by state authorities as agents of any kind. They were not even victims; rather, they were wards. Indeed, the official government narrative of both Camp Lincoln at Mankato and Fort Snelling's stockade was one of protecting vulnerable Indigenous bodies. In a letter dated December 6, 1862, the purpose of which was to list those warriors to be executed at Mankato, Lincoln wrote to General Henry H. Sibley that the remaining prisoners would be "held, subject to further orders, taking care that they neither escape nor are subjected to any unlawful violence."[24] His sense that "unlawful violence" would be done by white settlers to Dakhóta who had surrendered is borne out by Dakhóta accounts of enraged whites killing Dakhóta infants and women as they marched, in chain, for many miles to the camp at Fort Snelling.[25] Maybe just as striking, ethically if not legally, as this form of legal erasure is the fact that the camps remained in use for several months after Lincoln delivered his final Emancipation Proclamation on January 1, 1863. By May of that year, when the remaining "prisoners" of Mankato were forcibly removed to Camp McClellan in Davenport, Iowa, to remain there in *durance vile* and the surviving "captives" of Fort Snelling were removed by steamer boats to the Crow Creek reservation in South Dakota, they remained in forms of bondage that had become anachronistic but "necessary."

Despite capitalizing on Dakhóta people's legal indeterminacy, the concentration camps were known to Americans at that time as spectacles of punishment for perceived rebellion against the United States. Indeed, the material culture generated by the camps, their ephemera of newspaper advertisements, postcards, and stereographs, reveals a profusion of items that made the prisoners hypervisible while also obscuring the violence of the camps, even when that violence was observed firsthand. Before their removal, captives at Mankato and Fort Snelling were regularly visited by civilian outsiders, and among these were commercial photographers from St. Paul and Minneapolis, engaged in creating a profitable economy of postcards, or *cartes de visites*, many of which depicted sentimental images of lone, stoic "captives," as well as stereographs depicting prisoners and conditions in the camps (Figure 2). Newspaper ads in Minnesota newspapers featured advertisements, trumpeting that some of these photos "had reached collections in Europe" and were selling in St. Paul galleries "at New York prices."[26] Other objects, such as commemorative bowls, platters, and spoons (Figure 3),[27] recorded the hangings in more banal ways. Industries of ephemera grew from and reinforced the hypervisibility of Dakhóta warrior masculinity especially, as if preventing its resurgence required an ideological overkill, a translation into helplessness that went beyond criminalization and into humiliation. Such exterminatory industries created the discursive backdrop for the prisoners' letters, just as it would for Dakhóta and Lakhóta authors writing in the decades after the war, by authorizing only material that was the most innocuous and the most emasculated. Yet it was this demand—for what Elizabeth Povinelli calls not only an "[un]repugnant" indigeneity but a contrite one—that created the conditions for Dakhóta countertranslations that highlighted individuals' survival as well as the survival of the Oyáte.[28]

Of course, Dakhóta people continue to produce decolonial countertranslations. The spectacles of the tribunal and hangings are perhaps the best-known aspects of what would become the Dakhóta diaspora,[29] and Dakhóta people remember today the punishments of the camps and diaspora with great poignancy. In the opening of

FIGURE 2. Whitney's Gallery, *Stereoview of Six Dakota Men in the Prison Compound at Fort Snelling in 1862–3*. From the Minnesota Historical Society, http://collections.mnhs.org.

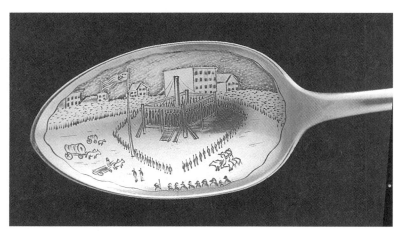

FIGURE 3. Unknown artist, *Mankato Spoon*, circa 1890–1902. From *History Detectives*, PBS.org.

a tribally produced documentary about the Mní Wakháŋ Oyáte, the chairperson, Myra Pearson, is seated on a couch while her grandson, Terry "T" Morgan, kneels on a rug at her feet, questioning her about Dakhóta history. As prologue to the rest of the documentary, Pearson says, "I believe it's now time to pass some of these stories and memories [from 150 years ago] onto you . . . but some of our memories are hard to speak of. My great-grandfather's brother was among the 38, the 38 who died at the place called Mankato." To which her grandson replies, "Is that why we live here at Spirit Lake? To get away from the people who hung great-grandpa's brother?" "Well, I guess you could say that. Sometime we'll have to visit again and I can tell you the whole story."[30] Although this conversation serves to introduce the documentary history that follows, the hesitation here signals not just a protective withholding of difficult knowledge but also an invitation to later engage with it.

Although the ad hoc legal machinery of the tribunals got the process of land theft underway, the concentration camps were the most expedient means to remove the Dakhóta from Minnesota. Gabriel Renville (Thíwakhaŋ, or Holy Lodge) was a "mixed-blood" who, because he was "not implicated in any of the outrages against the whites" during the war, was "given the privilege of being outside of the Indian camp, coming and going as he pleased."[31] From his position of relative freedom and mobility, Renville recalled that in the midst of an epidemic, when "children were dying day and night," the news of the Mankato hangings turned an already arduous situation into a brutal trial, making "a person . . . doubtful" whether "they would be alive in the morning."[32] Firsthand accounts like Thíwakhaŋ's reveal an anxious and prescient awareness of the specter of land loss. "How can we get lands and have homes again," he asks after news of the Mankato hangings reached Fort Snelling, adding that these "were the questions which troubled many thinking minds, and were hard questions to answer."[33]

Of course, this process of land theft had begun long before 1862. Charles Alexander Eastman (Ohíye s'a, meaning Wins Often or Winner), a Dakhóta physician and author who was separated from his father, Wakháŋhdi Óta (Many Lightnings), during the war, wrote that the situation of Dakhóta was one of "virtual imprisonment" long before the literal walls and chains at Fort Snelling.[34] Having treated away all but "a tract of land twenty miles by thirty," they found themselves unable also to access hunting and fishing grounds, and they grew more and more dependent on government annuities and traders' supplies for their survival. On entering the "new life" promised them by treaty, though, Eastman writes that "the resources so rosily described to them failed to materialize. Many families faced starvation every winter, their only support the store of the Indian trader, who was baiting his trap for their destruction."[35]

After the defeat and surrender of Dakhóta under Little Crow at Wood Lake, Minnesota, on September 23, 1862, 1,700 noncombatant Dakhóta and some mixed-blood Dakhóta, mostly women, children, and the elderly, were forcibly marched from their temporary detention by the U.S. Army in Camp Release.[36] For six days in early November, they were forced to walk in a three-mile-long chain of bodies to be imprisoned at a camp within sight of Fort Snelling, near St. Paul. Oral accounts of the forced march recall acts of violence committed by white audiences who inserted themselves into the spectacle of punishment in bloody ways, with some bringing "poles, pitchforks and axes and hit[ting] some of the [Dakhóta] women and children in the wagons," and others attacking whites and Dakhóta alike: "A boy was driving an ox cart and the white people knocked him down. Some Indians died from the beatings they received."[37]

Other Dakhóta oral histories remember an infant who was taken from his mother's arms and killed in front of her. She placed him in the crook of a tree so that his body could not be defiled by animals.

Episodes of rage on the part of whites such as these owed in part to the killings of some five hundred whites during the initial Dakhóta raids on white settlements, which were viewed through the lens of savagery rather than that of retribution for dishonest treaty dealings, failure to deliver on what treaty promises had been made, and the subsequent creation of famine conditions for Dakhóta. Gary Clayton Anderson, in his economic analysis of the origins of the war, links the failure of relationships that had existed since the early fur trade with this moment of crisis: "In the final analysis, a substantial number of Sioux men concluded that the white man had abandoned, seemingly forever, the obligations and promises of assistance that formed the basis for the Dakota communal existence and all relations with people."[38] My next section centers readings of prisoners' letters to tease out how Dakhóta thióšpaye ethics challenged this sense of cultural (or civilizational) incommensurability, and how those ethics endured in the face of the forms of state domination I have sketched so far.

Translating "God": The Davenport Dakhóta Prisoners' Letters

Missionaries of the American Board of Commissioners for Foreign Missions were the first and most numerous religious delegation within the concentration camps.[39] They established their first mission station at Lac qui Parle in Minnesota in June 1836.[40] With the aims of supplanting thióšpaye ties and communal responsibilities among Dakhóta, as well as breaking up community landholdings, they preached salvation along with ideals of national citizenship and individual property ownership. When Presbyterian missionary Stephen Riggs described the mass conversions in the concentration camps with Thomas Jefferson's phrase, as "a nation born in a day,"[41] we might say that nationalist and religious discourses of settler individualism intersected powerfully in the incarcerated bodies of the converted. Riggs described the Mankato prison in March 1863 as "one great school," adding that the inmates' desire for learning "is a perfect *mania*."[42] The reality, of course, was somewhat less divine than pragmatic. Riggs described how reading circles, overseen by "those who had been taught in our mission schools," were successfully transforming the Dakhóta into "civilized people."[43] But such reading circles furnished prisoners with pen and paper, as well as English literacy sufficient to write to relatives imprisoned at other camps and reassure them that they were still alive. Despite the importance of maintaining such thióšpaye ties as a motive for religious conversion, and despite the access to literacy that conversion provided, Riggs sees conversions as proof of the U.S. civilizing mission's success. In closing his remarks on education in this letter, Riggs suggests that the only way to account for the "progress . . . made by the Indians at Mankato and Fort Snelling, during the present winter," was that prison proved to be a crucible for the civilizing mission. In effect, Riggs concurred with Major Bradley, "who by the way was one of the Military Commission," and who "proposes as a theory, *that 'the best way to civilize Indians is to imprison them.'*"[44]

Dakhóta prisoners held in the other concentration camps at Fort Snelling, Minnesota, and Crow Creek, in what is now called South Dakota, also received literacy training from missionaries and produced letters. In the rest of this section, I focus only on the letters produced by prisoners held at Camp Kearney. The range of tones, subjects, and purposes they reflect reveal a richness of difficultly lived experiences: there are accusations of racism ("We realize that whoever sees us, and no matter what we say to try to defend ourselves, the white people will think of dogs," writes Wakháŋhdi Tópa [Four Lightning, or David Faribault Jr.]),[45] descriptions of harsh prison conditions, expressions of concern for relatives who were elsewhere, dutiful professions of Christian faith, gestures of what appear to be defiance ("There is one thing I want to set straight," writes Čhaské [First Born Son, or Robert Hopkins]; "I am looking forward to death and my execution at the appropriate time"),[46] and, of course, petitions for release. Given this complexity, and indeed ambivalence, they warrant further and more detailed readings than I can give here. However, reading the letters through for their singular accounts of thióšpaye ethics allows access to some part of their complex ethical articulations.

In his introduction to the collected letters, John Peacock remarks on running into translational difficulties in the process of editing a letter written by one of his own ancestors, Antoine Provençalle. Provençalle's repetition of certain Dakhóta phrases, including instances of "it is so" (the Dakhóta word *dó* or *yé*) and "my relative" (*mitákuye*), were so numerous that Peacock was at first tempted to remove most of them to "make them more idiomatically 'correct' in English."[47] Yet Peacock came to understand that these were more than "rhetorical flourishes." The "repeated invocation of kinship is not just a term of address; kinship is the very topic of the letter, of every paragraph, of each sentence. The rest of every sentence, of the body of every paragraph, then addresses what is predicated on kinship—exchange between kin."[48] A typical appeal based in thióšpaye ties is one like James Hepan Wakan's (James the Sacred Second Son). In a letter dated May 17, 1864, he asks Riggs "to mention ... [the] name" of his younger brother to those who might free him, as he is imprisoned "at the mouth of the Minnesota River" (Fort Snelling) and "his whole body is sick and in a weakened condition, and I don't expect him to last too long, I'm thinking [qa raramdote en misunka kaxkayanke cin he eya tanyan waunspekiya tuka tancan ocowasin xica qa on tehan iwaxake kte xni epca he cajedate kta wacin]."[49]

These appeals for help, or even just to inform relatives being held elsewhere, demonstrate how prisoners' desire for solidarity through the most basic acts of communication was one important motivation for the camp conversions. But thióšpaye bonds and norms extended beyond Dakhóta to non-Dakhóta as well. To a contemporary reader whose primary language is English, the repeated invocations of relational terms such as *mitákuye* (my relative), *mitákoda* (my friend), or *mihunkáwanži* (my one adopted brother) to describe Riggs (whom Dakhóta called Támakȟočhe, His Country) may seem like either formality or ingratiation. Perhaps it is something of both. After all, the prisoners drew on both Dakhóta customs of address and the literary manners of nineteenth-century epistolary convention. Their dire situation no doubt predisposed some Dakhóta to approach influential whites like Riggs in ways that might help them or their relatives. However, the sincerity of the thióšpaye address is beside the point. What matters is how the imprisoned used thióšpaye norms in quite Dakhóta ways, above all by leveraging it to call on Riggs and others to fulfill requests as matters of obligation owed to family. In this way the prisoners often constructed Riggs and other whites, through their address as relatives, as Dakhóta persons, subject to the norms of Dakhóta sociality—a strange reversal of power, given the extreme physical hardships suffered by Dakhóta in the prisons!

It is arguably mistaken to call this simply a reversal because the effect of Dakhóta people calling on white "brothers" was not to dominate them but rather to ask that they observe the obligations of reciprocity that were required of kin. For instance, in a letter dated June 2, 1865, to Stephen Riggs, Mr. Sagyékituŋ (Mr. Uses a Cane) opens what will become a request for help in gaining release from prison by citing his own fulfillment of favors asked by the missionary. "My relative," he begins,

I will write you a letter, and there is one thing I will say to you. There were many men imprisoned, and you took the Word of God [*táku wakháŋ wičhóie*, "some mysterious word"] to them, and you taught them. You told us to teach all of the men from the Mdewakantonwan people, and we did as you told us to [Mitakuye ito wowapi Wanji cicage kte qa taku wanji eciciye kte Wicaxta ota wicakaxkapi onkan en taku wakan oie kin en ayaipi qa Dakota waunspeyakiyapi Etanhan wicaxta tona mdewakantunwan oyate ocowasin waunspekiye onyaxipi qa ecen ecunqunpi].[50]

To this recounting of the initial favor asked by Riggs, Mr. Sagyékituŋ adds, with a hint of reproach, that one of these Dakhóta teachers named Bird Came Back had died, and that "you [Reverend Stephen R. Riggs and Reverend Thomas S. Williamson] were supposed to do this [take the Word of God to other Dakhóta], but instead you asked us to do it, so now we're finished." This last phrase in Dakhóta is "owasin onxtankpi iyececa okini niye ecanapi," and the English gloss that translators Clifford Canku and Michael Simon give suggests less a note of finality than of pride in their accomplishment: "and now all we finished is like maybe you did."[51]

However, this is far from pride in mimicry, as the rest of Mr. Sagyékituŋ's letter shows. After he explains that other of the small group of teaching Dakhóta "are going home at this time," leaving only himself and two other converts in prison, Mr. Sagyékituŋ gets around to stating his main purpose: demanding reciprocity. "Well," he writes, "there is one thing we want you to take a look at and think about it. The three of us want you to help us—it is so [ito taku wanji iwandake qa idukcan qa ito henaoz ounyakiyapi kta oncinpi do]."[52] Ultimately his grounds for asking for such reciprocity appeal to several different sets of norms: Dakhóta relational norms of mutual obligation ("We did as you told us to"), Christian rhetoric ("Those of us who live on this earth, and although we proclaim His Word, we are still the object of evil intention against us"),[53] and U.S. nationalism ("If the President saw the new program you have enacted, he would be thankful and say you did a good job, and he would commend you for your work").[54] Despite his savvy negotiation of various rhetorics, Mr. Sagyékituŋ returns to his thióšpaye-based appeal in the closing of his letter, reiterating to Riggs to weigh his obligation to the Dakhóta men, to "look at our actions and think about it." Then, in a reference that ostensibly suggests his valorizing of white culture, Mr. Sagyékituŋ notes that his petition has been written and therefore must be true: "Although our actions have taken place, they're all written down. There can be no lies about what we did, because it's all written down [Takomni token onkoranpi owasin owayanka kin hena woitonxni on hecen owa eonhnakapi nace epca]."[55] By citing the writtenness of his petition, though, Mr. Sagyékituŋ ironically plays back to Riggs the white fetishizing of print as supposedly embodying more permanent and civilized forms of memory—a fetishizing that was first expressed most fully, in the context of U.S. settler-colonialism, with the Bible.

Ethical singularities of the thióšpaye also show up in the vexed translations into Dakhóta language of core Christian terms denoting conversion. If the prisoners enjoined their white brethren to act as good relatives, then their letters also show them filtering a Christian vocabulary through a matrix of existing Dakhóta relational understandings, even, and perhaps especially, in their professions of faith— but faith in what, and in what degree? At one end of the translational spectrum is Ruban His Sacred Nest, who writes to Stephen Riggs, in a letter dated April 22, 1864, ostensibly with some irony: "They say the Holy Spirit alone is most great, I suppose for that reason, now we are men in prisons [Ecin taku wakan eyapi kin hecedan iyotan heon dehan koška unyakunpi wicašta]."[56] What appears here to be gallows humor becomes an unadorned accusation of white Christians bringing about an apocalypse for Dakhóta alone: "For myself, I think God is most Great and Good. Frequently I think about the second death [Judgment Day], that is something upon earth, it's not terrible, it's terrible for us alone [Tuka miš kaken epca waun Wakantanka hee iyotan qa wašte qa eya otakiyan awacin waun heon wicunṭe inonpa hee taku maka akan terika iyecece šni hee terika heon onkixnina]."[57] The letter writer's revision of the Christian Judgment to comment ruefully and with measured scorn on the actions of whites is a jeremiad in the truest sense, issuing a prophetic judgment on those whose morals have slipped. But the presence, in translation, of the word "God," for the Dakhóta compound word "Wakantanka," while in keeping with the translation used in early missionary materials written in Dakhóta, makes this writer's position of utterance quite complicated.[58]

It is complicated, first of all, by the fact that the Dakhóta conception of "Wakantanka" was no heavenly judge bent on righteous reprimand. To consider just the first half of the word "Wakantanka": the concept of wakháŋ proved to be something of a lifelong cipher to missionaries. For instance, in an early ethnographic tract, "The Theogony of the Sioux," Riggs describes the important concept of wakháŋ in the language of worship: "In the mind of a Dakota or Sioux Indian, this word Wahkon (we write wakan), covers the whole field of their *fear* and their *worship*. Many things also that are neither feared nor worshipped, but simply *wonderful*, come under this designation."[59] A sense of hierarchy infuses this passage, with fear and worship marking the extreme boundaries of an embattled ethical field. In fact, wakháŋ designates not what is wonderful, because the category of "wonder" is, like that of "worship," etymologically rooted in Christian theology and in a distinctly vertical or hierarchical sense of relation. Rather, it suggests in Dakhóta that which is remarkable or distinctive in a particular way. Riggs's entry for *wakaŋ* in his dictionary reveals a far more nuanced sense of this important concept than do his letters. Described in largely theistic terms as an adjective meaning "spiritual, sacred, consecrated; wonderful, incomprehensible," Riggs also notes that the word is "said also of women at the menstrual period," adding that its other meanings of "mysterious: incomprehensible; in a peculiar state, which, from not being understood, it is dangerous to meddle with" made it a poor translation for the Christian terms "holy" and "sacred," but also the "only one suitable."[60] The sense of danger in entering into relation with others that Riggs saw in the concept of wakháŋ, and saw as an obstacle to Dakhóta understandings of a Christian God, was in fact a central concept within Dakhóta ethics.

This sense of danger or risk is at work in a letter from February 1846 titled "Born Two Days Ago," where Riggs narrates his encounter with an elder Dakhóta man named Tokaheya.[61] The title of the letter does not refer to a Christian rebirth; instead, for Riggs, it captures the old man's retrospective sense of life's briefness, which Riggs compares to the biblical Jacob's pessimistic declaration that "few and evil have the days of the years of my life been."[62] Moved by illness, Tokaheya comes to Riggs to ask for a "small piece of cotton cloth," which he wants "to offer as a sacrifice" that may cure him. This statement leads Riggs to a theological commentary where he pronounces that the cloth would not be offered "to the true God" but instead to one of the sundry Dakhóta "gods." After Tokaheya describes a tortoise as the cause of his sickness, Riggs wryly comments, "the cotton cloth he wanted to sacrifice to his Aesculapius," before sermonizing to Tokaheya that Christ was in fact "the great atoning sacrifice, which made all others unnecessary." The old man's response is simple but hardly straightforward: "Well, don't give it to me."

Whether Tokaheya meant his reply as an outright refusal of Riggs's preaching and Christian theory of sacrifice or as a more conciliatory reply is not clear. What seems clear is Riggs's ignorance of Dakhóta ideas about disease causation and healing, or how tortoises within Dakhóta thinking can be beings capable of acting intentionally and responding ethically to other beings. As anthropologist Raymond DeMallie notes, Dakhóta cosmology has historically reflected mutual relations among human and other-than-human persons. The wakháŋ beings that made up Wakháŋ Tháŋka (great mystery), numbering sixteen according to "some holy men," included "sun, moon, wind, Thunder-beings, earth, rock, White Buffalo Woman, and a variety of invisible spirit forms." These beings were all bound together into a "oneness" that "was symbolized in kin relationships that bound all together and provided accepted patterns for interaction."[63] Their interrelationships formed the template for human interactions, such that "human relationships—parents and children, grandparents and grandchildren, brothers and sisters, husbands and wives—were reflections of these greater, more fundamental relationships established by the wakan beings."[64] By viewing Dakhóta religiosity as supernaturalistic and polytheistic, rather than based in relations of mutual responsibility between human and nonhuman beings, Riggs assumed an either/or mentality where one monolithic "belief system" replaces another. Because Dakhóta relationality had been understood from the get-go by Presbyterian missionaries in theistic terms, the conversion effort was cast in militaristic terms as a battle between "gods" and the "great God." Like his fellow American Board of Commissioners for Foreign Missions missionaries Thomas Williamson and Gideon Pond, Riggs saw the Yahwist call for renunciation of false gods and idols as being at the heart of what conversion was and how it was done. Tokaheya's treatment of the tortoise, however, reflected his sense that the tortoise's practicing of bad power or medicine required a reciprocal response, such as the threat of destroying the image he had drawn on a piece of cloth.

Riggs himself seems to have been aware of his own inability to fully, or even adequately, translate the Dakhóta concept of Wakháŋ Tháŋka, but he did not see that its translational difficulty stems largely from seeing it as atheistic—or socially vertical—concept rather than a relational—or socially horizontal—one:

> These historical facts have satisfied us that the idea of Great Spirit, ascribed to the Indians of North America, does not belong to the

original Theogony of the Sioux, but has come in from without, like that of the horse and the gun, and probably dates back only to their first hearing of the White man's God. The Dakota word is, "WAH-KON TON-KA"—*Great Wah-kon*—*Great Mysterious*, or *Great Spirit*, so called. . . . If this statement, in regard to the origin of the idea of Great Spirit, be true, as we believe it is, then, when we came to preach the gospel, and give the Bible to the Sioux in their own language, we simply *claimed our own*, in using WAH-KON-TON-KA for God. It is further to be observed, that, in the Dakota use of this word "wah-kon," some secondary ideas were worked out, as *sacred* and *consecrated*. Hence, in looking over the whole vocabulary, we found no word so fitting as this to represent "*holy.*"[65]

Apart from the rhetoric of ownership here ("we simply *claimed our own*"), Riggs characterized "the Dakota word" Wakháŋ Tháŋka as a necessary imposition, and in doing so, he believed that the imposed God concept would supplant nontheistic Dakhóta forms of relationality. The imposition of a God concept onto the relational concept—Wakháŋ Tháŋka, or "great mystery"—effectively elided from the missionaries' view Dakhóta customs of generosity and gifting, relegating these to secular practices with no spiritual import.

Monica Siems argues that Dakhóta epistemologies of the early 1800s were both nontheistic and latent in the "deep structure" of Dakhóta language, and thus did not simply change with the introduction of Christian vocabulary and concepts.[66] I find her questions—"What does God mean? What *could* 'God,' or a host of other Christian theological terms, mean in the language of a culture that had no corresponding referents?"—to be especially useful for thinking about how Dakhóta confronted their own imprisonment and missionization.

If we look to Dakhóta and Lakhóta sources for historical meanings of "Wakantanka," its meanings as a nontheistic relational or ethical concept become apparent. In a section titled "Nagipi (Spirits)," appearing in James R. Walker's ethnography *Lakota Belief and Ritual,* Lakhóta wičáša wakháŋ (ritual specialist) and phežúta wakháŋ (medicine man) George Sword describes Wakháŋ Tháŋka as part of a larger cosmology in which other spirits share power:

> There are many kinds of spirits (*nagipi*). All the spirits of one kind are the same as one spirit. There are four classes of spirits, and four kinds of spirits in each class. The *Wakan Tanka* is a spirit but it is

of four kinds. It is called *Wakan* because no man can understand it. The *Taku Wakan* is a spirit and it is four kinds and it is called *Taku Wakan* because it is akin to the *Wakan Tanka*. The *Wakan Tanka* and the *Taku Wakan* may be all called *Taku Wakan* because they are all akin to each other. When a prayer is made to *Wakan Tanka*, it is made to *Taku Wakan* also.[67]

In this passage, Sword sketches some of the complex, and indeed obscure, relational calculus of Lakȟóta/Dakȟóta cosmology through his description of the two ontological principles, or what Sword calls "classes of spirits," of Táku Wakȟáŋ (literally "something *wakan*," or relational) and Wakȟáŋ Tȟáŋka (what might well be translated as "great relational" but is often translated as "great mystery"). The sheer multiplicity of originary beings sketched here may make sense of Christian missionaries' impressions of Dakȟóta "religion" as being polytheistic. But if we recall Monica Siems's pertinent question about how one says "God" in a language that is fundamentally nontheistic, we can see a basic and crucial slippage in Ruban's letter in which he professes his Christian faith. Put simply, Wakȟáŋ Tȟáŋka and Táku Škáŋ are both figures for interpersonal relations that are governed by thióšpaye norms of reciprocity, power sharing, and economic generosity.

These interpersonal relations are further articulated in an 1894 essay, "The Sioux Mythology," by Charles Alexander Eastman, where Eastman evokes Wakȟáŋ Tȟáŋka through the image of the lodge:

The novice must bear in mind that purity and feast making are the foundations of the lodge, and pleasing to the Great Mystery. "Thou shalt often make a holy feast or a lodge feast to the God. Thou shalt not spill the blood of any of thy tribe. Thou shalt not steal what belongs to another. Thou shalt always remember that the choicest part of thy provision belongs to God." These were some of their commandments. It is a peculiar fact, already mentioned, that the Great Mystery was never directly approached except upon special and extraordinary occasions, such as the union meeting and dance of the "medicine lodges" once a year.[68]

Eastman's "thou shalt nots" place a premium on maintaining kin relations in ways that not only go beyond but actually invert the Abrahamic commandments' prohibitions against bad relations of various kinds with one's neighbor. They do so through their positive emphasis on preparing a feast "to the God" or "Great Mystery," which would have the effect of drawing people together in a ceremony of forging mutual obligations. Feasting was a social practice banned under the ethnocidal 1883 Religious Crimes Code, along with plural marriages, ritual specialists ("medicine men"), mourning and memorial giveaways (regarded by Indian agents and missionaries alike as "the destruction of property" that left the family of the deceased "in desolation and want"), the paying of dowries, and alcohol.[69]

Other letters illustrate the importance of other constellations of key terms denoting Christian conversion as portable but vexed concepts. The Dakhóta translation of the "Savior" concept used by Canku and Simon is especially fraught with meanings that reference norms of generosity as well as an ontology of power as something to be shared with those who lack it. In a letter dated May 3, 1864, Robert Hopkins (Čhaské, or First Born Son) writes, in a heartfelt letter to his "friend Rev. S. R. Riggs," about the disappearance of his wife and the constant threat of his own death. Even among other letters that describe the vulnerability and ongoing terror of prison life, his is remarkable:

> Today, I am writing you a letter. I am very sad today, and also very dependent on you for my existence—it is so. They said my wife has disappeared, therefore I am very heartbroken. Last winter, they said I was going to die. Lately, I just heard that, and then I began to suddenly think, when will I die? When I die, I hope it is quickly and I shall go to be with the Great Spirit in His home. I think I will not be afraid. At that time, whoever judges me, in the future, will receive judgment just like me, I think. Today, I now depend upon the one they call Savior—it is so [Nakaha ake Wowapi cikage tuka dehan wacinciyan tuka anpetu kin dehan nina cante mašica waun ye do mitawin tokiyaiyaya tanin šni keyapi kin heon nina cante mašica tuka wanihan maṭe kta keyapi nakaha he nawakiĥon onkan hehan kaken awacin makica tohan maṭe kte cinhan kohanna rin wakantanka ti kin ekta wai kta e nihinmiciya šni ke epca tokešta tuwe mayaco kinhan tokešta iš eya he tokata wayaco kin ihunni kta epca ecin dehan wanikiya eyapi kin he wacinwayedo].[70]

The ambivalence of this letter shows up as a crisis of relationality. On the one hand, Čhaské admits his reliance on the missionary Riggs ("I am . . . very dependent on you for my existence"), which reads conventionally as a statement about thióšpaye norms. But on the other hand, Čhaské also indicates his skepticism about the Christianity that Riggs represents, implicated as it is in the acts of white Minnesotans and the death of his wife. *Waníkiya*, the Dakhóta word for "savior" or "rescuer," implies in Riggs's own translation an ethical and existential paragon: "one who makes live."[71] Thus, when Čhaské declares himself a kinsman of Jesus, writing that he will "depend upon the one they call Savior," he calls on the generosity–dependence relationship that exists between relatives while adopting a wait-and-see attitude and critical distance from settler society ("the one *they* call").

This generosity–dependence relationship has an analog in the Dakhóta notion of pity. Of course one may have pity for the pitiful, whether in English or Dakhóta. However, the forms of social action that "pity" may normatively mobilize may be quite different. In the Dakhóta language, *uŋšika means "pitiful" but also "poor, miserable."*[72] For example, it is common—when Riggs assembled his dictionary, as it is still now—to say routinely to an infant, "Poor thing!" with the Dakhóta "Úŋšida!"[73] These words, and the existential condition of powerlessless or vulnerability that they describe, are vividly embodied in ceremonial giveaways: acts of generosity where the immediate relatives of a deceased person orchestrate a feast and gift giving to all who attended. William K. Powers describes the logic of the giveaway, a practice that appears not only after the releasing of the soul ceremony but also in many other Lakhóta contexts: "Once all their personal belongings have been given away, the donors are rendered destitute (*úŋšika*) and their neighbors and relatives will take pity on them."[74] Just as in the haŋbléčeyapi (crying for a vision), the immediate family of the deceased, in becoming úŋšika, elicits a generous response from those who are more powerful. In material terms, the giveaway makes possible the redistribution of economic resources, although this is more of a side effect of the practice than the reason for its being: "Usually within a year, at future giveaways, the original donors will become the recipients of goods and money, and eventually the original personal property that they gave away will be replaced."[75] The primary motive for giving is not solely economic; it is also existential and ethical, a celebration of solidarity made through shared relation, lost relatives, and grief. In light of this, Powers describes the memorial-feast giveaway as "a thanksgiving (*wopila*) in which the mourner and his or her family acknowledge the help received from neighbors and kin during the one-year period."[76]

Contrast this view of pity as an occasion for familial generosity with Presbyterian impressions about Dakhóta relationality. Thomas Williamson's early writings from his time at the Lac qui Parle mission (1835–46) provide one of the earliest missionary sources for understanding Dakhóta relational practices. Reflecting on "Indian Hospitality," the young Williamson writes to S. B. Treat in the winter of 1842 about the treatment that missionaries received before and after the introduction of the Gospel. Writing ten years later, he describes a relationship of mutual sharing, as "the Indians . . . mostly gave us three meals a day and always the best they had. When they were deficient in an important article of diet, as several times happened in regard to flour and sugar, we supplied the deficiency."[77]

Williamson himself contrasted this version of generosity with a pre-Christian one "before Christianity had made any progress among them" and within which, ethically, "the state of things was very different." He remembers,

> On arriving my baggage was carried in to one of the tents where I slept during my stay; but the owners of the lodge seemed to think affording a place to sleep in was their full share, and during my stay on only one occasion in that tent was I offered food, and that I understood was furnished by persons who were like myself only temporary lodgers there. During the first evening I was invited out to three feasts. Subsequently to one or two a day. These feasts in every case consisted of a single dish, mostly boiled meat, or boiled corn, or hasty pudding seasoned with salt, and on another dried cherries and water.[78]

In this early mission setting, what Williamson did not grasp was the importance of feasting as an ethical practice of relative making where Dakhóta feasted both Indigenous and white neighbors in order to extend networks of reciprocal social obligations.[79] Those who were feasted could in turn be expected to be obliged to provide support in times of need. Williamson's objections to such practices are in part aesthetic (he laments that the fare was merely "hasty pudding seasoned with salt") and in part moralistic, judging the practice of feasting to be evidence of Indigenous profligacy. Despite the continuities in Dakhóta customs of generosity, Williamson concludes that "the knowledge of and confidence in their old religion or superstitions is fast passing away."[80] He does this by separating out "religion" from ostensibly "secular" practices like feasting. Ironically, though, Williamson's account shows less evidence of Dakhóta Christianization than it does of missionary indigenization. By engaging in mutual obligations for feeding community members, Williamson's later account demonstrates that in "suppl[ying] the deficiency" of food in lean times, he must have seemed to be acting like a good Dakhóta in the eyes of his hosts.

Conclusion: Awáŋyaŋke and the Survival of Relatives

Returning to where this chapter began, it is clear that imprisonment worked powerfully together with the threat of dissolving the thióšpaye in motivating the mass conversions in the camps. However, what complicates this story is how, rather than replacing core ethical values in becoming converts, Dakhóta people continued to participate in thióšpaye relationships and thus maintained key epistemological differences from whites. In addition, a sort of mutual transformation took place between the missionaries and Dakhóta people. Some of Riggs's last writings, for instance, show evidence that key Presbyterian concepts had become indigenized. In the Dakhóta-language newspaper *Iápi Oáye* (The Word-Carrier), first printed at the Indian school in Niobrara, Nebraska, in 1871, Riggs's serial column on the history of the Dakota Mission defined several of the mission's key religious terms. "*Okodakecheya*, the Dakota name for church," wrote Riggs, "expresses the idea of a company of special friends. The pastor is a *Wechasta Wakaŋ*, a consecrated or mysterious man. The term *Hoonkayape* is used for elders—the *elders ones* among brethren. *Awaŋyake*, or *seeing over*, designates the office and work of deacons."[81]

Despite the apparent ease of moving between linguistic and cultural codes, internal tensions run through this short newspaper entry. Riggs, in attempting to lay out the church pecking order, uses Dakhóta words that have little meaning within a vertical ethical structure. For example, defining church as "a company of special friends," or a communal enterprise in which individuals exercise mutual responsibility and care, is a far cry from the quick judgment that Riggs renders in his early letter, and what Riggs calls "Okodakecheya" (to make friends of one another) here is a term he translates in his dictionary as "a league, covenant, communion, fellowship," with reference to the Dakhóta male friendship term, *khodá*.[82] Riggs translates the word *awaŋyaka* (in Yankton dialect but *awáŋyaŋka in other dialects*), in his dictionary published nearly twenty years after the Dakhóta newspaper, as a condition of "attending to," or of ethical responsiveness, rather than of overseeing, with its implied hierarchy and power relationship.[83] We might also translate it more simply as "caretaking."

Given the complex history of the Dakota Mission, as well as Dakhóta responses to it, the mass conversions at Mankato, Fort Snelling, and Camp Kearney do not read as either conciliation to missionary demands or even simply as a way of surviving. Rather, they point to how Dakhóta people reflected on the internal effects of colonization and on how settler-colonial representatives like missionaries challenged, undercut, or occasionally resonated with existing ethical concepts. The prisoners at the various concentration camps, in accepting Jesus, may have done so strategically, as a way to assuage white rage and to prevent further physical violence against them. What's more, the Dakhóta letter writers' citations of thióšpaye ethics under the guise of Christian dogma suggest that what missionaries took to be a total renunciation of Indianness may have been instead a nominal conversion belied by strong attachments to Dakhóta forms of sociality. Keeping such an epistemological translation in critical view is thus necessary to interpret the encounters between Presbyterian missionaries and Dakhóta during the thirty years of their relationship after the founding of the Dakota Mission at Lac qui Parle and through the establishment of the concentration camps, and allows a view of how Dakhóta converts may have practiced a Christianity whose ontological and ethical assumptions remained Dakhóta but were not legible to missionaries or within the civilizing framework of agricultural industriousness. In moving back and forth across lines of ethical difference, Dakhóta were able to maintain crucial ties to relatives while at the same time appearing to be dutiful converts and good citizens of the United States. Neither co-opted by God and radical individualism nor essentially untouched or unchanged, they adopted and adapted the performances of settler-colonial culture, filtering them through ethical norms that highlighted the normative possibilities of power sharing, sufficiency, and mutuality as core aspects of a peoplehood that was on the run but not extinguished.

First Interlude

Grace Lambert, Personal Interview, Fort Totten,
Spirit Lake Nation, August 10, 1998

This interview (it's really more of a freewheeling four-way conversation) happened more than twenty years ago in my grandma Grace Lambert's house in Fort Totten. I had dropped in with my mother, Donna Pexa (Charboneau), and my uŋčí (maternal grandmother), Rachel Charboneau (Langer Young). Grace was Rachel's sister, and they had grown up together not far from where Grace was living in 1998, at a district and place in Spirit Lake called Crow Hill. My voice is mostly absent from this conversation, although I really wanted to know about a town called Tokio (mostly because of its unusual name, which was a cipher to me, a weirdly Orientalized rez town). I was, I think, trying to be respectful, to listen more than to speak. In reality, I was just a bystander to an afternoon chat among three Dakhóta women. What still strikes me about the conversation is not only that it shows how remembering the past is transacted in ordinary conversations but also that it reveals what gifted storytellers my relatives were, and that Dakhóta women's storytelling and narrations of history do crucial work as the everyday acts of remaking tribal memory and recollecting the people. As Wazíyatawiŋ notes, although she "was not required to recite back to [her] grandmother accounts [she] had just heard," she later found herself in that position of responsibility with Dakhóta audiences who both quiz her on and impart to her "knowledge of and perspective on Dakota topics," and so "help preserve the integrity of the collective historical memory of the Oyate."[1] I include this and other oral histories in this book to evoke some small part of that memory, and to show continuities in thinking about belonging and relation between the assimilation-era authors writing at the turn of the twentieth century and my relatives speaking at the close of that century.

GRACE LAMBERT: So what do you want? [laughs]

CHRIS PEXA: Tell me about Tokio. I hear a lot about it.

RACHEL CHARBONEAU: Tokio, he wants to know. . . .

GL: What do you want to know about Tokio?

CP: Well, I don't know. What's it like?

GL: A real toughie town.

RC: That's what they used to say. . . .

CP: You know we just came from talking with Vern and he was telling us about the Peyote eaters.

RC: Ya.

GL: Oh yeah, that was way in 1919, I think it started.

CP: Are they still there?

GL: There's some. I don't know how many there is. Ain't very many families, I think Gabe Young's family, and the Blueshields. Did you see Martin Blueshield's family?

CP: We didn't get ahold of them, no. We drove by his house, I think.

GL: I think they're all peyote. And Rose, 'member she died. What's her name? The Littleghosts. They're watchacall, peyote. I don't think Ambrose is . . .

CP: Oh, he's not?

GL: Not Ambrose. Ambrose is in the real Indian church. He don't go to that.

CP: Which church is that?

GL: There is no church. They just have their sweats and their prayers, you know, right there, you know. That's the way they do it.

DP: Vern [Grace's son] said he goes to Ambrose's sweats.

GL: Ya, uh huh.

CP: It's got a reputation as a tough place?

GL: So many things happened there, you know. . . .

CP: What happened?

GL: A lot of crime. Well, at one time it might have been a good time. It started out all white people. It used to be a white people's town. Now and it's all Indian. I doubt if there are twenty white people there.

CP: It's part of the reservation, though?

RC: That's part of the reservation, isn't it?

GL: Ya, that's part of the reservation. See, the reservation runs way to Warwick.

DONNA PEXA: Yeah, we went by there, didn't we yesterday?

RC: No, that was Wood Lake.

CP: What's Wood Lake?

RC: That lake right there.

GL: By Tokio. You have to go off the road to get down to the lake. And there's lot of private houses down there that the rich people own from town.

CP: From Devils Lake?

GL: Ya, it's kind of a resort, like, you know.

CP: She was telling me about how the white farmers leased the land by Vernie's place.

DP: Out here, remember you were saying that was all reservation but most of it was leased to non-Indians?

CP: When did that start happening?

GL: Well, you know, anyway, our reservation is really not our reservation, I don't think, as far as reservations are concerned. . . .

RC: Really. . . .

GL: You know, like, uh, Pine Ridge reservation, Rose Bud reservation, them are really truly pure reservations. There's no white man locked in there, somewhere, who owns land. Here, this farmer up here, he own all this land in there, that's his.

DP: You mean it was sold?

GL: Sure! They sold 'em to 'em. You know, they were, what would you call them now, my dad had one too. Eee, that's my big problem, I always can't remember things. You remember they gave up their rights as Indian and now were going to live like a white man and work like a white man, pay taxes and everything. So they were given this land to farm. And my dad had one. He lived out there at Crow Hill, you know.

RC: Mm hm.

GL: What *did* they call that thing? But anyway, they made them shoot an arrow. You know all these Indians that wanted to be like that, that were given these . . . homestead. . . . Ya, that's what they called it I think, homestead or something. They were supposed to give up their Indian rights, they were never gonna pick up the Indian way again. And so they put them on these farms. But, see, they never, ever trained them to farm and to learn about the use of money, and how they should—that they are to pay taxes for this land, and all the property they had they had to pay taxes for that. They never showed them these things. So the Indian just went along and farmed, and when his crops came in and everything, why, they sold them and then they used the money themselves and never paid the taxes, so that land was taken away from them, right now, and given to a white man. And so the white man got in, in a certain year. I can't remember what it is. Maybe Vern told you.

CP: He gave me a big photocopy packet, a history.

GL: Ya, it probably tells in there what year the homesteads were all taken back and they were given, kind of like a rush. Like the gold rush. You remember they let all these white people rush to the place, and they stake out different places. . . .

DP: And they sold it to them? . . .

GL: . . . They didn't sell it to them, they gave it to them under homestead law. See, the homestead law was that you work this farm and after you have made it into a thriving farm, why then after so many years, it'll be your own, see, and under that ruling, these homesteads were given out to the white people. So you know they just cheated the Indians like a little old, I don't know what, even a mouse I think has more chance. . . .

RC: Ya.

DP: How could they allow that on the reservation?

GL: Because the Indian didn't know a thing then . . .

RC: Yeah.

GL: . . . at that time. They had no education, they never knew of any kind of farming or anything. So, you know, whatever, they presented it to them, they thought it would work all right, but when they tried it, then it would be difficult, because they didn't know how. And nobody else ever came and taught 'em anything. They had a box farmer. He went around and taught the Indians, of course, but that was later. That was *way* later.

CP: A lot of non-Indians on the reservation now, then?

GL: Mm hm. Ya. Our reservation is just a big checkerboard, just like Sisseton. Sisseton is the same thing. And now they're trying to say they have no boundary lines anymore at all, because there are so many white people that are on their reservation in Sisseton. But, you know, they're tough. They're demanding that the original land that they had given them is the line. . . . And so they I guess you know there's enough of them with education that they can override them. So they just give them what they can. Otherwise they are considered white, and then trying to tax them and all that. Really lose the land then. But now they're giving them the same chances that they give us. So we can buy these lands back, now that they're worthless, you know. [laughter]

CP: Do you know a lot of white people?

GL: A lot of them are leaving because of you know, no crops and all that. Right now there's gonna be no crops because of how dry it is. So it's really bad, the way the Indian has been treated. When I think of it, it makes me sad.

CP: Do they get along, the different populations, the whites and Indians, for the most part?

GL: Well, I don't know how it would be . . .

CP: . . . except in Tokio? [laughter]

GL: He's really stuck on Tokio, enit? [laughter]

RC: Well, that's where they told him to go. . . .

CP: Well, it's just, you always talk about it too, Gram. [laughter]

GL: Well, Tokio, you know. Last winter, all the crimes that happened then. First, it might have been in August, I think, yeah, I think it was in August. . . . First of all, this one boy went out and these four kids were raising hell outside I guess, you know, and doing something, and this guy went out, and he told 'em to cut it out. And he never came back in. And the kids, you know, they kind of went away so everybody thought everything was okay, and that the man, the guy had gone home or something. Next morning, here they found him by the side of the road. They had drug him there. They killed him, you know, then they drug him over there. They just dropped him on the side of the road. So that's where they found him. And these four kids killed that man, that boy. He's a young man, about twenty I guess. And these are all fourteen, I think the oldest was fourteen, and twelve, I think, and I think the youngest was nine. Mind you. Can you believe that?

CP: So what happened at Crow Hill anyway?

GL: Well, Crow Hill—didn't I send you the story? I wrote it down on a paper.

RC: I never got it. Who did you send it to?

GL: I sent it in that paper. Remember when you guys wrapped me a big bag, you know? Oh no, I gave it to you, I think, to take all them things in.

DP: I don't remember seeing that one, though. There was a record in there . . .

CP: . . . Vern said that they sun danced there.

GL: Ya, they had a sun dance there last summer. Last summer, that John Chaske or somebody made there. Some people from Pine Ridge or even Rosebud came up and directed them. Showed them how it was done, you know. . . .

CP: . . . Oh really, they had never done one before?

GL: . . . Ya, they had done one before by Devils Heart [Mní Wakháŋ Čhaŋté].

CP: Oh really?

GL: Ya, they had one there

CP: Same people run it, from Pine Ridge?

GL: I don't know who ran it. I think some people from Canada ran that one. And then this one here was run by people from Rosebud.

CP: So a fight happened at Crow Hill?

GL: Ya, that's how come that got the name of Crow Hill. . . .

RC: Ya, Crows.

FIRST INTERLUDE

GL: ... because Crow Indians got killed up (RC: Mmm hmm) on top of that hill. When they came there, you know, and down below it's a valley, a great big valley, and that's where the village was, the Indian village was down there. I guess them Crows came, they were scouts, they came to scout, you know, and I suppose to steal their horses or something, that's all they did, they were always stealing from each other, you know. And I've often just said that too, you know, I said, just think the Indians, there's lot of things you know that they held with honor, not crimes, like stealing you know. If they stole a horse from the enemy, they gained a feather for that as an act of bravery. And which is really true, you know. And so I said, we sure had to change a lot of ways, we really had to change a lot of our rules and things that, who we honored and respected before. That seems kind of funny. I always kinda notice these things, you know. I suppose because I go to church a lot, I always compare them. But anyway, these Crows went up there and they were scouting, I guess, and they were trying to see how many horses they could steal from these Sioux people that were camped down there in that village, you know, and here, there was some other Sioux that were scouts that were up there too, and they found them. And so they came dashing back down to the camp and told, they have a herald you know, so that guy heralds, you know, goes around and tells everything, so he told, so all the warriors got together, they went up and fought 'em. There was about thirty-eight of them. Thirty-eight of them, and they killed all of them, so that's where they're buried. And that's how come they call it Crow Hill. Khaŋǧí Pahá.

RC: Khaŋǧí Pahá.

GL: Khaŋǧí is a crow, Pahá is a hill.

CP: What about Devils Heart?

GL: They call it Mní Wakháŋ Čhaŋté. Ya.

DP: Who named it that, the Indians?

GL: It must have been named by Indians. I'm sure no white man came along and named it that. [all laugh] See, that means that that's the heart of the lake. Ya, that's what it means. See, the Mní Wakháŋ is this one [this lake], Mní Wakháŋ Bde. But then they call that Mní Wakháŋ Čhaŋté, so the heart belongs to the Mní

Wakȟáŋ. Then later years they had Devils Back and everything else (RC: Ya, Devils Tooth) and Devils Tooth, that's that little rock, you know. Then there's a little joke about that. Oh, they say it's true, though you know. This one little old lady, she came to the store and she bought a whole bunch of stuff. And the Indians honored the stone, which is no more than right, because I always read in my Bible about the rock being God. You know, and they honored the rock as, as a kind of, a god, you know. And they made sacrifices, they offered their little offerings to it, you know, and all that when they go there and pray. Well, this old lady came to the store and she bought a whole bunch of stuff and she was going back and she stopped by the Devils Tooth, and I guess she bought a little piece of red cloth and she—that's what usually they use is red cloth, too, for all kind of sacred occasions, ceremonies—and here, she covered the little rock with the red cloth and she took out her Bull Durham, 'cause they always used tobacco as a gift, you know. So she took the Bull Durham and she opened it up and took some out and she says "Tȟuŋkášida, čhaŋdí wéčau," you know, "Grandfather, I brought you tobacco as a gift," you know, and she put it on the little red rock. Suddenly in back of the rock, you know, a drunk was laying there, "I'm sleeping," you know, and he just woke up when she said, "Grandfather, I brought you some tobacco." I guess he got right up and said "Háu," and she grabbed her bundle and the rest of her stuff and flew down the road. She was giving a gift to somebody. Got caught. Oh, dear. They always tell that.

RC: How 'bout that alcoholic, coming home, the one you told?

DP: The one, the woman whose husband was an alcoholic or a drunk, went to see the priest?

GL: The one that told her to wear a devil's suit? Oh ya! Oh ya, she was married to an alcoholic, you know, and they lived a little ways from the town, so he walked in every day and stayed in the bar, I suppose till it closed up, and then he'd be coming back. He'd be singing, and you know, staggering along, coming back home. She got just sick of him. I guess she tried everything, you know. But she couldn't make him stop, so finally she went to her minister, whoever he was, and she told him, "You know, I've tried everything. But nothing fazes him. He won't stop drinking," she said. "I wonder what I should do. What would you suggest." And he said, "Well, I don't know," he said, "I don't know what to say either," he said, "but, I know what. You try something," he said, "maybe this might help," he said. He said, "I have a devil suit," he said, "you know, that they used in a play. I'll give that to you," he said, "and you can put it on." And you know, at the corner of where they live, why, there was a little clump of trees. And so he said, "At that little corner where the clump of trees are, you could hide there," he said, "and wait for him when you hear him coming. And when he comes right by, you know, you can jump up and say boo to him, you know, scare him." "I'll try it," she said, "I've tried everything, I may as well try it," so she said, she took the devil suit home, you know, and she waited, and finally he went again, so she put the suit on when she heard him, coming then, she went over to the little clump of trees and she was hiding back there. Pretty soon he got close, and he was singing and staggering close by, and she jumped out from the clump of trees and grabbed him and said boo! And he said, "Who the hell are you?" She said, "I'm the devil." "Oh," he said, "put 'er here! I married your sister!" [laughter] That was even her. Oh, that crazy . . . well, that's a drunk for you, enit?

You know, Grandpa used to always tell this one about these Indians, long time ago, they really were dedicated Christians, even the Presbyterians and the Catholics, everybody, they were really dedicated people. And here they had a revival or something, I guess, and this minister, you know, he was having his service early in the morning, so he was talking about the last, what do you call it, Passion, you know, where they had taken him before Pilate, and they were slapping him and spitting in his face and everything, and then finally they said they took him and put a crown of thorns on his head, you know, and they put a purple robe on him and they were bowing to him and saying, you know, "You Christ, you're king, king of the Jews." They were saying all that. Well, all this time, I guess, this drunk came in, you know, and he was sitting way in the back row and he was listening to all this, and pretty soon, why, it ended, and he [the preacher] said, "They crucified him, you know, and they killed him, at the end, they even tied him to the tree, and he died." Well then, that was the end. And he said, "Now we'll have dinner." So he said, "We'll all go the meeting hall, and we'll have dinner over there." So they all went down and got to the meeting hall, and they were sitting there, and the ladies got the table all prepared and usually they always called the men first, I don't know why, but the men were first to sit down and eat, you know, they honored the men. And the men had to come and eat, they said, so the men all went and sat down. That drunk, too. He was kind of a little bit sober, he was sobering up, and he sat down too. Of all things, the minister called on him to say the grace. So finally he got up, he stood up and he said, "You know," he said, "Jesus, you were a good man. You did everything for everybody," he said, "you even brought people to life, and you healed the sick, and made the lame walk, and the dumb talk, and those that couldn't hear," he said, "and yet they just tortured you and slapped you, and spit on," he said, "and then they put a crown of thorns on your head. Then finally they just nailed you to the cross and made you die on there. God damn it," he said, "if I was alive at that time. . . ." [laughter] I don't know what he thought he'd do. But everyone had to laugh. He got himself mad. Well, at least it hit him right. . . .

DP: He got carried away with himself. . . .

GL: . . . Ya. At least the story hit him right. Oh dear, my dad used to always tell us that. And he used to always tell us too about obedience, you know. He'd say, "No matter what you say," he said, "you got to be obedient." "But," he said, "there's always a temptation there to bother this little obedience." This minister was getting ready for his service Sunday morning, he had his desk all full of paper, you know, and he was standing there. Pretty soon his friend came in. "Well, good morning, preacher," he said, and he was talking with him. He said, "What's that little box there doing," he said, and the preacher said, "Oh, that's my sermon," he said, "that's my sermon for today," he said. So he said, "Don't open it," he said, "I'm going over to the church," he said, "to get things ready," he said, "I'll be right back, and I'll get it, and I'll see what, we'll have our service then." So he went, and this man was standing there, and he kept looking at that little box and thinking, "I wonder what it is that he has in there that he don't want nobody to open it," you know. "Well, I think I'll open it." So he went and he opened it, and here it was a mouse, he jumped out and it ran. So he started chasing it, you know, and he knocked all the papers all over the floor, but he

FIRST INTERLUDE

71

was still crawling around, and just then the minister came in. "What you doing there on the floor? And what is all this?" He said, "I told you," he said, "I wanted to know what was in that box," he said, "I opened it, and that little mouse got away." "See," he said, "that was my preaching," he said, "obedience," he said, "I told you, obedience. You always cannot obey, you know, you just had to go and open it."

DP: Caught him, huh?

GL: Ya. But that's true, enit? When they tell you not to do something, that's just when you go and do it. And sometimes you get yourself in some terrible trouble, too.

CP: What's that story about your grandma on the hill?[2]

RC: What? Oh, the one that got killed by lightning?

CP: What was that, what happened?

DP: Were you [Grace] there then?

RC: Uh huh, she was there. And Lily was there, too. I was a baby then.

GL: Ya.

CP: Where was that?

GL: At that homestead. That's how my dad quit that homestead, mind you. Of all things. I've always felt bad. But it must have struck him, you know, hard. That was his mother [Išnáwiŋ or Lone Woman], you know. And she had just lost his sister, that spring. And then this was in August. I always remember Grandma [again, Išnáwiŋ] in mourning. A long time ago the women never combed their hair, they always just wore it like that, when they mourned, you know. Some of them chopped it off with a knife too. And here, she was in bed, we all slept on the floor all the time 'cause not so many beds in them days, nobody had that much money to be buying fancy beds and everything, and I doubt if they even had them too, to sell, maybe, you know. Well, so we, my grandma slept on the floor with my brother Gabe and . . .

RC: Lydia.

GL: . . . my sister Lydia, and two Brown girls, Louisa Brown and Esther Brown. Them were her grandchildren. These were her grandchildren from that daughter that died. These were her daughters, and they were grandma's grandchildren, and they were there. And here there was a big bed here, and that's where me and Lily [Lillian Chase, Grace Lambert's and Rachel Charboneau's sister, whose interview appears as my Third Interlude] slept, on that bed. And there was a stove right in the middle of the room. A cook stove, with four little legs, you know, and it had little doors on each side. An old-time [stove]. . . . And then my dad and my mother slept on the side. That night there was a big storm, that's how come they moved in with us, they had a frame house, but I think they were scared because there was no foundation on it, and probably they were scared it might blow over. So they came over to the log house and they stayed with all of us. Here it must have been six o'clock in the morning, I think. It was early in the morning, I know. This was on August 6th, I think, or August 4th, I can't remember. Anyway, I woke up and here it was, there was a big bang, you know, like a clap, you know, just loud. Woke me up, so I woke up, and I was laying behind Lily. Lily was laying in front, she was pregnant, she was going to have Brownie that time, she was laying in front. I was laying in the back, I sat up in bed and here, right, this little stove here, with the chimney, you know, it just stove piped, and it went up, there was no chimney like you have now, like this one here, it's got a chimney, it just goes in and goes out. But it was just stovepipe, you know. I saw this blue flame just go up like that. That was that electricity that was going up. And then the room was just full of soot, just flying all over, mind you, little black soot, and then just a smell like gunpowder. You know how you shoot a gun and there's that smell? That's just the way it smelled. It was smoky. But my dad jumped up and I heard him, he said, "Must be the dog," šúŋka héd [the dog there]. . . . He went out, and I was sitting up, you know, I was sitting up and I could see my grandma and them down here on the floor, you know, and here it was grandma. "Ohh," she said, and she raised her hand like that. So I just called my dad, "Papa," I said, "it's grandma, Khúŋši." . . . He came back in, you know, and he grabbed her hand, he said, "Iná" [mother]. About the second time he said it, "Iná," he said, she said "Háŋ" [yes], but just soft, "Háŋ," she said, and then next time he called her she didn't answer no more. She had died. So they went, he went out, he told mama, he said, "You move her outside," and then me and Louisa, Louisa Brown, we had to run across the field, you know, and papa's field it was, oh, it was just high, too, just ready to watchacall, almost, almost ready to crop? But just ready to, watchacallit, grain? And here, we just ran across, we were just soaking wet by the time we got across that field, that was about forty acres, I think, we went through that, got soaking wet. Went to Joe Brown's and they were eating, and the old lady said "Oh thakhóža táku tókha hé? [my grandchild, what is wrong?]," she said, so I told her, I said, "Grandma got killed," and she started to cry. He said, "I'll get the team," he said, you know the old man, and he got up. So a team must have been close by, because in no time, why, he drove up. The old lady fed us and gave us some tea, you know, and some bread.

So we ate that and were driving in the wagon with them and came back to the house. By that time ma had the tent, you know, a regular tent, she had it up, and they had my grandma in there. Auntie Lily said that she helped her put the tent up, and then she helped her put the tent up and she said we drug grandma out on a blanket, she laid out on a blanket so they pulled her, drug her over there. Here, I always remember she was just all matted like, hair just to her skull, and then a great big pug here, that was all her hair that was long, you know, all in a great big pug. Mama said she couldn't get nothing out of her hair, it was so matted, you know, that she couldn't the comb through it or anything, so she had to leave her like that. But she put a scarf on her. But she didn't put a scarf on her right away because I always remember, gee, the people just came in no time, mind you, the neighbors, you know? They were all coming in wagons. The old man, that was his sister-in-law, she used to be married to his brother, and that's how come she raised Charlie Blackbird, that was Charlie Blackbird's dad, that she used to be married to, but she died. And then Charlie Blackbird's dad, his name was Zitkána Sápa [Black Bird], you know, and that was the brother to this Gray Hawk, and here he came in, he just looked at her, and he just, you know, I think there must be signs about these, the way they fixed her hair, like that, and electricity, what it does, because I always remember that old man, "Hé hé hé" [something like "Look here!"], he said. "It wasn't hard to do," he said. You know, I heard that. It stayed in my mind, but I never, ever said a word about it until way late, years after. I think I had children even. I asked my mother one time, "You know when grandma got killed," I said, "that old man came in here. I heard him say that. What did he mean by that," I said, saying, you know, that you made a mistake, that was as good as what he said, you know when he said. "It's easy to do," he said. But he meant, "Why didn't you do it?" And here, my ma said, "She was told to kill one of the grandchildren."[3] But she didn't want to. She thought literally she had to. But, see, she didn't have to, that's what the old man meant, when he said, "It was easy to do." I said, "Well what would she have had to do?" And here my ma said, he told them later, you know, I suppose after I wasn't around, maybe, when he explained that to them, I guess he said she could have taken one of the kid's clothes, like hers or Lydia's or my brother Gabe's, one of their coats, went over the hill and filled it with grass, and stabbed it or killed it, you know.

CP: Who told her to kill?

RC: Wakíŋyaŋ.

GL: Wakíŋyaŋ, the thunder. See, they were the ones who told things to the people, what they were to do.

RC: Ya, they believed in that.[4]

GL: See, they had to. That's why they were afraid of thunderstorms. That's why they all revered the thunder as a god, you know. So she could have easily done that, and here ma said that old man told them that even then, you know, when she had a knife and she stabbed that little cloth with the weeds in it, why, she said they'd scream too. And she said blood would kind of trickle out. And I always think about when the Lord asks Abraham to kill Isaac, remember? And here then next, when he was going to do it, he told him not to touch him, but he saw this ram, so he killed the ram instead, remember? So I always think, you know, I put these things together with the Bible, and they really lived by a good law, because these are all creations of God. God created the thunder and the lightning, you know. They had power, too. Just like us—we have the power to do what we want to do. That's our will. You can even be bad, or if I wanted to, I could kill you. [laughs]

DP: You had a story you were telling us last time we were here about the thunder, lightning, too, coming back. . . .

GL: Oh, that's how come, they always said they call this Mní Wakháŋ. Because there's supposed to be a great spirit in there.

My dad used to tell us that. I often wonder what hill that was these scouts were sitting on. But this was many, many years before any white people were around here, I guess. See, these guys, there's always scouts looking for different places where there's other Indians, you know, where they could steal from them, you know, food or whatever, you know. And I guess these scouts were sitting on some hill, but I always think maybe it's the one right behind where mama and them lived, remember? Because that's about the highest one. And I think from there you can see Mní Wakháŋ.

RC: Ya, you can.

GL: And you can see way over here. But my dad said that, and then over there, . . . at what they called Ȟé Skána, that's Little White Mountain, they call it. Hé means "mountain" and Ská means "white," so "White Mountain" they call it, but that was an island at one time, the water was all around it, and here, my dad said that this thing surfaced, this great big object surfaced, and these scouts up on that hill, sitting up there, saw it, this thing surfaced, and it started going on the lake here, and it was looking around, and they said you could see its eyes were just yellow, you know, just shiny, you know, and the sun I suppose was down, but there was a big storm coming up, and it was coming, and here, that storm just came and started to fight with this object that was on the lake, and he would fight back by throwing, you know, red flames from its mouth. And isn't that funny how they make cartoons like that, too, now? [laughs] And he heard these things were told many years ago, too, you know. That's really something sometimes when you think about these things. But the thunder, the lightning, would strike, you know, strike at him, and he'd fight back with his big flame. Kept on going and going and going until he got to that white hill, that white mountain island. When he got there, well, that was the end of it, the lightning struck, and he never fought back no more, and there was nothing to it and the storm just went off. And that was the end of it, and I guess he said that's why the water is called wakȟáŋ, sacred, because they figured that thing that was fighting the lightning was a god too, you know, a water god. They call them Uŋktéhi. I gave you that, enit?

CP: Oh, I don't know, I've just, I've heard that name.

GL: Oh, you've read about it. Uŋktéȟi they call them.

CP: So why is Mní Wakháŋ Ćhaŋte the heart of it?

GL: Well, because it was used as, like, when you go vision seeking, you go on that hill and you do it. And I suppose they considered it sacred because lot of things happened on there too, you know, like this man and his two ladies who were going to participate with him. I think he was trying to make a ceremony, they call it the horse dance, they make the horses dance, so that they can get water, I guess, or something. Well, they do all these things for a purpose, you know, like sun dance too, which is for water too, when it's real dry and they need water, they have them. And usually it rains, they say, you know, and water starts trickling down that little tree. They say the clouds start coming out. God answers them, I guess. And so it was with that hill, I guess. They used to go up there, and this old man and his two women that were to hold things for him while he was making the horses dance, you know, why, they were up there with him, and they had to be stark naked. Gee, someone must have been just watching them, enit? [all laugh]

DP: Someone got an eyeful, huh?

GL: Ya. Because they were all just stark naked, and this great big storm just came up, and it was just thundering and striking all over the place where they were, but it didn't strike them, it would just strike behind them and on the side of them, and then it was just pouring. But when they had started I guess they had, you always braid these sweetgrass, you remember, you braid them, well, they had that kind, and they lit them and they dug holes in the ground and they stuck them in there, so they were standing up and burning like a candle. And they said them two braids of sweetgrass never went out with all that rain that just poured. They stayed and stayed and stayed until they say the thunder went on.

CP: And that was all at the Heart?

GL: Ya, that was at the Mní Wakháŋ Ćhaŋté. And then years later, why I guess when the priests first started coming, of course right now these were all pagan doings, you know, and one thing or another, and this one priest I guess he made a cross, he made a cross and he drug it up there, and he put it up, on top of the hill. That night a big thunderstorm came, and they said that the lightning struck it and just splintered it to nothing. So that was telling the priest that they shouldn't do that, maybe, that that was a sacred place. That's how come they call it Mní Wakháŋ Čhaŋté. I think I wrote that down, too, mind you. And then I think I wrote down about how they moved that little church there at Crow Hill, that little church, they made it at St. Michaels, and then this was all wintertime, it was ice, you know, so [a] lot of them say it was hauled by team, but you know my ma said that it was hauled by oxen. And she said they were given oxen at that time as there first, whatchucall, what do you call it, what you journey in, their first vehicle . . .

DP: Transportation?

GL: Transportation, that's it, their first transportation, ya, were the oxen. And then she said later they were given horses, but she said they were given nothing but wild horses, and they were in payment for a lease of this Camp Grafton, and that was a lease that was signed by these tribal heads at that time, whoever they were. Of course they couldn't sign, but I suppose they put their thumb mark, you know, somebody probably witnessed for them. They leased that Camp Grafton for 99 years, and 99 years went by quite a while ago, in '71 I think, when I worked there, when I first started working as a culture, for this Indian culture in Lake Region College, you know? Well, that time, the guy that taught us how to go about, you know, doing it, why, he, I was telling him about it, and way about a month later, he said, "I've investigated in the Clerk of Court in Minnewaukan and I've investigated in the Clerk of Court in Devils Lake. There is no lease of any kind there," he said. "They've got records for years and years back, there's none," he said, "that says Camp Grafton was ever leased by the Indian people." I said, "Sure, they destroyed them! What the heck, that's easy to do," I said, "especially in them days," I said, "there was no Indian around there to say that they ever did," I said. "They done all kinds of dirty work, they sure can do that too," I said. "Well, I bet you're right," he said, "but there's no record, mind you."

CP: What about all those stories, Gram, you used to tell . . .

RC: About what?

CP: About the lake itself and the thing rising . . .

RC: Maybe that's the one she told . . .

CP: Oh, is that the one, too. And the black dog, and the black man?

RC: Oh, that's up at the fort they used to see that big, black dog, and a man all dressed in black. Mama used to tell that, when the soldiers were here, they used to see things like that.

GL: Oh, really?

RC: That's what she said.

GL: Ohh.

CP: What would they see? What would they do?

RC: They do nothing. They just go around the square, she said, and they tried to catch them, the soldiers. They couldn't catch them. The next night, she said, it'd be a big black dog going around there.

CP: And then the man in black?

RC: Ya, the man in black. Ya, she used to tell this stuff. She said she used to wash for the soldiers.

GL: Uh huh. Lot of them did, you know. That's how come there's so many white people, half-breeds. I was telling that to Father, you know, I said, "What about that, Father?" "That was no sin for them," he said, "because they did it for a cause," he said. They were starving, so they used to have to go and do the laundry for these soldiers that were here, you know. These soldiers had families out East, but they couldn't bring them 'cause there was no place to put them. And so they had to be there by themselves so they were allowed to just have, you know, take these women in with them, and then they gave them extra rations and stuff. And that's how come so many of our Indian women have . . .

GL: Ya. Remember where Lily's grandmother picked them up, and that's how come they, they came alive, because their mother dropped them and left. And she ran on into Canada and never, ever came back to even see them, him and his little sister. But see she had been living with a white man in Minnesota when they had this 1862 "massacre" they always keep calling it, well, I don't know about that. . . . Well, anyway, that's when they started all running, because the soldiers were after them after they had just cleaned up that town where they kept the rations. They said they had lot of rations but they weren't even giving it to them, poor things, and they were just starving. So they just went, but my dad used to always tell us about how, he said that they, it was started over an egg, he said . . .

RC: Ya, he always tells that . . .

GL: You remember that? He said that these two boys,[5] you know, they were Indian boys, they were going along in this little town here, somewhere in there was the building where the rations was kept for the village, you know, and the Indian village is over here somewhere, and its all woods around Fort Snelling. And these two teenage boys, they're about thirteen, fourteen years old, one of them belonged to one of the chiefs, you know there's always a chief for all the, several, there's several fires, you remember?[6] Even the Oglalas have that too. Sicangu and Spotted Tail and all them, you remember? Well, them over here too, they have that, and so they have these chiefs. Anyway, there must have been a couple of chiefs in that camp maybe, 'cause these camps weren't all together, because there's too many of them. Somewhere there's another camp, and somewhere there's another area. Well, anyway, these two, one of these kids belonged to the chief,[7] that was the chief's son, and they were going and here, they went in a chicken coop, they found an egg in there, you know, and they took it, you know, they came out and, right now, the farmer that owned the chickens and that place was his farm, why, he was watching out for them kids and when they got in sight I suppose, right away, he was watching them, and he came outside and he was standing with his shotgun set on the porch, on his little porch, to see what them kids were going to do. Soon they came out with the egg, and the other kid said, "I dare you to break it," and the crazy kid, I guess he just dropped it so it broke, and he just shot him. And they said that's what started that war. So this kid, the other kid, here he took off and ran, but the other one was shot. He got killed right there, you know, that was a shotgun. And the kid who got back to the camp and he told them that the boy was dead, you know, that guy shot him. So that's how come the uprising came up. All the warriors got together, and they went into the town and boy, they destroyed everything, cleaned that place just flat. That's how come they call it the massacre. And that was close to

Fort Snelling, so right now somebody ran over to Fort Snelling and told them, so the soldiers start coming and that's when the Indians broke camp and they ran each, every direction. Some ran towards the river, and some ran towards the open, this way. There was no towns and all these places, they weren't there then. Some went right into Canada. That's how come they have Sioux Valley, that's one of those places. And that's when the party that was running through the open area was Lily's grandmother, my sister Lily said her grandma was seventeen years old at that time. And her sister had these two kids, but she had been living with a white man. But see, when these Indians were starving to death, well, already they were kind of in an uproar. They were undecided about what they should do, but they were telling their people that all these people that were married to white men, they were going to kill them, you know, the men and their children, but they were going to let the women live. They were planning on that already then, so that Lily's grandmother's sister told her husband, or the man that she was living with, I don't suppose that they were married, you know, at that time. Well, she told him to go because they were going to kill him, you know. So I guess he went, so she was alone with her two little kids, and that was Luke McCay and his sister, Nancy Straight, them two, they're brother and sister. And so she had them two, so they started running right away because the soldiers, they were just a little ways, you know, so they started running right away. They must've left their camps and everything, enit? They were just running every which way, you know, grab whatever they could eat, you know, and that's all they ran with. And she was running with them, but Auntie Lily was telling me that her grandma said that they could just feel the shells falling on them when they were shooting above them. They weren't shooting at them, at least, the soldiers, but they were shooting above them, but all the pellets were just falling on them like rain. Must've been scary, uh? So they were just running, and I guess Lily's grandma said, "I was young at that time and I was really swift, you know, and fast, and always used to run at races and win all the time, so I was really running real way ahead of everything," but her sister was really keeping up with her too, but she had this one kid on her back, and then she had one, you know, and I suppose she was carrying the stuff maybe, you know, for them.

She looked, she said she didn't see her no more, so she looked and soon she went by here, and she didn't even have her kids, her sister, you know, she just ran by her, and she said she looked back and here she said she saw the poor little kids laying on the ground way in the back. She just dropped them and left them. So she just ran, ran back. She said, "I ran for a little ways," but, she said, "I just couldn't, couldn't do it, so, I just. . . ." You know, they always say kanakana, that means you kind of give a hoot or what, I don't know what. She ran back, and she put one on her back and carried the other one, she never had any children before so I imagine she could really run, and she just ran. But she said she never saw her sister again. She just ran right on.

And you know Mrs. Yankton? She was a good friend of mine too, she would talk to me all the time, and she was telling me about her mother, was a baby too, and they dropped her too. Her mother dropped her too, and she said there was a whole bunch of them, and she said they all got caught over here somewhere, you know, and that's how come this was a fort, they were just now beginning to make this, this was a fort made for relay mail. You know, Pony Express. See, that's what they were making these forts for, so the mail would go. . . .

DP: So it was a fort before it was a reservation?

GL: Ya! Uh huh. That's why the soldiers were here. Ya, this was a fort, and it was supposed to be a Pony Express stop, see, where they could change horses, and ride a different horse to the next post. The next one would probably have been Fort Buford, and then maybe up into Fort Peck. See all these . . . anyway, they got caught here, close here, anyway, they weren't exactly here, you know, but they got caught further back, Fort Abercrombie? What do they call it? Something, anyway, I can't never say that. Anyway, there, I guess they picked up all the little babies, you know, the soldiers did, came along in wagons you know, and they picked up all these babies, and this is the story that Mrs. Yankton is telling me, and she said that her ma said that, her mother told her, when they got over here, why, they just examined all of them to see who all were nursing babies. You know, I suppose they show, your milk runs off when you're nursing a baby, so I guess they found out. Put all the nursing mamas in a wagon and they took them back, and that's where they took them, to that Fort Abercrombie or whatever you call it, they took 'em there, and here there was a great big room, big building, you know, it was just no partitions or anything, it was the whole, solid room. And they took us in there, her grandma told her mother, "They took us in there, and here," she said, "we went in and there was all you poor little babies, you were all sitting in a row. Each one had a slab of bacon, they were sucking on bacon. [laughter] So that's how we learned to give our kids a slab of bacon," she says. That's where they learned that. Wasn't that cute, huh? So they all found their little babies, you know, and see that woman could have found her babies. But see Lily's grandma kept them and brought them up. She just kept them and brought 'em up.

CP: So when did they . . .

DP: Make this a reservation?

GL: Later!

CP: Well, I was going to ask when they put a fence around the fort. Who controls that now?

DP: Is that the state or the city that took over control?

GL: It's a state historic place. Ya, see it was turned back to the tribe, the whole thing belonged to us. That was one good thing Louie Goodhouse did. He said we will never be able to keep it up. That will be a lot of expense. It will be a torn and broken-down place, just like the old hospital and that old school at St. Michaels. It will be like that, he knew. And so he said we'll give it to the historic, the North Dakota historic. He probably got some money out of it, maybe. But maybe he put it in for the tribe too. But maybe it's never recorded, or maybe it is too—we don't know. Nobody has ever checked in on it, I guess, I don't know. But see, that's what he did, and he turned that into the Bismarck Historical Society. So they turned it over and that's how it's kept up, that's why it's kept up. It's a historic place.

CP: Did you both go to school there?

RC: Mm hm. I went to school there when it was a boarding school.

GL: I didn't. The sister school was over here.

RC: I went over there, too.

CP: You [Rachel] went to both?

RC: Ya.

GL: Ya, it burned down. It burned down in '25, huh, 1925 or '26.

RC: '26.

GL: I know I was in Flandreau then, and you must have been in Bismarck maybe, or you were here?

RC: Here.

GL: Oh . . .

CP: The Grey Nuns ran both of those?

GL: No no no . . .

RC: No no. Just that one. But when that burned down they all came over here, the Grey Nuns, they kept them . . .

GL: And taught . . . taught their own students that they got from over there. Because they were too many when they crowded them here.

DP: You know I wanted to ask you before we forget, Vernie gave me this list, you know, the old census? of Louie Longie, you know, being the father, and then Rosalie Adele and the rest, you know, Joseph, Antoine. . . . Who is the mother? There's no mother listed on here.

RC: Ya, our grandmother, who was she?

GL: My mom used to always call her Susanna.

RC: Huh?

GL: Susanna. I suppose Susan or something, Susanna, but . . .

RC: No last name?

GL: I don't know what her last name would be. Ah, what's her name, you know, that Cap Cavanaugh's daughter. She lives in Warwick. She came here, you know, and she had a great big family tree. And she has the Indian name, but I can't remember. It's something about Makhá . . .

CP: Yeah, that's what Vern said.

GL: Makhámani or something. . . . "Walks the Earth" or something. I don't know now. Don't write it down because maybe . . .

RC: Maybe that's not the one.

GL: . . . might be someone else's name and here we'd be accused of stealing it. [all laugh] No? You should see her. I wonder where you could see her.

DP: Who is that now?

GL: Kelly. Her name is Kelly. I don't know her last name, but she is Cap Cavanaugh's daughter. She had the family tree, you know, the, the—it's a great big one, kind of like a map, you know, it's got all the watchacall. . . . And she has that name, because they come from Rosalie.

DP: Is she around here?

GL: Mm hm. Well, Kelly lives over here, at Warwick. But I really don't know her last name, so I wouldn't know whereabouts you'd find her, but she lives over there anyway. But you know what? Her mother, I don't think she's very interested in things like that, but I think she's . . .

RC: Who's her mother?

GL: Marianne Green

RC: Ohh.

GL: Marianne. You remember mama's . . .

RC: Cousin?

GL: Cousin, but she became her sister because our old grandpa married her grandmother.

RC: Ohh.

GL: See Marianne Green . . .

RC: Isabel?

GL: Ya, Isabelle. Isabelle is Marianne Green and them's grandmother. But see their father's name was Francis Longie, and that was supposed to be our grandpa's brother. So our grandpa married his sister-in-law.

DP: Hmm.

GL: It's about earth, so you could write "earth" anyway, but I don't know what else. Don't put the "Máni" on there because maybe it might not be right! [laughs] So many nowadays are just really concerned about names. "They stole our name!" And oh my, how do they know! Oh dear. Ya well you can write maybe "Marianne. . . ."

DP: What are they doing to the church [Seven Dolors Catholic Church]? Are they fixing the basement, or—?

GL: They're building a ramp. They're going to put a ramp there, instead, you know because we have so many wheelchairs and I guess everybody . . .

RC: Oh ya, that's good.

GL: . . . just says, you know, we're in a wheelchair, we can't go to Mass, we can't climb them steps. So they're putting on a ramp.

DP: Who's the priest there now?

GL: What is it, Chuck? Lute?

RC: He used to be in Pine Ridge, uh?

GL: Ya, he was at Pine Ridge for sixteen years. They say he talks fluent Lakȟóta.

RC: . . . He knows everybody.

DP: Father Lute?

GL: Huh? Ya.

RC: Father Chuck.

GL: Ya, we always call him Father Chuck. You know, he's supposed to be part Indian, on his father's side. But he's Sac and Fox, from Iowa, I can't remember where. But I remember that time when he was first ordered to come, you know they told us, he's part Indian, they said, and I guess somebody went and asked Tony McDowell. "Tony, do you know the name of that guy? Do you know what tribe he belongs to, that guy that's supposed to be coming?" "Ya, I guess he's a sexy fox." [all laugh] "Isn't he sexy?"

RC: Sexy fox . . .

GL: He's Sac and Fox and here he said, "Ya, he's a sexy fox." Crazy Tony. Are you just hungry now?

CP: I'm getting there, yeah.

GL: Oh dear, I wish I had something to feed you. You know that guy said you wanted to roast a chicken, and I said no, I said, we'll roast them to death! [all laugh]

DP: I think I'm the only one that's roasting here.

GL: But you know what? This guy down the store here, what time is it? Is it before six, I think. . . .

RC: It's quarter, quarter to five.

GL: Oh, well, that's open. You could buy whatyoucalls down there. You can buy chicken, and stuff, put it in the, what do you call these little ovens?

DP: Microwaves.

GL: Ya. They're right there. You can heat them all and everything. You're gonna have a good meal.

CP: Good!

GL: There's a restaurant there, but I don't know if it's open all day.

DP: Oh ya, at that little mall?

CP: Luis Cafe?

GL: Ya! He serves real good meals too.

RC: Who is he?

GL: He's a Mexican. He's a Mexican, but his wife is part Indian. She's, uh, remember Susie Black Fox? That's her daughter. You remember Ambrose, Ambrose Little Ghost? That's his sister's daughter, that girl. But see, when she had her, she gave her up for adoption, so she said, "I was adopted by white people," you know, "white people brought me up," but she said, "I want to know about my Indian side." She is white, you know, her father must be white. But her mother was Indian. She came from Susie Black Fox there.

DP: Changing the subject, but is it Auntie Grace's tape that's all in Sioux? Have they put any subtitles on your video, do you know yet?

CP: The ones they did for the college, the video?

DP: For the school up here? Eugene Hale?

GL: Huh?

DP: 'Member when they videotaped you and Auntie Lily?

GL: Uh huh. What about it?

DP: Yours is all in Indian [Dakhóta language]. But in Auntie Lily's, they put subtitles underneath so they put it all in English underneath. Have they done that with yours yet?

GL: I wouldn't know. I wouldn't know. I never go over there. I never bother myself about them.

DP: 'Cause we have them.

RC: Ya, she's got the tapes.

DP: I bought a copy of each one last time I was here, and they said, as soon as we get the subtitles made for yours, they were gonna let me know, they were gonna send me one.

GL: Ohh.

DP: We're gonna go over there and see them too, if they're still there.

RC: Well, it's almost five, they won't be there.

DP: Oh, they won't be there right now, so maybe tomorrow. You want to get together with Auntie Grace again?

CP: Yeah, I would like to.

RC: She'll get tired of you pretty soon. [laughs]

GL: You know, that's gotta live on. If somebody's interested, I think it's worthwhile to let them know.

2 (Il)legible, (Il)liberal Subjects

Charles Alexander Eastman's Poetics of Withholding

> *I am an Indian; and while I have learned much from civilization,*
> *for which I am grateful, I have never lost my Indian sense of*
> *right and justice. I am for development and progress along social*
> *and spiritual lines, rather than those of commerce, nationalism,*
> *or material efficiency. Nevertheless, so long as I live, I am*
> *an American.*
>
> —Charles Alexander Eastman (Ohíye s'á), *From the*
>   *Deep Woods to Civilization*

> *Inarguably, there is a satisfaction in dwelling on the degree*
> *to which the power of our enemies is implicated, not in their*
> *command of knowledge, but precisely in their ignorance.*
>
> —Eve Kosofsky Sedgwick, *Epistemology of the Closet*

Ohíye s'á (He Wins or Winner) headed south across the medicine line as a fifteen-year-old exile returning from Manitoba, ever so reluctantly, to a United States whose armies and militias had pursued him, his family, and his people to the point of death. With him was his father, Jacob Eastman, whom he had thought hanged with other Dakhóta warriors at Mankato, and whose new life as a Christian convert and homesteader the younger man despised, calling it "a false life! A treacherous life!" At his father's homestead in Flandreau, Dakota Territory, Ohíye s'á would himself convert, becoming Charles Alexander Eastman (1858–1939), the Isáŋyathi (Santee) author, physician, and intellectual whose life and writings navigated the assimilationist demands of U.S. settler society in relation to his own sense of Indigenous peoples' enduring epistemic and ethical differences from white "civilization."

The position of Eastman is complicated: born into a Waȟpéthuŋwaŋ (Wahpeton) Dakhóta family in 1858, a graduate of Carlisle Indian

School and Beloit College, a star football player for Dartmouth, and trained at Boston University as a physician, he was also one of a small group of Native American intellectuals comprising the leadership of the SAI, an assimilation-era (1879–1934) and progressive-era (1890–1920) organization that worked to air Indigenous grievances and lobbied for the passage of the Indian Citizenship Act. Over his cosmopolitan career, Eastman was often described as a cultural mediator who bridged irreconcilable worlds. One Chautauqua brochure for a 1904 Eastman lecture touted, "This strong and interesting Sioux American . . . has come to be regarded as the literary spokesman of his race" and emphasized his position at the brink of both the "natural" world of his "tribal" boyhood and the "artificial" one he encountered at Dartmouth College and Boston University.[1] Such a reception, typical of Eastman's white audiences, reproduced what K. Tsianina Lomawaima calls the "false dichotomies" of "wards and citizens, savagery and civilization, past and future, Native tribe and U.S. nation."[2] On one side of these dichotomies is a sort of ethnological Eastman, lauded as a "representative of his race" and "full-blooded Sioux" orator and writer. Such epithets appeared not only in his remarks at the First Universal Races Congress in London and in Eastman's obituaries but also during his life: in many of his books' frontispieces (including the first edition of *Indian Scout Talks*), Eastman appears in a feathered war bonnet. Likewise, Kiara Vigil wryly notes, "One article from Manchester's *Union* in 1939 provides an extensive obituary titled: 'Dartmouth's most famous Indian grad dies in Detroit, Dr. Charles Eastman '87, A Full-Blooded Sioux Known as Ohiyesa, Recognized as Most Learned Member of Race.'"[3] On the flip side of these images, though, is the activist Eastman of the SAI, whose strong advocacy for citizenship and the elimination of the Office of Indian Affairs aimed at ending tribal wardship.[4] Eastman's best-known autobiographical work, *From the Deep Woods to Civilization* (1916), seems in its title alone to avow the irreconcilable differences between his Indigenous upbringing and the white "civilization" in which he served as both a lobbyist and popularizer of Dakhóta politics, culture, and philosophy.

Ironically, contemporary critics have tended to place Eastman within a binary of assimilation and resistance. Penelope Myrtle Kelsey, for instance, argues that Eastman was a "resistance writer" for having tried to set the record straight about "Dakota cultural practices, identity, and thióšpaye to a presumably misinformed audience."[5] For other critics and historians, his close involvement with the United

States government, first as the only physician at the Lakȟóta Wounded Knee massacre, later as a translator of Dakȟóta names for allotment rolls, and ultimately as a congressional insider and lobbyist for Indian citizenship, mark him as a kind of patsy. Robert Warrior reads Eastman's oeuvre as an attempt to gain "sympathy from white audiences for the difficult . . . process [for Native Americans] of being American citizens," adding that Eastman's memoirs are "highly sentimental accounts of his childhood in which he portrays Natives as needy for, worthy of, and ready for inclusion in mainstream civilization."[6] Such a view captures the mediating aspects of Eastman's life and work, but unfortunately ascribes an assimilationist motive to both.

This chapter continues chronologically from the story of prisoners' conversions I recounted in chapter 1, where I explored the meanings of their ambivalences as a means of self- and community protection and as subversive withholding. Here I further develop a method for reading the meanings and varieties of that withholding, examining how Eastman's representations of Indian life appealed to white regimes of legibility, playing up his innocuousness while also celebrating and renewing Dakȟóta peoplehood. I am not interested in locating Eastman on a scale of biographical heroism or infamy in terms of resistance. Instead, I focus on how his idealizations of Dakȟóta ethics perform a certain kind of labor within and for Dakȟóta communities as covert acts of reterritorialization. As this chapter's title indicates, what is hidden or illegible is thus key to my reading of Eastman's depictions of Dakȟóta life, and I follow James C. Scott's sense of legibility as an optics through which modern states have tried to "get a handle on its subjects and their environment."[7] By the early twentieth century, these ways of seeing included reservations, tribal rolls, and blood quantum, but they also extended to expectations of simultaneous Indigenous authenticity and vanishing, or what in the realm of citizenship amounted to incorporation and erasure of Indigenous individuals. Like other SAI members who advocated for Indian citizenship, Eastman's insistence on being both American and Indian reveal him to be negotiating a structural crisis defined by stark binaries of insiders and outsiders, citizens and aliens, the purportedly civilized and wild. Assimilation's demands were marked by a settler-colonial logic of Indigenous authenticity that became figured as "Indian blood" or "competence" as well as by a logic of incorporation and elimination of indigeneity.[8]

Rather than resolving these dialectics, the force of Eastman's work rests in his keeping both terms of the dialectic in play. His writing thus occupies what Kevin Bruyneel calls a third space from within which Eastman asserted the (illiberal) possibilities of Dakhóta life across the boundaries of U.S. political time, highlighting how Indigenous Americans, as (potential, not yet) dual citizens, occupied a space that was not fully assimilable.[9] But problems of representation in Eastman's case complicate Bruyneel's reading, including how Eastman often couched his assertions of critical Indigenous difference in a primitivist rhetoric of the vanishing Indian. His use of white hate speech ("savages" and "wild Indians" abound) and settler tropes of detribalized indigeneity, or what Lucy Maddox calls his "persistent turning to the abstract, the ideal, the generic," make difficult any straightforward celebration of him as a third space anticolonialist.[10] Yet that is partly my point: his is the unheroic decolonization of an emergent peoplehood discourse that was typical of many assimilation-era Indigenous people, especially of elite brokers who worked many sides and angles in pursuing a specifically Dakhóta sovereignty. Where that ideal vocabulary (i.e., "the wild Indian" who is also "the natural man") reads for Maddox as an effacement of Dakhóta elements in his work as well as a symptom of "the flight from the political competitions that he found so disillusioning," I see it is a complexly mediated move toward the tribal political. These turnings are vexed by a poetics of withholding that complicates both Bruyneel's reading of Eastman and Homi Bhabha's notion of hybridity; these point to the presence of what we would now call a critical Indigenous theorizing of representation and agency.

By poetics of withholding, I mean there is something of the closet about Eastman's writing, where the closet is defined less by sexual difference than by the perpetually uncanny existence of Indigenous people in a settler-state. Eastman was arguably celebrated because he fulfilled, in some of his work, this settler-colonial vanishing act. As Eve Kosofsky Sedgwick observes, though, "in the vicinity of the closet, even what *counts* as a speech act is problematized on a perfectly routine basis."[11] In keeping with my use of translation in my introduction, I approach Eastman's writings as covert resurgences of Dakhóta politics and ways of knowing. His writings are part of a broader set of countertranslations through which Dakhóta confronted state forces (legal, educational, religious) and the coercive processes whereby state agents sought to make Indigenous people increasingly legible, knowable, and controllable. Writing about the founding of the Bureau of Indian Affairs by Secretary of War John Calhoun, Eastman described how Calhoun's new bureaucracy responded to this hidden domain with its own translational demands: "In 1824 the United States required of the tribes in this region to define their territory, a demand that intensified and gave a new turn to their intertribal warfare."[12] Here Eastman implies that "intertribal warfare intensified" as a result of the strict delineation of territory that occurred because of state demands to tie geographical territories to tribal sovereignty. Foreclosing the possibility of overlapping territories and tribal jurisdictions, as well as mobile or fluid geopolitical boundaries, the United States government's requirement sought, as Mark Rifkin notes in a Mahican treaty-making context, "to manage modes of political recognition in ways ultimately conducive to U.S. aims and interests."[13] These modes of management had negative consequences for intertribal diplomacy. Eastman diagnoses these attempts to pin down what were highly mobile Indigenous boundaries as causing the escalation of intertribal warfare and creating a "truly 'savage' warfare" that grew "in bitterness until it culminated in resistance to the Government, in 1862," in the war between allied Dakhóta bands and U.S. army and state militias.

His brief account of one of the causes of the U.S.–Dakhóta War underscores not only how state territorializations were settler-colonial translations but also how Indigenous peoples voiced critical countertranslations, in this case narrating their own identities as "nations" whose "resistance to the Government" appeared through both outright warfare and more subtly as Indigenous modes of reckoning relatedness and community, of collective decision making and diplomacy. These ways of reckoning relatives are based in theories of the individual and the people that are of course tribally specific, but that Eastman universalized (as the "Red Men's") while drawing substantially on his knowledge of Dakhóta people. But universalizing is one variety of what I regard as Eastman's translational ruses, through which he depicted indigeneity as a detribalized object that was immediately apprehensible to whites: the generic Indian who, in a settler-colonial logic of replacement, could be imitated, absorbed, and co-opted. This process has been described by Indigenous studies scholars under the rubric of "playing Indian." Here and throughout this chapter, however, I use that phrase in a different sense than Philip Deloria in *Playing Indian*, Shari Huhndorf in *Going Native,* or Eve Tuck and K. Wayne Yang in "Decolonization Is Not a Metaphor," where such play appears as the privileged practice of whites. My sense, which is closer to Monika Siebert's formulation in *Indians Playing Indian*, is that this game of mimicry was played by Indigenous people too, and played in canny ways to protect tribal ways of being, knowing, and doing. Where Siebert's argument describes how Indigenous people have resisted multicultural incorporation through performances of tribal-national histories, I am interested in a species of absence: how Eastman, like other assimilation-era Indigenous intellectuals, appealed to white regimes of legibility even as he safeguarded Dakhóta knowledge from white consumption and co-optation. From a Dakhóta perspective, his amiability is a pose of smiling opacity.[14]

As I will show, the content of Eastman's nostalgias was quite Dakhóta, and there is great specificity to the ways in which he cites a Dakhóta relational epistemology. My use of the term "ruse" signifies a kind of cunning or stratagem rather than an act of duplicity. This sense of the term draws on its earliest recorded usages in Middle English where it describes "a detour or turn made by a hunted animal in order to elude capture."[15] The ironies of this usage are not lost on me, given Eastman's own canny ways of handling associations of "wild Indians" in a settler-colonial imaginary. If anything, it makes the term all the more appropriate because Eastman was fond of owning and reworking these associations, converting animals into Indians (and vice versa) for the sake of criticizing this imaginary.

One aspect of this rusing or poetics of withholding lies in how Eastman ciphered Dakhóta knowledge by downplaying its intertextuality: withheld from view are its many and nuanced relationships with his other writings and with Dakhóta thióšpaye discourses in other oral and written literatures. From the pat moral lessons of his animal tales to the apparently straightforward how-tos of his scouting manual, Eastman's invitations to "play Indian" thus offer mostly floating signifiers. Part of my task in this chapter is translational. I identify some of those intertexts—not for transparency's sake but to show the extent and effects of Eastman's withholdings. It may be helpful to locate this withheld intertextuality in terms of other subversive rhetorical traditions, such as Henry Louis Gates Jr.'s account of black vernacular tradition in *The Signifying Monkey*. Gates gives a picture (schematic diagrams and all) of black callbacks to literary and oral antecedents, describing how the practice of signifying draws for its rhetorical meaning on a double voicedness, and quotes Gary Saul Morton's "elaboration" of this doubling effect: "The audience of a double-voiced word is therefore meant to hear both a version of the original utterance as the embodiment of a speaker's point of view (or 'semantic position') *and* the second speaker's evaluation of that utterance from a different point of view."[16] In Morton's account, this idealized audience gets the punning that goes on in a genre like "playing the dozens"; they are the source of its critical power to displace regimes of white signification.

This doubling is both similar and dissimilar to the rhetorical ruses in Eastman's (and arguably in other assimilation-era Indigenous authors') writings. It is similar in that, as with black double voicedness, there is an emphasis on intertextuality, or a text's relationships with other texts, which in Eastman's case include his other writings and Dakhóta genres of oral history like the hithúŋkaŋkaŋpi (long-ago stories) that I read later in this chapter. Likewise, his citations of these literary and oral intertexts would have been opaque to white audiences of his time because he points, often with little or no context, to certain Dakhóta ethical ideals and practices. These read as cognates or Gatesian homonyms to white notions of "physical excellence," "citizenship," and "God," to name a few, so that despite repeated invitation to identify with Indians, there is an entire level of withheld signification barring the fulfillment of that invitation. It remains only a tease.

But Gates's account of subversive meaning may be supplemented by highlighting precisely what lies outside or beyond language: the nonlinguistic aspects of Indigenous experience in homelands. Eastman's how-to guide, *Indian Scout Talks*, brims with details of Dakhóta places. In his chapter on "The Language of Dress," the litany of feathers alone (eagle, raven, Canada goose, cut, notched, split, dyed, not dyed, and so on) would confound even the most ambitious Boy Scout, especially those who do not live in what is now the upper Midwestern United States—that vast Dakhóta territory described in Eastman's prose. Confoundment also occurs because what falls out in any enactment of these how-tos is their narrated environment. Because that environment is narrated rather than encountered through the body, Eastman effectively solicits his white readers into relationship with what Diana Taylor calls an "archive" rather than a "repertoire," because in the latter, "live, embodied actions . . . , [as traditions] are storied in the body, through various mnemonic methods, and transmitted 'live' in the here and now to a live audience."[17] Further complicating Eastman's poetics is the fact that the Native environment in his accounts is mediated by Dakhóta norms (Eastman constantly places the body in an ethical field of relationships with human and other-than-human persons). Because Dakhóta communities who inhabited those environments upheld those norms, in their absence, and in the absence of a regulating Indigenous community, the lessons offered by Eastman are an ersatz ethics but a real reminder of why that absence existed: the ethnic cleansing and exile endured by Dakhóta after 1862.

My method for reading here focuses on citations of Dakhóta ethics as the kind of idealized ontology of earth Elizabeth Povinelli describes, in which "the irreducible unity of earth and people" appears in the service of imaginative "reoccupation and return rather than redemption."[18] In a similar decolonial spirit, David Martínez has argued that Eastman is maybe best seen as a "Dakota philosopher" whose writings promoted Dakhóta epistemologies.[19] I extend Martínez's account to examine how Eastman mobilized nostalgia as a politics for reindigenizing lost territory and renewing the Oyáte within a Dakhóta decolonial imaginary. That is, I view Eastman's translations as acts of Dakhóta reoccupation and return—and expressly not as efforts to indigenize white Americans or "to explore the possibilities for cross-cultural understanding and identification that might exist on the common ground of childhood," as Tony Dykema-Vanderark asserts.[20] On the contrary, Eastman's translational withholdings are foundational to how he narrates Dakhóta presence and the possibility of flourishment in the early twentieth century.

We might think of this rewritten peoplehood as the outcome of a cultural translation that is subversive not because it *resists* but because it *insists,* and insists specifically on embodied Dakhóta archives—of physical practices, exercises, yes, but also of the feelings that various places and their inhabitants inspire. Eastman's situation as a cross-cultural broker is usefully understood as responding to the demands of white audiences for unvarnished depictions of "authentic" indigeneity. In this regime of cultural translation, Eastman would indeed seem to enact the trope of the vanishing Indian—and serve as a settler-colonial agent—by giving access to an Indigenous original that could be appropriated and performed at will by whites. But as Lawrence Venuti argues, to insist on mediation within a regime of what he calls "fluent translation," in which the translator works "to make his or her work 'invisible'" and the resulting translated text seem "'natural,' i.e., not translated," would be to deny the reader access to "what is 'present in the original.'"[21] If such denials operate in Eastman's writings, then his translations of Dakhóta life disrupt expectations of Indigenous legibility, transparency, and apprehensibility even as they rely on expectations of the very same.

Eastman asserted Dakhóta meanings about familial and communal attachments, embodied practices, and relational understandings, crystallizing what he called "the Indian" into something like what Saba Mahmood describes as a "positive ethics," or "the specific gestures, styles, and formal expressions that characterize one's relationship to a moral code."[22] The basis for such a code in Eastman's work was the thióšpaye, which furnished an embodied ethics that, as Ella Cara Deloria argues, was central to Dakhóta peoplehood. In *Speaking of Indians*, Deloria writes that the thióšpaye, as a term, "was essential in describing tribal life," noting that it "denotes a group of families, bound together by blood and marriage ties, that lived side-by-side in the camp circle."[23] Deloria underscores how the thióšpaye worked to inculcate relational values and practices, as when elders "put the correct words and formal speeches into . . . [a child's] mouth for him to repeat to this or that relative," and so enacted an "informal but constant system of education in human relations and social responsibility."[24] In his own literary work, Eastman deployed thióšpaye discourses of generosity and hospitality to suggest Dakhóta ways of reckoning, and dwelling in, territories.

The basis of thióšpaye ethics lies not only in human interpersonal relationships but also in relationships with other-than-human occupants of land, water, and sky. Within this ontology of earth are prescriptions to behave as a good relative. These prescriptions were formally and originally transacted as treaties and constituted both human and other-than-human territories.[25] The conceptual and cosmological implications of how people live moral codes in relation to other powerful persons (human, other-than-human animals, spirits) runs throughout Eastman's depictions of thióšpaye relationality, and by writing about the land as an affectively rich web of human and other-than-human relatives, Eastman articulates individual citizenship as grounded in richly storied and felt relationships to Indigenous homelands. The effect is to repersonalize and reanimate what property discourses of federal Indian law and U.S. citizenship had rendered as lifeless. For readers attuned to thióšpaye discourses, Eastman's invitations to non-Native children to play Indian push back against a settler metaphysics by positioning white bodies, through their play, in a field of Dakhóta relationality.

More Than Talking Animals

In the last tale of *Red Hunters and Animal People* (1904), Eastman's earliest published collection of tales from Dakhóta oral tradition, three young men visit their brother-in-law, Sheyaka, who the text calls a "renowned" Sioux hunter. As Sheyaka regales them with stories of talking animals, his audience begins to voice doubts about the veracity of his account, and their dialogue reads like a Platonic interrogation of animal language, intelligence, presence, and, finally, collective presence or peoplehood. Near the start of their conversation, though, one of the three young men, Kangee, insists, on the basis of his observations of a mother doe and her fawn, "that there is good ground for saying that the wild animals have a language to which we have not the key." But Katola, "the doubter," counters: "He [Kangee] has made the doe and fawn real people. They can neither speak nor reason . . . and the fawn hides [from hunters] because it is its nature to hide, not because the mother has instructed it."

Katola's doubt, in its ascribing to nature essential differences between humans and animals, forms an analog to categories of race by which Euro-Americans historically viewed Indigenous peoples as savage, as less than human. Through Katola's doubt, Eastman ironically maps a genealogy of racial difference onto the animals whom (or which) human beings, enfranchised by their ability to ponder the ontological status of other-than-human others, sit around and leisurely discuss. But instead of carrying the analogy of Dakhóta human being to Euro-American colonizer to its full extent, Eastman's story ultimately refuses any absolute ontological distinction between human beings and animals. Instead it asserts across boundaries of difference the ways in which human beings are like animals in behaviors they have learned from them. Roving from one animal example to another, recounting the bear's "drunken" ferocity and vanity, the wolf's cunning, and so on, Sheyaka concludes that his people have learned mimetically from the actions of all the different animals. "We Red people have followed their example," says Sheyaka. "We teach our children to respect and obey their elders." This summing up by the "old story-teller" effectively forecloses the prior debates about animal language and intentionality, declaring instead that not only are animals exemplary peoples but also that their peoplehood, as with that of human beings, inheres in maintaining norms of intergenerational respect and obedience.

Recalling that Eastman's animal stories began to appear in *Lippincott's Magazine* in 1893, the same year Rudyard Kipling's *Jungle Book* tales were published, we might imagine an Eastman whose aesthetics reproduced, or in some sense apologized for, a settler-colonial status quo. But this would be to mistake style for substance. Instead, these stories invoke and evoke Dakhóta stories, Dakhóta knowledge, and the thióšpaye networks embedded in them as political frameworks with which to analyze and criticize the United States' thefts of Dakhóta lands. Instead of positioning Eastman along an axis defined by the poles of either traditionalism or assimilation to settler civilization, his talking animals recover and rearticulate Dakhóta peoplehood, along with the thióšpaye-based ethical relations of gift giving and receiving at its core, as an imaginative act of decolonization. His idealizations of Dakhóta modes of sociality are a means for him to rework and reinvigorate what were and remain historically sovereign forms of relation based in Dakhóta cosmology. Neither purely traditional nor assimilated, his fictional remakings of the thióšpaye demonstrate the flexible adaptativeness that Scott Lyons describes when he asserts "the reality of Indian time on the move."[26]

In finding Eastman's fiction to be grounded in a relationality where power appears as something to be shared among human and other-than-human beings and where the political is mediated by kinship norms of economic sufficiency and reciprocal giving, we may enrich existing tribal-nationalist approaches[27] to the reading of Native American literatures within their relevant intellectual, cultural, and political contexts. We may also further develop Penelope Myrtle Kelsey's view of Eastman as a "resistance writer." While Kelsey orients us through her readings of "tribal genres" toward meanings that, all told, loosely signify Dakhóta peoplehood, she does not explicate the relational logics underlying those genres.[28] Nor does her reading reveal how the tribal nation form—and its provocative extensions of relation to and with other-than-human beings—effectively narrates nonstatist possibilities while also producing a veiled decolonial imaginary.

More than an expression of sovereignty rooted in structures of federal recognition or in mimicking the narrations of Indianness enacted in federal law, Eastman's voicing of political criticisms by animals attempt to defederalize Dakhóta peoplehood. That is, his animal tales do precisely what Joanne Barker (Lenape) has called for in Native Americans' present-day decolonization struggles: "to get outside the political legacies of plenary power doctrines, colonialism, and racism and to reimagine the possibilities for Native governance and social relationships."[29] Such a reimagining of his work demands, at least from a settler culture's perspective, something of a temporal shift, in that the peoplehood imaginary of Eastman allows him to remember forms of sociality and diplomacy that existed before the creation of reservations, when human beings and animal people inhabited a complex network of nations whose boundaries were continually made, transgressed, and reasserted. Instead of simply giving voice to wolves and bears, the voicing of political critiques and demands for the recognition of rights for animal persons acts as a decolonizing gesture and a reclamation of thióšpaye practices that were quite literally outlawed under federal Indian policy. Eastman's cast of human and other-than-human characters throughout Red Hunters dramatize thióšpaye ties, or their abrogation, as the result of diplomatic accords upheld or failed. They also implicitly argue for a form of peoplehood that, because it claims not just equality but also ethical superiority for nonwhites, and so contests United States legal definitions of Native Americans as being constitutively inferior.[30]

In order to trace the place-based ethics of Eastman's animal tales, I now turn to an explication of the thióšpaye, its main differences from liberal notions of the individual and of Christian citizenship, and its resistive possibilities. I then move to the criticism of U.S. "civilization" that appears in Eastman's *From the Deep Woods to Civilization*, contrasting its renderings of U.S. temporality with a temporality of pausing that is implicit in the Dakhóta storytelling genre of hithúŋkaŋkaŋpi (usually glossed as "myths"). I then briefly read Eastman's descriptions of Dakhóta philosophy in his autoethnography, *The Soul of the Indian* (1911). By viewing his animal tales as critiques of U.S. settler-colonialism, criticisms that by the time Eastman writes *From the Deep Woods* become far less oblique, we may see more clearly his innovative translation of Dakhóta politics into narratives that at once sentimentally appeal to and challenge the United States. We also see that these challenges come specifically through citations of Dakhóta conceptions of peoplehood, power, and gift.

Throughout *Red Hunters*, Eastman's animals model good thióšpaye behaviors that attest to their status as distinct tribes, nations, or peoples[31] that are inassimilable to other tribes, nations, or peoples. This modeling constitutes a Dakhóta formation of peoplehood that contests settler structures of the racialized, atomized family in the liberal nation-state. Such structures drove Indian policy in its adoptions of compulsory education programs for Native children, whose removals from their families into residential and day schools depended, as Beth Piatote asserts, "upon public understandings of family and tribal-national domesticities as aberrant formations that were hostile to the settler states of the United States and Canada."[32]

While trying to break up Indigenous families through educational reforms, the settler-state also attempted to transform family and property relations through the 1887 Dawes Act, also known as the General Allotment Act, which granted landholdings, usually of 165 acres, to individual American Indians, replacing communal tribal holdings and extending U.S. federal law and protections to the new landholdings. The language of the act contained explicit provisions for the civilizing of the Indian, making adoption of "the habits of civilized life" a condition of the act's extension of United States citizenship.[33] This construal of the liberal individual as not only the bearer of rights but also as the locus for reckoning relatedness is based broadly in the progressive rhetorics of the nineteenth century.[34] The merging of civilizing, Christian, and individualistic discourses typified a heterosexual imaginary in which the nuclear family was enshrined as paradigmatic. As Lucy Maddox notes, this conflation was invoked by white Protestant reformers like Lyman Abbott and Merrill Gates, who saw "the reservation Indian" as a "generic figure, shaped—and limited—entirely by communal, tribal values and thus unfit for the kind of individualizing competition that characterized Christian citizenship."[35] Thomas Biolsi describes how the state constructed new kinds of Lakȟóta individuals beginning in the 1880s through four main modes of subjection: property ownership, determination of competence (to own land), recording of blood quantum, and recording of genealogy.[36] Although Biolsi places the beginning of the construction of the modern Lakȟóta individual in the reservation period (after 1878), the settler-colonial imposition of a modern subject began in earnest among Eastern Dakhóta as early as 1830, when the American Board of Commissioners for Foreign Missions established their Dakota Mission at Lac qui Parle, in what is now Minnesota, bringing with them a progressive rhetoric that wed Jesus with the plow.[37]

Against such antitribal pressures of early missionization and later allotment policy, Eastman deployed thióšpaye ethics and notions of peoplehood as assertions of tribal solidarity, persistence, and resilience. As Rifkin argues, Native peoplehood discourses may describe "modes of indigeneity—knowledge, relations to place, and forms of collectivity—that defy state narratives and survive despite being targeted for eradication."[38] Other Native studies scholars have asserted important linkages among long-standing relations to land, kinship, and political resistance in their efforts to make more legible the political stakes of peoplehood discourses.[39] The issue of legibility is especially crucial in Eastman's case because I read his children's tales as criticizing United States settler-colonialism on the basis of tribal epistemologies that were probably missed by his largely white audience and that are still relatively obscure in the secular academy—existing liminally, as Jodi Byrd writes, "in the ungrievable spaces of suspicion and unintelligibility."[40]

The visions of relationality that Eastman's talking animals invoke are political ones rooted in the thióšpaye, or extended family as historically lived through the unit of the band. As Alan Trachtenberg explains in his reading of Luther Standing Bear, a Lakȟóta (Sičháŋgu and Oglála) author, "The word *Tiyospaye* might be understood as meaning those ties of affection and obligation typical of Native families."[41] Trachtenberg's description relies on a public/private binary typical of liberalism, stripping away any potentially politically meanings of "affection and obligation." More accurate to evoking a sense of the thióšpaye's joining of affect and politics is what Ella Cara Deloria simply calls honoring, which is both a precondition and an ongoing guarantee for social being: "To have standing, one must have someone, or some persons, who *cared* for him; cared for him enough to honor him; to benefit others in his name."[42] As a social object that individuals realize through maintaining those ties, thióšpaye also creates and reproduces communal values, or "the customs and expectations that gave the *Oyate* its distinctive character, what might be translated into Western terms as its *national* ideals."[43] It is a shorthand for the matrix of kinship relations that help bring about the good life.

The basis of thióšpaye ethics lies not only in human interpersonal relationships but also in relationships with other-than-human occupants of land, water, and air. The thióšpaye is grounded in an ontology of earth where obligations to behave as a good relative, formally and originally transacted as treaties, constitute both human and other-than-human territories.[44] The conceptual and cosmological implications of how people live moral codes in relation to other powerful persons of various kinds runs throughout Eastman's depictions of thióšpaye relationality, and by writing about the land as an affectively rich web of human and other-than-human relatives, Eastman articulates individual citizenship as grounded in richly storied and felt relationships to Indigenous homelands.

Eastman's citations of Dakȟóta ethics engage and indict the ongoing settler-coloniality of the U.S. settler-state while also imagining Dakhóta peoplehood as emergent from the embodied, everyday acts of living in long-occupied lands—acts that he describes as being governed by an ethic of sufficiency and a critical Indigenous relationality. In practice, the extended family bridges cosmology and political action; it is the basic unit of Dakhóta territoriality because it provides the familial metaphors on which gifting, whose ritual sharing of power is at the heart of diplomacy, is founded. In the thióšpaye, one sees the dynamic relationship between Dakhóta and non-Dakhóta forms of land tenure and how the Dakhóta historically reproduced, through a broad constellation of social forms—including ceremony, myth, hunting and fishing, and household practices—the enduring, flexible networks of relatives. Instead of being a static entity that was forced forever to retreat from the state, Dakhóta people have continually remade ourselves by remaking our thióšpaye connections to our environment and to one another. Thióšpaye and gifting ultimately suggest a view of cosmological plenitude, of the courage to adapt and endure as a people.

Deloria notes that observing the dictates of a nonbiological kinship was "the ultimate aim of Dakota life"[45] and that kinship held "all Dakota people . . . together in a great relationship that was theoretically all-inclusive and co-extensive with the Dakota domain."[46] By "domain" she means not only ancestral lands but also the affective and ethical textures of lived experience and relationship with other Dakhóta persons. Her defining of kinship against the liberal ideal of the individual thus refuses convergences of race, class, and gender around heterosexual, monogamous marriage and the nuclear family. By widening kinship to include animals, spirits, and the land, she troubles the distinction between nature and culture and so sets the stage to recover, as a site of resistance, a nature that federal Indian law has discredited by instrumentalizing it and regarding it only as property. Peoplehood, then, is a fluid sort of relationality; it is national or political but not statist, with communities rather than individuals as the bearers of rights. I gloss this articulation of thióšpaye ethics as critically relational: nonstatist norms of gifting, reciprocity, and material sufficiency mark the moral limits, if not the failures, of state capitalism.

The Pause

The affable storytelling style of *Red Hunters* (one 1905 reviewer notes that "the book is simply and pleasantly written, with no affectation or mannerism") earned Eastman a settler readership that saw the animal stories as differing "not as widely as might be wished from the white man's animal tales now so numerous."[47] Yet the stories also repeatedly cite Dakhóta oral traditions and their relational frameworks. They demonstrate what Bruyneel calls the refusal of "false choices" between political positions "framed by the imperial binary"[48] of savagery and civilization. Eastman's citations of Dakhóta oral tradition, while couched in a capitalistic discursive field (Euro-Western publication), and written mainly for a white audience, refuses any temporality in which boundaries exist "between an 'advancing' people and a 'static' people, locating the latter out of time."[49]

Historically, stories from Dakhóta oral tradition were heard with careful attention as they were passed down from grandparents to grandchildren. Wazíyatawiŋ describes this ethic of careful listening as being "rooted in a deep sense of kinship responsibility, a responsibility that relays a culture, an identity, and a sense of belonging essential" to her life.[50] Listening and remembering, both ways to uphold one's thióšpaye obligations, are also profoundly relational activities, grounding the audience "in the needs and concerns of the people whom these narrative actions ultimately benefit in terms of collective memory and social cohesion."[51] Oral tradition, and the stories Eastman drew from it for his collection, consequently embody one significant mode of Dakhóta historicity.

In his foreword to *Red Hunters,* Eastman explains, "The main incidents in all of . . . [the tales], even those which are unusual and might appear incredible to the white man, are actually current among the Sioux and deemed by them worthy of belief." The narrative genre he is working in is something like a fable but is different in that it is more than fiction: "When the life-story of an animal is given, the experiences described are typical and characteristic of its kind. Here and there the fables, songs, and superstitious fancies of the Indian are brought in to suggest his habit of mind and manner of regarding the four-footed tribes." If he is straining here to define genre within a realist–imaginary (or historical–mythic) dichotomy, his marking of the stories as belonging to a preexisting kind bypasses these dichotomies altogether, as they predate modernist binaries. The Dakhóta genre of storytelling Eastman draws on is called hithúŋkaŋkaŋpi, which, as Wazíyatawiŋ notes, "refers in general to stories from the elders that teach about the past and often involve things of a mysterious nature, not easily explainable. . . . Some of the kinds of stories included in this category are the Uŋktomi stories, those of the Oceti

Šakowiŋ, or the Seven Council Fires, stories about animals (whether the rabbit, wolf, bear, eagle, or others) . . . and other 'how they came to be stories.'"[52] To this pedagogical list she adds that these stories are also a gift from the ancestors to help ensure the survival of the people, and that they "have been passed down through the generations and should only be told in the winter when snow is on the ground."[53]

Wazíyatawiŋ's mention of the seasonal specificity of hithúŋkaŋkaŋpi is evocative of Dakhóta ways of reckoning time: the hithúŋkaŋkaŋpi, and of Eastman's retellings of them in *Red Hunters*, locate their animal–human interactions in a Dakhóta time that is distinctive in several ways. First is the pedagogical pause in the telling of the tales, from one night to the next. Because hithúŋkaŋkaŋpi are often didactic, with a moral, and because their audience is primarily children, the daily gaps are necessary for the listeners to digest the teachings. Second is the grand pause of winter itself, when the thióšpaye encamps until hunting season begins, so the storytelling is framed by the seasons. Another of Eastman's early collection of hithúŋkaŋkaŋpi, *Wigwam Evenings* (1909), describes the sadness of one of the fictional storytellers, Smoky Day, "when the village breaks up for the spring hunt, and story-telling is over for the season."[54] Finally, in its political aspect, the pause interrupts the forward-moving time of the United States and its progressive, civilizing rhetorics.

In *From the Deep Woods,* Eastman's criticism of "the warfare of civilized life" focuses frequently on the failure of white Americans to share wealth and on both the cause and symptom of this failure: the mechanistic or spiritually evacuated quality of American society.[55] A crucial part of what made up civilization's state of perpetual "warfare" for Eastman was the existence of social inequalities and what he came to view as a corrupt, corrosive relationship to capital. Describing his travels across the western states and Canada as a representative of the YMCA, he relates his disappointment in seeing the religiosity of "white[s] and nominally Christian Indians" lead "often to such very small results."[56] Such religiosity "was a machine-made religion" and, further, "was supported by money, and more money could only be asked for on the showing made; therefore too many of the workers were after quantity rather than quality of religious experience."[57] Eastman's disappointment with the failure of Christian civilization to live up to ideals of equality reads as a jeremiad against spiritual materialism. He critiques the wealth making and wealth keeping that stood against both Dakhóta and Christian ideals of generosity.

Understanding the close ties between modern nationhood and domination, Eastman deployed the term "civilization" derisively to mock U.S. policies and political practices, reserving the term "nation" for Dakhóta, other Indigenous nations, and animals.

Other critical articulations of nationhood further reveal the implications of Eastman's machine metaphor to characterize the American civilization as capitalistic. Benedict Anderson finds that the social space of modernity is distributed in "homogeneous, empty time," likening the nation both to the "old-fashioned" (French realist) novel and to a sociological organism. This temporality, reified as calendrical simultaneity and born of print culture, forms one basis for imagining the nation and is created through our participation in the reification of the nation's temporality. But for Partha Chatterjee, this reification is capitalistic: "Empty homogenous time is the time of capital. . . . But by imagining capital (or modernity) as an attribute of time itself, this view succeeds not only in branding the resistances to it as archaic and backward, but also in securing for capital and modernity their ultimate triumph, regardless of what some people believe or hope, because after all, as everyone knows, time does not stand still."[58] By historicizing Anderson's notion of temporality—as Eastman historicizes American progressivism—Chatterjee lays the groundwork for his later claims that the time of modernity is utopian, constituting only one possible imagining of temporality. "Politics here," concludes Chatterjee, "does not mean the same thing to all people. To ignore this is, I believe, to discard the real for the utopian."[59] A utopian narration of the nation works to subdue alternative concepts of temporality and intersubjectivity. Chatterjee's resistance to Anderson's universalizing sense of temporality may be applied to Eastman's literary resistance, on the basis of specificities of place, to the claimed universality of United States national time.

A pause, because it is created by and through exchanges—like the sharing of a story between family generations or the more tangible exchanging of gifts that accompanied treaty ceremonies—is time not organized by universally reified spaces but instead born of the embodied encounter with a specific place. As such, it is basically anticapitalistic. The story "The Gray Chieftain" from *Red Hunters* underscores the importance of gifting among the Dakhóta and also depicts gifting's place-based, relational contexts. The titular gray chieftain is a spoon-horn ram named Haykinshkah, who is surveying with his mate the sun setting over the "inner circle of the Bad Lands." This landscape harbors the gray chieftain's "ancient castle," a butte that "had been the peaceful home of the big spoonhorns for untold ages" and becomes home for Haykinshkah's lamb, who is born that night. This story, as many of Eastman's animal stories do, casts the spoonhorns as a people who define themselves by customs and a continuous history of occupying the land of their ancestors. These customs are revealed in the ewe's caring for her lamb:

> She gave suck to the lamb and caressed it for some time before she reluctantly prepared its cradle, according to the custom of her people. She made a little pocket in the side of the cave and gently put her baby in. Then she covered him all up, save the nose and eyes, with dry soil. She put her nose to his little sensitive ear and breathed into it warm love and caution, and he felt and understood that he must keep his eyes closed and breathe gently, lest bear or wolf or man should spy him out when they had found her trail.

The ewe's breathing into the lamb's ear "warm love and caution" and the lamb's resulting understanding, which involves both affect and intellect, recall Wazíyatawiŋ's remarks on Dakhóta oral tradition as something intimately familial, "the story of one family, one lineage, reflecting the ancient village structure and the community that united those with a collective identity and memory."[60] It also reflects the power of hithúŋkaŋkaŋpi to "mark" their listeners with knowledge or "leave an imprint on the listener," as do habits of others carefully observed.[61] Likewise, the making of a cradle out of earth literalizes rootedness and performs an Indigenous ontology of intimacy with homelands. The spoonhorns' continuous occupation of territory and their enduring customs describe a common temporality grounded in the bodily knowledge that the land imparts. When two "wild hunters" named Wacootay and Grayfoot appear, having set out for Cedar Butte to kill a ram, we overhear them debating the location of their prey. "'I think, friend, you have mistaken the haunts of the spoonhorn,'" says Wacootay, "to test his friend." In reply, Grayfoot stresses the similarities between human beings and other-than-human beings in matters of attachment to certain places: "'This is his home—I know it,' replied Grayfoot. 'And in this thing the animal is much like ourselves. They will not leave their old haunt unless forced to do so either by lack of food or overwhelming danger.'" Grayfoot's remarks point out how attachment to a place may constitute a sense of home; they also reference Dakhóta resistance to dispossession by settlers.

As the hunters continue their search for rams, they begin to see how affective attachment adds another dimension to responsibility for the land and for the others who live on it. When the two sets of characters, human and ram, meet, the hunters catch their first sight of the gray chieftain, who "stood alone upon a pedestal-like terrace, from which vantage-point it was his wont to survey the surrounding country every morning." In a conspiratorial aside, the narrator adds, "If the secret must be told, he had done so for years, ever since he became the head chief of the Cedar Butte clan." With this aside, though, the story's description of the ram as a chief becomes more specific, more historical, and more bound to place. Further, in the rehearsal of the ram chief's credentials, it includes an ethic of sufficiency:

> It is the custom of their tribe that when a ram attains the age of five years he is entitled to a clan of his own, and thereafter must defend his right and supremacy against all comers. His experience and knowledge are the guide of his clan. In view of all this, the gray chieftain had been very thorough in his observations. There was not an object anywhere near the shape of bear, wolf, or man for miles around his kingdom that was not noted, as well as the relative positions of rocks and conspicuous trees.

Haykinshkah's survey of the land from the vantage of a central point, a nodal point for the ram people's relations with other animals, conveys more than a generalized noting of his perspicacity. His daily vigil and observations emphasize how the ram is intent on the survival of his clan and how that purpose informs both a sensuous knowledge of his kingdom and so also a legitimation of his people's place there. Vine Deloria Jr. describes a "sacred center" in "Indian tribal religions" that "enables a people to look out along the four dimensions and locate their lands, to relate all historical events within the confines of this particular land, and to accept responsibility for it."[62]

In the spoonhorn story, this responsibility appears as an ethic of sufficiency. Despite the spoonhorn chief's past vigilance, the hunters happen upon Haykinshkah during a lethargic moment, when the "younger members of the clan" were to assume the watch, and as he looks off "toward the distant hills," they debate whether they should shoot him. Grayfoot, impressed by the fact that the ram "is a real chief" who "looks mysterious and noble," argues for a delay: "Let us

(IL)LEGIBLE, (IL)LIBERAL SUBJECTS   109

know him better. . . . I never care to shoot an animal while he is giving me a chance to know his ways." He also notes, "We have plenty of buffalo meat. We are not hungry." This sufficiency argument shows up repeatedly throughout Eastman's writings and is foundational to his criticism of the United States' claim to be a greater civilization. Eastman's characters receive this argument in different ways. Grayfoot, for instance, speaks it as if it were a matter of universal knowledge among his tribe, while his friend, Wacootay, admits to his friend and to himself that "he had never thought of it in just that way before," being "chiefly moved . . . in the matter of the hunt" by "the desire for meat." Such differences index intratribal politics but also the need for, and possibility of, a Dakhóta condemnation of the capitalistic logics of extraction and accumulation. After not shooting Haykinshkah and agreeing instead to track a ewe whose trail had excited their curiosity, they come upon the cave where the mother ewe had buried her lamb in its "cradle" but reveals the hiding place with "a faint 'Ba-a-a!'" Again, Wacootay impatiently reaches for an arrow to kill the lamb, but Grayfoot stops him by reminding his friend, "We want horn for ladles and spoons. The mother is right. We must let her babe alone."

After the ewe has fled with her lamb, the narrative elaborates its sufficiency argument by explaining why taking more than is needed from animals is wrong. "After a long silence," Grayfoot invokes an affective commonality beyond linguistic differences: "So it is . . . that all the tribes of earth have some common feeling. I believe they are people as much as we are. The Great Mystery has made them what they are." In this summation, he conveys his sense of why accepting responsibility for both a place and those who dwell in it is appropriate if not necessary. Observing first an equivalence among "all the tribes of earth," which bars ontological division among them, Grayfoot returns to the story collection's opening problem of viewing language as a marker of persons. A kind of sympathetic communication exists between humans and animals. In "seem[ing] to understand their thought," Grayfoot locates this power to communicate in a broader narrative of shared cosmological origins, in which "The Great Mystery [Wakhán Thánka] has made the animals what they are"—that is, the "silent people" as Eastman calls them in the foreword of *Red Hunters*.

The Nation-State, Translated

The complex figure of Wakhán Thánka, which is often translated as "Great Spirit," appears as a nexus for interpersonal relations in both

Eastman's writings and Dakhóta philosophy. In his essay "The Sioux Mythology," Eastman evokes Wakháŋ Tháŋka through the image of the medicine lodge and a distinctly Dakhóta version of the biblical commandments: "Thou shalt often make a holy feast or a lodge feast to the God. Thou shalt not spill the blood of any of thy tribe. Thou shalt not steal what belongs to another. Thou shalt always remember that the choicest part of thy provision belongs to God."[63] Here, the "thou shalt nots" place a premium on maintaining good relations with relatives in ways that not only go beyond but also actually invert the Mosaic commandments' prohibitions against bad relations with one's neighbor. Through their emphasis on preparing a feast "to the God" or the Great Mystery, they have the effect of drawing people together in a ceremony of forging mutual obligations. As Raymond DeMallie notes, Dakhóta cosmology reflects mutual relations among human and other-than-human persons. The wakháŋ beings that made up Wakháŋ Tháŋka, numbering sixteen according to "some holy men," included "sun, moon, wind, Thunder-beings, earth, rock, White Buffalo Woman, and a variety of invisible spirit forms."[64] These beings formed a "oneness" that "was symbolized in kin relationships that bound all together and provided accepted patterns for interaction." This oneness was the template for human interactions, such that "human relationships—parents and children, grandparents and grandchildren, brothers and sisters, husbands and wives—were reflections of these greater, more fundamental relationships established by the *wakan* beings."

The foreword to *Red Hunters* expresses this relationality succinctly, naming the "grandfather" of "these silent people," the animals, as "the Great Mystery," because they know "the laws of their life so well!" "They must," concludes a "philosopher and orator of the Red Men . . . have for their maker our maker. Then they are our brothers!" More than just affirming ontological solidarity, invoking "the Great Mystery" here authorizes a discourse of adoption that is dramatized in the opening story of *Red Hunters*, "The Great Cat's Nursery." Eastman stages Dakhóta adoption practices, which resulted from white territorial encroachments, through the character of a puma mother who adopts another puma's kit. The kit "was the age of her own baby which she had left not long before, and upon second thought she was not sure but that he was her own and that he had been stolen. . . . So she took him home with her. There she found her own kitten safe and glad to have a playmate, and Nakpaksa decided, untroubled by any pangs of conscience, to keep him and bring him up as her own." The adoptive mother, who is later killed by white hunters, is not simply the victim of settler aggression: Eastman is playing on and extending familial sympathies while also showing the empathetic (and thus political or diplomatic) failures of whites who act as if they have no relatives.

In *Red Hunter's* most pointedly decolonial tale, "On Wolf Mountain," a "tribe" of wolves convenes a council meeting to debate what should be done about a rancher's violent encroachment on their territory. The rancher, Hank Simmons, regards the wolves as mere nuisances until, starved, they attack his herd of sheep and threaten to kill him. By asserting wolves' rights to the land, based on their ontological (rather than historical) relationship with it, and by representing their slow starvation at being driven off their land, Eastman replays Dakhóta dispossessions that resulted from the 1851 Treaty of Traverse des Sioux: "The large Mayala wolf with his mate and their five full-grown pups had been driven away from their den on account of their depredations upon the only paleface [Hank Simmons] in the Big Horn valley. It is true that, from their stand-point, he had no right to encroach upon their hunting-grounds."[65] The wolves are not simply enemies of all human beings; they made alliances in the past with the Dakhóta. A Dakhóta–wolf reciprocity appears, for example, in hunting practices, about which Eastman recounts the custom of humans leaving behind "much meat upon the plains for the wolf people." Out of this mutual respect, this hunting together with "these Red hunters as guide and companion," an accord takes shape, in which the wolves and Dakhóta act together to drive away Simmons, whom the narrator derides as "quite another kind of man who is their [common] enemy."

Examining United States–Dakhóta treaty history reveals how a thióšpaye logic extended to the land and its occupants. The wolf–human reciprocity in Eastman's tale serves as a basis for evaluating that history and the actions of settler society. In the 1851 treaties of Traverse des Sioux and Mendota, Eastern Dakhóta tribes ceded all but a thin strip of land along the Minnesota River.[66] The treaties made them largely dependent on annuities, many of which were withheld or lost to graft among Indian agents over the next ten years. The 1862 U.S.–Dakhóta War was a direct result of the United States' failure to uphold the kinship obligations that had been formed through the treaties and of the starvation among Dakhóta stemming from this neglect. This was followed by a resolution by the thiyóthipi, or soldiers' lodge, who convinced the reluctant former spokesman for the

Bdewákhaŋthuŋwaŋ chief, Thaóyate Dúta (His Scarlet People, or Little Crow), to lead the fight.[67] The motive for these attacks was similar to that of the wolves on Simmons in Eastman's story. Before the attack, the wolves hold a council meeting in which they air their grievances against the human encroacher:

> A gaunt old wolf, with only one eye and an immensely long nose, occupied the place of honor. No human ear heard the speech of the chieftain, but we can guess what he had to say. Doubtless he spoke in defence of his country, the home of his race and that of the Red man, whom he regarded with toleration. It was altogether different with that hairy-faced man who had lately come among them to lay waste the forests and tear up the very earth about his dwelling, while his creatures devoured the herbage of the plain. It would not be strange if war were declared upon the intruder.

A scout, after taking shelter in a cave where the wolf people reached their decision to declare war on the rancher, returns to a Dakhóta council meeting to report the news: "'The paleface,' said they, 'has no rights in this region. It is against our interest to allow him to come here, and our brother of the wandering foot well knows it for a menace to his race. He has declared war upon the sheepman, and it is good. Let us sing war-songs for the success of our brother!'" In both of these passages, the explicit statement of rights and the claim to territory (the council does not "allow" the rancher "to come here") powerfully show that the brotherhood between the Dakhóta and the wolves is more than an abstract figure of solidarity. It is a citation of both treaty history and knowledge of wolf–human relationships, as Luther Standing Bear recounts in his collection of Lakhóta tales, *Stories of the Sioux*, and Ella Cara Deloria writes in the "The Rock-Cave Dweller." Both these texts speak to the importance of wolf–human reciprocity and personal sacrifice as ethical norms. In one of Standing Bear's tales, alliance is founded on an act of sacrifice by Marpiyawin, an old woman who leaves her camp and human relatives to look for her dog even though a blizzard is immanent.

The alliance obligates the human beings to join the wolves in war for their mutual success. Kinship between the wolf and Dakhóta people thus serves as an organizing logic for military and political action. This alliance is further motivated by the genocidal intentions of the white settlers, whom Eastman represents as wanting to poison the entire wolf nation. A trader, chiding Simmons for his lack of initiative, says that extermination would have saved his ranch: "Well, I told you before to take out all the strychnine you could get hold of. We have got to rid the country of the Injuns and gray wolves before civilization will stick in this region!" Here Eastman's portrayal is designed to show that the settlers' image of himself as a civilizing agent is distorted. As in a Lacanian mirror, non-Dakhóta readers see themselves for the first time reflected back grotesquely. His purpose is not only to show the wolves' and Dakhóta's ethical superiority but also to shame his white readers. This tactic, based on the hope that non-Dakhóta readers will recognize themselves in the trader and Simmons, may well be mistaken because the social work that shaming does is quite different in Dakhóta and other Indigenous contexts than in liberal, secular societies, where, per Marx and Engels, forms of relation are transformed by competition into ones that are "purely monetary."[68]

Because of this capitalistic transformation, Eastman's writings and citations of Dakhóta oral tradition stand as utopian efforts to enact noninstrumental relations. In *The Soul of the Indian*, Eastman recounts the world's "first treaty," made between a human being, Little Boy Man, and the animals, because the animals recognize Little Boy Man's superior hunting ability. Inishnaechage, the "First-Born," created a "being in the likeness of a man, yet more than man."[69] Little Boy Man was made out of Inishnaechage's loneliness, who sought to make "not a mate but a brother." And although Little Boy Man is Inishnaechage's brother, he is also very much like a son, receiving "rules" and "counsels" from his elder brother, to whom, Eastman writes, "we trace many of our most deep-rooted beliefs and most sacred customs." The conflict between animal people ("who were in those days a powerful nation") and Little Boy Man begins when Uŋktómi, the Spider, who sees the lone human being growing "in wit and ingenuity," advises the animal people, "who all loved the Little Boy Man because he was so friendly and so playful," to kill him before "he will be the master of us all!" In a scene that recalls the death and rebirth of Osiris, the water beings act on Uŋktómi's advice, killing the first human being and hiding his body in the sea, only to see him "given life again" by First-Born in an inípi (purification ceremony).

The mutual trust and thióšpaye relationship between the first human being and the animal people is only interrupted by Uŋktómi. Little Boy Man, after his death and rebirth, resumes his peaceful life with the animal people, learning their languages and customs, until

Uŋktómi again "sowed dissension among the animals, animals, and messages were sent into all quarters of the earth, sea, and air, that all the tribes might unite to declare war upon the solitary man who was destined to become their master." First-Born, seeing his brother sorrowful, "naked, and alone," arms him for the coming battle, which finds Little Boy Man fighting buffalo, elk, bears, thunder beings, and swarming insects, "the little people of the air." With the help of his elder brother's advice, Little Boy Man overcomes all of his animal opponents, who sue for peace and make the first treaty: "They must ever after furnish man with flesh for his food and skins for clothing, though not without effort and danger on his part." In return, human hunters honor those animals for the sacrifice of their lives, and the hunter, out of "respect for the immortal part of the animal, his brother, often leads him so far as to lay out the body of his game in state and decorate the head with symbolic paint or feathers. Then he stands before it in the prayer attitude, holding up the filled pipe, in token that he has freed with honor the spirit of his brother, whose body his need compelled him to take to sustain his own life."

The human–animal relationship outlined in Eastman's recounting of the first treaty, determined by both physical need and ethical agreement, demonstrates that the political realm extends to other-than-human persons who are bound to human beings in a web of thióšpaye rights and obligations. It also describes when war is justified when waged in defense, and so is a decolonial assertion about the just cause of Dakhóta in the 1862 war. The account is told not out of nostalgia but as a politics meant "to educate a derelict treaty partner," as Robert A. Williams Jr. puts it, and to allow "once alienated groups to imagine themselves as connected in a world of human diversity and conflict."[70] Eastman's rhetorical purposes in the Little Boy Man story become evident: to educate, certainly, but also to shame, and thereby draw back into proper ethical relation those who broke their promise to act as a good relative should, with generosity and sharing.

Whereas commodity forms of the gift predominate in a market society, gift giving among the Dakhóta, as among other Indigenous peoples, is strongly linked to establishing and maintaining relationships at personal, communal, and cosmic levels. Kenneth Morrison argues that "if 'power' differentiates between personal entities who otherwise share the same manner of being, then the category 'gift' becomes the central ethical trajectory of religious practice."[71] Although he writes in the context of seventeenth-century Algonkian philosophy, this statement, and his further observation that "positive, powerful others share; negative, powerful others withhold," apply well to Eastman. In linking power with gift, Morrison elucidates how kinship relationality, as a way of allying with those outside of one's people, went beyond metaphorical analogy to motivate behavioral responsibility and material practices of sharing. Instead of viewing whites as ontologically different from the Dakhóta, Eastman regards them as powerful others whose negativity lies in their withholding of generosity. That the Dakhóta were and are historically entangled with whites (note that Eastman was married to a white woman, Elaine Goodale Eastman) adds moral force to the shaming.

Eastman translated the nation form into Dakhóta terms through writings that sought to undercut the designative authority of United States law and that asserted the primacy of Indigenous ethics as a long-standing and legitimate basis for sovereign political action. In writing about the past, Eastman pointed to the failures of a national model based in a temporality of abstract capital and on liberal assumptions about the necessity of individual ownership of property—an ownership that has lacked certain ethical protections offered by consensus politics based in a relational cosmology. The grossly unequal distribution of wealth, graft, and a Christianity evacuated of communitarian concern that Eastman observed in his life up to the publication of *From the Deep Woods* find a powerful tribal retort in his animal stories. Their commitment to an acknowledgment and respect for persons of various kinds out of a sense of the power inherent in alterity and their commitment to an ethic of reciprocal gifting constitute a model of peoplehood (and by extension nationhood) that was and remains relevant as an alternative to the settler-state and its tendency to abuse power. In constructing a tacit theory of political legitimacy that recognizes multiple centers—indeed, a vast field of peoples made up of human and animal collectives—Eastman suggests not just the critically corrective potential of Dakhóta philosophy and forms of governance for non-Native society but also their rehabilitative role for tribal communities in the ongoing work of decolonization. In my next section I detail how Eastman's political translations intervened not only at the level of the people but also at the level of the individual citizen.

Citizen Kin: Eastman's Indigenizing of Indian Citizenship

In 1911, Eastman served as the representative of the "North American Indian" at the First Universal Races Congress in London, where he joined W. E. B. Du Bois in a panel session discussing "The Modern Conscience in Relation to Racial Questions (The Negro and the American Indian)." In his talk, titled simply "The North American Indian," Eastman's remarks on the political place of Native Americans in the United States vividly frame an Indigenous politics of the land. In that politics, embodied and relational contexts push back against a national citizenship model based in racialized, settler-colonial logics of assimilation and absorption.[72] Eastman broaches this politics almost innocuously, in a kind of ethnographic-nostalgic mode, through what he calls the "friendship" of "the first North American":

> A loyal and disinterested friendship was one of the finest things developed by the first North American, who knew how to be a true comrade, even to death. Intelligence combined with patriotism meant leadership, and was always at a premium. Of culture in the technical sense he had none, but that his mind was logical and keen is sufficiently proved by his oratory and generalship. His children were taught to obey: silence, self-control, self-denial, these were the foundations of character-building. There was a school of the woods in which the young were systematically trained in body and mind, by sports and Native arts of many kinds, nature-study and wood-craft, together with a thorough drill in tribal history, tradition, and folk-lore.[73]

Here the merging of loyalty and disinterestedness recalls treaty language, where the perennial "peace and friendship" vowed between Indigenous and settler nations was often underscored with pledges of noninterference in one another's social and political lives, or in other words by recognition of mutual sovereignty.[74] Indeed, treaty discourse may have been the most effective means for Eastman to voice his twofold concerns in this speech: first to argue for an end to government paternalism and to secure greater protections for Indigenous individuals, and second to achieve these protribal goals through national incorporation. By framing friendship in terms of "intelligence" plus "patriotism," in which the latter is infused with Indian ideals of service, Eastman turns what might be taken as a nostalgic and racialized performance into the voicing of political questions that would inform the debate over Indian citizenship over the next decade: how may an Indian (or Dakhóta) politics of the land move outward—from the stolen physical and epistemological grounds of the tribal na-

(IL)LEGIBLE, (IL)LIBERAL SUBJECTS 117

tion to those of the settler nation—as a tribal-national supplement to U.S. citizenship?[75] And how might that "school's" lessons also move inward—within the tribal nation—to reindigenize and reterritorialize long-occupied Dakhóta homelands?

Eastman's translational withholdings around notions of Indian citizenship show up perhaps most clearly through juxtaposition. On the one hand is Eastman's most overtly political work, *The Indian To-day* (1915), which reads in many ways as an argument for Indian citizenship even as it expresses the desire to end federal paternalism and Indian wardship. On the other hand are two texts that deal with children's physical and moral education: Eastman's ostensibly apolitical handbook for children, *Indian Scout Talks* (1914), and his essay "What Can the Out-of-Doors Do for Our Children?" (1920). The latter two works grew out of Eastman's close involvement with the Boy Scouts of America. Although he was never credited by name in the Boy Scouts manuals, Eastman wrote *Indian Scout Talks* specifically for the Boy Scouts and Camp Fire Girls, and he served as a camp director and national councilman.[76] *Scout Talks* and the 1920 essay catalog embodied techniques of prereservation Indian life, evoking a Dakhóta place-based imaginary that persisted in spite of an agency system that put Native peoples under the charge of often unscrupulous Indian agents and within the harsh pedagogical structures of mission and boarding schools aimed at eradicating all traces of Indianness.

Recent theorizing of citizenship emphasizes its performative and embodied aspects.[77] In Eastman's hands, Indian citizenship appeared in these terms, and he also idealized it in specifically Dakhóta terms as critically relational. As Mark Rifkin asserts, subjective self-determination or the sovereignty of the subject may correctively be thought in terms where "subjectivity arises from a recognition of interdependence in which the borders of selfhood are envisioned as a transfer point within necessary sensual flows of touch, taste, and smell," and where the porously sensual subject serves as touchstone for viewing "interdependence and vulnerability as positive principles of peoplehood."[78] In this view, self-determination inheres less in isolation than in an ongoing negotiation of the dimensions of embodied experience in which identity is predicated on a simultaneous acknowledgment of autonomy, the distinctness and integrity of "'I' and 'you,' and of necessary relation, a 'we' (re)created through the potential for vulnerability and penetration by others' impact on the senses."[79] Rifkin's insight is useful for reading how Eastman's narrations of embodied experience perform Indian citizenship in ways that are substantially different from an individualistic and abstract vocabulary of rights, despite Eastman's deployments of a racist vocabulary of Native "wildness" in his political tract, *The Indian To-day*.

The Indian To-day appeared in a series titled "The American Books: A Library of Good Citizenship" that purported, as the volume's title page puts it, to be "a series of authoritative manuals, discussing problems of interest to-day." As such, Eastman's volume was uniquely positioned to advance an Indigenous critique of national citizenship. From its table of contents alone, though, *The Indian To-day* has an innocuous quality, with some headings replaying dominant ideas of Indigenous disappearance and "uplift" by white society: "The Indian as He Was," "The How and Why of Indian Wars," "The Agency System: Its Uses and Abuses." Yet while no heading in the volume is overtly inflammatory, a civil tone of redress runs through them. Eastman's stated purpose follows this sort of measured critical stance. "It is the aim of this book," he writes, "to set forth the present status and outlook of the North American Indian. In one sense his is a 'vanishing race.' In another and an equally true sense it is a thoroughly progressive one, increasing in numbers and vitality, and awakening to the demands of a new life."[80] Aiming to historicize the state of Native nations in the present, as well as forecast their future within the larger body of the United States, Eastman frames the latter aim, which investigates "the outlook of the American Indian"[81] in terms of U.S. citizenship and through conventional liberal vocabularies of rights and obligations.

Eastman's version of liberalism was grounded in his view that Dakhóta sovereignty had and continued to exist in the body. That is, the persistence of the embodied constituted a critical remainder even after Dakhóta were incorporated as citizens into the United States. "In order to answer these questions," he writes in *The Indian To-day*, of "what position" the Native individual "fills in the body politic," Eastman asserts that we must turn to what may be called a Dakhóta habitus:

> We ought, first, to consider fairly his native environment, temperament, training, and ability in his own lines, before he resigned himself to the inevitable and made up his mind to enter fully into membership in this great and composite nation. If we can see him as he was, we shall be the better able to see him as he is, and by the worth of his native excellence measure his contribution to the common stock.[82]

Here what Eastman calls the "native environment, temperament, training, and ability in his own lines" represents a system of cultural capital that had not disappeared, but whose persistence, as embodied techniques that constitute a particular kind of Dakhóta subject, was foundational to contemporary forms of Dakhóta citizenship. In Eastman's construction, what "was" and what "is" in terms of Dakhóta presence become equal.

This temporal equation also extends to Dakhóta understandings of place. As David Martínez describes the "natural world" in Eastman's writings and in the popular American imagination at the turn of the twentieth century, "Nature was something 'out there' as opposed to the Dakhóta of Eastman's memory, who regarded it as 'right here.'"[83] Throughout *The Indian To-day*, Eastman likewise insists on the presence of the past not only for Dakhóta understandings of "nature" or "native environment" but also as a means of correcting the emphasis placed within a liberal citizenship imaginary on individualism and imagining of land as a space abstracted away from intersubjective, sensuous relations. Instead, Eastman depicts Dakhóta territory as a commonplace—a self-evident sign of Dakhóta historical presence in traditional homelands as well as a place held in common through which the Oyáte might be remembered and remade. Just as "nature" stands in for "Dakhóta territory," Eastman substitutes "the Indian" for "Dakhóta." As Kiara Vigil observes about Eastman's fellow SAI member Carlos Montezuma, this essentialist usage highlighted "the founding objective of the SAI as a pan-tribal organization" to provide a unified platform for waging the fight for citizenship for all Native people.[84] Eastman did appeal at times to a pan-Indian ideal in order to gain political traction. But Vigil's reading of Eastman's idealism is incomplete without consideration of the specifically Dakhóta content his generic "Indian" mobilized.

For instance, a passage from Eastman's speech to the Races Congress reveals him gesturing toward thióšpaye philosophy, a turn that Eastman would repeat throughout his writings and thinking about Indian citizenship: "Above all he must be a spiritual man; one who loved the Unseen God, and whose motives were in accord with the 'Great Mystery.'"[85] Here Eastman's ambivalent attitudes toward Christianity relate directly to his thinking about citizenship. Eastman converted to Christianity as a teenager, and in the 1890s he worked as the Indian secretary of the YMCA, extensively touring Western reservations in order to assess and improve the different organizations on reservations and in Indian schools.[86] Yet his later account of this work in *From the Deep Woods to Civilization* suggests that his views on Christianity were strongly influenced by contact with what he calls "the racial mind."[87] He was especially moved by an encounter with "an old chief of the Sac and Fox tribe," who verbally rebuffed Eastman's proselytizing and who criticized "the white man" for trying "to buy God with the by-products of nature."[88] From this tension, some early biographers and critics diagnosed a syncretistic view[89] in which boundaries between opposing terms slip away in an assimilatory blur: to be a good Dakhóta was also to be consummately a Christian.

Often Eastman is actually antisyncretistic in his accounts of "religion," privileging Dakhóta philosophy and its complex figure of the "Great Mystery," or Wakháŋ Tháŋka, rather than the Christian God. His citing of Wakháŋ Tháŋka in "The Sioux Mythology" suggests Eastman's commitment to an essentialized depiction of Dakhóta ways of reckoning relatives, where Wakháŋ Tháŋka figures as a nexus for interpersonal relations between different kinds of agential beings, including spirits, animals, plants, and rocks. By using terms like "mythology" and "religion" to stand in for a wide range of embodied practices within a thióšpaye imaginary, and by couching these citations within the terms of white hate speech (i.e., "The savage holds that the key of heaven is vested in the visible phenomena of the universe"), Eastman stakes out a position within the dialectic of savagery and civilization that doesn't simply invert but also actively deconstructs both terms of that dialectic.[90] Translating "religion" into thióšpaye terms removes Dakhóta practices of reckoning, making, and breaking kin from the sphere of deficiency within which settler society historically located all Native Americans, not just Dakhóta, as irreligious or "pagan," and which enabled legal and political interventions (mission boarding schools, for instance, but Indigenous wardship and congressional plenary power more broadly) as remedies for perceived Native irreligiosity and sovereign lack. In other words, invoking thióšpaye ethics here pushes back against views of savagery as paganism—not by refuting accusations of godlessness but by replacing, figuratively and literally, key terms of colonization into Dakhóta social practices and the lands from which those practices grew.

Eastman's other writings on citizenship also tacitly assert Dakhóta forms of sociospatiality that survived U.S. attempts to eradicate them, because of or despite being couched in progressive discourses of physical "improvement." In a 1920 essay entitled "What Can the Out-of-Doors Do for Our Children?" written by Eastman for the journal *Education,* Eastman proposes that American schools should incorporate into their curricula a program of citizenship training based in Dakhóta thióšpaye philosophy and argues for its potential to be a physical and ethical corrective for the settler-state's children: "I predict that the time will come when we shall have an entirely out-of-door school."[91] White children of "the formative age," he argued, should not get their exercise in a gymnasium but "should season their muscles in the sun, in the fresh air, in the spring water coming down from the mountain, with a jump into the clean brooks and lakes of the mountains. That is where you get your nerve tonic."[92] What complicates this project of healing the nervous diseases of the nation is the fact of Eastman's outdoors rhetoric being legible within (and thus able to be appropriated and domesticated by) the physical education culture of post-Victorian America.

Although I have so far stressed the tacit and the indirect in Eastman's citizenship discourse, more explicitly Dakhóta prosovereignty moments appear that assert key differences from a white reformist movement like the YMCA's. Bodily techniques guaranteeing good health of body and mind appear in Eastman's account as sovereign locations, but the marking of those bodies as Indian bars any easy passage over onto/into white bodies: "And you must begin with the child. Why, the old Indian man used to rub the child's legs with snow and then wash it off with ice water, and after that he would rub him with hot oil, and the little fellow was waterproof! They probably knew that God made all these laws, and we are creatures of habit, and we can get back into that habit."[93] Here the archaic appears in the practice of insulating small children from the cold, marking it with poignant difference through the intimacy of the intergenerational contact Eastman describes. That difference is amplified by the mention of "God" here—a reference not to the Judeo-Christian god but to Wakháŋ Tháŋka as the author of "these laws," or bodily habits, that made possible Dakhóta survival in a harsh climate. But the imperative voice that opens the passage also links its particular care of the self to intergenerational norms of the thióšpaye. By the time he asserts that "we can get back into that habit," Eastman has thus already moved away from inclusivity. In its place is the urging and urgency of reclamation and the suggestion that embodied Dakhóta pasts, despite settler-colonial genocide, ethnocide, and land theft, are always recoverable. The fact that "God" or Wakháŋ Tháŋka underwrites this availability is significant, given that "God," like the thióšpaye, serves as a metonym for practices of making and keeping relatives here and throughout Eastman's writings. What this metonym implies is that the making of relatives can restore individuals' relations not just to one another but also to places and locations that are encountered in exile from ancestral homelands.

Eastman further elaborates on thióšpaye relationships between humans, Wakháŋ Tháŋka, and the out-of-doors by recounting a meeting with an elder chief in Washington:

> It was not long ago that I sat with an old, old chief in Washington, and translated to him a few things that were in the Congressional Record. I came to the words, 'raw material,' and he said, "What do you mean by that?" I said, "Earth, and trees, and stones, uncut, unpolished, unground. That is what the white man calls raw material." He shook his head and he said, "There is only one raw material, and that is fresh air coming through rich sunshine. All things live on that; all things come from that, the animate and the inanimate—and inanimate things are animated by it."[94]

This exchange is compelling for its positioning of Eastman as the recipient of an elder's knowledge. At this moment Eastman is no longer the austere three-piece-suited representative of his race, and conversely no longer the headdress-wearing paragon of an essentialized Indianness. Instead, the corrective headshake of the "old, old chief" reconstitutes Eastman as a Dakhóta person involved in a respect relationship of youth to elder, subject to the gently disciplinary corrections entailed in that relationship. Because of this interpellation, and in ways that Eastman would perform throughout his writings for non-Native audiences, "the old, old chief" may remind Eastman of cultural knowledge that has been obscured by instrumental language—language that Eastman, almost foolishly it seems, elaborates: "stones, uncut, unpolished, unground." Returning to the ontological foundation of "fresh air," which in Dakhóta philosophy correlates with breath or spirit *(wóniya)*, Eastman makes a summary translation: "The point of it is, out-of-doors means God; out-of-doors means mystery, and that means God."[95] Here again the placement of Dakhóta cosmology alongside the white physical education term "out-of-doors" demonstrates a reworking of white ideals through their placement alongside Dakhóta concepts.

Alongside such valorizations of Dakhóta philosophy within Eastman's citizenship discourse are examples of more entangled or enmeshed relationships between whites and natives. For instance, Eastman's closing chapter in *The Indian To-day*, while again explicitly linking thióšpaye practices with becoming enfranchised citizens of the United States, frames that citizenship in terms of both persistent Indigenous philosophies and miscegenation, or "the interfusion of his [the Indian's] blood with yours [the non-Indian]."[96] As a complication of how and what such "interfusion" means, Eastman's concluding chapter enumerates the important roles in "service" to the nation that Native individuals have played: first as soldiers and scouts for the U.S. military but also as guides for explorers ("The name of Washington is immortal; but who remembers that he was safely guided by a nameless red man through the pathless wilderness to Fort Duquesne?), and finally as "historic Indian women" (Pocahontas, Sacajawea, and Catherine, "the Ojibwa maid" who saved Fort Detroit from being wiped out by Pontiac).[97]

While significant, both these social forms of interfusion and the biological ones of marriage and sexual reproduction are less important than a contribution that Eastman reckons in terms of Indigenous philosophies. The book's closing sentences assert "the contribution of the American Indian, though considerable from any point of view, is not to be measured by material acquirement. Its greatest worth is spiritual and philosophical."[98] More than a nostalgia for a vanished or lost world of Dakhóta "tradition," Eastman seems here to predict that Indigenous persistence will lie in another both–and situation: "He will live, not only in the splendor of his past, the poetry of his legends and his art, not only in the interfusion of his blood with yours, and his faithful adherence to the new ideals of American citizenship, but in the living thought of the nation."[99] This citizenship does not aestheticize "the Indian" out of existence or sublimate Native bodies into a liberal philosophy. Rather, it ambiguously marks "the nation" (the U.S. settler nation? the Indigenous nation? both?) as the location where Native "living thought . . . will live." If not an outright assertion of persistent tribal nationhood, Eastman's prediction here stakes out discursive space for Indigenous temporalities beyond the settler-state's, asserting both the incorporation of "new ideals" as well as ongoing Dakhóta claims to lands ("the splendor of his past").

Published in 1914, several years after the first American edition of the *Boy Scouts of America Official Handbook* (1910), Eastman's *Indian*

Scout Talks recounts in great depth and detail (complete with illustrations and diagrams) the physical training, civic ideals, and philosophical disposition of young Indian boys and girls. Its idealizations of a prereservation Indian life appeared in the context of a broader out-of-doors discourse that underscored the physically and morally restorative force of "nature" for an America that had become sickened by modernity. As in *The Indian To-day*, Eastman refuses "nature" as a universal category through his citations of thióšpaye philosophy, revealing complex ways of making available, and withholding, Dakhóta ways of being in place. Embodied practices, and their physical and social milieus, appear as exercises for fortifying, and even indigenizing, the moral character of boys whose contact with civilized life "has ... deprived [them] of close contact and intimacy with nature."[100] But in spite of this remedial purpose, as with other of Eastman's autobiographical works, an assimilatory overlay—as in the use of terms of Native abjection in the close of the volume's introduction—complicates this intervention. "How gentle is the wild man when at peace!" he writes, "How quick and masterful in action! Like him, we must keep nature's laws, develop a sound, wholesome body, and maintain an alert and critical mind. Upon this basis, let us follow the trail of the Indian in his search for an earthly paradise!"[101] Although this depiction of the "wild man" sanitizes violent or retributive forms of Native wildness ("how gentle ... !"), there is also an immanent utopianism here in which "the Indian" appears as being always already in pursuit of what Eastman calls "an earthly paradise."

Rather than being consigned to the past, "the Indian" undertakes his "search" in Eastman's narrated present for this paradise through physical and mental training that is in accord with "nature's laws." As I have argued, the term "nature" references the figure of Wakháŋ Tháŋka and a thióšpaye philosophy. Accordingly, the "earthly paradise" here appears as a figure for not only traditional Dakhóta homelands but for the complex and ethically regulated interpersonal matrix of relations between different occupants of those lands. The fact that Eastman frames this potential for tribal reclamation and reinvention as an invitation to the physical and ethical training of white children is significant. It is not as a gesture of tribal inclusivity but a reframing of citizenship in terms of white ethical-physical engagements with Indian lands. This reframing, however, is ultimately a ruse because it presumes an ethical training whose norms would have no community to uphold them. The greater part of what Eastman describes, which is essentially a training in Indian ethics, would be simply unavailable to his average reader.

By merging Indigenous "wildness" with the possibility of ongoing resistance to white encroachments on Native lands and bodies, Eastman asserts the ongoing possibility of a decolonial freedom. His citations of treaty discourses, grounded in thióšpaye norms of intergenerational obedience and respect like those underlying his account of human–animal relations at the outset of *Indian Scout Talks*, thus counter a settler logic of possession. Describing how his uncle used to send him for water over and over again, Eastman notes how "no protest or appeal escaped my lips, thanks to my previous training in silent obedience." This obedience recalls the moral training described by Eastman's contemporary, Iháŋkthuŋwaŋ (Yankton) anthropologist Ella Cara Deloria. In *Speaking of Indians* (1944), she describes how addressing a relative demanded the correct "term, attitude, and behavior" rather than just the correct term of relatedness. Such a moral training, into which "one simply was born," ensured that "a socially responsible Dakota might not thoughtlessly indulge his moods."[102] For Deloria and Eastman, subjectivation through norms of speech, thought, and body (or "term, attitude, and behavior") appears less as oppressive regulation to be resisted than as constitutive of Dakhóta interiority and intersubjectivity. Deloria explains, "You see, everyone would be rated well as a relative had to *make* himself feel and act always in the same way. . . . But it wasn't [monotonous]. For there was as great a variety of permissible attitudes and behaviors as there were kinds of relatives."[103]

Likewise, Eastman's account of "wild animals" and "wild Indians" idealizes an ethic of circumspect noninterference or "friendship" as the basis for Dakhóta subsistence hunting as well as for peoplehood. Just like the friendship invoked in the Races Congress speech, the one between humans and wild animals is a metonym for both Deloria's account of Dakhóta moral training and historical treaty relationships. Observing that the ferocious wild animals of white children's "books of adventure . . . are mainly highly spiced fiction," Eastman asserts that "it is well known to Indian hunters that no animal offers battle to man except under very strong provocation," and that "hand-to-hand combat with beasts were few indeed." Although Eastman does not explicitly link this assumption of wild animals as bloodthirsty to anti-Indianism, the implication is clear enough. As an alternative, Eastman suggests several "general truths" that briefly sketch a Dakhóta ontology of place-based relationships as it outlines a decolonial politics of respect: "First, the animals are accustomed to mind strictly their own business and are not likely to interfere with you unless you molest them first. Second, there is a way to learn the peculiarity of each and make his acquaintance. Third, it is possible to influence them greatly, even in critical circumstances, by firmness and self-control." Here the valorized "firmness and self-control" points toward the moral training that Deloria would later idealize in her autoethnography *Speaking of Indians*. The suggestion that little white boys would do well to act more Indian, especially by adopting an attitude of "disinterested friendship" toward animals, is obviously a tease, in both the pedagogical and comic senses. In the first sense, it is a ruse of apprehensibility that Eastman stages here. To be subjected to the moral and physical regulation of the thióšpaye—and this is exactly what he outlines in this innocuous passage—apart from Dakhóta lands and communities is clearly impossible. With the invitation to play Indian remaining on the verge of apprehensibility, approachable but always unclaimable (because to be Dakhóta would be to recognize the thióšpaye as those to whom one is ultimately responsible), Eastman quietly chastens misanthropic settler-colonial attitudes toward Indigenous people.

The final chapter of *Indian Scout Talks* extends these tactics and criticisms to U.S. citizenship, reflecting back on how the previous twenty-five chapters constitute, all told, a "School of Savagery" that is simultaneously a "Training for Service."[104] The chapter's title inverts the ward–pupil relationship of federal Indian law, so that in this savage school, which Eastman explains is "no haphazard thing, but a system of education which has been long in the building," even the civilized will experience "wonderful things."[105] Eastman continues, continuing to invert and elevate the figure of the savage: "Ingenuity, faithfulness, and self-reliance will accomplish wonderful things in civilized life as well as in wild life, but, to my mind, individuality and initiative are more successfully developed in the out-of-door man."[106] Beyond simple inversion, or more precisely, within it, are Eastman's revisions of U.S. national citizenship along the lines of thióšpaye ethics. He concludes, "Where the other man is regarded more than self, duty is sweeter and more inspiring, patriotism more sacred, and friendship is a true and eternal bond."[107] Of course, his argument for selflessness may read as passé to non-Dakhóta. In his linking together of the physical, or embodied, and the ethical, Eastman would appear to be a Christian gentleman of his time, and his notion of virtue and its relation to what he calls "physical excellence"

(IL)LEGIBLE, (IL)LIBERAL SUBJECTS   127

in *The Indian To-day* admittedly resonates with the ideals of a group like the YMCA.

By locating physical excellence in techniques like the inípi, which would read as exotically Indigenous to his white audience, Eastman departs from Christian formulations like the YMCA's. The effect of this exoticized Indigenous difference is to endorse Eastman's claims that Native Americans offer settler society a redemptive moral and physical compass for national citizenship. But as with his method for making friends with wild animals, Eastman once again stages his citizenship talk through an act of withholding. In a chapter on "Indian Methods of Physical Training," Eastman first describes the inípi, in what seems to be a ham-handed effort to accommodate his white reader, as "the original Turkish bath."[108] He adds that the process of sweating, jumping into icy water, and sleeping while wrapped "in a buffalo robe with the hair inside . . . makes him a new man." But in what does his newness consist? Eastman here makes an assertion with no clearly available referent. In contrast, Eastman's earlier text, *The Soul of an Indian* (1911), gives further context for this "bath" when he states that the origin of the "eneepee" is in the Dakhóta creation story of the First Man, and that the inípi "has ever since been deemed essential to the Indian's effort to purify and recreate his spirit." He writes,

In our Creation myth or story of the First Man, the vapor-bath was the magic used by The-one-who-was-First-Created, to give life to the dead bones of his younger brother, who had been slain by the monsters of the deep. Upon the shore of the Great Water he dug two round holes, over one of which he built a low enclosure of fragrant cedar boughs, and here he gathered together the bones of his brother. In the other pit he made a fire and heated four round stones, which he rolled one by one into the lodge of boughs. Having closed every aperture save one, he sang a mystic chant while he thrust in his arm and sprinkled water upon the stones with a bunch of sage. Immediately steam arose, and as the legend says, "there was an appearance of life." A second time he sprinkled water, and the dry bones rattled together. The third time he seemed to hear soft singing from within the lodge; and the fourth time a voice exclaimed: "Brother, let me out!"[109]

Unless would-be Scouts were familiar with Eastman's entire literary output, it is unlikely that they would have had access to this story or to Eastman's further citations of Dakhóta philosophy, such as when he explains that the boulders are called "'Tunkan,' a contraction of the Sioux word for Grandfather."[110] What is withheld is a vast and enduring relational ontology, and in this withholding is a protective opacity, a sovereign silence.

As with his reinvestment of tropes of Indian wildness and savagery, Eastman retools the key terms ("mind, body, and spirit") of the YMCA's brand of muscular Christianity with Dakhóta ethical content, as he describes the Dakhóta Everyman in his wilderness school:

> He knew that virtue is essential to the maintenance of physical excellence, and that strength, in the sense of endurance and vitality, underlies all genuine beauty. He was as a rule prepared to volunteer his services at any time in behalf of his fellows, at any cost of inconvenience and real hardship, and thus to grow in personality and soul-culture. Generous to the last mouthful of food, fearless of hunger, suffering, and death, he was surely something of a hero. Not "to have," but "to be," was his national motto.[111]

At one level the passage is a jeremiad against the unequal distribution of wealth within the United States—a prophetic critique that Eastman voiced in *From the Deep Woods to Civilization* and one that was taken up widely by others, including the YMCA, during the assimilation era. The premium Eastman places on volunteerism, for instance, certainly echoes the ideals of the YMCA, especially in its emphasis on physical work that contributes to social stability. Far from assuming a singular law of generosity, though (Jesus's command to his disciples to "Go, sell everything you have and give to the poor"), and especially a law that reproduces social classes through unequal demands for self-sacrifice, this articulation of generosity is maybe best read in the context of Dakhóta notions of gifting.

One of these forms is in the making of offerings to other-than-human persons. Accounts from contemporary Spirit Lake Nation oral histories reveal how a portion of the land itself—a particular rock—appears as the sign of an ethical failure and a reminder of the need to keep good kinship relations. Eastman likewise emphasizes the living presences of other-than-human persons as the means for constituting oneself and others in relationship, and this particular story about a place called Crow Hill (Kanǧí Pahá) likewise shows how a rock's presence is vital, vibrant, and instructive. In it, my grandmother Lillian Chase, a Dakhóta woman who grew up at Crow Hill, recounts the origin of its name, switching between English and Dakhóta languages at different points in her narrative, with considerably different implications for the place-name in each language. While the full account appears in my Third Interlude, I'll quote a portion of it here to allow for comparison with Eastman:

> Then that big rock [Íŋyaŋ Watháŋka] over here. These guys should put that rock up and honor it. They call that the Devils Tooth. They've been calling it that for a long time, but my grandma said that it is a woman. That stone, that's a woman sitting there. They had a Fourth of July on top of that hill. There was a bunch of them there and they were all busy. Then there was this guy and this girl. He must have hit her, so that girl was running away with her baby on her back. She went down the hill and that guy followed her. He was getting close so she sat down like this and, here, she turned into a stone. So he lost his wife there [laughs]. My grandma used to tell me that. So that's a woman sitting there. She had a baby on her back and she made herself into a rock. They should write out a big story about that and honor that rock. Now the white people themselves call it Devils Tooth, and it's not like that.[112]

Here the land holds memories of violence and sacrifice that come together in the rock, or Íŋyaŋ, called Devils Tooth by "the white people." Like with Eastman's "idealized" accounts of bodily habits that lead his reader "toward perfecting an out-of-door body and a logical mind,"[113] and which also assert Dakhóta ways of knowing, Lillian's story has an affective and historical density that may not readily be apparent.

Her use of íŋyaŋ, the Dakhóta word for "rock," recalls the appearance of Íŋyaŋ as a figure in Dakhóta creation stories, where Íŋyaŋ is a powerful originary being. In nineteenth-century anthropologist James R. Walker's transcription of Oglála cosmology, Íŋyaŋ is described as "soft and shapeless but he had all powers. . . . He longed for another that he might exercise his powers upon it. There could be no other unless he would create it of that which he must take from himself. If he did so he must impart to it a spirit and give to it a portion of his blood. As much blood as would go from him, so much of his powers would go with it."[114] Walker's account genders Íŋyaŋ as male, and his desire for relation, for dialogue out of isolation, is what drives his act of creation—an act where power is recognized ("he had all powers"), where it is thought to be insufficient in itself ("he longed for another"), and where it is shared ("as much blood as would go from him"). Contained within Walker's version of the Íŋyaŋ story are the seeds of Dakhóta/Lakhóta understandings of power as unfolding between various classes of beings—beings who relate to one another in purposeful ways. Íŋyaŋ thus embodies a relationality that is epistemologically and ontologically precise in how it understands and engages with difference.

Lillian's sister, Grace Lambert, whose full interview with me appears in my Second Interlude, also tells a story about the place called Íŋyaŋ Watháŋka (Devils Tooth). Because it also illustrates how gift giving mediates social relationships among Dakhóta, it is worth quoting as a supplement to Eastman's idealization of generosity:

> One time there was an old lady, she left an offering. Did they tell this before? This old lady went to the store to buy some groceries. She started home with her groceries. Where that rock is, there was a man, who got drunk the night before. When he woke up, he layed down by that rock and went to sleep. The old lady was walking toward that rock. She stopped by the rock, and in them days they only buy Bull Durham [tobacco]. She pulled her Bull Durham out. First she put some material on top [of the rock]. She said, "Grandfather, I brought you some offerings and have pity on me and pray for me." She was saying, "Grandfather, I brought you some tobacco." By that time the man with the hangover was laying behind the rock. He woke up by that time and he said, "Haŋ" [(feminine) yes]. He scared the old lady. She ran all the way home from there.[115]

Grace's telling of the joke about the drunk reveals a few important things. First, it places land in the context of gifting between human and other-than-human persons. The old lady brings tobacco to honor Íŋyaŋ in order to acknowledge their kinship relation where Íŋyaŋ is "Grandfather" and to acknowledge her position of existential need ("have pity on me and pray for me"). Second, the joke historicizes Dakhóta ways of being in place. By making a man with a hangover ventriloquize the figure of Íŋyaŋ, and so acknowledge alcohol's long shadow, Grace draws a line connecting prereservation ceremonialism with one especially harmful consequence of settler-colonization. And because it is a joke, she demonstrates one key guise survival may take: laughter. What places hold are not just names or good jokes but also ways of knowing, including knowing what is funny, what is seriously

(IL)LEGIBLE, (IL)LIBERAL SUBJECTS 131

funny, and what is not. This is a matter of aesthetics as much as ontology, and it is to aesthetics of naming that I now turn.

Troubling Translation

In a chapter of *The Indian To-day*, pointedly titled "Inheritance and Other Frauds," Eastman expresses anxiety over the dispossession of Native lands through illegal claims made by supposed heirs of deceased allottees because "the law provid[ed] that the allotments of deceased Indians may be sold for the benefit of their legal heirs" before the twenty-five-year holding period had passed.[116] Pointing to the massive and sudden land losses that occurred among the White Earth Ojibwa, who were victims of "the theft of over two hundred thousand acres" after legal restrictions on mixed bloods allowing them to sell lands, Eastman expressed how regularizing allotment rolls would protect against further thefts.[117] As he saw it, the intent of the translation project was primarily economic, meant to ensure the smooth operation of inheritance laws provided for by both the allotment system and the 1906 Burke Act's modification of that system to do away with its twenty-five-year holding period. In 1903 President Theodore Roosevelt appointed Eastman to regularize Dakhóta names for allotment rolls. The bureaucratic task of translating traditional names into "American" ones—a task that took Eastman five years to complete—may of course read as evidence of his unvarnished faith in assimilation, in the same way that his work as a field physician at an army camp after the massacre at Wounded Knee and his involvement with the SAI suggest his assimilationist intent. However, Eastman's motives for "systematiz[ing] the Indian nomenclature" and for writing about it at various times in his life cannot be summarized so easily.[118]

For one, giving Westernized names to Dakhóta individuals worked to protect against continued graft and land losses. With English names came greater legibility, and in matters of deciding property inheritance and transfer of titles among families, legibility offered protection against unscrupulous claimants. Less instrumentally, Eastman understood his role as a translator as a means of preserving Dakhóta life, and in doing so communicating something of its philosophical underpinnings to non-Dakhóta. For instance, he discusses the American names he devised in terms of Dakhóta aesthetics, or as examples of standards of beauty. Although perhaps not immediately apparent, the relationship between Dakhóta names and sociospatial environments—of how the body and the places it occupies are constituted in thióśpaye terms—is also key for understanding Eastman's possible motives in his work on translating tribal allotment rolls into English. Writing about this "special appointment," Eastman describes some key principles governing his project:

> It was my duty to group the various members of one family under a permanent name, selected for its euphony and appropriateness from among the various cognomens in use among them, of course suppressing mistranslations and grotesque or coarse nicknames calculated to embarrass the educated Indian. My instructions were that the original native name was to be given the preference, if it were short enough and easily pronounced by Americans. If not, a translation or abbreviation might be used, while retaining as much as possible of the distinctive racial flavor.[119]

Here what Eastman calls the "distinctive racial flavor" of Dakhóta names encoded several possible cultural logics. For example, a child could be named according to birth order. Eastman's given name, Hakeda, means "last-born son," as his mother died during childbirth. Only later in his life, after proving himself through physical competitions among his peers, would he earn the name Ohíye s'á (Wins Often or Winner). This change of name demonstrates another logic of naming: the bestowal of honor.

In *Indian Scout Talks*, Eastman details two other classes of names besides "birth names," including "honor or public names" and "nicknames." Refuting the erroneous claims of "white men that an Indian child is called after the first noticeable thing his mother sees after his birth," as well as the idea that "some event occurring near the child's birth established its name," Eastman recounts the ceremonial conferral of honor names "by the clan medicine-man at a public ceremony."[120] As with other ceremonial occasions, this "christening" is accompanied by feasting, and importantly, by "gifts presented to the poor of the tribe in honor of the occasion. These needy folk, in their turn, leave singing the praises of the child by his new name."[121] Eastman elaborates this making of gifts, explaining that "by giving away their property to those in want, his parents intend to teach him love and good-will toward his fellow-men," adding, "if, when he grows up, the boy fails to sustain his honor name, he is no longer called by it."[122] The act of receiving a name immediately situates the child within a field of efficacious ceremonial action and moral expectation, and as the child grows older, these valences continue to resonate and be remembered in the name itself.

Elaborations of such honor names, in what Eastman calls "deed names," further situate the Dakhóta individual within a social field of other-than-human persons, indexed by "bird and animal names" as well as "those of the elements" that are used "to express temperament" or to remember and celebrate remarkable achievement. Here Eastman describes how "loftiness or beauty of character" is conveyed through references to the sky or clouds, as with the names of "well-known chiefs" like "Red Cloud, Touch-the-Cloud, Blue Sky, and Hole-in-the-Day."[123] Deeds "requiring great physical courage" would "often be celebrated by giving the name of some fear-inspiring animal, such as Bear or Buffalo, or one of the nobler bird names—those of Eagle, Hawk, and Owl."[124]

As with naming practices, the notion that the physical environment should always be thought and met in relational terms is something Eastman underscores in his statement that the meaning of Indian citizenship entails remembering the "native environment," in the sense of making that environment whole again through memory and story. Linda Tuhiwai Smith has observed that as a result of colonization, "the land and the people have been radically transformed in the spatial image of the West." She goes on to describe that "spatial image" in terms of a way of seeing and simplifying local knowledge, much like what James Scott describes in his use of the term "legibility."[125] If the translational process of settler-colonial law converts Indigenous place into space and homelands into property, then Eastman's recollections of those homelands and places tread on forbidden (because unimaginable within the settler property imaginary) ground. In Eastman's citizenship discourse, there is a tacit theory not just of reclaiming Native lands but also of Dakhóta poesis as and through kinship with the land and its other-than-human inhabitants. The performative remaking of long-standing forms of sociality and repersonalizing the land infect U.S. citizenship with relational meanings.

Reanimated Futures

I imagine that Orson Welles might give an embarrassed smile at the pun at the notion of a "citizen kin." I hope he might at least be sympathetic to the critical possibilities it suggests. Welles's depiction of

Charles Foster Kane, after all, could have appeared in a number of Eastman's own criticisms of a morally bankrupt American civilization. At the very least, Kane's insatiable desire for power, his acting as if he had no relatives, painted him as the consummate wašícu, sometimes translated as "fat-taker," contrary to Eastman's idealized Dakhóta citizen. Eastman's idealization and veiled citations of Dakhóta forms of belonging perform an incisive critique of exclusionary forms of citizenship, but they also wager a utopian bet on the resurgence of those older practices. Eastman narrated embodied techniques of Dakhóta land tenure and forms of relationality to force young whites to think through their bodies about thefts of Native lands and to disturb their own naturalized sense of belonging. Eastman's citations of thióšpaye philosophy reveal a sovereign, if suppressed, form of Dakhóta territoriality, so that his scouting manual becomes, in the light of thióšpaye philosophy, less a how-to guide for whites playing Indian than a representation of a Dakhóta lifeworld that Eastman asserts as being latent in the "living thought" of the settler nation. By insisting on the aliveness of Dakhóta epistemologies of home places, Eastman writes the Oyáte as an unassimilable presence. In describing the lives of Dakhóta before the reservations, a certain nostalgia is at work, but it is a nostalgia with future-oriented political stakes because it rehearses Dakhóta criteria for settler-national and tribal-national belonging as enduring alternatives to liberal criteria for citizenship.

In this sense of future making, Eastman's nostalgic performances of Native wildness anticipate contemporary debates over tribal citizenship. Then, as now, Native nations strive to define internal standards for belonging, and they do so as a basic exercise of sovereignty. Far from creating a climate where anybody can be an Indian, this process of negotiating citizenship standards is in dialogue with Indigenous pasts where communal belonging was predominantly reckoned through relational philosophies and laws. Joanne Barker (Lenape) writes that such "Native customary laws" that were and are used to determine "membership, relationship, and responsibility are incredibly discriminating" rather than being an open door to any would-be tribal "Wannabe."[126] Spanning a range of legal, social, and geopolitical sites, or what Barker identifies as "genealogical practices, relationships to ecosystems and specific lands, inheritance laws, customs regarding adoption, marriage and naturalization, and beliefs about social responsibilities within extended family units," these diverse forms of kinship theory and practice continue to challenge settler-colonial notions of recognition.[127] As Barker puts it, instead of turning to nontribal sources (like the U.S. government) for answering the question of who is and who is not Native, "why not treat these practices, and the cultures and epistemologies in which they are defined and from which they emanate, as the authority?"[128]

Why not indeed? Eastman implies this same question in his depictions of human–land relations, the depictions of which, because of or despite their appearances in a scouting manual, form a critical supplement by introducing a tribally specific philosophical dimension to legal discussions in which land appears in instrumentalized forms as disembodied and inert. Eastman's muted repersonalizing and reanimating of the land through his writings certainly also complicates his later political writings, including *The Indian To-day*. Eastman's remembering and reconstituting of himself as a Dakhóta person in relation to Dakhóta lands destabilizes discourses of blood and their exclusive modes of citizenship, which by 1887 had become naturalized within not just U.S. law but among many Indigenous communities as well.

My next chapter examines Nicholas Black Elk's accounts of travels and mock ceremonies he and other Lakhóta did for tourists in the mid-twentieth century, and how their forms of movement across state geopolitical boundaries and across boundaries separating the human from the other than human were reactivations of Oyáte ways of knowing. I describe how Black Elk invoked Lakhóta relationality with other-than-human beings as a return to older ways of knowing and thinking about boundaries that exist between not just humans and other-than-humans but also between settlers and Lakhóta, men and women. By renewing relationships with powerful other-than-human beings in Lakhóta homelands, Black Elk's performances were implicit critiques of the settler-state's biopolitical management of bodies and populations, its hierarchies between genders, and between those considered as having life versus not having life. In conversation with that chapter's focus on how critical relationality transgresses settler-colonial hierarchies, the Second Interlude that follows provides an oral history of my grandmother, Grace Lambert, describing the various bands of the Oyáte. Her account of the Thíthuŋwaŋ sun dance describes it as an exchange of power between human beings and powerful other-than-human beings, through which Thíthuŋwaŋ people would receive life-giving water during drought times. However, as usual, she demurs after telling only this brief anecdote, saying,

"That's all I know about the sun dance. That belongs to the Plains people. Today they call it traditional dancing. That one is a sacred dance." I love her humility in that moment because there are worlds within what she described—and within the word "sacred." As I will show, the sacred appears in Black Elk's transcripts in relations of circular reciprocity, or generous gift giving—a vastly different version of the old anthropological notion of the gift that I interrogate and rewrite from a thióšpaye perspective.

Second Interlude

Interview with Grace Lambert, Taté Tópa Dakhóta Wóunspe (Four Winds Dakota Teaching) Program, March 10, 1993

This interview was conducted by Eugene Hale, a citizen of the Spirit Lake Nation and first-language speaker of Dakhóta, and is part of an oral history archive housed at the Taté Tópa Tribal School in Fort Totten, North Dakota. The archive holds video recordings of elders speaking in the Dakhóta language, or sometimes in a mix of English and Dakhóta. The interviews were meant to be used for language and culture instruction in the Dakhóta Wóuŋspe (Teaching) Program, and Hale's questions focus on local places and on what happened "long ago," or before the making of the Devils Lake reservation in 1867.

Here, my grandmother, Grace Lambert, discusses such topics as honoring enemy warriors who had been killed, hard work as a way to survive, sun dances, the various thióšpaye at Spirit Lake, the origin of the name Mní Wakháŋ, or Spirit Lake, and medicine men. She emphasizes the interweavings of personal intentionality and causality in the affairs of persons of many different kinds, especially when she describes the relation between Lakȟóta people, water, and the sun dance as being about the performance of need before powerful other-than-human persons who, in seeing one's need, respond by giving rain. I grew up hearing a lot of what she talks about here, both from her and from my unčí Rachel. But as with the other Interludes, I have tried to stay out the way of her tellings by giving minimal annotations to her words, noting only historical contexts and dates where appropriate.

EUGENE HALE: What is your name?

GRACE LAMBERT: Grace Lambert.

EH: Do you have any stories, or any teachings? We want to know, if you could tell us? About the things that happen around Fort Totten, stories, and other things, or the things you remember. Did you grow up here?

GL: Yes, I grew up here; I was born here. I grew up here, went to school here, I finished school elsewhere.

EH: Do you know any stories?

GL: What kind of stories?

EH: Stories like what the Dakhótas did a long time ago for entertainment, powwows, or sun dances?

GL: Long time ago when I was little, our grandma raised us. They tried to teach my mother and father how to farm. They gave them land, horse, a wagon, and farm tools. All the tools a farmer needs. They must've been the first ones here.[1] They picked certain ones that could work. They were given a homestead to support their families. That's why my mother and father were given those things. We always lived with our grandmother. Our grandmother raised us. I had two younger sisters, a brother, an older sister. She stayed around until she got married and moved away. When we lived with our grandma; she was our teacher. She taught us things that were taught a long time ago to children—how to live and survive. These were teachings from our grandmother. Maybe that's why our grandma raised us. "Listen!" my grandma used to say, "and look around. Don't be daydreaming, because you aren't going to learn anything." That's what grandma would tell us. "During the day make use of your hands. Learn to do something and do it. Learn how to sew 'cause you're a woman." That's what she used to say to me. She would tell my brother go to the barn and water the horses and feed the chickens, help your mother and father out. That's the way we grew up. "If you listen well you won't have heartaches. Keep your eyes open because you're going to learn from that." That's what she said. She even told us to watch an ant. "These are the best workers." All day they would run around. They would haul all their food into a hole for the winter. They would haul and get things ready. That's what she said. "If you're willing to work, you're going to be thankful for it. You have ears for something, so listen! When someone talks foolishly, they always run into something, my grandchild." This is what she would say. "If you hear something good and tried to live that way, you'll be thankful. Don't let your hands hang there; make use of your hands. Check the roads real well or you might get lost." As we

SECOND INTERLUDE 139

were growing up, this is some of the teachings our grandma taught us. I remember these things to this day.[2]

EH: Long time ago did they have sun dances around here?

GL: No, not that I remember, I never heard anything about it. But my dad, long time ago, he would say, "Long time ago, before the Dakhótas were given this reservation, they used to travel a lot. We are Santees. The ones that live out on the prairies. They're the ones that sun dance." The ones on the prairie, they're not close to water. Santees in Minnesota lived along the Mississippi River. That's where us Santees lived, and that's why we had plenty of water and made good use of it. The ones that live on the prairies—on some days the river would dry up. They would have it hard without water. Through that tree, they would pray to the sacred one [Wakháŋ Tháŋka]. That is why they would dance to the sun. He gives them water so they can live in a good way. This is why they sun dance. That belongs to the prairie people. The Thíthuŋwaŋ and Iháŋkthunwan lived along the Missouri River. On the days they didn't have water, they would sun dance. The Santees never did that. Maybe they should have done that too. They used prayers and sacred dances [wakháŋ wačípi]. This is what they used. These men were medicine men. They would gather together, perform this dance. If you were not one, you couldn't be there. It only belonged to that clan. Like a membership. They would gather together at a sun dance. One day out of the sun dance, they would cook their sacred food [or perform the kettle dance].[3] This is one of their ways. That's all I know about the sun dance. That belongs to the Plains people. Today they call it traditional dancing. That one is a sacred dance. The women stand up front with a feather. In the middle of the song they would wave this feather. When they honor a man with words in a song, they would wave this feather or fan around at this time. Long time ago, they used to do that. They call it traditional honor dance. When a man goes to war and kills an enemy and scalps him, and takes the scalp back with him, it's an act of bravery. That's why they take the scalp. Then they honor these men.

The Dakhóta people always honor their people. The man never pretends. When a man brings it [a scalp] back, they put on an honor dance. The woman, like your wife, she would carry that scalp for him, and dance with that. They're not dancing because they killed. They're dancing because they feel sad. This is because [so that] the enemy's spirit would not bother them. That's why they do this. This is what they used to tell us, when we were little children.

EH: On this reservation, how many tribes are there and what kind of tribes? The Santees [Isanti], Cut-Throats [a derogatory name for all dialects and bands of the Oyáte], are there more of them, that you know of? They're Dakhótas, but different bands.

GL: You mean clans? Yes, Santees have seven different clans. Tetons have seven different clans or fire places. Tetons, I don't know their ways too good. Some Santees are called Sacred Lake Village People, Shoot the Leaf [Waȟpékhute], and Leaf Village People [Waȟpéthuŋwaŋ]. The ones they call Sacred Lake People [Bdewákhaŋthuŋwaŋ] is because they live along the Sacred Lake. Shoot the Leaf People, they're called that because they shoot the leaves. That used to be a game for them. They would shoot at three leaves. That's how they got their name, from that game. The ones that are called Leaf Village Clan are Wahpetons. Then they're some—the names are Dry It on the Shoulder. This is one of the Santee clans. When they go hunting, they get buffalo and dry the meat. Sometimes they get attacked or move to other campsite. While they are traveling, they put the undried meat on the horse's shoulders. This is what they do. That's how they got their name: Dry It on the Shoulder. Each one of these clans has their own leaders. Then the Sisíthuŋwáŋ [Sisseton]; the word *sisíthuŋwáŋ*, nobody can't translate or explain that word. There are different stories about that word, but I don't know the right explanation. The Mississippi River, Minnesota River, and the Red River, they stayed along these rivers. West from the Mississippi River this way, the Sisseton's tribes and all over this way. The Santees lived. The Tetons lived by the Missouri River and down south. Down the other way, Rosebud and the Black Hills and down there. This is where they live. That reservation over there belongs to them.[4]

I want to tell you something, and it's the truth. My dad used to say this: the Dakhótas never say, "This is my piece of land." That's what he would say. Because all the land belongs to them. They don't own an acre. They own the whole thing. This is one of their strong beliefs. In the beginning, they took their names down on paper and gave them land. A lot of them didn't want that. That's what they said. This was not their belief. They believed that all the land was theirs. All of it. Nobody had one acre.... [English translation missing] this is my land. They even got the Dakhótas saying that.

EH: The Sacred Lake Heart [Mní Wakháŋ Čhaŋté] or Sacred Lake, and some call it the Backbone. How did they get these names, or did you hear it from somebody?

GL: The Sacred Lake always did have that name from a long time ago. It always has been Mní Wakháŋ. Never was Devils Lake. Long ago before Christianity came here, nobody believed in the evil spirit ways. The Dakhótas only believed in the spiritual ways. They only believed in the Holy One [God] and respected him. There wasn't such a thing called Devil, and I never heard of it. When ever we did something wrong, they would say, "Don't do that; it's sacred [he wakháŋye]." Our grandma, whenever we do something wrong, she would never say, "Don't do that. It's evil." Instead, she would tell us, "Don't touch that, it's sacred." This is the way we listen. Nowadays we tell them don't, that's bad. It's a challenge for them. They would go ahead and do it. This is the way I understand it. These are my own understandings, the things I've told you.

Oh, about Mní Wakháŋ—each family has a different story. And they understand it and tell it differently. And the stories aren't the same. I'll tell you something, but this is me and my family's belief. There were some men sitting on Crow Hill looking toward the lake, and they saw something big come out of the lake. And the men that were sitting on the hill. At that time, the lake was right below here and clear to Minnewaukan [a mostly white border town just west of the reservation]. That isn't the real name; it's Mní Wakháŋ.[5] That town, they call it Minnewaukan. By Minnewaukan there is a landmark, and that's how far the lake was. From there and back this way was all water. Over there by Wilson Howard—I mean Dwayne Howard. By his house there is a hill, maybe you seen that. That hill used to be an island—our family's, which is what the stories are about. This thing that comes to the top of the water.[6] That creature is real big. The ones that were sitting on the hill. That creature would look in their direction. They seen its eyes, and it looked like there was fire in its eyes. It started to swim west on top of the water. Over here towards where the sun goes down [west] and it was rainy, windy, and a big thunderstorm—bad storm, anyway. They said one was coming. The creature and the thunders had a battle. This thing—this, this, the creature the one that was swimming. The electricity, I forgot how to say lightning. . . . He battled with the Thunder Beings [Wakíŋyaŋ]. The thunders would shoot lightning bolts at the creature, and the creature would fire back. And it looked like flames of some kind. It got as far as the island, and the Thunder Beings fired a lightning bolt for the last time. From then on, that thing [creature] was never seen again. The people that were sitting on the hill saw the whole thing. They're the ones that said, "That lake is sacred [wakháŋ]." This is how it got its name, Spirit Lake. That's how I heard it. That's what they told us. Nobody said or wrote about it, that's all I know about it. This is what we been told by our family.

EH: How about that rock over there [Devils Tooth]?[7]

GL: That rock. I never heard too much about it. They always had sacred ceremony over there and leave offerings there. One time there was an old lady, she left an offering. Did they tell this before? This old lady went to the store to buy some groceries. She started home with her groceries. Where that rock is, there was a man, who got drunk the night before. When he woke up, he laid down by that rock and went to sleep. The old lady was walking toward that rock. She stopped by the rock, and in them days they only buy Bull Durham [tobacco]. She pulled her Bull Durham out. First she put some material on top [of the rock]. She said, "Grandfather, I brought you some offerings and have pity on me and pray for me." She was saying, "Grandfather, I brought you some tobacco." By that time the man with the hangover was laying behind the rock. He woke up by that time and he said, "Haŋ" [(feminine) yes]. He scared the old lady. She ran all the way home from there. That's the only story I know about Devils Tooth. After Christianity came, everything was labeled "devil." The backbone, I don't know too much about that one. They just started that one not too long ago.

    The Heart of Spirit Lake [Mní Wakháŋ Čhaŋté], that was

there a long time ago. The people—I think it was the Tetons that used to make offerings up there. That's what they said when the Black Robe People came. The Spiritual People were showing the Black Robe People the Dakhóta spirit ways. One of the Black Robe People said, "The Dakhóta spiritual ways are no good; it's towards the Devil. I'm going to make a cross and put it on top of the hill to show this is the right way." So he built a big cross, and he carried it to the top of the hill and stood it up on top of the hill. From that I used to think. Long time ago the Dakhóta ways they believe in the Great Spirit for a long time. They always say, "The holy ones [táku wakháŋ]." They never say, "It's an evil being." They always say, "The Great Spirit told us this." This is a way of life. We lived here on earth for thousands of years and nobody knows for sure. Nobody can't tell us how long we lived here. This is what I believe; you believe in Great Spirit, you're going to live. This is how I understand it. Today I'm a Christian. Whatever beliefs that my grandfather and grandmother had, that belongs to them. I have respect and believe in these things. I can't live like that because it's different today. Even those days are different. The days are not the same, so you can't go back. Long ago the Dakhótas had Indian names.

EH: Do you remember any of them?

GL: Yes, well, I forgot. I can't remember a thing. The Indian names? I don't know. I can't think of one.

EH: Long time ago, a man or medicine men, they used to call them long time ago. There was one or two of them that could change themselves into animal forms like a bear or a snake. Do you know any? That someone told you? Do you remember any stories? There used to be a lot of men like that. They called them spiritual persons and there were many. They used to be on our reservation. Do you know any of them?

GL: No. There was one, a man, my mother's male cousin, my grandmother, my mother's mother. Her brother or her cousin. That's her boy. That's my grandmother's cousin. She said he was blind. That's what my mother told me. My mother's cousin, that's the one who was blind. My mother said her grandmother raised him too; she raised all of them. They all lived together as a family. Some were orphans, so my grandma raised them too. The cousin, the one that was blind. There was a log cabin, a small log cabin next to the house, and nobody was living in it. They moved him in there. For many days they had the windows blinded, and they always kept the door locked. So he sits there in the dark. His grandma always brought him food. She took him some food one time. He said, "Grandma, next time you come, bring a piece of paper and a pair of scissors." So his grandma took him a piece of paper and scissors. My grandma wasn't blind, so she left the door open, because she wanted to see what he was doing. And here he cut a snake out of paper. He said, "Watch this, grandma." The cut-out paper snake—he threw it on the floor. It turned into a snake and started to crawl towards his grandma. His grandmother screamed and ran out the door. From that time on that man was sacred. He did a lot of spiritual things.

Then there was a man. His name was Black Pumpkin and he was a medicine man. They said he was a strong medicine man. Black Pumpkin was a twin. Then there was another man, a twin too. His name was Flat Wood. His real name was Announces Good. That was his real name, Announces Good. I don't know why they called him Flat Wood. This man was really kind-hearted. Him and this Black Pumpkin, I mean Announces Good. These two were different twins. The elders used to say twins are sacred people because they are different. They're born in twos. Normally we are born one at a time. Then they are born in a pair; they're sacred people. And here, this man, [the] one that made that snake, he does a lot of sacred things. He even doctored himself so that he could see. He even cured his blindness. They considered him a sacred man, so they always depended on him. They know that he knows about different medicines. Black Pumpkin went to this person. "Grandson, they said you're a holy man. I want to challenge you." He said, "Okay, where are we going to do this?" "We are going to the back of the woods. You can use your spiritual powers, and I'll use mine. You see this tree?" "Yes!" They said it was an oak tree. It was big, really big. "From this tree we will take several steps backwards. This is where we'll have that stand off. This is one of my powers," and it was a deer hoof, they said. He held it in his hand and threw it at the oak tree. You could see the hoof sink halfway into the tree. This one, my mother's cousin said, "This is one of my powers," and it was down. You know, down! Fine feathers. Plumes. Oh! plumes. He said, "This plume here is one of my sacred things." So he got into a good position. He held his red-dyed plume, and he threw it at the tree. The plume went through the oak tree and came out the other side. This old man knew he was getting old. Black Pumpkin said, "Grandson, you won," and he shook his hand.

EH: How did Crow Hill get its name?

GL: You mean, you don't know that? You from here?

EH: Yes, I'm from here. We want to know about these things.

GL: Oh! Well, it goes like this. Below Cross Hill, that valley where Junior Joshua, Paul Yankton, and Boke Thomas—that whole valley the other way, where Walking Eagles live. The Dakhótas used to camp all over there. They always put scouts out so they can watch out for danger and trouble for the people. These scouts, they were walking through the woods towards Crow Hill. When they got up there, in Crow Hill, the biggest hill, that's the one they call Crow Hill. On top of the hill there were some Crow scouts. They must have checked out the camp to see where the horses were at. They like to steal horses. The Dakhóta people stole good horses from the Crow. Maybe they were going to steal them back. Maybe that's why the Crow scouts check out the camp. The scouts came down and told somebody to spread the word. So the people got ready. The ones that were warriors got word and sneak up the hill. They said they killed all the Crow scouts and buried them right there. That's why they call it Crow Hill.

3 Territoriality, Ethics, and Travel in the Black Elk Transcripts

*At a give away, we do them often at pow wows, the family honors
one of our own by thanking the people who jingle and shimmer
in circle. They are with us. We give gifts in both generous show
and as acts of faith in sufficiency. One does not future hoard.
We may lament incomplete colonial conversions, our too little
bank savings the circle we hope will sustain. We sustain it. Not so
strange then that I declined to hoard love and another's body for
myself. I cannot have faith in scarcity. I have tried. It cut me from
the circle.*

—Kim TallBear, "Disrupting Settlement"

In my first two chapters I argued that Indigenous decolonial politics and agency in the assimilation era were often couched in terms
of a settler-colonial representational regime that, through juridical
means such as blood quantum and censuses and through rhetorical
means such as notions of Indian vanishing and backwardness, created
Indigenous people as increasingly visible and legible subjects of the
settler-state. The practice of Dakhóta intellectuals was not to endorse
those politics, however, but instead to use this regime of legibility to
cipher Dakhóta knowledge to settler society. This encrypted remaking of the Oyáte worked as a kind of love letter to future generations
of Dakhóta: a decolonial reactivation and offering of thióšpaye ethics
based, as Kim TallBear's epigraph above about a powwow giveaway so
beautifully suggests, in notions of giving and sufficiency.

I have called such offerings "unheroic decolonialisms" for a few
reasons: first to evoke the negative affect attaching to Indigenous survival within a settler-colonial state, and second to suggest that while
they may be performed by individuals, such decolonizing modes are
foremost in the service of the collective, at the level of the thióšpaye,
or extended family, and secondarily at the level of the Oyáte or the
people. Third, these decolonial modes are unheroic because they

appear as colonial co-optation when one privileges heroic, by which I mean individualistic, rhetorics of revolt and refusal, or that view nostalgia as mobilizing cultural essentialism in naive or colonially complicitous ways. Yet this is the essential misprision relied on by assimilation's unheroic decolonialist: to seem utterly harmless to settler audiences while actually working to decolonize and rebuild Indigenous communities.

Where I previously looked at how the threat of settler-colonial violence structured Dakhóta self-representations after the end of the U.S.–Dakhóta War, resulting in practices of withholding peoplehood from view under the sign of good (individual) Indian citizenship, this chapter examines how thióšpaye ethics, or what a number of scholars now term critical relationality or radical relationality, furnish the means for translating and reworking settler-state mandates about Indigenous identity, land, and territory.[1] In this chapter I rework my analytical term of translation as proliferation, using it as a figure for how the law, as Judith Butler asserts, opens up liberatory spaces when the locations of its bodily performance "proliferate the domain of the bodily beyond the domain targeted by the original restriction."[2] State regulation of Thíthuŋwaŋ (Teton) or Lakhóta[3] bodies through blood quantum, ethnocidal laws like the 1883 Religious Crimes Code, and residence/confinement on reservations created Lakhóta as juridical subjects of the United States, thereby institutionalizing liberal settler norms of individualism, heteronormativity, and sovereignty. However, as Butler notes about the repression of desire—such as Indigenous desires for free movement, anarchical nonheterosexual intimacies, and noncapitalistic forms of relation—the "criminal codes which seek to catalogue and institutionalize normalcy become the site for the contestation of the normal."[4]

This contestation is evident in military resistances like those of Crazy Horse and Red Cloud. But here my focus is on complicit performances of tribal regeneration, where Lakhóta webs of kinship proliferated "the domain of the bodily" beyond a settler territoriality founded on the heterosexual monogamous couple and the nuclear family who possessed, inhabited, and transmitted property.[5] As Qwo-Li Driskill, Chris Finley, Brian Joseph Gilley, and Scott Lauria Morgensen assert, "Settler colonialism is the historical, institutional, and discursive root of heteronormative binary sex–gender systems on stolen land."[6] This chapter draws inspiration from the critiques of Driskill et al. and others of settler-colonialism, and from their insight that colonial sexual

TERRITORIALITY, ETHICS, AND TRAVEL 149

violence took place structurally at the level of peoples. As Driskill et al. put it, "Indigenous *peoples* were queered by colonization, so that all Indigenous people today are called to question heteronormativity as part of decolonization."[7] My analysis also draws on TallBear's premise that challenges to colonial hierarchies around categorizations of animacy/inanimacy and personhood also challenge the gender binary, infused as it is with judgments about agency and the capacity for vibrancy.[8] Specifically, I examine how Lakȟóta thióšpaye ethics of sufficiency and gift giving create nonhierarchical spaces in which responsibility is transacted ceremonially between human and other-than-human beings. In teasing out the dynamics of those spaces I build on TallBear's sense that "monogamy and marriage are . . . part of sustaining an animacy hierarchy in which some bodies are viewed as more animate, alive, and vibrant than others."[9]

The central texts I read here are the transcribed and translated interviews of Heȟáka Sápa, or Nicholas Black Elk (1863–1950), as they have been collected by Raymond DeMallie in *The Sixth Grandfather* (1984), with my readings of these focusing on the intersection of territory, gender, and kinship.[10] Specifically, I argue that Oglála wičáša wakȟáŋ (literally "man mysterious" or powerful, but meaning ritual specialist and healer) and Catholic catechist Black Elk's example reveals how place-based logics of relation—or what I call a critical relationality grounded in an ethic of economic sufficiency—challenge statist notions of sovereignty as something bound to a particular territory. Put another way, in Black Elk's account of his life, ceremonial performances make Lakȟóta territorial claims by mapping cosmological locations and relational norms of the thióšpaye across boundaries imposed by the settler-state. Lakȟóta territoriality, as mobile relationality, is centrally important in Black Elk's case not only because of his status as a celebrity, as a show Indian who frequently traveled outside the reservation, but also because his life story underscores how Lakȟóta concepts of land and family survived the state's assault on communally held homelands, turning them into reservations and tracts of private property. As I argued in my last chapter, this colonial translation involved time as much as space, imposing a settler-national temporality defined by abstract flows of capital in "empty homogenous time." In the span of just over twenty years after the 1868 Fort Laramie treaty, the Great Sioux Nation was created as a discursive object bound to a particular territory: the Great Sioux reservation. This territory would be greatly, and illegally, diminished through a series of treaties and congressional acts, the first of which occurred just seven years later, when Custer's treaty-breaking expedition to Ȟé Sápa (Black Hills) discovered gold. The final reductions in Lakȟóta territory took place in 1889 after a prolonged military resistance against the United States.[11]

Mishuana Goeman (Tonawanda Band of Seneca) observes how Indigenous women writers have remapped place in terms of "connections to multiple other spaces, histories, and people" rather than as "homogeneous, bounded, and temporally linear."[12] Likewise, Black Elk's travels and ceremonial performances reproduced long-standing geographical circuits of travel and tenure for Lakȟóta people, including territories that painter and author George Catlin described as spreading "from the banks of the Mississippi to the base of the Rocky Mountains."[13] Black Elk, especially in his later years, often traveled to Colorado in the hope of establishing an Indian pageant there—a form of ecumenical performance with territorial implications that I discuss toward the end of the chapter. Further, and closely related to these physical movements, travel routes validate venerable forms of Lakȟóta affiliation with other Indigenous peoples. Black Elk's visits as a Catholic catechist to the Wind River reservation, for instance, affirm his regard for Arapahos and continue the practice of Oglála wičáša wakȟáŋ visiting Wind River to conduct healing rituals for Arapaho families. By examining the ethical texture of those networks and rituals, I highlight how individual Lakȟóta did decolonizing work for themselves and for the Oyáte, even in England and France, where Black Elk performed in Buffalo Bill's Wild West show and in performances for tourists, like those at the Duhamel Indian Pageant in South Dakota. I ask how and to what extent these travels not only reaffirmed Lakȟóta geopolitical boundaries and claims to territory but also performed thióšpaye ethics as decolonizing opacities.

Black Elk's decolonizing work shows up in two main ways: as the reclamation of Lakȟóta warrior masculinity and in the reanimating of Lakȟóta homelands as affective and storied territory. Traditional gender understandings of the Oyáte were explicitly targeted by the settler-state in the criminalized and murdered bodies of the Dakȟóta in the post-1862 war concentration camps. The shadow cast by the bodies of those warriors fell across generations of Dakȟóta and Lakȟóta, barring performances of Indigenous warrior masculinity except to bolster white masculinity as superior, as with Wild Wests that, like Buffalo Bill's, staged an "Attack on a Settler's Cabin by Hostile Indi-

TERRITORIALITY, ETHICS, AND TRAVEL 151

ans" and culminated with Buffalo Bill himself repulsing the attack.[14] Ironically, Black Elk played this role in his tours with Buffalo Bill's and other Wild West shows. However, in his later performances of mock ceremonies, which enacted one of the visions he received as a child, Black Elk invoked thióšpaye ethics to reclaim a Lakȟóta warrior masculinity that would bring decolonial courage to other Lakȟóta. He was perhaps well positioned to do so because of his role as a heyókȟa—a thunder dreamer or clown—which by locating him as a multiply gendered person allowed Black Elk to embody gender and animacy/inanimacy inclusiveness as a means of decolonial praxis.[15] His example further suggests how Lakȟóta territoriality under assimilation reemerged in the mobile relations of the thióšpaye, which furnished idioms for Lakȟóta relational philosophies and territoriality through foundational narratives and ceremonies to include human beings who are not Lakȟóta but also other-than-human beings and spirits. In Black Elk's transcribed interviews, the thióšpaye's place-based and embodied norms of gifting are unheroic decolonizations performed through mock ceremonies.

Translated Lands, Lost Being

Complicating any reading of Black Elk is his iconicity. Holy man and detribalized Indian hero, the essentialized Black Elk is radiantly tragic, a "spiritual" (jacket blurbs, some penned by no less than Vine Deloria Jr., still call *Black Elk Speaks* a "religious classic" and "one of the best spiritual books of the modern era") and cultural spokesman who is often enlisted to stand in for all Lakȟóta, and even for all Native Americans. This metonym maps ideologically onto the image of the vanishing Indian, a convergence that John Neihardt attempts to inscribe in the ending lines of *Black Elk Speaks*, when he ventriloquizes Black Elk as pronouncing the death of his people: "And I, to whom so great a vision was given in my youth,—you see me now a pitiful old man who has done nothing, for the nation's hoop is broken and scattered. There is no center any longer, and the sacred tree is dead."[16] This two-sentence summary, penned by Neihardt and never spoken by Black Elk, has proven to be incredibly soluble in the settler nation's Indigenous imaginary. Some twenty years after *Black Elk Speaks,* Ruth Underhill would review Joseph Epes Brown's *The Sacred Pipe*, a volume that recorded Black Elk's versions of Lakȟóta ceremonies. There, she lamented, with maternal concern for "the beautiful but dying ceremonies of the American Indian," Black Elk was the "last custodian of the ancient rituals and already made famous through the sympathetic book by Neihardt."[17] As Michael Steltenkamp puts it, an essentialized Black Elk has proven to be itself a highly mobile signifier, "expropriated and utilized on behalf of diverse forms of special pleading" rather than representing the struggle to reclaim and rebuild Lakȟóta peoplehood after the Wounded Knee massacre.[18]

Other scholars have underscored the political dimensions of Black Elk's interviews, reading them as a response to U.S. colonialism. John Carlos Rowe examines settler concepts of territoriality and identity politics in the Black Elk transcripts, observing the enormous shift in federal policy that took place between allotment's use of Native wardship and the Indian Reorganization Act's move to greater tribal autonomy.[19] I draw here on his attention to how Lakȟóta forms of land tenure were especially targeted in U.S. laws and policies. Key to both allotment and Indian Reorganization Act discourses of Indianness were racialized and essentialist versions of not only blood or individual identity but also land. The Indian of the 1934 Indian Reorganization Act (IRA) was defined largely by settler-colonial standards of biological lineage and physical territory: "The term "Indian" as used in this Act shall include all persons of Indian descent who are members of any recognized Indian tribe now under Federal jurisdiction, and all persons who are descendants of such members who were, on June 1, 1934, residing within the present boundaries of any Indian reservation, and shall further include all other persons of one-half or more Indian blood."[20] Recognizing "descendants" as the legitimate offspring of heterosexual monogamous unions, and renewing the federal government's commitment to "blood" as a measure of identity, the IRA reproduces the heteronormative logic that the earlier Dawes Act brought into existence as a matter of formal policy. This happened despite the IRA's reformist aims at undoing the harms done by allotment's emphases on assimilation and individual land ownership, and devolving greater decision-making power away from the Bureau of Indian Affairs and to tribes.[21] Scott Lyons notes how the IRA's defining of Indian deployed a constrained view of both jus sanguinis, or right of blood as "Indian descent," or blood quantum, and jus soli, or right of soil as "residing within the present boundaries," while omitting culture and language. Lyons concludes of this omission, in a moment of sympathy with "the traditionalists" of Indigenous communities, that "there is no peoplehood possible in such definitions, no privileging of language or traditions, and thus no cultural survival."[22]

However, the diagnosis for Indigenous peoplehood under a reformist but still settler-colonial regime like the IRA was obviously not terminal—which is to say that the "right of soil" has been and continues to be exercised in ways that work to the side of state definitions, and especially through anticapitalist views of land. It may be an obvious but nonetheless important thing to note that the IRA's definition of Indianness is based on a view of Indigenous territories as being fundamentally inert and affectless. This is typical of a Lockean liberalism and a capitalistic temporality in which land gains its ontological status only through the addition of human labor. Subversion of this disenchanted territoriality through movements of various kinds—physical, ethicopolitical, aesthetic—is key to making sense of Lakȟóta responses to confinement on reservations, especially in cases where kinship networks and Lakȟóta/Dakȟóta cosmologies define alternative political geographies to those of the settler-state. In what follows I identify how Black Elk performed these alternative temporal geographies in relation to the settler-state's juridical sovereignty, focusing on how ceremonial performances—even in mock-up versions—reclaimed relationships with ancestral homelands.

Competing Territorialities

Just as the 1862 U.S.–Dakȟóta War would transform Eastern Dakȟóta's relationship with homelands into one of exile, our western relatives, the Thítȟuŋwaŋ (Lakȟóta), experienced pressures brought on by the incursions of settlers into Ȟé Sápa (Black Hills) in the years leading up to Custer's defeat at the Little Big Horn (1876), and of settler outrage following that battle. Not long before that watershed, Lakȟóta faced a settler population eager to claim lands that had been represented as unoccupied. Drawn by the allure of what Lieutenant James Calhoun, in his journals from the illegal 1874 Black Hills expedition, described as a land whose gold Custer believed "would open a rich vein of wealth calculated to increase the commercial prosperity of this country,"[23] and which the team of newspaper reporters embedded with the military described as "fairy-land," white miners began to flood into Lakȟóta lands that had been "set apart" by the 1868 Fort Laramie treaty "for the absolute and undisturbed *use and occupation* of the Indians." As Jeffrey Ostler argues, the federal government's commitment to upholding that article of the treaty was always tenuous because it faced petitions from private interests like the Black Hills Exploring and Mining Association—formed by speculators in the town of Yankton—and from the Dakota territorial legislature, who in their petition to Congress to open the Hills to "scientific" expeditions, alleged that the only use the Lakȟóta put the Black Hills to was as a "hiding-place to which they can flee after committing depredations upon the whites and the friendly Indians."[24]

In Black Elk's account of this historical moment, and of Lakȟóta land tenure practices in Ȟé Sápa, he describes camping as a child at Mní Lúzahaŋ or Rapid Creek, the main waterway running through Ȟé Sápa, from which men would embark to collect thípi poles in "the thick of the forest."[25] These tall lodgepole pines were used by Lakȟóta and other Plains tribes, and at this time, before white inundation, "there were lots of slim poles, for no one at this time had bothered them at all."[26] Far more than a "hiding-place," Ȟé Sápa was the locus of subsistence activities and was so abundant with game that Sitting Bull called it "a treasure to us Indians," adding that it was "the food pack of the people."[27] In addition to providing for subsistence, the hills were the locus of Lakȟóta ceremonial life. The morning after the pole gathering, the encamped Lakȟóta "began building a sweat tipi [*inipi*] for a medicine man by the name of Chips," who "was the first man who made a sacred ornament for Crazy Horse to use in the war." Black Elk speculated that "probably this [in Ȟé Sápa, somewhere along Rapid Creek] is where Crazy Horse was made bullet-proof and got his power."[28]

In his brief anecdote about Crazy Horse, and again and again in the account of his great vision, Black Elk highlights how Lakȟóta ceremonies centered around Ȟé Sápa and around the place Black Elk identified as its center: Íŋyaŋ Káǧa Pahá (Stone Made Mountain; in settler parlance, Harney Peak). Ȟé Sápa has been represented as the nexus of a web of kinship relations between Lakȟóta and powerful other-than-human persons, and contemporary accounts underscore how Lakȟóta ceremonial life in Ȟé Sápa sought to maintain good relations with these relatives. When a Lakȟóta sacred site, Phešlá, was put up for sale, Arvol Looking Horse commented, "Our creation story comes from the Black Hills, from the heart of Mother Earth. We came up from the caves which are connected under our Black Hills, and we received very sacred places to do ceremony. . . . Phešlá is one of these central ceremonial places."[29] Looking Horse's invoking of creation stories here links Lakȟóta ceremonialism with the ceremonial responsibility of maintaining originary ethical relationships. Looking Horse's interviewer, Chase Iron Eyes, adds that the sun dance, "one of seven sacred ceremonies given to the Lakȟóta by Pte Skaŋ Wiŋ" (Ptesáŋwiŋ or White Buffalo Calf Woman), is a ceremony "of sacrifice and renewal: participants re-enact the sacrifice of a spirit, Íŋyaŋ [stone], who spun himself and sacrificed himself until his blood became water. The ceremony ensures that nature's process of renewal continues so that, for example, water, plants, and animals remain abundant."[30] My point in replaying these accounts is to underscore that to be cut off from Ȟé Sápa is to be cut off from powerful lifegiving relatives. The loss of Ȟé Sápa meant more than just the loss of food; it also meant losing a portion of being itself. Black Elk's ceremonial performances for tourists brought him back into relation with Ȟé Sápa, and enactments of his great vision permit the reclamation of a critically relational view of land as a means of overflowing and unsettling settler boundaries.

Indigenous territoriality always challenges the presumed universality of settler territoriality. As Paul M. Liffman observes in a Huichol context, Indigenous territoriality involves "more than acreage, or administrative control to include kinship, historical land tenure, ritual networks, and their representation."[31] From the perspective of the settler-colonial state, however, Indigenous claims to place are often affixed with the tags of "failure" to assume statist forms of governance. Such an assumption has a historical lineage dating back at least as far as Sir Henry Sumner Maine and Henry Lewis Morgan, whose evolutionist schema for understanding differences in social structures contrasted a (primitive) kin-based prestate society with a (civilized) society based in territory.[32] This distinction has since undergone meaningful and significant revisions,[33] although not a complete dismantling. In the present, this distinction persists in the assumption that nonstate actors are incapable of, or unfit for, making territorial claims and thus exercising authority over lands and citizens. However, Anne L. Clunan and Harold A. Trinkunas suggest that the contemporary moniker of "ungoverned spaces" to describe nonstate territories is "a misnomer" that "arose from the state-centered conceptualization developed by many governments and international organizations confronting the apparent emergence following the Cold War of politically disordered territories." "In reality," they argue, "many so-called ungoverned spaces are simply 'differently governed.'"[34] In the same volume, Loren B. Landau and Tamlyn Monson observe that "in almost all cases, authority and power are shared among actors in dynamic ways that are not necessarily state centered, state authored, or informed by clearly articulated and unified strategies of control."[35] From a hegemonic point of view, it seems that the admission that non-state articulations of governance and sovereignty exist is still a heresy.

As hegemonic jargon, "ungoverned spaces" sounds a lot like Bishop Henry Whipple's musings in a letter to President Ulysses Grant over the U.S. government's dealings with Lakȟóta toward the end of the presidential term, in 1876, one year after Custer led nearly a thousand soldiers into the Black Hills on a "scientific" expedition, in violation of treaty terms made between the U.S. and Lakȟóta nations. Whipple, who intervened on behalf of Dakȟóta condemned to be hanged after the 1862 U.S.–Dakȟóta War, persuading Lincoln to commute the sentences of all but thirty-eight warriors, was the first Episcopalian bishop of Minnesota. He was generally well regarded by Dakȟóta. In a letter dated July 31, 1876, Whipple registers his distaste for the recent treaty violation: "We persisted in telling these heathen tribes that they were independent nations," he writes. "We sent out the bravest & best of our offices . . . because the Indians would not doubt a soldiers honor—They made a treaty and they pledged the nations faith that no white man should enter that territory."[36] "The whole world," he continues, "knew that we violated that treaty."[37] But this "friend of the Indian" goes on in the same letter to prescribe a three-part policy for dealing with the Indian problem once and for all. His solution would bypass all the complexities involved in making and upholding treaties:

> The end may be reached by a simple method—1 Concentrate the Indian tribes—viz place all the Indians in Minnesota on the White Earth Reservation, the Indians of New Mexico Colorado & Sioux in the Indian Territory [Oklahoma]—The Indians on the Pacific Coast upon two reserves. . . . 2. Whenever an Indian in good faith gives us his wild life & begins to live by labor give him an honest title by patent of 160 acres of land and make it inalienable. . . . 3 Provide government for every Indian tribe placed upon a reservation.[38]

Here Whipple bemoans what he views as an anachronistic regard for Indian nationhood. His recommendation ("Will you pardon me to make a suggestion") to "concentrate" the Indians into several massive

TERRITORIALITY, ETHICS, AND TRAVEL   157

reservations recalls the Minnesota ethnic-cleansing campaign, where the strategies of bounties, rounding up, imprisoning, and forcibly removing Dakhóta were meant to ensure that no Dakhóta person would remain within the state's borders. Likewise, his call to "provide government," primarily under the guise of applying federal law to punish crimes in Indian country, reveals his sense that Indigenous peoples lacked governance of their own.

Whipple's "concentration" solution to the Indian problem assumes territory's essential fungibility. The realities of Indigenous peoples' moral and ontological landscapes, and their affective relations to the land, simply do not register for him. As Uday Singh Mehta argues, territory's distinctive landscapes are largely invisible within liberalism; their ways of constituting "both a symbolic expression and a concrete condition for the possibility of (or aspirations to) a distinct way of life"[39] stand as a challenge to liberalism's oddly abstract, placeless conception of politics. Rather, territory has and continues to gather together "many of the associations through which individuals come to see themselves as members of a political society."[40] Many such associations appear at the intersection of land or environment, the gendered body, and concepts of family or relatedness. In Black Elk's case, Lakhóta ceremonialism is an embodied practice that creates and maintains intersubjective relations and relations to place, which is reckoned in personalistic rather than objectivist terms. It is thus also a means of remaking ethical and political relationships across the abstract physical space of the settler-state.

Whipple's scheme of genocidal confinement and assimilation was one prominent proposal for consolidating U.S. national space in Dakhóta/Lakhóta territory. Although Grant eventually did suggest to a group of Lakhóta delegates a move to Oklahoma (his suggestion was ignored by the Lakhóta delegates), the United States ultimately relied on tactics of incorporation and translation. In 1980, the U.S. Supreme Court case *U.S. v. Sioux Nation of Indians* held that the Black Hills—spanning what is now called South Dakota and Wyoming—were illegally seized by the United States over one hundred years earlier, in 1877, and that just compensation must be paid. The facts of the case centered around the Treaty of Fort Laramie, where the U.S. government pledged that the territory of the Great Sioux reservation, including the Hé Sápa, would be "set apart for the absolute and undisturbed use and occupation"[41] of the Great Sioux Nation. Further, the Fort Laramie treaty specified that no treaty could cede any part of the resulting reservation unless signed by at least three-fourths of adult male Lakȟóta. Despite this provision, and in retaliation for the Battle of the Little Bighorn, Congress passed an act in 1876 that ratified an "agreement" which had been circulated among the Lakȟóta, but which had in fact been approved by only 10 percent of the adult men.

In effect, the illegal abrogation of the Fort Laramie treaty, and the federal seizure of the Black Hills, converted Lakȟóta homelands and key hunting grounds into unhomely national space. This conversion further imposed a legal calendar in which Lakȟóta ways of reckoning time—and forms of relation—were suppressed and criminalized. For instance, the 1889 Indian agent report for Dakota Territory describes the passage of a law on the Rosebud Agency prohibiting a ceremony in which the spirit of a deceased relative would be kept for a period of time after death. This keeping and releasing of the "soul" in "ghost lodges" was outlawed at the same time as were otúȟ'aŋpi (giveaways), where the immediate relatives of a deceased person would orchestrate a feast and gift giving to all who attended. William K. Powers describes the logic of the giveaway, a practice that appears after the ceremony of releasing the soul as well as in many other Lakȟóta and Dakȟóta contexts: "Once all their personal belongings have been given away, the donors are rendered destitute [úŋšika, a term commonly translated as 'pitiful'] and their neighbors and relatives will take pity on them."[42] Just as in the hanbléčeyapi (crying for a vision ceremony), the immediate family of the deceased, in becoming úŋšika, elicit a generous response from others. In practical terms, the giveaway makes possible the redistribution of economic resources, although this is more of a side effect of the practice than its reason for being: "Usually within a year, at future give-aways, the original donors will become the recipients of goods and money, and eventually the original personal property that they gave away will be replaced."[43] In these giveaways, the primary motive for giving is not economic but existential and ethical—a celebration of solidarity made through shared kinship, lost relatives, and grief. In light of this, Walker describes the memorial feast giveaway as "a thanksgiving (*wopila*) in which the mourner and his or her family acknowledge the help received from neighbors and kin during the one-year period."[44]

I can recall when my grandma, Lillian Chase, whose interview appears as my Third Interlude, passed away. I was very young, maybe seven, but I remember there was a wake in the basement of the Seven Dolors Catholic Church in Fort Totten, and many members of my im-

TERRITORIALITY, ETHICS, AND TRAVEL 159

mediate and extended family were there. Grandma Lily was a fabulous quilter, and some of her work was hanging on the wall as mourners gathered to pray, drink endless cups of Folgers coffee, and sit next to grandma Lily's casket. At the giveaway, some of those quilts went to those who had helped with the wake and funeral. When my maternal grandma, Rachel Charboneau, died, I was grateful to feel the help and prayers of so many people, and it made me see the very different ways of imagining and performing responsibility to relatives who exist between settlers and Dakhóta. My point in recalling these forms of what Kim TallBear calls caretaking, or "more expansive forms of connection and belonging beyond those produced by monogamy and non-monogamy, and their sex centered understandings,"[45] is to suggest that Dakhóta and Lakȟóta people have managed to keep the functions of the thióšpaye going in spite of ethnocidal and genocidal settler laws and policies. Even in conditions of radical subjection, thióšpaye ethics have been mobilized to decolonize relationships, define territory, and remake the Oyáte through everyday actions.

A cosmological explanation for these expansive and generous forms of caretaking appears in Black Elk's account of the origins of the Oyáte. In a series of interviews or teachings given to Neihardt in 1944, Black Elk recounts a story about the culture hero and first chief or headman, Slow Buffalo:

> A long time ago before we have a history, as far as the Sioux could remember back, it used to be they had the seven bands and in these seven bands there was a chief by the name of Slow Buffalo. I figure they were living way out toward where you always face (south) along the edge of the ocean. One day the seven bands got together and they were going to scatter all over the universe. This Slow Buffalo was a chief of the whole seven, but before that this tribe of Indians might have [been] two tribes or one. They expanded and grew to have seven bands. Slow Buffalo, probably his great grandfather, was a chief of one band, but as they grew up and expanded it was getting so it was quite a tribe, so he called all the men and they had a council. He said: "We are seven bands and from now on we will scatter over the world, so we will appoint one chief for each band."[46]

The absence of an objective physical referent is important here (Black Elk's guess that "they were living way out toward where you always face . . . along the edge of the ocean" is as close as it comes), as the account foregrounds how Lakȟóta people inhabited a relational landscape whose boundaries were constituted by an invitation.

The story of Slow Buffalo elaborates the logic of this form of critical relation as being expansive but not possessive, drawing into a thióšpaye relation various lands, peoples, and other-than-human beings through the act of naming: "At this council they named the animals and things. He told the chiefs: 'The Mysterious One [Wakȟáŋ Tȟáŋka] has given us this place, and now it is up to us to try to expand ourselves. We will name every person and every thing.'"[47] This account suggests how the original call to "expand ourselves" means widening the web of peoplehood and extending kinship obligations through sharing of power, material goods, and territory. In practice, the thióšpaye bridges cosmology and political action; it was the basic unit of territoriality because it provided the familial metaphors on which an ethic of gifting, whose ritual sharing of power is at the heart of diplomacy, is founded. The thióšpaye is also where one sees the dynamic relationship between Lakȟóta and non-Lakȟóta forms of land tenure, revealing how Lakȟóta historically reproduced through a variety of social forms, including ceremony, myth, hunting and fishing, household practices, and the enduring, flexible networks of relatives. As Kim TallBear notes in discussing the thióšpaye as an itinerant and migratory social form, "Resisting settlement, whether that's settlement in place, whether that's settlement in a particular discipline or form of knowledge, or whether that's settlement in a particular intimate relationship, especially one sanctioned by the colonial state, that resisting that is not unhealthy, and it's not settling down, but that those kinds of movements constitute healthier relations with all the relations that we need to be attuned to . . . [than the consumptive ones] the settler state has compelled us to build."[48]

Here TallBear invokes resistance to describe movements that are epistemologically unsettling. However, I have sought to show how epistemological reactivation and reclamation during the assimilation era, and something like the rebuilding of "healthier relations with all the relations that we need to be attuned to," occurred in situations that might not seem the least bit resistant or unsettling. I now turn to Black Elk's narrative to examine the ways in which it affirms the importance of mobility again and again for the health of the people in images of the "good red road," a spatial metaphor for decolonial relation that crosses the "hoop" of Lakȟóta peoplehood,

TERRITORIALITY, ETHICS, AND TRAVEL   161

and how one early location for recovering that "road" was in mock ceremonial performances for tourists.

The Ethical Landscape of the Great Vision

In fall 1873, as many Oglálas and Brulés were traveling toward the Rocky Mountains, a nine-year-old Black Elk fell ill while encamped along the Greasy Grass River (Little Bighorn). His legs, arms, and face became badly swollen, and he heard someone say, "It is time, now they are calling you." Lying in his thípi, Black Elk saw two men descend from the clouds, and after announcing that his grandfather was calling him, the men went back into the clouds. Black Elk followed them on his own cloud "and was raised up." As he climbed higher, he saw his father and mother looking at him, and this made him feel sorry to leave. "This all came suddenly," said Black Elk. One key aspect of his narrative is the entrusting of the young boy, by the Six Grandfathers (Black Elk says "they are really the grandfathers and great grandfathers way back which the tribe came from"), with the task of restoring, or "making over," his "nation."[49] Called the "great vision" by scholars and by Black Elk's biographer and (colonial ghost-writer), John Neihardt, this event provided Black Elk with not only power and knowledge to become a healer but also the obligation to restore Lakȟóta to the "good road" of ethical relation that had been lost as a consequence of colonization and the United States' genocidal war. Despite Neihardt's framing of it, the great vision and its later enactments by Black Elk—the horse dance and the heyókȟa, buffalo, and elk ceremonies—constituted a decolonial politics rather than a tragic Indigenous object of settler consumption or the sellout of a former "show Indian." Besides articulating a history of colonization from a Lakȟóta perspective, Black Elk's vision depicts an anticapitalistic logic of circular reciprocity where gifts are given to actively acknowledge relatedness rather than in expectation of a countergift.[50]

To explicate this logic, I focus my reading on the horse dance, as this was Black Elk's vision's central ceremony, and one he saw as the main ceremonial means for decolonizing the Oyáte through unsettling the territorial and psychological confinements created by the reservation system. Black Elk's vision registers how Lakȟóta historicized U.S. settler-colonialism as causing a lack of relatedness among not just tribal peoples but among animals and the earth.[51] This lack, along with the eroding of thióšpaye relationality that is its symptom, are at the heart of what Black Elk means when he says the hoop of his nation had been broken, casting Lakȟóta into the day-to-day situation of despair that Frantz Fanon calls *les damnés*. Fanon writes that "the colonized person . . . perceives life not as a flowering . . . , but as a permanent struggle against an omnipresent death."[52] Laying out some of the structural causes of this sense of life-or-death struggle, Fanon observes that "this ever-menacing death is experienced as endemic famine, unemployment, a high death rate, an inferiority complex and the absence of any hope for the future. All this gnawing at the existence of the colonized tends to make of life something resembling an incomplete death."[53] Typically decolonization has been imagined through individual and collective acts of resistance. But as I have argued throughout this book, decolonizing and remaking communities can occur through, rather than apart from, encounters with oppressive others, and may occur in actions whose political significance appears outside a binary of subversion and resistance.

For instance, Black Elk's mock ceremonial performances of his vision to white tourists sought to transform the disabling effects of settler-colonialism on the psyches of the performers even as they educated white audiences by demonstrating the humanity of Lakȟóta. His performances embodied a radical translational poetics that enlisted whites' participation in what must have seemed an eminently consumable display but that deployed thióšpaye ethics in ways that were unintelligible within an anthropocentric, capitalistic, disenchanted worldview. Because the main decolonial transformation involved in the horse dance is the taking on of the vibrancy of the Wakíŋyaŋ, or Thunder Beings, who are powerful and fearless relatives, one would have to hold to a radically relational—that is, decolonial—view to adequately interpret the performance.

This transformation proceeded from an ethic of the gift, the first indication of which is the act of beholding the other. The act of beholding holds central importance in Black Elk's account of the horse dance, which opens with the appearance of horses from each of the four directions. Black Elk describes these not as cardinal directions but cosmological ones corresponding to different manifestations of power. Indeed, it is an other-than-human power, or spirit, who introduces Black Elk to the visionary horses, saying, "Behold them, for these are your horses. Your horses shall come neighing to you. Your horses shall dance and you shall see. Behold them; all over the universe you have finished."[54] After this, four virgins appear, one of them carrying "the sacred pipe" bundle that was given to Lakȟóta by the cultural hero White Buffalo Calf Woman (Ptesáŋwiŋ) as the means of maintaining Lakȟóta peoplehood.[55] Her presence here grounds Black Elk's vision in Lakȟóta history and its founding ethical gesture, where Ptesáŋwiŋ gives the people a medicine bundle, enabling the ceremonial means for continued relation with all beings. In the originary scene that follows the virgins' appearance, the black spirit of the western powers begins to sing the horse dance:

> My horses prancing they are coming from all over the universe.
> My horses neighing they are coming, prancing they are coming.
> All over the universe my horses are coming.[56]

In reply to this song, one of the horses, a "dappled black stallion," also emanating from the west, "where his home was," begins to sing:

> They will dance, may you behold them. (four times)
> A horse nation will dance, may you behold them. (four times)[57]

The four repetitions of each of these speech acts invoke both the reply of the horses, as "dance," and the black stallion's addressee, Black Elk, to "behold" not just individual horses but "a horse nation"—itself a term that could imply all horses everywhere and through all times, as well as being a common name for Lakȟóta—signaling a call-and-response where the horse's dancing, as acknowledgment of one's existence, only becomes actualized when it has been beheld. "May," then, expresses a conditional possibility: if one attends in a manner that does not grasp or foreclose the being of the other but instead acknowledges and assents to their freedom through beholding, then dancing, as an exuberant reply and mutual nod, will occur.

At this point in the vision, the song of the black stallion "went all over the universe like a radio and everyone heard it," including "all the fowls, beasts, and every living thing heard this horse sing." Because the horse's voice "was more beautiful than anything could be," "everything danced to the music of the horse's song. It was so beautiful that they just couldn't help dancing." This exchange suggests a view of power negotiated between beings—whether human, spirit, or animal—who demonstrate intentionality and who express mutual responsibility, or the refusal to extend the same, toward one another. Rather than being subsumed by the petitioner in the act of being called, they attend in a relation that sustains difference while nonetheless posing an ethical reply. Presence itself becomes the gift here, and as a closer look into the vision's cosmological roots will show, the gift of one's being may work transformatively in a number of ways, not least of all to make a decolonizing rupture in the settler-colonial imaginary. Black Elk's ceremonies perform the gifting of a form of relation that is a negation: not of the material fact of imperial conquest in the name of a greater "civilization," but of the nonrelational attitude undergirding U.S. settler-colonialism. Thus, in each of the performances of the major ceremonies of his vision, Black Elk challenged the fetishizing of natives as anachronistic, doomed, and beautiful.

Some further contextualization around the notion of the gift may elaborate how relation itself might be given, and how gifting works to cut across racialized ontologies to become a means of decolonization. While commodity forms of the gift predominate in a market society, gift giving among Lakȟóta is strongly linked to thióšpaye discourses and to establishing and maintaining relationships at personal, communal, and cosmic levels. Kenneth Morrison argues that "if 'power' differentiates between personal entities who otherwise share the same manner of being, then the category 'gift' becomes the central ethical trajectory of religious practice."[58] Although Morrison is writing about seventeenth-century Algonkian philosophy, these, and his further observation that "positive, powerful others share; negative, powerful others withhold," nonetheless hold true in Black Elk's case. In linking power with gift, Morrison elucidates how kinship, as a way of allying with those outside of or other than the people, went beyond metaphorical analogy to motivate behavioral responsibility and material practices of sharing.

This form of gift giving is tantamount to sacrifice, but in a different sense than that term appears within an exchange paradigm like that of anthropology's oft-theorized notion of the gift. In accounts like Marcel Mauss's and Georges Bataille's, sacrifice cannot transcend the dialectic of debt and repayment, but only seeks freedom for the subject within the dialectic's horizon by converting loss into something positive. Bataille, in his critique of capitalistic utility, names this "constitution of a positive property of loss" as the "sacred" quality of the gift, where he valorizes the gift—particularly in its "archaic" form—as a "sumptuary loss of ceded objects." Although Bataille is interested in finding alternatives to the necessity of a thing-based utility, where value is tied to "the inertia, the lifelessness of the profane world," its fungible objects, and its subjects caught in endless self-objectification, there are significant differences between this and the forms of gift giving and sacrifice seen in, say, the horse dance. Indeed, Bataille's account of how sacrifice allows the one who makes the sacrifice to "enrich himself with a contempt for riches," trading the sacrificed thing in for a power—of symbolic expenditure, that alone for Bataille bars the fetishizing of mere usefulness—strikes me as unrecognizable within the Black Elk transcripts. Still, there are some important resemblances to that context. For one, Bataille's gift enables the recovery of a "lost intimacy" between individuals, and between individuals and the world; this pushes powerfully against the objectifying (both self-objectifying and other) tendencies that undergird state territoriality.[59]

In the symbolic realm, Bataille's notion of sacrifice as "creation by means of loss" points to the example of the isolated individual, the poet who "frequently can use words only for his own loss," because poetry for Bataille is quintessentially the elegiac, the "expression of a state of loss."[60] His poet is one who "is often forced to choose between the destiny of a reprobate, who is as profoundly separated from society as dejecta are from apparent life, and a renunciation whose price is a mediocre activity, subordinated to vulgar and superficial needs."[61] Bataille projects this profound alienation, which is the alienation of an exchange economy—an economy from which Bataille never fully escapes—onto "primitive" or "archaic" customs of exchange such as the potlatch ceremony. Here he bases his reading on the comparative ethnography of Marcel Mauss in *The Gift* (1925), an urtext for anthropological thinking about "primitive" economies. Here Bataille superimposes a capitalistic framework on the potlatch that makes it really into a caricature of a debt-and-repayment model of exchange: "*Potlatch* excludes all bargaining and, in general, is constituted by a considerable gift of riches, offered openly and with the goal of humiliating, defying and *obligating* a rival."[62] Bataille's version of obligation depends on an escalating competition of surfeit, the ideal form of which would lead to forms of destruction, or what he terms "the spectacular destruction of wealth," and ultimately to forms of destruction to which there can be no reply. The "ideal" of a "primitive" process of gifting, writes Bataille, "is realized in certain forms of destruction to which custom allows no possible response."[63] Here gifting forecloses response rather than inviting it; in such an economy, solidarity would be the scarcest of resources. Is this not to be caught within the adversarial realm of the exchange? Despite Bataille's nostalgia for the lost spectacles of wealth and their enduring subversive potential, doesn't this sneakily reproduce the relations of dominance and subjection that are always present in those spectacles?

In contrast, the horse dance vision remakes an ethical economy based on the circulation of gifts. It does this chiefly through its description of what will become, in ritual performance, the transformative adoption of spirits' powers. That the stallion comes from the west is cosmologically meaningful, for instance, because the west is the home of the Thunder Beings, or Wakíŋyaŋ. Julian Rice, in his exegesis of the Black Elk transcripts, captures the density of meanings surrounding the Wakíŋyaŋ: "*Wakinyan* represents the potency and potentiality of the warrior spirit. He begins a process that culminates in the manifestations of tree-splitting destruction and life-giving rain, just as atmospheric percussion becomes the thunder of a *cega* (drum), the hail of a *wagmuha* (rattle), the neighing of a *šunkawakan* (horse), and the words of a *walowan* (singer): 'anpao/hinape/cinhan/šunkawakan wan/hotonwe' 'daybreak/appears/when/a horse neighs.'"[64] The predominant Lakȟóta metaphor of this struggle for realization is that of mounted combat. Frances Densmore's transcriptions of the thunder or heyókȟa vision of Lone Man opens with the dreamer's report of hearing thunder from the west becoming "the sound of hoofs, and I saw nine riders coming toward me in a cloud, each man on a horse of different color."[65] Nine riders then come from each of the other directions, and the men tell him, as Black Elk was also told, to kill an enemy and thereby become "'a member of their company' so that he might 'always call on them for help in time of need.' Although these riders come from four directions, they are all Thunder beings."[66] Rice draws here on ethnomusicologist Densmore's account of the Wakíŋyaŋ, hence the close attention to the aural dimension of the horse dance.

In my family, the Wakíŋyaŋ are a remarkably storied people. My grandma Rachel used to tell me a story about how they took her grandmother's, Makȟáhenamaniwiŋ's, life. One way I heard the story was that the electricity traveled down a stovepipe, jogged a short way across the floorboards, and moved up the metal bed frame and into her sleeping body. My maternal grandma and her sister, Grace, were sleeping in the same bed, but they somehow got away with only minor burns. When the lighting escaped my grandma's neck, it broke with tremendous force, leaving a smell of scorched hair and ozone. But there

TERRITORIALITY, ETHICS, AND TRAVEL

was another image, one that seemed forever untethered from the rest. The morning before the storm, my grandma saw Makháhenamani-wiŋ wailing outside the cabin: facing the hill, and with her back to my grandma, she seemed to be imploring someone who wasn't there. But imploring for what? I had to wait a decade to find out from my grandma Grace. When I asked her, she described how friends and relatives arrived in wagons, and after a rapid-fire genealogy, explained her own puzzlement at something one of them had said:

> They were all coming in wagons. The old man, that was his sister-in-law, she used to be married to his brother, and that's how come she raised Charlie Blackbird, that was Charlie Blackbird's dad, that she used to be married to, but she died. And then Charlie Blackbird's dad, his name was Zitkana Sapa [Black Bird] you know and that was the brother to this Gray Hawk, and here he came in, he just looked at her, and he just, you know, I think there must be signs about these, the way they fixed her hair, like that, and electricity, what it does, because I always remember that old man, "*Hé hé hé*," he said. . . . "It wasn't hard to do," he said. You know, I heard that. It stayed in my mind, but I never, ever said a word about it until way late years after, I think I had children even. I asked my mother one time, "You know when grandma got killed," I said, "that old man came in here. I heard him say that. What did he mean by that," I said, saying you know that you made a mistake, that was as good as what he said, you know when he said. . . . "It's easy to do," he said. But he meant, "Why didn't you do it?"

Grace's wondering about "that old man" saying "it wasn't hard to do" reveals the last turn of the story, which involved a sacrifice:

> And here, my ma said, "She was told to kill one of the grandchildren." But she didn't want to. She thought literally she had to. But see she didn't have to, that's what the old man meant, when he said "It was easy to do." I said, "Well what would she have had to do?" And here my ma said, he told them later, you know, I suppose after I wasn't around, maybe, when he explained that to them, I guess he said she could have taken one of the kid's clothes, like hers or Lydia's or my brother Gabe, one of their coats, went over the hill and filled it with grass, and stabbed it or killed it, you know.

But who told her to kill one of the grandchildren? Was it the Wakíŋyaŋ? And why did the grandma not know that a mock-up version of a grandchild would do as a sacrifice?

The question of using a mock-up in acts of ceremony is one I will return to in a moment. As for who asked for the sacrifice, I can only assume it was the thunders, and when their demand wasn't met, either through misunderstanding or neglect, they claimed my great-great-grandma's life instead of her daughter's and grandchildren's. But from Grace's telling, it seems the keeping of good relations only called for the intention and gesture of sacrifice, not an actual death. In this misunderstanding of the terms of caretaking, there's something of the radically unpredictable that I would later learn was also associated with Wakíŋyaŋ, who in turn are associated with heyókha, or one who dreams of thunder, whom Black Elk's narrative associates with being in close relation with Wakíŋyaŋ. In fact Black Elk's vision is rooted in the contradictoriness of Wakíŋyaŋ and in the radical openness to otherness which that contradictoriness enables. This openness or vulnerability takes on warrior aspects in oral accounts where Wakíŋyaŋ flies from his perch atop a high mountain and flies north to repel what Rice calls "the enemies of growth—greed, pride, and the other invasive wakan šica (bad spirits)."[67]

In a reclamation of a criminalized identity, Black Elk's warrior power, given in his vision through the gift of the "soldier weed of destruction," or soldier medicine, would be used as a decolonial power to settle the "dispute of nations."[68] Presumably this means he would end the settler-colonial occupation of Lakhóta lands, or maybe of all Indigenous lands on Turtle Island. In any case, it's significant that Black Elk refuses to fully act out the duties of this powerful gift. Black Elk accepts the herb that he encounters in his vision just after the horse dance as valuable, perhaps even necessary, but he shows reluctance to ceremonially act out this portion of the vision, where four riders, having been made sacred by the grandfathers, charge into battle. Amid the smoke and "rapid gunfire" of their attack, Black Elk hears "women and children wailing and the horses screaming in fear, dogs yelping." In a parenthetical aside, Black Elk adds that his ritual performance of this power would have made him a chief, but at apparently too great a cost, admitting, in a parenthetical aside, "(I am glad that I did not perform this killing, for I would have not only killed the enemy, but I would probably have killed the women and children of the enemy, but I am satisfied that I have not been well off. Perhaps I would have been a chief if I had obeyed this, but I am satisfied that I didn't become a chief.)"[69] Despite his only partial acceptance of its destructive power, this warrior power remained a powerful decolonial medicine for individual Lakȟóta. At the close of this portion of the vision, Black Elk looks down and notices for the first time "how [he] was dressed," being "painted red" with joints that "were black" with "a white stripe between the joints all over" his body. Black Elk here realizes that he has fully embodied Wakíŋyaŋ as well, not only in the power to destroy but also by assuming Wakíŋyaŋ's location and presence in the sky: "Whenever I would breathe, I would be breathing lightning. My bay horse had lightning stripes on it. The horse's mane was like clouds."[70]

While there is a Bataillean kernel of the simultaneously destructive and creative power of the gift in this account of the soldier medicine, Black Elk's first performances of the horse dance in 1881 reveal its purpose to be liberatory in a different sense: in transforming an interiority of subjection through a ritual sharing of Wakíŋyaŋ's powers. Rice views this moment as "the ritual introduction of fear" that "is a necessary infusion of the force that will become the power to grow."[71] The black horse riders of the vision "incarnate the emergence of courage from fear" by incarnating Wakíŋyaŋ himself, facing the coming storm and singing until it suffuses them, transforming themselves into thunder:

I myself, made them fear.
Myself I wore an eagle relic. . . .

Myself a lightning power I wore.

Myself, hail-like powers I wore. . . .

I, myself, made them fear.

Behold me![72]

After this transformation, Black Elk sees the grandfathers in the clouds (Black Elk adds, "I could see myself too on the clouds as in the vision, but I was on earth really"), who sing to Black Elk, "At the center of the earth may you behold a four-legged." At this, all the horses present begin spontaneously to neigh and prance in affirmation, neighing to the each of the four directions or powers,[73] and processing in a circle with the human participants, themselves offering prayers and petitions for the powers' help to each quarter. Each of these prayers addresses some aspect of renewal: of being unšika, or pitiful and in need of renewal ("Grandfather, behold me. / My people, with difficulty they walk, / May you behold them and guide them. Hear me."), of taking on the power of the thunders that is also the power of the horse nation by becoming one's horse ("My horse neighing as he ran, prancing as he ran. / In a sacred manner he ran. / Behold me!"), or of declaring renewal achieved ("A good nation thus I have made over").[74]

This process of empathizing with what is fearful, to the point of embodying its power, suggests that the ritual renewal of the people that Black Elk sought to achieve hinged on an ethic of power sharing that was not a matter of exchange but of pure gift. The thunder beings respond to the existential condition of being unšika by destroying fear, then giving their cosmic courage as a seed for the renewal of the people that is still to come. This is not a gift of indebtedness but of unilateral sharing. I don't mean to suggest by this that all Lakhóta at all times are utterly selfless or to posit an overly idealized form of ethical behavior. Rather, I want to suggest that the ethical structure of the horse dance gives a fairly direct context and meaning for Black Elk's language of making over his nation, one where gifting creates and recreates enduring bonds of relation or kinship. Gifting does this not through creating obligations but by creating and circulating affective and economic attachments to one another and to the land that do not demand indebtedness or accumulation. Rauna Kuokkanen gives a pan-Indigenous definition of this circulation of gift as a Marxian form of "extended circulation":

> In reciprocity as practiced in terms of indigenous worldviews, gifts are not given primarily to ensure a countergift later on, but to actively acknowledge kinship and coexistence with the world; without this sort of reciprocity, survival—not just of human beings but of other living beings—would be impossible. Thus the main purpose of circular or ceremonial reciprocity is to affirm myriad relationships in the world; from these relationships arise an acknowledged collective and individual requirement 'to act responsibly towards other forms of life.' This kind of reciprocity implies *response-ability*—that is, an ability to respond, to remain attuned to the world beyond oneself, as well as a willingness to recognize its existence through the giving of gifts. This sense of responsibility

embedded in the gift is the result of living within an ecosystem and being dependent on it.[75]

What Kuokkanen describes here as a circular form of reciprocity is what I want to underscore as a Lakȟóta ethic of gift giving that Black Elk's vision and ceremonial performances reactivated in order to provide for the well-being of the people and to sustain peoplehood itself by affirming relationships that help to sustain the people. This aim of renewal at the levels of thióšpaye and Oyáte is repeatedly made by Black Elk in his transcripts, as well as at the end of his account of the horse dance, where he recalls how his people "looked like they were renewed and happy. They all greeted me and were very generous to me . . . , and congratulated me, giving me gifts. Especially the sick people had given me gifts."[76]

One might object here that Black Elk participated in an exchange economy because the gift of his ritual healing was repaid by "the sick people." A phežúta wičáša (medicine man, herbalist, or doctor) conventionally would be given a gift, such as tobacco, in response to the performance of a ritual. I certainly don't want to suggest that there was a single logic of gift giving among Lakȟóta in the early reservation period. Indeed, quite the opposite is true; just as different idioms of kinship bound Lakȟóta to non-Lakȟóta in different ways and for different purposes, with brother-to-brother kinship being reserved for intertribal peacemaking and the relationship of parent to child often being used in diplomatic endeavors with Europeans and Americans, so different forms of gift giving were mobilized for different persons and purposes. The relation between the ceremonial horse riders and Wakíŋyaŋ stands outside of an exchange paradigm and its cult of accumulation, giving a clear alternative to the accumulatory and utilitarian logics of settler society. Bataille is right in saying that the spectacles of loss may create value not caught within this logic. But Black Elk's assessment of his people as being made happy articulates what his ceremonial performance adds to an individualistic and competitive notion of gift giving: it is ultimately the people, and not the individual, who stand to benefit from the generous gifting behaviors of powerful others.

To bring the discussion back to territory, we might now say that Black Elk's performance of the horse dance moves across boundaries demarcating reservation from United States, tradition from future, and even Lakȟóta from non-Lakȟóta. In offering the gift of transforming the fear of colonization, ceremony becomes portable and potent—most of all to those who can read its symbolic content, but affectively, and perhaps to a lesser degree even to outsiders. To some extent, though—and it is not clear from Black Elk's interviews or writings what exactly that extent might be—the extending of relation that was absolutely ordinary and normative within Lakȟóta life may have been one of the intentions behind Black Elk's mock-ceremonial performances to non-Lakȟóta. While there are ceremonial means for the making of kin such as the hunká ceremony, the making of relatives is historically not something especially or necessarily formalized. A contemporary of Black Elk's, Ella Cara Deloria, whose writings I will examine in final chapter, describes how simple awkwardness in conversation resulting from a lack of relatedness might lead to a surprising opening. On her first visit to "a youngish Oglala woman at Pine Ridge who was not related to anyone I knew" (Deloria was a Yankton Dakȟóta), she was obliged "to converse only in Dakota because" the woman "knew no English, and again it was too formal and distant to be 'natural,' without a kinship relationship." "Evidently she felt herself at a disadvantage too, for she remarked on the second day, 'Too bad we are "nothing to each other." I guess we have no one in common.' Then she said later, 'I never had a sister.' She must have had many, at least classificatory [i.e., socially, through kinship], sisters; everyone has. She meant that she was the only daughter of her parents."[77] Deloria reminds us that for Lakȟóta, as with all Dakȟóta bands, to be unrelated is tantamount to social nonexistence, as the woman's expression, "to be nothing to each other," implies. That is, one has no particular social existence outside of the framework of familial relatedness. Deloria goes on to show how this lack of relation could quite easily be overcome and could confer a form of social being and belonging that was "unspeakably comforting." Seeing a "good opening," Deloria tells the woman, "Well, I shall have to be your sister," laughing as she said it "so as not to seem presumptuous, in case that should not be her idea."[78] Even here, when a distant formality governs the dialogue, Deloria displays a certain sensitivity to the ethical texture of their exchange, avoiding the appearance of presumptuousness because it is a decidedly non-Lakȟóta quality. We find then that "apparently it was" her idea as well, "for she agreed eagerly. Right off, then, we began calling each other by kinship term. I said *cuwe* [čhuwé or elder sister], and she said *mita* [mitȟaŋ or younger sister], and as though by magic we were instantly at home with each other. This was a case of establishing kinship without a mutual relative."[79]

My point in closing this section with Deloria's anecdote, and in linking thióšpaye ethics with spatial practices, is to suggest that Lakȟóta ways of making relatives constitute a mobile and flexible geopolitics that decolonizes relations the settler-state attempted to fragment, reify, and isolate. Among Dakȟóta and Lakȟóta, relatedness may be, as Deloria says of her čhuwé, "fabricated out of nothing," replacing that "nothing" with the emotional reassurances of being treated as a family member, often without any further expectation other than to reply in kind. These humble performances of solidarity invoke the original scene of Lakȟóta relation, mapping onto Lakȟóta lands the ethical attitudes that join the present with a deep past. As such, any act of kin making historicizes Lakȟóta relation beyond the moment and symptoms of domination. Turning thióšpaye values into personal and communal relationships is more than simply an act of connecting with the past, though, however the past might be configured. It also is forward looking, a matter of conceiving a future in which ethical relations of the thióšpaye and Oyáte have been reconstructed. An adaptive and expansive notion of territoriality is at work in such ethics, as well as a dynamic interplay between past traditions and future peoplehood. Slow Buffalo's command "to try to expand ourselves" through naming "every person and every thing" thus incorporates others into the social life of the family and band as a gift of relation rather than as indebtedness. Instead of annihilating difference, then, adoption sustains it while extending ethical responsibilities and imperatives for reciprocities. Next I will examine how Black Elk's ceremonial performances offered non-Lakȟóta an encounter with whiteness's other in the guise of the wild Indian in ways that at once appealed to that fantasy while keeping his tribally oriented work out of view.

The Duhamel Indian Pageant: Sharing the Gift

The main purpose of Black Elk's vision was to facilitate Wakíŋyaŋ's giving the gift of decolonial courage as a means of rebuilding the Oyáte. Curiously, perhaps, Black Elk sometimes performed for white tourists to achieve these goals. In doing so he remade thióšpaye bonds across the state-imposed boundaries of reservations and among relatives. In addition to these intrinsically Lakȟóta aims, his performances also unsettled the attitudes of his white audiences. This outward-turning gesture is consistent with the ecumenical approach to difference that we see in the origin story of Slow Buffalo and its imperative to extend kinship to others through diplomacy, adoption, and economic trade. This juxtaposition of audiences and performative roles may draw out the politics of what might otherwise read as playing Indian in a retrograde sense.

In the summer of 1934, Alex Duhamel, a Rapid City businessman and owner of a "trading post" in its downtown, invited Black Elk to perform in an Indian pageant at Sitting Bull Crystal Caverns, a tourist attraction in the Black Hills. Black Elk accepted the offer, and almost every spring and summer for the rest of his life, he traveled with his family, "picking up children en route who had been attending boarding schools during the year."[80] One aspect of Black Elk's participation in the pageant resonates with this image of boarding school children joining the family caravan. Making the drive from Pine Ridge in a truck, rather than in Black Elk's "little Model A Ford," the caravan involved families from multiple reservations all migrating together for the seasonal camp. Black Elk's granddaughter, Olivia Black Elk Pourier, recalls that "people had everything with them, their bedding and all that. If I remember right, about three or four families went and we rode with them. . . . Anyway, we rode in a truck, and we really enjoyed it, because it was open, and we could just see everything."[81] I deliberately avoid calling such travel "seasonal work" because these "migrants" had motives for travel that went beyond simple utility. Or maybe more precisely, their seasonal caravanning was framed by seasonal travels to Hé Sápa that predated reservations, would still be part of living memories (such as Black Elk's), and was motivated as much by the pleasure of being together, through the remembering of traditional gathering, as it was by making money. When the pageant moved from Sitting Bull Caverns to a campground not far away, at Crystal Cave, the number of the encamped grew. David O. Born writes that

> a minimum of twenty-five Native Americans were usually in the . . . camp, although it was common for there to be as many as fifty or more. Families would drift in, stay and participate for a few days or weeks, then move on. The Duhamels provided a secluded campground, water, food, and a 25 percent share in the daily gate. According to Bud Duhamel, the pageant rarely broke even, but "it satisfied the Indians and it satisfied us, so what the heck! What's the difference if you made money or not?"[82]

TERRITORIALITY, ETHICS, AND TRAVEL　175

In other words, the pageant gathering of Lakȟóta was much more than either a spectacle for white consumption or a means of subsistence for the performers; it reasserted the solidarity of human kin as well as of affective relations with Ȟé Sápa. Performing in the pageant allowed Black Elk and his family to reconnect in bodily and storied ways with lands and locales that were historically precious to them. Pourier describes how Black Elk "used to show us where they got their wood and their lodge poles, and then they used to do the sun dance in certain places in the Black Hills."[83] Black Elk then maps the sun dance's location "way back in the Hill—over here by Smithwick, in that direction." Just as the loss of the Black Hills struck at the heart of Lakȟóta peoplehood, the ability to encamp in the proximity of these lands, and to engage in traditional activities like collecting lodge poles, meant a restoration, however temporary, of a portion of Lakȟóta being.

In a remarkably similar way, another major Lakȟóta and Dakȟóta gathering, the Catholic Congress, drew together thióšpaye while being viewed by non-Lakȟóta in ideological terms as contributing to the fight against Indian customs and superstitions. Indeed, the congresses were touted for the role they played in Native peoples' successful transition to "civilized" life. A *New York Times* article from 1892 notes that the second annual Congress, held on the Cheyenne Agency in South Dakota, "opened Sunday with a show of patriotism seldom excelled in civilized communities," with "eight thousand Sioux Indians" traveling "overland in wagons from points from 60 to 600 miles away," and were attended by "all the famous chiefs . . .—Grass and Gall, Little White Bull, Judge Sawn, Hump, Chaska, Campbell, Cora, Belle, and the Babies."[84] This writer states that the main purpose of the Congress was "to dedicate the new church and mission house erected here by Miss Drexel of Philadelphia, and incidentally to celebrate the renewal of cordial relations between the Catholic Church and the Indian Bureau."[85] This hegemonic reading, however, ignores forms of Lakȟóta and Dakȟóta travel and sociality—forms that continued under the sign of "pilgrimage" and "worship," but that also renewed Dakȟóta peoplehood through powwows and feasting. Importantly, they involved all of the Oyáte's reservations and thus gathered together the various thióšpaye into one location. That this gathering would have had great significance for the attendees as an occasion for celebrating solidarity only requires that we remember that the Wounded Knee massacre occurred just two years earlier, and only one year before the first Congress was held. Jesuit historian Louis J. Goll observes that Catholic religiosity did not change the core dynamic of Dakhóta social life, which was based in the circulation of food and hospitality, asking: "When people are willing to be hospitable to visitors out of friendship, why should they change their attitude when religion is added to friendship?"[86]

Goll's rhetorical question captures the ethical continuity between Black Elk's secular or touristic ceremonies and those done for relatives. The congresses were near reenactments of older forms of moving and forming summer camps for sun dances and buffalo hunting.[87] Even when the automobile would have been a commonplace, many congress participants arrived on horseback (Figure 4). As a remembrance and redeployment of tradition, then, this event concentrated a far-flung bunch of relatives into a single location. The act of travel itself redrew the map of Lakhóta territory as continuous rather than being made sundry and conflictual by reservation boundaries.[88]

Like the attendees at the Catholic congresses, the performers involved in the Duhamel Indian pageant negotiated between multiple sets of motives, including settler co-optations of Indigenous identity and intratribal ones of revitalizing the Oyáte. From even a cursory reading of an advertisement for the pageant, it would seem these latter resurgent motives remained opaque to white audiences, who were lured by the promise of an Indian spectacle. As with other venues, like Wild West shows, the pageant framed Indianness as nostalgia or as violent spectacle (as with Buffalo Bill's war scenes), by which Indianness could be rendered harmless and consumable. A postcard advertised the pageant's reenactment of "old time tribal ceremonies" as "Interesting, Historical, Educational, Glamorous."[89] Faithful to this hodgepodge of motives or effects, the pageant staged ethnographic aspects of supposedly traditional Lakhóta life, including a burial rite, oratory, pipe ceremony, healing ceremony, "love call," sun dance, and horse dance—one program lists seventeen different acts. "Glamor," presumably, resulted from how the spectacle went beyond static, museum dioramas of an anthropological, "aspects of social life" narrative to include real, live "Sioux Indians." Part of the affective payout of the pageant for settler audiences was the return of the repressed, neatly summarized by a postcard advertisement's closing lines: "The war cry of the last savage mingling with the soft beat of the tom tom will make your blood tingle" (Figure 5).[90] The postcard expectedly conflates the Indian pageant with the cavern's geological timelessness and

FIGURE 4. "Procession on Horseback at Catholic Sioux Congress, 1923." Marquette University Archives, Bureau of Catholic Indian Missions Records, Milwaukee, Wisconsin, ID 10294.

naturalness, equating the "blind fish" swimming in the underground pools with the Indian performers. For other audience members, it was an opportunity to engage in a less salacious form of exchange. Some, writes Raymond DeMallie, "were seriously interested in Indian culture, like Reginald and Gladys Laubin, students of Indian dance and traditional arts and crafts, who visited the pageant in order to talk with Black Elk and the other old men."[91] Still others, including Lakȟóta from nearby reservations, came to join in the dancing.

Despite these exoticizing narratives, the pageant ceremonies participated in a highly mediated form of gifting, enlisting settler publics as unwitting participants in a ceremony of tribal renewal, in that the pageant partially reenacted Black Elk's horse dance. One way it did so was through enactments of Black Elk's visionary ceremonies. DeMallie, for instance, views Black Elk's touristic ceremonies as mobilizing Lakȟóta culture beyond both the individual practitioner (Black Elk) and beyond existing geopolitical boundaries (like the Pine Ridge reservation). This expansive and marginally inclusive mode of performance thus helped Black Elk to live up to his obligation to share his vision. DeMallie argues that by helping to "bring about a better understanding of his people" through an appreciation of "their moral worth," Black Elk made real his wish "to make his vision 'go out.'"[92]

FIGURE 5. "Duhamel Sitting Bull Crystal Cavern and Sioux Indian Pageant." Postcard circa 1940s.

This reading of the pageant highlights one aim as the humanizing of Indigenous people. Rather than being solely the commodification of an exotic other, certain stagings and venues brought white audiences into close proximity with Indigenous performers. Similarly, the brochure's descriptions of Lakȟóta tools like the travois refuse any fundamental difference between the "Sioux" and whites. Describing how "the travois were the wagon of the Sioux," the brochure seems to debunk a social evolutionist view:

> It is claimed by experts that the Indians never used wheels because they never traveled far enough to learn their benefits. However, the writer disagrees with this as the Sioux traveled hundreds of miles each year, and the reason they never hit on wheels was because, in the first place, they didn't have heavy enough loads to overburden the horse, and then too the travoy would follow right side up any place the horse could go, where with a two or four-wheeled vehicle this is practically impossible.[93]

In the actual stagings of the pageant—about which we know very little, given the scarcity of accounts[94]—there is in addition to making the vision "go out" also a kind of conservation motive at work. Rather than making Lakȟóta culture transparent, commodifiable, and im-

TERRITORIALITY, ETHICS, AND TRAVEL

mediately apprehensible through full performances of ceremonies, the versions that tourists saw were fictions. Black Elk's grandchildren note that the pageant's ceremonies "weren't the real thing—it was a pageant."[95] When asked by their interviewer whether what was shown were "actually sacred ceremonies," Black Elk's grandchildren's reply is disarmingly direct: "No, they wouldn't do that." If that is so, and the empty pot reads as a figure for crucial meanings withheld from the performance, it might be easy to conclude that the pageant didn't refer to any tribal reality. But given Black Elk's self-positioning as a teacher of Lakȟóta and non-Lakȟóta alike, it's possible that Black Elk's staged performances cordoned off certain tribal knowledge while also assuming—as his vision demanded—a decolonial stance toward whites. In this sense there is an insistence that some aspects of Lakȟóta life remain opaque (we can perhaps hear the decolonizing cry of Édouard Glissant's call for "the right to opacity for everyone"[96]), as well as the possibility that a certain obscurity maintains despite a literally dramatic, or staged, opening up of local knowledge.

Black Elk's granddaughters recall a kettle dance that was performed during the heyókȟa káǧa (literally, to make heyókȟa), a ceremony performed by Lakȟóta who had dreamed of the Wakíŋyaŋ. The kettle dance songs are performed by the heyókȟa, who dance around a pot filled with boiled dog meat, upon which everyone feasts at the end of the ceremony. They thrust their hands into the boiling water and complain, as a contrary ought, that it is too cold. In the pageant version, however, Esther Black Elk DeSersa remembers that "they did not really have anything cooking in the pot; they just danced around it."[97] Nonetheless, the cosmological context for embodying and sharing power is present here, through sharing and eating food that had been transformed by the heyókȟa. Likewise, the sun dance didn't involve actual piercing of the flesh or prolonged dancing; instead, "dancers were tied to the center pole by ropes attached to halters worn around the back." According to one account by Emma Amiotte, a friend of Bud Duhamel's, "the dancers blew on their eagle bone whistles, straining on the ropes, giving a good impression of a real sun dance."[98]

Black Elk's later conferring of Lakȟóta ceremonial knowledge to non-Lakȟóta also speaks to his motivation to expand the hoop of Lakȟóta peoplehood. In a letter dated May 15, 1947, Black Elk writes to his friends, Claude and Frances Hansen, about his wish to travel to Denver to work in a pageant there. Black Elk addressed and regarded the Hansens as "grandchildren," and had given them the names Curly

Bear and White Buffalo Calf Woman as a formal recognition of social kinship. Black Elk's letter reveals a mingling of financial and religious concerns. On the one hand, Black Elk is concerned with securing work for himself and his family, and expresses his frustration with the Duhamel pageant. "I want to get away from the other show in Black Hills," he writes, where a "richer white guy wants to use me as a chief of the whole show but I rather be in Denver this summer. My son Nick Jr. will get a job to work there while I take in the show job so we planned it."[99] The identity of the "richer white guy" is not clear from these late letters from Black Elk to his Denver kin; nor is it important for our purposes. Rather, Black Elk's distaste for being made "chief of the whole show" signals an important shift in the discursive focus of the pageant—one that moved away from a more broadly inclusive representation of Lakȟóta domestic and religious life and toward an uncomfortably individualistic spotlight on Black Elk as an iconic front-man. Against this turn of events, Black Elk shows a desire in this letter to teach his adopted Denver grandchildren about Lakȟóta ceremonialism, writing, "I sure like [indecipherable] makes me teach you + lots of cultures about that Peace Pipe Ceremony: so that's why I'd like to come to Denver." A letter written a year later, in 1948, by Black Elk's son, Benjamin, describes his spending time with his father at the Sioux TB Sanitarium, in Rapid City, where Black Elk was recovering from a stroke. "I was with him all winter," he writes, "and learned a lot from him all that I learned is written down, in Sioux dialect. Besides the history of the Portable Altar, The pipe."[100] This history of "the pipe," or the ceremonies given to Lakȟóta by Ptesáŋwiŋ, was told to Joseph Epes Brown by Black Elk the previous year and was published as *The Sacred Pipe: Black Elk's Account of the Seven Sacred Ceremonies of the Oglala Sioux* (1953). Black Elk's stated purpose behind this collaboration was to help Lakȟóta and, more generally, to restore proper relation to all peoples. At the end of the dedication to *The Sacred Pipe*, he writes how he "wished to make this book through no other desire than to help my people in understanding the greatness and truth of our own tradition, and also to help in bringing peace upon the earth, not only among men, but within men and between the whole of creation."[101]

Do we conclude from these acts of sharing that Black Elk thought Lakȟóta ceremonialism, as given by Ptesáŋwiŋ long ago, would transform settler society? Maybe. But more, it seems that he thought that in transmitting what he would call in a letter to Curly Bear and White

Buffalo Calf Woman the "good words and the light of the once proud Sioux Indian Religion,"[102] a transformation among Lakȟóta people would occur. That his non-Lakȟóta friends were impresarios in Denver mattered a great deal to Black Elk, as their patronage meant that the rituals of his vision would continue. Black Elk suggests to them that, as with the pageants, "reading this [*The Sacred Pipe*] through your knowledge. . . . Indians will be deeply understood. I take courage, Curly Bear for the Indians need you and your ability."[103] This letter reveals both a conviction born of friendship (Black Elk reveals in another letter to his family that he wanted to give the name "Slow Buffalo," after the Lakȟóta hero, to Curly Bear) and a savvy understanding of how discourses about natives circulated in non-Indigenous communities through commercial venues like pageants. Black Elk's letter to Curly Bear shows a faith in the transformative potential of ritual performance to broker the giving of power as decolonial courage and relational empathy.

Through his words, visions, and travels, Nicholas Black Elk occupied a uniquely ambivalent position of Indigenous celebrity and unheroic decolonizer. But instead of being disabled by confinement on the Pine Ridge reservation, he used his renown to travel across settler-colonial borders, remaking as he went long-standing networks of Lakȟóta movement, reconnecting especially with Ȟé Sápa by camping there in the summer while performing in Alex Duhamel's Indian pageant throughout the 1940s. Couching the resurgence of thióšpaye ethics of gift giving and sufficiency in tourist's shows, he ciphered these in the empty kettles and unpierced breasts of his and his fellow performers. But as my family's story about the Wakíŋyaŋ demonstrates, even a mock-up may get the job done, and in the case of Black Elk's pageants, that job was to demonstrate to other Lakȟóta a more egalitarian and entangled relationship with other beings than what the settler-state had imposed through its privatizing of land and family. This opening of representational territory for the Oyáte was preliminary, as with Dakȟóta prisoners' letters to their relatives and Eastman's literary output. In my next chapter I show how Dakȟóta author and ethnographer Ella Cara Deloria's novel *Waterlily* sought to place an unciphered thióšpaye ethics as the basis of the Oyáte, and in full view of settler audiences.

4 Peoplehood Proclaimed

*Publicizing Dakhóta Women in
Ella Cara Deloria's* Waterlily

All that which lies hidden in the remote past is interesting, to be sure, but not so important as the present and the future. The vital concern is not where a people came from, physically, but where they are going, spiritually.

—Ella Cara Deloria, *Speaking of Indians*

I notice that in the Sioux country, children of white men and Indian mothers are steeped in folklore and language, but children of white mothers and Indian fathers are often completely cut off from the tribal folk-ways. If every Dakota woman disappeared today, and all the men took white wives, then the language and customs would die, but otherwise I do not see how they would.

—Ella Cara Deloria to Franz Boas, August 7, 1940

In "There Is a River in Me," Dian Million (Tanana Athabascan) remarks how academic proprieties can mark off certain stories and experience as illegitimate forms of knowledge. She explains how survivors' testimonies about residential or boarding schools in Canada and the United States are an especially powerful form of Indigenous knowledge and theorizing in that they "engage in questioning and reformulating those stories that account for the relations of power in our present."[1] Testimony or story, she argues, "*is* Indigenous theory."[2] In the Interludes of this book, the stories of my relatives bear out how such Indigenous theory—whether about decolonization, Indigenous peoplehood, relationality, or otherwise—does not need to take the form of abstract propositions in order to offer richly felt interpretation, self-reflection, and ways of experiencing the world. There is theory, as the enculturing of place and the refusal of sexual violence, when my grandma Lily said about the place called Íŋyaŋ Watháŋka on the Spirit Lake reservation, "Then there was this guy and this girl. He must have hit her, so that girl was running away with her baby on her back. She went down the hill and that guy followed her. He was getting close so she sat down like this and, here, she turned into a stone . . . So that's a woman sitting there. She had a baby on her back and she made herself into a rock. They should write out a big story about that and honor that rock."

Her story about a radical failure to respect one's partner is in dialogue with the literary depictions of the Oyáte I examined in my other chapters, and as a whole, this book also participates in a larger story that reframes Dakhóta reemergence and resurgence under an assimilationist regime. I have traced the beginnings of Dakhóta resurgence to the translational citing, reclaiming, and adapting of the thióšpaye's core ethics under assimilation policy, and how these modes of relating to one another were taken up and reworked in the wake of the 1862 U.S.–Dakhóta War to articulate the people, the Oyáte, away from the gaze of the settler-state. The ethics they hold are not essential and unchanging things but rather fragile ways of life under constant surveillance and assault. Yet I agree with Million's view that in spite of the violence done to Indigenous peoples, it is not victimry that orients our storytelling, our theorizing, but rather enduring locales, including those most intimate locales of the body that have held us close: "The life-affirming stories of [our] enduring experiences in these places, these places that are inhabited by our ghosts, our spirits, the spirits of the potentia, the life force itself."[3] This final chapter turns to the locales of Dakhóta/Lakhóta femininity as foundational to a resurgent peoplehood as it appears in Yankton anthropologist and novelist Ella Cara Deloria's (Aŋpétu Wašté Wíŋ, or Beautiful Day Woman) literary and ethnographic writings.

Deloria was born in 1889 at White Swan on the Yankton reservation and was raised in Wakpala on the Standing Rock reservation. By one of few Indigenous novelists writing in the United States during the first half of the twentieth century, her only novel, *Waterlily*, went unpublished until 1988. Deloria's father was Philip Joseph Deloria (Thípi Sápa, or Black Lodge), one of the first Episcopal priests to be ordained among the Dakhóta. Her mother, Mary Sully Bordeaux, was French Dakhóta and had been raised speaking Dakhóta, which remained the first language in the Deloria home. This linguistic and cultural backdrop positioned Deloria to work with Franz Boas at Columbia University, a collaboration that would lead to the collecting and transcribing of traditional Dakhóta tales that she published in 1932 as *Dakota Texts*. Building on my previous chapter's analysis of the decolonial space carved out by nonhierarchical or anarchic Lakhóta concepts of animacy/inanimacy, my reading here examines Deloria's reclamation of a Dakhóta/Lakhóta gender binary and gender roles, and how she ciphered these in and through the genre of the straight romance novel as a way of disaggregating the compulsory monogamous heterosexuality that held over from allotment policy. By invoking the determinate language of gender roles, I should add a precautionary note here at the outset that I regard gender performatively or as fundamentally revisable. My readings of Dakhóta/Lakhóta gender depictions, whether in Deloria's work, in the ethnographic record, or in living oral histories, begin from the assumption that gender, as a discourse about the sexed body, would be almost infinitely variable, were it not for that variability being foreclosed, as Judith Butler puts it, "by certain habitual and violent presumptions."[4]

As a Dakhóta woman and strong advocate for the church, Deloria was a cultural broker who shared the ambivalent positioning of the other Dakhóta intellectuals in my previous chapters. At certain moments in her career, she portrayed Indigenous peoples in starkly assimilationist terms, writing in *Speaking of Indians* that "tribal life is only a phase in human development anyway," and that "the next step, for every people, is national life."[5] She concedes in that same work that "nobody knows and appreciates the fact any more than Indians themselves that there were splendid disciplines in the old culture to sustain and strengthen its people," but that "as time goes on, those disciplines lose their force."[6] What could fill the void was the church because "no other institution is so well-equipped to offer friendship, sympathy, wise counsel, and unselfish assistance to all who need it."[7] This may seem an unequivocally proassimilationist declaration, but it is softened and made complicated by Deloria's accounts in the same text of kinship as "the ultimate aim of Dakota life," because to "obey kinship rules" and "be a good relative" was to be "a good Dakota" and so "be humanized, civilized."[8]

Her novel *Waterlily*, written after *Speaking of Indians* during the 1940s, elaborates this positive portrayal of kinship values. Based heavily on ethnographic field notes gathered during the 1920s through the 1940s, it imagines Dakhóta life in the 1830s, before the imposition of the reservation system and the arrival of missionaries like those of the American Board Commission of Foreign Missions. *Waterlily* tells the story of a young Thíthuŋwaŋ (Lakȟóta) woman named Blue Bird, whose thióšpaye is destroyed by an enemy war party in a raid. She and her grandmother "wandered blindly" across the plains, but for only two days, after which they are taken in by another camp circle whose "people were their kind and spoke their dialect."[9] Even in its narrative setup, it describes an act of communal reconnection and familial reconstruction.

Other scholars have emphasized the pedagogical and reconstructive role of *Waterlily*'s depictions of thióšpaye life. Maria Cotera argues that the novel is a project of tribal revitalization that was in line with the IRA politics of the 1930s and 1940s, which purported to preserve Indian customs. She adds that its focus on women "was a consummately political one and that it represented (for its time) a fundamentally new approach to the project of tribal survival."[10] Mark Rifkin asserts that Deloria's novel mobilizes the political potential of kinship in the thióšpaye to provide alternative ways of imagining social relationship that allotment policies had suppressed.[11] These illiberal forms of relation, Rifkin argues, remained the de facto objects of administrative regulation in spite of the Indian Reorganization Act's claims, or as John Collier puts it, to "set up permission to the Indians to work out self-government which is appropriate to the[ir] traditions."[12]

My reading of *Waterlily* is largely sympathetic with both Cotera's and Rifkin's, and especially with Cotera's reading of Deloria as a decolonial author who reclaimed preallotment women's roles as an imaginative means to remake the Oyáte. I give ethnographic and literary flesh here to Cotera's analysis by reading *Waterlily* alongside *Dakota Texts*, Deloria's ethnographic field notes, and her "Pageant: The Wohpe Festival." I juxtapose these in order to account for the omission of certain ethnographic material from the novel that Deloria had originally intended to include, such as the wíŋkte, or Dakȟóta/ Lakȟóta third gender, and the "perpetual virgin," or nonreproductive woman. Rifkin reads Deloria's decision to cut what she called "all that winkte element" as both a form of protective withholding and evidence of taking "the bribe of straightness."[13] As the former, it suggests "the presence of social room for the winkte while not outright naming the role as such and perhaps signaling that Deloria can be understood as fulfilling a traditional role in the novel's act of ethnographic remembrance."[14] As the latter, it illustrates a dynamic where "marginalized persons and groups . . . play aspects of normality against each other as part of a counterhegemonic claim to legitimacy, distinguishing themselves from other, more stigmatized modes of deviance."[15] Here Rifkin's enlisting of Deloria and other Native authors in a present-day project of queer critique, and his subsequent disappointment with her performance of it, projects a kind of ahistorical desire for sex/gender resistances to the settler-state. I raise this point in appreciation of Rifkin's otherwise excellent reading and to note how it prevents us from seeing how Deloria's gender depictions across her writings assert not just cultural difference (as tradition, from the vision of Indigenous sociality endorsed or mandated by the IRA) but also Dakhóta/Lakȟóta indigeneity as radical or incommensurable difference.

I focus in particular on how Deloria's centering of Dakhóta women's perspectives and social power as caretakers of the thióšpaye and guarantors of the Oyáte appear as a resurgent gender politics. Deloria packaged her gender politics within a conventional heterosexual romance, the conventionality of which facilitates an ethnographic ruse of tradition that appears harmless to settler sex and gender norms. Like Black Elk, Eastman, and the Dakhóta prisoners I examine in my previous chapters, I argue here that Deloria's ambivalent relationship with straightness provides opportunities for subversive withholdings and future-oriented translations of Dakhóta/Lakȟóta life, and her omissions of certain content from the novel's final version are best understood in terms of this positioning rather than editorial contingencies or personal conservatism. While Deloria's sex and gender depictions are no doubt heteronormative, the matrilineal and matriarchal aspects of the novel, and not just the thióšpaye's extension of family to a wide array of relatives, are ultimately refusals to participate in norms of the monogamous couple and nuclear family.

In a letter to anthropologist Ruth Benedict, Deloria wrote about her mixed feelings over her unpublished ethnography, *A Dakota Way of Life*, noting how it contained "a practical demonstration of some of the cross-currents and underneath influences of Dakota thinking and life," but that she "can't possibly say everything *frankly*, knowing that it could get out to the Dakota country." Despite Deloria's reluctance over scandalizing both her settler and Dakhóta audiences, *Waterlily* depicts some of the "underneath influences" of thióšpaye life, including figures like the nonreproductive perpetual virgins and the sexually promiscuous Double Women. These citations are muted translations or traces of some of the material collected in her ethnographic fieldwork, including gender identities beyond a heterosexual binary and accounts of female sexual immorality. Her accounts of powerful negative women who demonstrate selfish or excessive behaviors are just as pedagogically important as those of powerful positive ones, like Woȟpé and White Buffalo Calf Woman, whose generosity is foundational to Lakȟóta peoplehood. Although these presences are muted in *Waterlily* (in this I agree with Rifkin, who notes them as "traces"), they are available to those in the know. Creating readers who were in the know was part of Deloria's hope for her ethnographic archive. In her preface to the 2009 edition of *Waterlily*, Susan Gardner notes how Deloria "hoped that her materials would be made available to graduate students in anthropology,"[16] including, I imagine, Dakȟóta/Lakȟóta like herself. This orientation toward the future Oyáte is worked out within settler structures of Indigenous legibility, as Deloria's granddaughter, Joyzelle Godfrey, states in an interview: "Deloria's primary goal in both her ethnographic research and her writing was less about making the Dakȟóta people intelligible to whites than it was about providing Dakȟóta people with a body of information about traditional culture with which to rebuild an autonomous and thriving nation."[17]

Godfrey's reading of audience underscores the politics of legibility and opacity that I have discussed throughout this book under the term of decolonial translation. Because Deloria was an anthropologist, her readers, then and now, might assume that she was invested in at worst collecting data about the Lakȟóta for the sake of gaining settler understanding and at best creating an archive for future Lakȟóta. In any case, her involvement with ethnography as a means of producing a knowable racialized or ethnic subject brings her into orbit with what Denise Ferreira da Silva, Audra Simpson, Andrea Smith, and others have called "ethnographic entrapment": the condition of Indigenous subjects' eminent knowability and simultaneous effacement of Indigenous access to power and historical knowing.[18] For Indigenous anthropologists like Deloria, ethnographic entrapment is an opportunity for intervention and critique, as Smith has argued, in the refusal to reveal certain details.[19] But it also requires engaging with larger structures of settler-colonial oppression and racialization within which the ethnographic is the description of a difference that is always already available to be narrated and contained. As such, ethnographic entrapment is part of the politics of recognition like those of the IRA, which, despite its efforts to devolve decision-making power back to tribes, did so by regulating "the old Indian traditions of self-government," or by "permitting" powers of self-government that

PEOPLEHOOD PROCLAIMED 189

revolved largely around settler notions of "acquiring and managing property" and making contracts.[20]

Indian Reorganization and the Liberal Bargain

The second section of *Speaking of Indians*, titled "A Scheme of Life That Worked," is Deloria's scholarly meditation on the Dakhóta ideal of kinship. She argues there that the main purpose of kinship was to insure against the existence of social atomization, or "haphazard assemblages of heterogeneous individuals" who would be left outside of relation as such, and so outside of being human.[21] Without the aim of obeying kinship rules and being "a good relative . . . the people would no longer be Dakota in truth. They would no longer even be human. To be Dakota, then, was to be humanized, civilized." Deloria's linking of the human with being Dakota through kinship—or more precisely through the performance of kinship, by upholding kinship law rather than simply by accident of birth—invokes historical meanings of the adjective "dakhóta" as one who feels affection for another, or is friendly.[22] This reworking of the meaning of civilization not only inverts the imperial binary of center and periphery, asserting settler society's utmost periphery—the tribal—as the location for humanness and law, but also transforms the criteria by which civilization may be known. Like Eastman did through his animal stories and autobiographical works, Deloria rewrites civilized as a function of ethical relation rather than being evidenced through material power, and as the negation of uneven economic development or unequal distribution of capital rather than their guarantor. She comments, for example, that, "by kinship all Dakota people were held together in a great relationship that was theoretically all-inclusive and co-extensive with the Dakota domain."[23]

By linking kinship with the utilitarian suggestion of her section title, "A Scheme of Life That Worked," Deloria attempts a difficult mediation. How to make the concept of kinship intelligible within a liberal framework of rights that accrue to, as Deloria calls them, "heterogeneous individuals"? Legal historian Gloria Valencia-Weber describes this problem of intelligibility in her claim that "the unique collective right that tribal sovereigns insist on retaining does not fit the usual constitutional conversation about the individualized 'who' and 'what' activities shall be cognizable and protected."[24] For Deloria's fellow Dakhóta and assimilation-era author Charles Alexander Eastman, one way was to sue for rights from the U.S. government through claiming the legal subjectivity of a unified people. But despite Deloria's negotiating forms of scientific racism and a cult of anthropological salvage that regarded Indigenous peoples, languages, and lifeways as artifacts, her response to liberalism was less mediated than Eastman's. Indeed, it was more of an outright separatism. Her defining of kinship against the liberal individual is a refusal of social constellations where race, class, and gender have converged around heterosexual, monogamous marriage and the nuclear family. By widening the domain of kinship to include animals, spirits, and the land, Deloria disturbs the distinction between nature and culture, and thus sets the stage to recover, as a site of political resistance, a discredited nature that federal Indian law has instrumentalized and regarded only as property.

Waterlily responds to the damage wrought by adopting settler notions of family and the subsequent damage of disavowing one's kinship with other Dakhóta by declaring them to be inferior. Sociologist Amalia Sa'ar describes this dynamic of internalized racism as one effect of taking the "liberal bargain": the process by which "members of disadvantaged groups become identified with the hegemonic order, at least to a degree."[25] The specific mode of identification she examines is one whereby a member of what she calls a marginalized group stands to gain benefits from liberal orders, despite their "hierarchical and selective character."[26] Rather than viewing such identification simply as necessarily a sellout or betrayal of other forms of identity, Sa'ar sees the liberal bargain as a site of socially "intermediate and dynamic states" in its adoption of "modes of knowing" that include "different levels of commitment ... [which] tend to range from internalizing and actively promoting liberal authority, to working with it for short-term gains while avoiding conflicting emotional investment, to passive and active forms of resistance."[27] While Sa'ar's analysis focuses on the liberatory potential of taking the liberal bargain in a contemporary Palestinian context, highlighting how it may be used by people living under oppressive conditions, I would highlight how Deloria shows its negative potential to disable existing forms of subjectivity as well as peoplehood.

This negative potential appears as a continued assault on thióšpaye ethics despite the formal ending of federal allotment policy in the midst of Deloria's most productive period of writing in the 1930s and 1940s. In 1934 Congress passed the Wheeler-Howard or Indian Reorganization Act, which sought to reverse assimilationist policies and begin an era of greater Native self-determination. It proclaimed "to conserve and develop Indian lands and resources; to extend to Indians the right to form business and other organizations; to establish a credit system for Indians; to grant certain rights of home rule to Indians; to provide for vocational education for Indians; and for other purposes."[28] The act had three main goals, which historian Frederick Hoxie summarizes as halting the individualization of Indigenous community resources, restoring tribal institutions and forms of collective decision making (such as the thióšpaye), and endorsing the compatibility of U.S. and tribal citizenship. In total, these goals would help to ensure that Indianness would have a continuing place in American life.[29] Like allotment, though, the IRA was framed within an ideal of progress, no longer cast in terms of outright assimilation to "civilizational" ideals of bourgeois individualism and property, but instead as a matter of establishing tribal business and governance in bourgeois and representational democratic molds. In so doing, John Collier declares, "it does not seek to impose on the Indians a system of self-government of any kind," but only "sets up permission to the Indians to work out self-government which is appropriate to the traditions, to their history and to their social organization."[30]

While the IRA proclaimed in this way a de jure end to the forms of detribalization—via the imposition of liberal forms of land ownership and individualism—inaugurated by the General Allotment Act of 1887, in effect it did not constitute a radical makeover of federal Indian policy. For one, allotment had created a fair number of assimilated Native individuals who objected to a systematic return to older social forms, and in particular to forms of communal life. One prominent institution that promoted an assimilationist discourse in its most radical rhetoric was the American Indian Federation, a national organization founded in June 1934 that aimed to repeal the IRA, remove the Indian commissioner, John Collier, and abolish the Bureau of Indian Affairs. The arguments made for these abolitions were multiple, of course, and not entirely attributable to a disavowal of kinship bonds or other markers of Indigenous identity. For one, the AIF held that the IRA was emergency legislation designed to end further Native land loss, and was therefore most applicable to nations like the Oneida in Wisconsin, who had lost 99 percent of their lands under allotment policies, but irrelevant to other Native peoples such as the Seneca, who had not been allotted, and who had an elected system of governance since 1848.[31] This critique was essentially of the federal "one size fits all model" of Native governance.

Other arguments levied by the AIF asserted that the IRA would increase, rather than lessen, federal supervision over Indian country, and that the act's defining of Indianness according to blood quantum perpetuated allotment's racial logic rather than devolving the definition and regulation of tribal citizenship to Native nations, many of which followed kinship logics of matrilineal or patrilineal descent to determine enrollment.[32] In its more radical statements, though, the AIF decried the IRA's advocacy for a return to communal forms of land ownership and decision making by using a far right rhetoric. Historian Laurence M. Hauptman notes that "the organization frequently red-baited and thus received nationwide attention. It accused to the commissioner and his program of being anti-Christian, atheistic, having the support of the American Civil Liberties Union, and being communist inspired."[33] Mediating these critiques was another position that deployed a rhetoric of rugged individualism and that viewed government intervention as damaging to individual initiative. This view was represented most prominently by an Oklahoma faction of the AIF leadership. One Cherokee named Lone Wolf, at one of the congresses where community members debated the IRA, insisted on Native incorporation within the federal economy (and ideology), and declared that he would rather "pay taxes and be a man among men than a useless Indian forever."[34] The AIF revealed a vocal contingent of Native politicians who did indeed see the liberal bargain as a means of promoting both individual and tribal autonomy.[35]

Deloria's ethnographic work for Boas in the 1920s allowed her a unique perspective on the extent to which allotment and reorganization policies had affected Dakhóta kinship laws and bonds. In Deloria's 1937 unpublished transcripts of her interviews with Dakhóta men and women, "Dakota Autobiographies," one interviewee, an Oglála woman named Emmy Valandry, reveals an introjected racism as she recounts her memories of the aftermath of the Wounded Knee massacre. The excerpt, worth quoting at length because it lays out the (liberal) contrast to Deloria's kinship-based depictions of gender and ethics, begins with Valandry musing about the ghost dancers she had seen before the massacre, and wondering why they did not assimilate as she and her husband had done:

> "Why are they so foolish? why don't they simply give themselves
> up and settle down somewhere peaceably and unmolested," I was
> thinking to myself. ...

> People kept going there to look on, but as for me, I only went that once; I didn't like them, so I didn't go again. Smelling of blood, looking so dirty, they were spoiling our church; they were yelling so hard now, when really it was their own fault for being intractable.
>
> One of the wounded was a young woman with a gunshot wound this big, opening into a dark hole, and her gown was all but torn completely off her; and she sat with her hair coming unbraided, and she moaned with every breath.[36]

Following this passage is a long description of similar scenes of suffering in a church that served as a makeshift hospital for survivors of the massacre. It shows Valandry striking a similar pose of scornful judgment, as when she faults the wounded and dying for their unwillingness to modernize: "People kept going there to look on, but as for me, I only went that once; I didn't like them, so I didn't go again. . . . Really it was their own fault for being intractable."

Valandry shows no sympathy toward the dying, laying blame for their deaths on their lack of a civilizational identity as respectable individuals. This lack is indicated most clearly by their "intractable" practice of ghost dancing. Here racism joins with classism and religious intolerance, while all of these forms of objectification pass through repressed loyalties to relatives, as well as through older or "traditional" gender constructions. Ironically, her mother and other women enact these in their preparing of food and coffee for the sick: "I went with my mother to the commissary, and she selected deliberately the cuts of beef and other foods, and they were turned over to her. An employee brought the things to our place and immediately my mother made a broth, and coffee, and several women assisted her in taking the food to the sick."[37] What results is a complex picture of how colonial ambivalence could be disabling, as with Valandry still being bound to responsibilities of her immediate nuclear family (for instance, with helping her mother at the commissary) but having renounced those same kinship obligations to other members of her thióšpaye.

What Deloria arguably finds most reprehensible in Valandry's story is her disavowal of a kinship relation to a grandchild who has "brown eyes." Deloria's notes to the transcribed interview show her revulsion at what seems to her a double betrayal—first in refusing affective bonds to one's grandchild, and second in citing race to render that refusal somehow legitimate:

This informant loves to stress her unfamiliarity with things Dakota, but she does speak the [Dakota] language as shown in this paper. It will be noticed she takes extra pride in being the child of a white soldier and the stepchild of a white teacher, and that he wanted them to dress un-Indian, and live in a house, etc. Incidentally, she is particularly proud of one granddaughter who married a white man with blue eyes and idolized the youngest of their children because he also had blue eyes; and when they lost that youngest child, this old grandmother with her whiteman complex was so exercised that she made some ridiculous remarks about how extra hard it was to lose that one—that she could spare either of the others more easily as their eyes are dark anyway.[38]

Deloria's disgust here takes the form of a prolepsis; it becomes the critique that Valandry, as a colonially interpellated subject, should have made of herself. The "whiteman complex" that Deloria sees in Valandry's admiration for blue-eyed progeny demonstrates the pervasive and invasive ways that phenotypes associated with settler culture came to dispace kinship bonds with one's dark-eyed grandchildren. What Deloria finds "ridiculous" is maybe not the love of blue eyes as such but how this biological supplanting of affective bonds based in kinship and care threatened to disintegrate Lakȟóta families.

The tale, "A Woman Kills Her Daughter," from Deloria's collection of hithúŋkaŋkaŋpi, *Dakota Texts*, presents an exaggerated and dramatized version of this absent mother–child bond. It tells the story of a mother and her two children, a boy and a young woman, and a man who marries the young woman. Living all together in the same thípi, and soon enough with the young couple's newborn baby, the mother becomes "enamoured of her son-in-law" and, becoming "very silly in her actions" (the Lakȟóta word that Deloria gives as "silly," *ohanwitkotkoki* or *owitkoko*, translates as "foolish" but also as "crazy") kills her daughter by weakening a riverside swing's rope, drowning her. The baby's hunger drives the rest of the plot, which has the murdered woman's brother taking the baby away from camp so its crying won't disturb the witkó mother. At the stream, the murdered daughter appears "from the waist up," nurses her child, and explains to her younger brother how she was done wrong and how she was now a fish from the waist down. After several nursings, the husband follows the baby and brother-in-law to the stream, and when he sees his beloved, he slashes her in half with a knife, "made a sweat-bath [inípi] and restored the young wife to her former self." The mother, of course, is swallowed by an "abyss" that opens where the man has drawn a line on the ground. The restoration of the young woman's life through the inípi echoes the hithúŋkaŋkaŋpi of Little Boy Man, the first human being, who was killed by animal people at the behest of the trickster Uŋktómi. Its form of caretaking places other-than-human ancestors like Íŋyaŋ (rock), the rock over which water is ladled, as her restorer. The young woman's nursing of her child, even in her half-human state, inverts and exaggerates her own mother's selfishness, placing giving and taking life in direct contact, and plays out a maxim voiced by the mother of the title character in *Waterlily*: "When you marry, my daughter, remember that your children are more important than you. Always the new life comes first. Your duty to your children must be in accordance to this rule."[39]

Where uncontrolled sexual desire overrides familial sympathies in this tale, and thióšpaye forms of caretaking restore order, Valandry's example presents a more trenchant pathology where racialized subjects of federal Indian law turn against each other. Mark Rifkin argues that such affective displays signal the naturalization of administrative forms of control. These forms of self-subjectification emanate from a logic of recognition between tribes and the federal government, such that "the pursuit of federal acknowledgment requires that a people narrate themselves in ways that fit the *tribal* mold of U.S. administrative discourses."[40] Here Rifkin is interested in capturing, through a queer theorizing of heteronormative notions of biological legitimacy in offspring, those "occluded" moments that he gathers under the term "shame histories." These forms of abjection include, broadly speaking, any features of life "that are pathologized when measured against a racializing, heteronormative standard."[41] Although his analysis centers on the uses of genealogies to establish tribal rolls and implicates how biologically reproductive logics are bound up with the reproduction of social forms such as membership and citizenship, Rifkin's methodology is portable to other contexts through which such discourses generate structures of feeling.

Valandry's case reveals how assertions of an individual identity legible within allotment law worked to distance herself from those traits with which allotment law and policy had negatively invested the notion of the tribal. These specifically had to do with imagining the tribal woman according to a logic of not only blood quantum, or racial identity, but also in ways that pathologized affective relations and forms of expressing communal solidarity, such as caring for the sick or dying, or in the case of "A Woman Kills Her Daughter," with sustaining a child's life, with which Dakhóta women would have been traditionally charged. In this way, allotment regulated gendered identities and activities through the imposition of ostensibly nongendered norms of "civilized" life such as individual property ownership, thrift, and agriculture. Valandry's response to these forms of interpellation is to misread them, and in doing so to displace and misplace her rage. Valandry's feelings of deep insecurity at being made a gendered subject by the state do not take "the form of a critique of the *craziness* of settler superintendence of their identity."[42] Instead her insecurity becomes directed at other Indigenous people as bourgeois condescension and racialized hate.

Valandry's account contrasts sharply with a scene from the opening pages of *Waterlily*, where Blue Bird, having left the caravan of Thíthuŋwaŋ for another camp to give birth, looks into her child's eyes for the first time. Before she does, though, her eyes are drawn to "the waterlilies in full bloom" all around her as she kneels at the water's edge to wash the birth blood from her hands:

> Then, hardly knowing why, she rained a few drops gently on the little face that fitted nicely into the hollow of her hand. But, try as she would, she could not concentrate on the wonder she held there. All around the waterlilies in full bloom seemed to pull her eyes to them irresistibly, until she turned to gaze on them with exaggerated astonishment. How beautiful they were! How they made you open your eyes wider and wider the longer you looked—as if daring you to penetrate their outer shape and comprehend their spirit.[43]

Here the blurring of boundaries separating flower from self might at first suggest a typical instance of the sublime, which appears through negation of sensory detail and leaves only subjectless gazing behind. But the individuating work that "spirit" does in this passage is significant as a refusal of romantic sublimity: indeed, the spirit of the blooms is only a potentiating force for the scene of motherly recognition that follows, a recognition that creates the bond of love as "she glanced from one [bloom] to another, and suddenly it was impossible to distinguish them from her baby's face." Instead of desubjectification, "a new sensation welled up within her, almost choking her, and she was articulate for the first time."[44] To be articulate here inverts

Valandry's articulate disavowal of kin, as Blue Bird cries, "'My daughter! My daughter!... How beautiful you are! As beautiful as the waterlilies. You too are a waterlily, *my* waterlily.' She sobbed with joy."[45]

Outside of Lakȟóta and Dakȟóta epistemology, such a scene reads as mawkish. But Blue Bird's likening of her newborn daughter to the waterlilies demonstrates one typical scene of Dakȟóta naming, where a person would receive a name after an event that occurred during or near the time of his or her birth. Waterlily's naming, though, is something different even from a commemoration. Based in Blue Bird's existential recognition of a life force held in common by flowers and infant, her encounter with this force or power and her recognition of personal responsibility for its safeguarding ("You too are a waterlily, *my* waterlily") stand as an originary analog to the kinship bonds that Deloria's novel goes on to elaborate and celebrate. As a gesture that reaches across the boundary separating self from other, kinship recognitions/creations like the one exchanged between Blue Bird and Waterlily dissolve—imaginatively, and through apposition—the racial logic and phenotype fetishes of Valandry's account.

Deloria's reply to settler hierarchies is not to assert an ontology of her own but instead to recover a space where existing categories of difference are nascent but not yet cemented into being, and thus assert a relational logic of kinship that uses familial metaphors for this particular bicultural subject while not limiting the application of those metaphors to the realm of sheer biological descent. In so doing, the social labor that *Waterlily* performs is pedagogical and decolonizing, performing the critical task of negation implied by Fanon's claim that "in an age of skepticism when ... sense can no longer be distinguished from nonsense, it becomes arduous to descend to a level where the categories of sense and nonsense are not yet in use."[46]

Waterlily's Gender Binary

Waterlily's rendering of the thióšpaye is normatively heterosexual, appearing as a pedagogical concern of the novel's characters who inculcate "proper" gendered behaviors in children and reinforce these behaviors over the characters' lifetimes. This depiction is not heteropatriarchal, though, because Deloria stages critiques of sex-based forms of inequality and abuse through *Waterlily*'s gender binary. The most dramatic of these stagings takes place near the end of the novel, when a traveling group of Dakȟóta encounter an isolated family in the middle of a blizzard. At this point in the novel, which opened with Waterlily's birth, Waterlily is expecting the immanent birth of her own child, though her husband, Sacred Horse, has recently died and she is living with his family. Seeing her daughter's homesickness, Waterlily's mother-in-law arranges for her to make a winter trip back to her home camp. In the middle of their trip, accompanied by a war party for their protection, Waterlily and her family are forced to stop by a blizzard when they meet "some strange people" comprising "a man and his wife, both well over fifty, two girls, their daughters, and three small children," where "one of the daughters was with child."[47]

Here a Dakhóta family's isolation from the rest of the thióšpaye would signal not only an unusual antisociality but also the possibility that other, more serious, thióšpaye norms had been transgressed, including prohibitions against incest. Added to this possibility is the fact that the man talks too much: "Only the man talked, plausibly enough, accounting for their unexpected presence out there. But he was plainly evading the truth."[48] The wife's relative silence further signals aberrant gender politics, with Deloria describing how, "as if she were their mother the little ones kept close to the man's wife, a stupid-looking woman who said not a word more than necessary."[49] Here the narration's point of view follows Waterlily's condemnation of the immorality of the ostracized husband's wife, which shows up in her "stupid-looking" and closed-mouthed appearance. Her scorn comes out of a sense of female responsibility—not just to safeguard one's children's emotional and physical well-being but also to censure and possibly divorce a husband who has violated their trust. The wife is "stupid," in other words, for not asserting the power accorded to her as a Dakhóta woman and mother.

As the scene continues, the responses of the (male) warriors in the migrating party register their disgust, but unlike Waterlily's, theirs is couched in orthodox thióšpaye terms: "'It is unspeakable,' the war chief went on. 'No wonder that those who offend so heinously against kinship do not have the courage to mingle with decent folk, preferring to hide out where the other beasts are. He would not have ventured here, but hunger drove him in.'"[50] Despite their distrust of the strangers, the traveling party received the visitors and "extended hospitality to them and, out of human decency, sent them away with quantities of jerked meat and other foods." In their observance of these masculine forms of hospitality, the warriors were protecting "their own reputation as hosts" with the unstated rule saying "in effect, 'Treat as a man any stranger in your tipi who bears the physical semblance of a man.'"[51] Here "man" mainly signifies a human being who is deserving of what the narrator calls "human decency,"[52] regardless of "what sort the man might be," and in observance of this rule, the encamped men share jerked meat, "included the man in their conversation, even handing him the pipe."[53] But here the phrase "who bears the physical semblance of a man" importantly, if incidentally, also opens up sexual identity to its performance, as the responses of the thióšpaye's men show.

Dakota Texts collects a tale titled "Incest" that gives a redemptive take on thióšpaye hospitality, identifying it as a way of restoring relation after its radical wounding. The story begins in a thióšpaye where a young man lives, "the only son of his parents" and so "greatly loved" that he was given "a special tipi in the manner of a boy-beloved."[54] One night a woman enters his thípi and lies down next to him "to tempt him," but he is not able to discern her identity. The next morning he asks his father for a bowl of red paint to place beside his bed, and when the next night "the woman entered again and bothered him," he dips his hand in the paint and covers her dress with it as best he can. He still can't tell the next day who the woman was, but she reappears to him for a third night. This time he covers her face in paint, and later, during a shinny game (similar to field hockey), he sees the face of the elder of his younger sisters, "as if dipped in blood."[55] When she visits him again at night, he brands her face with a hot iron and sends her out of his thípi. In revenge, the elder sister causes him to meld into a tree that quickly grows from his thípi and rises above the camp. After the sister runs away into the woods, Deloria reveals in an aside that she "had the deer spirit,"[56] which represents a nonreproductive female sexuality, or the spirit of "the enticing woman."[57] Soon after she leaves the scene, a stranger appears with deer meat that he instructs the younger sister to roast and feed to her brother. To make a long story short, the brother is rescued not just by this sharing of food and care but because the young sister agrees to marry the stranger. When he reveals that he is actually a "thunder man," or Wakíŋyaŋ in human form, he kills "many buffaloes," makes cakes of pemmican with the meat, and ultimately restores the camp by inviting them back and feeding everyone.

In its merging of sexual violence within the thióšpaye with the appearance of a stranger whose other-than-human power is dangerous and ultimately restorative of harmonious relations, "Incest" both replays and goes beyond the realist stranger episode in *Waterlily*. Its portrayal of female sexuality as destructive might seem misogynistic to our sensibilities now. But its closing action of feeding the camp circle with the flesh of the transgressive elder sister, who was after all a "deer spirit," suggests that the real danger to the thióšpaye was not the specific crime of incest, let alone nonreproductive forms of female sexuality. Instead, the powerful presence of the other than human, both as deer spirit and thunder man, shows the vulnerability of the human world and thióšpaye to those powerful others, and the need for protocols to regulate relations with them. In this case, sacrifice is that protocol—in the deer-woman's death and in the younger sister's marriage to the thunder man. And in both cases, the sacrificial responsibility as well as the agency to restore moral order belong to women.

Unlike the scornful response shown by the men to the incestuous strangers, Waterlily and her mother are moved by the children's lack of decorum. For instance, "it was the little ones . . . who excited Waterlily's real pity," as she turns to the children, who had already shown that "they had no manners at all" when they "devour[ed] the food offered them, forgetful of their surroundings [i.e., their position as guests] in their eagerness to eat."[58] Their exchange (or lack of it) draws together issues of kinship, respect, and gender:

> With a smile she reached out a friendly hand to them and was shocked by their sudden reaction. All together they shrank back and began wrinkling up their noses belligerently at her with a lightning rapidity and a precision that made it comical. Then they settled back against their mother, who made no show of correcting their unfriendly action. And next, from the folds of her wrap, they stuck out their tongues repeatedly while Waterlily gazed on them in amazement. Instantaneously they had turned into wild cubs, ready momentarily to resist being picked up and carried away. After such a complete rebuff, Waterlily sat listening to the men's talk and forgot the strange children for a time. Much later when accidentally she again looked their way, there they were, all quietly staring at her with fear and hostility in their shining black eyes, which never wavered once, lest she make another attack and they be caught off guard. Friendship had been omitted from their experience, along with everything else that makes life warm and pleasant.[59]

The daughters' near feral responses to Waterlily's gestures of care show affects that have been untethered from thióšpaye regulation.

Without this regulation, and in the aftermath of the father's sexual violence, "fear and hostility" replace the possibility of friendly relation. In an inversion of a civilized–savage binary, Deloria's narrator describes the children of the stranger family as being unsocialized to proper kinship rules and because of that being caught "in a benighted state."[60] Waterlily notes the importance of an ethic of hospitality that operates not through following strict rules like those of the thióšpaye system but rather is marked by adaptability—an openness to relation as such—and underwrites all other norms: "It was better to stay with other people and try to do your best according the rules there. Waterlily of course did not say this in so many words, to herself; nevertheless, it was what she sensed keenly as she sat watching the children."[61]

The stranger episode and "Incest" are both negative accounts of thióšpaye ethics—that is, what kinship is not—as they relate to particular performances of gender. At other moments in the novel, femininity and the pedagogical role of elders in gendering children show up in positive forms. When one of the main female characters, Blue Bird, is preparing for the birth of her daughter, Waterlily, she is showered with attention and favors from her sisters-in-law, who are themselves reminded to do these favors by Blue Bird's mother-in-law, Gloku:

> Secretly she prodded her daughters to be dutiful toward their brother's wife. "Daughter, set up your sister-in-law's tipi for her when we make camp; drive the anchoring pegs for her. That wooden mallet is none too light," she would say to one of them as they journeyed, when the people were moving about again. To the other one she suggested, "Why not cook enough for your brother's family as well as you own tonight. Your sister-in-law seems tired."[62]

These "translat[ions of] . . . kinship obligation . . . into a helpful deed" for the expectant mother would become pampering, however, were it not for the expectation that Blue Bird would begin to refuse them beyond a certain point, as a sign of her continuing independence. Indeed, the "prevailing attitude" is that it is "much more becoming for a woman to be independent" rather than to expect "special consideration" for being pregnant, and in the build-up to the birth, we see Blue Bird negotiating a complex web of gender expectations in order to gain her in-laws' respect.

As the birth approaches, Deloria gives an ethnographic commentary that positions such gender role-playing as being in the service of not only biological but social reproduction:

> Here then was Blue Bird's delicate role: to accept the attention showered on her by Rainbow's sisters with appreciation and grace, and at the same time with tact and restraint. These intense loyalties between collaterals of opposite sexes were deep-seated, the result of lifelong training. They had been going on long before her time and would continue long after she was gone—as long as Dakotas remained Dakotas and their kinship sanctions endured. Everyone knew and accepted them and aimed to play his or her part within their framework, and then relationships remained smooth.[63]

The equivalences drawn here between a core Dakhóta identity, "kinship sanctions," and the "intense loyalties" between those of "opposite sexes" suggest Judith Butler's analysis in *Gender Trouble* of the metaphysical unity of sex, gender, and desire. In Deloria's fiction, however, the last term is pitched toward desire for long-term social reproduction of peoplehood more than toward individual erotic desire for an opposite gender or toward sexed/gendered identity as such. While this is certainly also what Butler, after Foucault, calls a "regulatory fiction," or a "culturally restricted principle of order and hierarchy," it is Deloria's account of that order and hierarchy that I want to question, as well as the particular metaphysics—the "abiding substances"—that attach to its gender ontology and to institutions like marriage.[64]

Deloria's extensive comments on kinship in her ethnography and in *Waterlily* corroborate Rifkin's sense that gender and sex understandings of the thióšpaye are quite different from those enshrined in allotment policy, being predominantly heterosexual yet complicated and crosscut other by gender possibilities like the wíŋkte and "manly hearted woman," or warrior woman, which I will discuss in a moment. But I want to emphasize how Deloria's gender depictions are also, in their celebrations of matrilineality and matriarchy, important refusals of the monogamous couple and nuclear family that remained enshrined in the IRA as a continuation of allotting lands to "the head of a family or single person over the age of eighteen years."[65]

Charles Alexander Eastman observed in *The Soul of the Indian* that Dakhóta were historically matrilineal, noting, "The wife did not take the name of her husband nor enter his clan, and the children belonged to the clan of the mother."[66] Eastman adds that within this matrilineal structure, "all of the family property was held by her, descent was traced in the maternal line, and the honor of the house was in her hands."[67] Through the phrase "honor of the house," Eastman expands the sphere of female activity beyond the material present and into a vision of Dakhóta futurity. This futurity in turn certainly has biological continuation as part of its makeup, but to a far greater degree it comprises a thióšpaye ethic that places responsibility for communal survival squarely with women. Godfrey notes that all of children's daily activities "were supervised by their mother" or by other female family members, and "this is the traditional way of being."[68]

She adds to Eastman's statement that Dakhóta society was historically matriarchal as well as matrilineal, citing Deloria's interviews with "the traditional people" (presumably this refers to Deloria's interviews with Dakhóta individuals whose living memory extended beyond the beginning of reservation life):

> The papers—Ella's papers of interviews with the traditional people—the Sioux culture was actually "matriarchal," where the women owned the home, and everything in it. They owned the front yard and the back yard. Even though that "front yard" and "back yard" really changed a lot, as they roamed over the prairie. But everything in the home belonged, *belonged* to the women. The man owned his regalia—his war regalia—and his clothes, and his shoes, and his personal things, and his horses. But his items of ownership were away from the home. The woman's ownership was the home and everything that was in her domain. So men didn't interfere in the raising of the children. Women had that responsibility.[69]

This sketch of property and child rearing fits the gender binary more generally described in *Waterlily* as well, with masculinity inhering largely in war and hunting "away from the home." Given this gendered division of labor that might be said to begin in marriage but does not require that institution beyond a certain point—say, when a Dakhóta woman divorced her husband—we might find that the responsibility for ensuring the survival of Dakhóta kinship is disjoined from marriage. After all, children were often raised outside of marriage, because they belonged to the mother's line and women were not dependent on men for recognition of lineage. Wazíyatawiŋ corroborates this lack of dependency with a positive evaluation of female responsibility, writing, "There was never a fear that if a woman left her husband that her children could not be claimed."[70]

Deloria depicts female independence and camaraderie as central to Dakhóta thióšpaye ethics and reclamations of peoplehood. In fact, *Waterlily* begins with a scene of divorce in which Blue Bird has just left her abusive husband, Star Elk, to join another Thíthuŋwaŋ band. The novel withholds all mention of Blue Bird's husband until after she has given birth. This delay magnifies her apparent isolation from the rest of her band, but it also sets apart the birth and its moment of kinship recognition/creation from any male involvement. As the narrative continues, her isolation is couched in terms of an ethic of respect that Deloria uses interchangeably across her writings with the term "avoidance." At first Blue Bird feels unable to tell her mother-in-law that she needs to dismount from her horse and walk because her mother-in-law is walking with her father-in-law:

> The young wife Blue Bird could scarcely sit her horse another instant. Oh, to dismount! But the kinship rule of avoidance kept her silent as long as it was her father-in-law who walked ahead leading her horse. At last, mercifully, he handed the rope to his wife and dropped behind to walk with a friend.
>
> "Now I can speak. She too is a woman; she knows how it is with me." But even then Blue Bird waited as long as she dared before saying, "Mother-in-law, let me get down. I must walk."
>
> "Very well. If you must you must. But say when you want to ride again," the older woman replied, then added, sighing, "Ah, child, we do you wrong to travel today—but try to bear up. Already we have made the three stops, so the next will be the last. It can't be far now." That was all. The respect customary between two persons in their relationship made them hesitate to discuss freely the cause of their mutual anxiety.[71]

While this passage marks Blue Bird's sharing of anxiety about the immanent birth as normal, especially within kinship rules governing the relationship between mothers- and daughters-in-law, it may seem overly restrictive or even dangerous. The "kinship rule of avoidance" here, though, is the "respect relationship in the family of marriage," as Deloria discusses in her ethnographic notes, *The Dakota Way of Life*.[72] The Lakȟóta word for this is *wištelkhiya*, which Deloria translates as "to be bashful towards," adding that "it is a formal 'bashfulness'" that is observed in the presence of certain relatives, but especially among in-laws, who occupy a class Deloria terms "respect relatives."[73] She writes, "In all kinship etiquette the respect relationships are the most demanding. When a respect relative is present, one must behave in a dignified and formal manner unvaringly. And whenever possible, it is best to avoid such a relative altogether."[74] Deloria gives the reason for this avoidance according to a distributive logic: "The reason why the entire network of kinship seemed to be so regulated is that in any given group those whom some persons must respect and avoid are sprinkled randomly."[75]

A range of affects, often negotiated at the same time, comes from this random distribution of heightened formality. For instance, one's encounter with a formal relative "causes one to make a quick change of manner to suit the moment," but this change can be done "quietly while still associating with informal relatives. . . . If talking excitedly in frivolous mood, one feels oneself suddenly on guard and one's erstwhile exuberance gradually dying down."[76] Deloria's ethnographic example demonstrates the suppleness of relational regard and respect created by such avoidance, describing how the arrival of a "new avoidance relative (mother of the new brother-in-law)" among a group of "women collaterals " (sisters and cousins) hushed their uninhibited "chatting."[77] "Thereupon," Deloria notes, "without 'seeing' her, they sat up and focused their united attention on a cunning child playing near, and so they preoccupied themselves while their 'mother-in-law' passed swiftly out of sight, without 'seeing' them."[78] The aim was not to deceive but rather to calm "their talk and laughter out of respect for her." Here self-effacement works to safeguard the dignity of one's in-laws, a dignity of relations between relatives of opposite sexes that "remains so essential that it is actually preferable to ignore the other's inevitable moments of embarrassment rather than offer help and sympathy directly."[79]

Indeed, Blue Bird's upholding of this rule forbids her from dismounting her horse until her father-in-law was no longer nearby. Deloria idealizes her observing of avoidance rules so that she upholds "Teton modesty" while she is in labor and when she decides to leave the group to give birth alone. Maybe ironically, her exaggerated performance of the dictates of such modesty allows us to witness her childbirth, the narration of which identifies clear possibilities of female agency within Dakhóta gender prescriptions. Woven into the narration of Blue Bird's childbirth is her recollection of her own grandmother's advice, or sayings, creating a dialogue between different generations of Dakhóta women:

> On the young girl's brow stood beads of sweat icy cold. Against a spinning world she struggled to think coherently. Just what was it her grandmother once told a woman—something about the best position to induce an easy birth? Or was it quick birth? What was it, anyway? She groped for it in her confused mind. Suddenly it came like a flash. And with it something else the grandmother once said: "No woman cries out like a baby; people ridicule that. To carry a child is an awesome thing. If one is old enough to bear a child, one is old enough to endure in silence."[80]

As with the novel's accounts of how children are directed toward gendered forms of behavior and identity, Blue Bird's memory of her grandmother brings out the pedagogical role in kinship relations among Dakhóta, and particularly between members of the same gender. The modesty of avoidance rules becomes here a gendered injunction to "endure in silence" while giving birth—in part because to cry out while the entire camp was on the move might draw the attention of enemies but also because, as Deloria writes, "self-control was always admirable, even under severest pain."[81] But the grandmother's logic, while quite demanding in some ways, also invokes—as a justification for its demands—the privileged position of children within Dakhóta culture. Despite how they are cherished, however, children are not evidence of some heteronormative premium on biological reproduction, because in the widened family that is the thióšpaye one could be childless while also having many responsibilities (as an auntie or uncle, say) for helping to care for children.

The Dakota Way of Life corroborates this ethic of mutual caretaking and the indulgence with which children were treated by nonbiological kin. Describing how children were, "on the whole . . . trained to keep still," she elaborates on how this was not any sort of harsh disciplining but rather the effect of group care for the child, who would be still as a consequence of being "humored" constantly by relatives.[82] She describes the "humoring" of children who were "very dear" by reason of some unusual circumstance, like those "who had been wished for, and perhaps prayed for, or one who almost died at birth but lived, was often not succeeded by another child for some years," describing the physical layout of the camp circle and how, in its clusters of a "family group of several homes," there was always "some grownup that was free to humor the child, thus giving it no chance to whine or scream.... Only orphaned children, those for whom nobody cared, are, as a rule, reported as crying so the entire camp could hear. 'Why is she crying here, like an orphan?' someone will say."[83] Here Deloria speculates for a moment, seemingly the objective ethnologist, and gives a sort of functionalist explanation of a shared need "for the tribe's safety" for the communal ethic of caring for children: "I think it was partly the need in each family group to keep the babies quiet, so as not to seem anti-social, so as not to seem irresponsible of the tribe's safety." She immediately softens her detachment, though, by adding that an instrumental concern for safety transformed into affection, which "made every grownup feel it her duty to guard, amuse, and humor the children, and made the children become very much attached in return, to the one who spent so much time with them."[84]

In *Waterlily*, too, the expansive set of interfamily relations among members of the thióšpaye shows up in a web of mutual maternal care for children, even when they are grown. During the novel's sun-dancing scene, a young man named Lowanla, whom Waterlily would eventually marry, impetuously vows to receive one hundred cuts as his part in the ceremony. He does so after his father dies, when Lowanla "ran away to the hills and prayed and wailed all day, 'Great Spirit, you alone have the power to give my father back to me. Give him back, and you shall have one hundred pieces of my living flesh.' At sundown he returned home and found his father just coming back to life."[85] Because of his entering into this reciprocal exchange with the Great Spirit, and having made a vow—the upholding of which is the crux of the sun dancers' displays of courage and scarification, rather than the spectacle itself—Lowanla is obliged to follow through with his promised sacrifice. This is something the rest of the thióšpaye finds at once admirable and pitiable, as such a vow, though "not unheard of, certainly," was made by "fighting men . . . seasoned warriors, with great fortitude, who nevertheless knew from many battle wounds how it would hurt."[86] The scene of Lowanla's actual scarification shows the depth of affection shared between nonbiological kin. When Lowanla had had ten pieces of flesh taken from each shoulder, "with eighty to go," his female relatives stage an intervention:

> The grieving people watched in silence, knowing that this was something that must be done and that any protesting in his behalf

would be out of order. But after the man had taken ten pieces from each side, with eighty to go, two elderly women who were the youth's aunts rushed out, frantically tearing away their gowns and baring their shoulders as they went, and demanded that the remaining cuts be made on them instead. This was extraordinary. Nothing like it had ever been known before.[87]

Despite their hesitation at the lack of precedent for the aunts' action, some of the male "mentors" present decide to allow them to stand in as proxies for their nephew, declaring that "it is admirable of sisters to honor a brother by being good to his child."[88] After these aunts in turn received fifteen cuts on each side of their shoulders, having given "sixty pieces and would have given more," Lowanla's two elder sisters step in and "quietly offer to give the remaining twenty."[89] The distribution of suffering that the Lowanla scene depicts is powerfully evocative of how a gendered identity may be constitutive of new forms of solidarity—experienced collectively as astonishment at the "extraordinary," but also individually in the women's barring of further suffering for their beloved kin—in its disruption of an expected or scripted gender performance. What is compelling about the scene is not so much that transgression leads to something new but that that newness strengthens relations within and across genders in the community.

Where the Lowanla scene dramatizes the power of affective bonds to provoke caring, even maternal, responses beyond the immediate, biological family, Deloria's accounts of multiple marriages further articulate Thíthuŋwaŋ notions of family as being transgressively different from those of the allotment family. Polygamy, one of the "immoralities" that the 1883 Religious Crimes Code sought to regulate, forms an integral part of the thióšpaye's life. When Blue Bird comes to the new camp with her grandmother, they are regarded as falling "into the category of the humbler folk of the community," as they had no "male relatives to give them backing." Rather than signaling a subordinate position in the camp, though (we are told "their lowly station in no way degraded them in the popular esteem"), they are exempted from certain social obligations, like the giving of feasts and giveaways. It is in this context of how Thíthuŋwaŋ discerned (or refused) class differences partly through a gendered marriage economy that the narration broaches the subject of multiple wives. Far more threatening than polygamy to both individual honor and the thióšpaye were forms of sexuality unregulated by marriage. Consequently, much earlier in the novel, and afraid that her granddaughter might "come to ruin" by the wooing of "reckless young men," Blue Bird's grandmother speculates that a marriage arrangement would be timely. "I am too old for this," she laments. "Perhaps I should simply give the girl away in marriage now, to some kind and able householder, to be a co-wife. Then she can be honorably married before any trouble can befall her. Yes, that would be best."[90]

Avoidance of sexual "trouble" may seem to echo settler society's prohibitions of sex outside the conjugal marriage as deviant. But if this is a repetition, it also contains significant differences. Its morality is construed in terms of the survival of the thióšpaye, where unregulated (biological) reproduction would have strained the people's subsistence. Also, the normal presence of multiple marriages among Dakhóta signals a profound difference from settler society's marital norms. Where the Indian code pathologized multiple marriage partners as an instance of unchecked erotic desire, the cowives of *Waterlily*'s thióšpaye worked to increase social cohesion by creating new kinship bonds. Deloria's ethnographic notes, for instance, give evidence for how multiple wives also served as multiple mothers. Writing in *The Dakota Way of Life,* Deloria observes that a "partial check" of "six families where there had been plural wives" revealed that in three of the families, "the co-wives were already sisters or cousins and were therefore 'Mothers' to one another's children anyway, even if they had different husbands."[91] By "sisters" here Deloria does not restrict her meaning to a biological relation; rather, she is describing how polygamous marriage founded kinship relations between cowives, who "as co-wives . . . became sisters, as was the custom."[92] This multiplying of the maternal role in turn helped to ensure thióšpaye care and stability, since "if one co-wife died, there was no question where he [*sic*] own children should go. They remained in their father's home where the surviving wife was their mother, and her children their siblings, according to the kinship system." By extending kinship relations and responsibilities beyond immediate kin, polygamy obviated patriarchal notions of lineage legitimacy: "All my informants spoke with gratitude and affection regarding the mother who brought them up. And unless I asked, they did not separate themselves in a different camp from their half-siblings. They were all brothers and sisters without distinction."[93]

These examples of multiplicity in the thióšpaye articulate a kinship that differs significantly from the heteronormative kinship of the state, perhaps above all because Dakota genderings and ways of reckoning kin are in the service of sustaining Dakhóta peoplehood. Just as Deloria's accounts of kinship are in definite ways a refusal of the biological, so too is "the people" constituted nonbiologically through the performances of ethical behavior toward one's relatives and, as I showed with the figure of the stranger, through nonrelatives as well. This leads to something of a tautology: to be Dakhóta is to perform the (gendered) thióšpaye roles and responsibilities befitting a Dakhóta. However, despite the apparent fixity of the historical gender binary depicted in Deloria's novel and ethnographies, there are also important gender slippages.

Slippages in the Dakhóta Gender Binary

Exceptions to the stark gender binary depicted in *Waterlily* necessarily complicate any determinate reading of its gender constructions. Deloria introduces the gendering process in the novel as a kind of warning against the appearance of a third gender: wíŋkte in Lakhóta, or wíŋkta in the Iháŋkthuŋwaŋ dialect: "The tribe's concern was that its girls should become women and its boys men through normal and progressive steps without complications. And in the case of boys, this was a peculiarly delicate matter because of the belief that a boy who was allowed to play girls' games and wear female dress was liable to come under a spell that would make him behave in a feminine manner all his life."[94] Here Deloria describes gender crossing as a one-sided affair, applicable only "in the case of boys" but not of girls. As if to illustrate the affective consequences of gender boundary transgressions, Deloria follows her mimetic theory of how one becomes a wíŋkte through imitating normative gender behaviors and dress with an account of Little Chief being scolded for sleeping in on the morning of a hunt. Reproached by his social uncle, Bear Heart, who is the brother of the clan leader, Black Eagle, Little Chief feels most wounded by Bear Heart's attack on his fledgling masculinity. Bear Heart, glaring at Little Chief and his cousins, who are still lying in their grandmother Glosku's thípi, chides the boys: "'What? Are they still in bed?' He appeared disgusted. 'Up with you, every one of you! Up with you—unless I have been mistaken in thinking you were males!'" This, the narrator explains, "cut deeply. To be a female was all right if one was born so, but for a male to be called a woman was intolerable."[95]

The passage recasts a story from Deloria's ethnographic notes about a man named Makula whose father woke him during an especially cold morning to announce that buffalo were nearby. Like Bear Heart, who is the novel's prototypical warrior and who plays a key role in training the young boys, Makula's father tells his son, "Come, come! Women may stay warm in their beds at a time like this but real men must go forth!" Deloria's comment on the Makula story suggests that the gender binary and techniques of training young Dakhóta in gender norms were sometimes stark. "It was the reference to his maleness that challenged him," writes Deloria, "for to be compared to a woman was the worst possible insult, whose effect was to drive many a boy into assuming a man's role regardless of danger and possible death."[96]

Anthropologist Raymond DeMallie comments that Dakhóta gender differences constellated around notions of courage, or "hardness of heart."[97] The contradictions between the symbolic freighting of male courage through acts of war and the reluctance of families to actually see their sons go to war registers some of the psychological fissures and slippages in the Dakhóta gender binary and in the presumption of strongly determined gender expectations, such as male courage in warfare. After an attack on the Black Eagle camp leaves three children dead and one girl "spirited away," Bear Heart assembles a war party. When Little Chief, who is at this point in the narrative no more than nine years old, implores his uncle to allow him to come, Bear Heart observes a distinction in the types and purposes of warfare, and consequently of courage. After he "puffed away" on his pipe "for some time," considering his nephew's naive bravery, he answers, "I have to say no, for a good reason. This is no trip for you, my nephew. This is an angry errand, a determined one. Unless we are victorious, we mean to die on the battlefield. There may be no one to bring you back safely."[98] Bear Heart's response evokes a do-or-die form of masculine courage—a tragic, sacrificial courage that may have been familiar enough to Deloria's white audiences even in 1944, when film stereotypes of Native braves abounded. But as Bear Heart continues his explanation to Little Chief, he draws out a more nuanced dimension of masculine courage oriented around sporting displays of mock killing, as in the practice of counting coup: "If this were to be the usual kind of warpath, a mere seeking after adventure for the sport and glory of it, then I would say yes. But let me make you a promise. When next I go on such a warpath, you shall go with me."

When Deloria describes the six "ancient societies" in the camp circle, she identifies an exception to compulsory male soldiering:

"The executive Chiefs' Society and the advisory Owl Headdress were composed of elderly, venerable worthies who did much sitting and deliberating. The remaining four, known as Badgers, Stout Hearts, Crow-keepers, and Kit Foxes, were military orders ever alert for action. It was not demanded of them, or of any man, to go to war unless he wanted to go."[99] The suggestion here that going to war was a voluntary choice for Thíthuŋwaŋ men, as well as the distinction between a retributive warfare and a symbolic one based in "sport and glory," outline a theory of courage that, although certainly gendered in clear ways, cannot be seen as corresponding to settler gender constructions. If anything, Deloria's underscoring of the dual and contradictory roles of voluntarism and courage, and of making space for forms of courage that refuse warfare, seems something of a protest to U.S. drafting of soldiers during the first and second world wars.

So too does the Lakȟóta/Dakȟóta wíŋkte interfere with determinate readings of *Waterlily*'s gender politics, suggesting the possibility of reading an oppositional politics in Deloria's articulations of gender along the lines that Mark Rifkin suggests in *When Did Indians Become Straight*. The term *wíŋkte* or *wíŋkta* can be translated as "wants to be a woman" or "would be a woman" (*wíŋyaŋ*, "woman"; *-kte*, "shall or will"). Rifkin views Deloria's "flirtation with the figure of the winkte" as "avoiding outright charges of savage perversity while indicating the presence of accepted options other than marital manliness."[100] This claim seems uncontroversial to me, and I agree with it on the whole. However, the historical status of wíŋkte varied across the divisions of the Očhéti Šakówiŋ. Among many of the Eastern Dakȟóta bands, they were ostracized to the point of exile, while among the Thíthuŋwaŋ bands, including Deloria's Iháŋkthuŋwaŋ (Yankton), wíŋkte held a certain esteem as wakȟáŋ persons, or persons with some unusual degree of power. Sue-Ellen Jacobs notes that for wíŋkte and female "warrior women" alike, there was a similarity in the sanctioning of gender reversals through what she calls "supernatural" means, with women changing gender identities through recurrent dreams and men doing so through hanbléčeya, or vision quest.[101]

Following from this differential valuing of wíŋkte across Dakȟóta/Lakȟóta communities, the Thíthuŋwaŋ category of the wíŋkte also historically involved more than sexuality alone, often including the performance of ritual roles among the people. This is not to discount the importance of the wíŋkte within/outside the structure of the conjugal family, only to add that the identity of the wíŋkte was bound up with other social roles and responsibilities. As Beatrice Medicine has noted, the equation of wíŋkte "with male homosexuals in most introductory anthropology texts and classes" obscures "other facets of action . . . bounded within the winkte gloss—ritualist, artist, specialist in women's craft production, herbalist, seer, namer of children, rejecter of the rigorous warrior's role, 'mama's boy.'"[102] In performing these roles, adds Medicine, wíŋkte continued to engage in "masculine" activities such as accompanying war parties, and they often supported themselves through hunting.

Rifkin observes how Deloria's character, Woyaka, demonstrates the characteristic power of and receives the respect traditionally accorded to wíŋkte, as do the perpetual virgins like White Dawn, whose "indisputable purity" allows her to "move with ease and serenity, and to look any man in the face without flinching."[103] In addition to the presence of these characters, Deloria's depictions of gender binary diverge significantly from allotment gender subjectivities, perhaps most of all in their differing purposes: where allotment severed ties between Dakhóta gender identities and kinship ethics, Deloria asserted these ties as crucial to decolonizing and remaking the Oyáte. My final section will read how she invested especially the role of the female storyteller—expansively defined to include grandmothers, novelists, and academics, among others—with this critical, decolonizing responsibility.

"Speech Is Holy": Storytelling and Pageantry in the Performance of Dakhóta Femininity

My second epigraph at the start of this chapter describes the crucial role that grandmothers play in the transmission of Dakhóta culture. Something of this importance comes across in the Dakhóta words for grandmother, kúŋši (paternal grandmother) or uŋčí (maternal grandmother), which also appears in the ritual language used by wičáša wakháŋ and healers to communicate with spirit beings. There uŋčí is the word for sun, and it carries with it a connotation of life-giving beneficence.[104]

Waterlily narrates early nineteenth-century Dakhóta life from the vantage of two generations of Dakhóta women. This text is more than a humanizing account of Dakhóta life generally; it reveals the central importance of women's roles for Dakhóta cultural survival. Storytelling is one of those roles, although here the term "story" must itself be bracketed as having specific gendered and ethical meanings. Wazíyatawiŋ notes in *Remember This!* that of the several genres of traditional Dakhóta storytelling, some are the province of women only. The category of stories from elders "that teach about the past and often involve things of a mysterious nature,"[105] called hithúŋkaŋkaŋpi, are most often (but not exclusively) told by women. Charles Alexander Eastman's animal stories, which I read in chapter 2, are a good example of hithúŋkaŋkaŋpi, as are Black Elk's tellings of the "how they came to be" stories and the stories of the Očhéti Šakówiŋ that I discussed in chapter 3. The capacity of these stories to influence their listeners is part of their ethical texture, which Wazíyatawiŋ describes as a kind of marking. She explains how her grandmother, Naomi Cavender, described the action of hithúŋkaŋkaŋpi in terms of "how a child is influenced by someone with whom they spend time. A man, for instance, may have certain habits, and if a child sees this he may also develop these habits because he has been marked by his relationship to the man. These stories may have this same kind of influence in that they become imprinted on you and become a part of your thoughts. In essence, they become a part of you."[106]

Deloria similarly dramatizes the central importance of storytelling through a male character, Woyaka, who embodies Deloria's own work as a novelist, storyteller, and pageant writer.[107] Woyaka's recounting of his training by his grandfather points to the importance of the tribal historian. In giving the winter count, which summarizes key events that fall within living memory, Woyaka remembers being chastened by his own grandfather for failing to remember what he had just heard:

> Well might you think my childhood was austere, for at any instant and without warning my grandfather would grip me firmly by the shoulder until I winced, he being a powerful man. "Now tell me," he would say, "what was that you heard last night?" And woe to me if I could not give it step by step without a flaw! Gravely he would then tell me, "Grandson, speech is holy; it was not intended to be set free only to be wasted. It is for hearing and remembering." Since I did not like to disappoint him I refused to trifle my time away on nothing. If I wakened during the night or too early to get up at dawn, I fixed my mind on remembering a new story or in going over what I already knew or in recalling some incident in all its details, just for practice.[108]

As Waziyatawiŋ explains, stories' and histories' importance in Dakhóta oral tradition were part of a matrix of relational responsibilities that informed who one would be or become.[109] The learned stories' importance comes through in the ferocity of the grandfather's gesture, which attempts to convey the strong correlation between language and being. Just as Waziyatawiŋ notes how the performative, embodied aspects of hithúŋkaŋkaŋpi may mark their listeners ethically because the stories often highlight some aspect of thióšpaye law, Deloria's portrayal of Woyaka signals a key means by which Dakhóta/Lakhóta ethics are reproduced over time.

Fiction and ethnography were not the only literary genres through which Deloria performed the role of the powerful female storyteller who culls tradition and preserves it for future generations of the Oyáte. Deloria also wrote and produced community historical pageants over twenty years for a number of Indigenous communities, the Episcopalian Diocese of South Dakota, the Haskell Indian Institute in Lawrence, Kansas (now called Haskell Indian Nations University), the Camp Fire Girls, and the YWCA. Susan Gardner argues that this form of colonially "embedded" pageantry developed over time from an accommodation within Euro-American institutions to more resistive performances of "Indian identities under siege" and reveals Deloria's growing ability "to encode a rhetorical strategy of dissidence within hegemonic and canonical Euramerican narrative forms."[110] Indeed, Deloria's statement from a 1927 letter to Episcopalian bishop Hugh Latimer Burleson that "pageantry is great" because "you can show so much that you would not dare to talk about" would seem to validate Gardner's reading of Deloria's pageants as expressive vehicles for the sexually transgressive material that Deloria was reluctant to publicize to fellow Dakhóta. Although this may be the case with some of the pageants, others reveal forms of resistance that are perhaps not so apparent in their content but more in the formal fact of Deloria having authored and produced them.

Deloria worked within a fairly orthodox, some might say settler-colonial, narrative frame in her 1940 pageant "The Life-Story of a People, for the Indians of Robeson County and Adjacent Areas."[111] This work was commissioned by the U.S. Department of the Interior's Office of Indian Affairs and the federal Farm Security Administration as part of a community-building effort for Indigenous communities who had suffered greatly during the Depression. Telling the story of the Lumbees through the narration of a "Modern Questor," which is effectively a persona for Deloria in her guise as ethnographer, the pageant frames the Lumbee people and their "folk-ways" (chief among them, not surprisingly, "hospitality") as having survived colonization, enslavement during the American Civil War, and ultimately making "consistent progress in all fields: Religious, economic, social, and educational."[112] The last third of the play especially reads as a résumé of "civilized" traits, and one senses that one of Deloria's purposes was to help Lumbees in their cause to gain federal recognition.

An earlier pageant from 1928, "The Wohpe Festival," offers a more compelling comparison to Deloria's gender portrayals in *Waterlily*. Based on a girl's puberty ceremony, its audience and performers were non-Natives, being "arranged especially for Schools and Summer Camps."[113] Its subtitle elaborates on the person of Wohpe: "Being an all-day celebration, consisting of ceremonials, games, dances and songs, in honor of Wohpe, One of the Four Superior Gods of the Dakota Pagan Religion; Goddess of Nature and Patroness of Games, of Adornment and of Little Children."[114] The theistic terms "god" and "goddess" are mistranslations (though an interesting confusion of Wohpe's gender) of the powerful aspects of an other-than-human person like Wohpe, who in Lakȟóta cosmology appears as one aspect of Wakȟáŋ Tȟáŋka (great mystery), a conceptual nexus for Dakhóta kinship understandings. Deloria's gloss, "one of the four superior gods," seems to directly cite the amateur ethnographies of James R. Walker, who lived for eighteen years (1896–1914) on the Pine Ridge reservation as an agency physician. Walker notes in a 1915 letter to anthropologist Clark Wissler from the American Museum of Natural History in New York that Walker's recent interviews with an Oglála man, Finger, had turned up information that challenged Walker's earlier understandings: "Finger's discussion of Wakaŋ Taŋka agreed with that given in part of my paper on the sun dance submitted to you, except relative to Skan and the relative existence of the four superior Gods." Walker summarizes the mapping of Wakȟáŋ Tȟáŋka's different aspects, in which Wohpe appears as a feminine power ontologically identical with the earth.[115]

Maybe most emblematic of Dakhóta regard for women's power in the pageant is the figure of Ptesáŋwiŋ or Pté Ská Wíŋ (White Buffalo Calf Woman). Although unmentioned in Deloria's work, Ptesáŋwiŋ's role as a female culture hero who founds an ethic of respect for women is evident in Deloria's regard for women as bearers of culture.[116] The story of Ptesáŋwiŋ remains, moreover, as Beatrice Medicine notes, a "charter for Lakota belief systems"; she describes the arrival of a beautiful young woman to encamped Lakhóta.[117] Finger, the same Lakhóta informant who recounted the cosmology in which Wohpe appears, describes Ptesáŋwiŋ as an incarnation of Wohpe. Finger's account is long, and a full recounting of it here is not necessary, but some of its details are worth mentioning. The story begins with two young Lakhóta men atop a hill:

> They saw a long way in the distance a lone person coming, and they ran further toward it and lay on another hill hidden so that if it were an enemy they would be able to intercept it or signal to the camp. When the person came close, they saw that it was a woman and when she came nearer that she was without clothing of any kind except that her hair was very long and fell over her body like a robe. One young man said to the other that he would go and meet the woman and embrace her and if he found her good, he would hold her in his tipi.[118]

This opening scene of sexual threat poses the ethical question of how best to respond to otherness. Thus we see the desiring man's companion "caution[ing] him to be careful for this might be a buffalo woman who could enchant him and take him with her to her people and hold him there forever," an injunction that captures Lakhóta understandings of the presence of power in other persons as being ambiguous (and so promoting ethical comportment toward all unknown others). Indeed, unchecked desire leads the young man to throw aside such caution:

> His companion saw him attempt to embrace her and there was a cloud closed about them so that he could not see what happened. In a short time the cloud disappeared and the woman was alone. She beckoned to the other young man and told him to come there and assured him that he would not be harmed. . . . When he got there, she showed him the bare bones of his companion and told him that the Crazy Buffalo had caused his companion to try to do her harm and that she had destroyed him and picked his bones bare.

Here the reference to the power of the "Crazy Buffalo" is not simply a metaphor for sexual aggression; it also points to an ontology where power can be variously efficacious or dangerous. It consequently points to the need for ethical circumspection.

Wohpe ultimately enters the Lakȟóta camp, which she has directed to prepare a feast in honor of her arrival, and which she binds to a promise of restraint: "The men must all sit with their head bowed and look at the ground until she was in their midst. Then she would serve the feast to them and after they had feasted she would tell them what to do: that they must obey her in everything; then if they obeyed her in everything they would have their prayers to the Wakaŋ Taŋka answered and be prosperous and happy."[119] Following these injunctions, the feast is prepared, and Wohpe arrives, drawing "low exclamations of admiration" from all the women. What follows is a scene of hospitality that becomes mapped onto subsequent gender roles, as does the implied connection between Wohpe's femininity and her power to both create and, as with the young scout, destroy:

> Then the woman entered the circle and took the food and served it, first to the little children and then to the women and then she bade the men to look up. They did so and saw a very beautiful woman dressed in the softest deer skin which was ornamented with fringes and colors more beautiful than any woman of the Lakota had ever worked. Then she served the men with food, and when they had feasted she told them that she wished to serve them always; that they had first seen her as smoke and that they should always see her as smoke. Then she took from her pouch a pipe and willow bark and Lakota tobacco and filled the pipe with the bark and tobacco and lighted it with a coal of fire.[120]

In bringing the pipe to the people, like with the thunder man's gift of buffalo meat in Deloria's "Incest" tale, Wohpe gives a ritual means of renewing affective bonds of solidarity through the performance of gender roles and so help to ensure the survival of Lakȟóta as a people. Her serving the men with food becomes at once a figure for the nourishment that she (as pipe) would provide ceremonially to Lakȟóta peoplehood and an articulation of the sexual deference men would pay to women, and the affective harms that would come of it they failed in that obligation.

To return briefly to Deloria's rendering of Wohpe, we see one of its sections, "The Peace Pipe Ritual," reenacting Wohpe's gift of the pipe to Lakȟóta. There, the pipe is filled with "kinnikinnik," or tobacco mixture, by "The Server," who then speaks "mystically the following chant: 'I can bring my people good, / I can bring my people good, / When my friend does this for me / I can bring my people good," which Deloria glosses as "I can give my people pleasures and good things when my friend the Sun grants me a favorable day."[121] As in Finger's account of Wohpe's distributing food to the people, the "giv[ing] . . . my people pleasures and good things" invokes a gesture of hospitality that is physically and ethically restorative. As the pipe ceremony continues and the pipe carrier addresses the different directional powers, who are identical to the cosmological powers enumerated by Finger, Deloria's references become more coded: "Next he [the Server] kneels on one knee and lays the Pipe for a moment on the ground murmuring 'All-Mother!' which the people repeat. Rising and pointing the stem upwards he says aloud: 'Great One Above; accept this Pipe. We have also offered the spirit of the smoke to your messengers, the Four Winds and to the All-Mother. Westwind will tell you when you pass by his tipi this night that today we honor Wohpe the Beautiful, and through her, the Mysterious Four-Four.'"[122] Whether non-Lakȟóta performers of the pageant would have any reference point for "the Mysterious Four-Four," let alone the invoking of the directional powers or the story of the pipe's origin, is unclear from Deloria's notes, although she is explicit about the pageant being "a device for teaching the people that they must, as children of Nature, recognize a kinship with all her other works,—all animals, birds and growing things." The overall rhetorical effect she envisioned for white performers, however, was more aesthetic than ethical, and she reports having found, "in experimenting with this material, that it helps for everyone to play Indian all that day," adding that "with a beaded band around the head, a feather in the hair, a pair of moccasins when possible, and a blanket here and there, an entire camp or school is instantly changed into an Indian tribe before the days of Columbus, and the events are carried through with charming spontaneity."[123]

The pageant's invitation to "play Indian all that day" reads as something more than a retrograde performance for settler consumption. For contemporary Dakȟóta audiences, it is an invitation to reindigenize oneself and one's communities through remembrance and reenactment of a story that recalls how the Oyáte was originally constituted in and through relations to homelands. Deloria's fiction and ethnographic work repeatedly call for, as a matter of "spirit," the renewal of thióšpaye ethics and forms of caretaking through the performance of long-standing gender roles. These appear within a gender binary and emphasize collective forms of care and affection, of anarchic power sharing rather than hierarchy. They observe the sustaining power of Dakhóta women to remake the Oyáte, in part by passing on stories that are theories—of how to be Dakhóta, of how to treat those who are not Dakhóta, of how to treat your relatives so all may survive. Rather than being evidence of having taken the "bribe of straightness," as Rifkin asserts, *Waterlily* gives settler audiences the heterosexual romance they expected while gesturing toward other texts and archives that remain out of settler view.

Although Deloria's depictions of the thióšpaye assert a gender ontology and call for her readers to recognize the historical forms of femininity and masculinity that have worked to sustain Dakhóta peoplehood against the gender redefinitions of the state, it is an ontology that holds within itself the possibility of its own critique. Whether through the wakȟáŋ status attributed to individuals falling outside the gender binary, same-sex friendships like that between male kȟolá (male friend of a man) or between female cowives, or the ceremonially sanctioned renunciation of marriage and childbearing, Deloria's representation of gender binaries underscores both their slippages and their being in the service of a more fundamental ontology: that of peoplehood. As I have suggested throughout this book, Dakhóta authors writing during (and in Deloria's case slightly after) the assimilation era deployed thióšpaye ethics of gifting and sacrifice as an invitation to continue making vital and relevant those kinship ethics of generosity that cut across and potentially redefine metaphysics of race, class, and gender. Deloria's giving voice to Dakhóta women's experiences, in her ethnographies and pageants, but above all through *Waterlily*'s female protagonists, show her making this gesture, and doing so not as an anthropologist or a novelist but as a Dakhóta woman and storyteller.

Third Interlude

Interview with Lillian Chase, Taté Tópa Dakhóta Wóunspe Program, Fort Totten, Spirit Lake Nation, February 26, 1993

Lillian Chase was another of my grandmothers and the eldest of my unčí Rachel's sisters. She passed away when I was still a young child. This interview, like most conducted by Eugene Hale as part of the Dakhóta language learning program at the Tate Topa Tribal School, focuses on both present-day and older places and place-names on the reservation. Uŋčí Lily spoke in a mix of English and Dakhóta for this interview, and when I hear her now, I am struck at how her words speak the animacy of the land. Her opening description of an Uŋktéhi, or water spirit, which appeared out of Mni Wakȟáŋ, or what's now called Spirit Lake, in the form of a snake, and her account of Íŋyaŋ Watháŋka (Devils Tooth), which remembers an act of violence against a mother and her child, describe a world populated with powerful beings and stories. She also recounts a story about a fairly recent performance of the horse dance, a ceremony that traveled well beyond the Pine Ridge reservation, and whose life-restoring capacities show up here in the telling of a good joke.

LILLIAN CHASE: At one time . . . this creature, you could see his shining eyes and people would run and hide.[1] They would all stay in their thípis. They'd stay in their homes because his breath was bad. At certain times he would go back in the water. On the west side, the Dakhóta built a bridge out of great big rocks, you know. They used it for a road. They said whatever that is that comes out from the water would bust up the bridge—three times. Yeah, that's what they said.

EUGENE HALE: They said it was a big snake?

LC: Ya, my grandma[2] used to tell a lot of stories because she was just a little girl then, and she grew up here.

221

222　　　THIRD INTERLUDE

EH: Where did Devils Heart and Devils Tooth get their names? Do you know?

LC: Ahhh. The white people keep saying that—Devils Heart. They're giving names to them. And then "Backbone," they say that.[3] Then that big rock [Íŋyaŋ Watháŋka] over here. These guys should put that rock up and honor it. They call that the Devils Tooth. They've been calling it that for a long time, but my grandma said that it is a woman. That stone, that's a woman sitting there. They had a Fourth of July on top of that hill. There was a bunch of them there and they were all busy. Then there was this guy and this girl. He must have hit her, so that girl was running away with her baby on her back. She went down the hill and that guy followed her. He was getting close so she sat down like this and, here, she turned into a stone. So he lost his wife there [laughs]. My grandma used to tell me that. So that's a woman sitting there. She had a baby on her back and she made herself into a rock. They should write out a big story about that and honor that rock. Now the white people themselves call it Devils Tooth, and it's not like that. And then there's Devils Heart. My grandma used to say that it's just a hill.

　　On top of there a long time ago, when just Indians [Dakhóta] lived here, they made a big cross and they put it on top [aside: that was hard to do . . .]. They said when the thunders[4] came they destroyed it into splinters so they had to take it away. There must be something in there, they said, in Devils Heart [Wakháŋ Čhaŋté]. I said nobody should live close to that place. It might blow up [laughs].

　　My grandma used to tell me a lot of things like that.

　　At one time over here, a creature used to come out of the lake.[5] This creature, you could see his great big shining eyes, and people would run and hide in their thípis. The Indians all had to go in. They would stay in their homes because his breath was bad—poison. Over here, that bridge, three times they fixed it over, because that creature would destroy it.

EH: A long time ago, did you ever see them make horses dance?

LC: Huh?

EH: They said there is a man in Montana who is really good at that.

LC: There was one that did that here. I seen it with my own eyes, because I followed it. You know how kids are, they're nosy. They

THIRD INTERLUDE 223

like to see everything. That's how we were, me and another girl. We followed it. He must not be spiritual [nína wakȟáŋ, "really wakȟáŋ," or really having power over life and death] because that evening the thunders [Wakíŋyaŋ] came—rain and wind, and it was terrible. They said that [an] old man was seen [hiding] between two feather mattresses [laughs]. I don't know how true that is, but that's what they were telling.

Well, I seen it. He [the horse dancer] had, I think it was a gunnysack on his head. On his forehead he had a mirror. He had that all over himself. He had four horses that followed. One was Alex Yankton's. The others, I don't know. Those four were on horseback, and they're the ones that's supposed to dance. Three of them didn't dance; just the one, Alex Yankton, was riding. It was dancing real nice, like this [gestures with hand in air, a chopping motion]. That's the only one that danced. The other three, they tried to make them dance, but they got out of hand. Maybe they were scared of him. There were four women. I remember them women, too. There was Mike Yankton's mother and her sister, and then Lou Merrick's wife. The last one I don't remember. They all had their hair down and they had red dresses on and they were following the ones who were dancing, like this [gestures again]. They were following him with small pans, like this. In the meantime they tried to make the horses dance, but they didn't want to. Alex Yankton's horse was the only one that danced. And here there was a woman behind them too.

This woman, her name was Gun [Mázakhaŋ]. She was on horseback. She had on a red outfit. She let her hair hang loose and she was riding a horse. The horse was kind of jumping around. Something happened and she fell off her horse. Maybe she wasn't supposed to do that. Instead it's supposed to be a man.[6] But still she rode that horse. And then he [Alex Yankton] didn't finish it.

By that time the thunders were coming back, so they had to quit. Everybody started pounding their tents, the stakes down on their tents. It was just awful. That big tent, how do you say that now—big top? It was a big white one that they set up. That's where they were dancing. They were sitting underneath there pounding on a drum. The whole thing fell on them. They said them guys couldn't get out of there [laughs].

[pause]

And then over there by the dump grounds, from there, the other way. The hills go like this some place over there. It goes like that. That's the Devils Backbone. That rock over there is called Devils Tooth. They said that's a woman. She ran away from her husband and here, she turned into a stone.

[leans in] Long time ago there were a lot of sacred people. They could do anything to you. It was scary. Khúŋši [paternal grandmother] used to tell there's a gang. They gathered on a certain day. They would rub sacred herbs on their arms and legs, and they would fly around. They fly around. The ones that are home have to tie a bundle of medicine above their front door. The ones that didn't have those, they raise hell with them. That's what grandma would tell us. It was really scary, long time ago.

She said when they were moving camp, there's an old lady that's got an eagle. She has a gift for eagles, that's why they were always together. That bird was lazy. My grandma said, "He doesn't try to fly. He likes to ride horseback, that eagle. He didn't want to fly" [laughs]. When they moved camp, he would ride on a horse and follow along. She used to tell me that, whenever the enemy was coming. . . . That eagle would let her know. So they all get ready.

One time she told a story about three lady cousins. The older one said, "We'll stop here. There's wild turnips all over.[7] We'll get off here and dig out turnips." There were three of them got off. The rest of the family members kept on going. They got off and they started digging wild turnips. One of them stopped and said, "Listen!" There was something making loud noises. They all straightened up. It must be in a coulee. They looked up toward the hills. They saw the enemy on the hills all around then. The young one started to cry. She cried, "If we make a run for it, we're gonna be dead. They're gonna kill us."

The older one said, "Don't cry! Whatever I tell you, do it. That's the only way we're gonna live." So they went along with her word.

She turned them into little rabbits—those small ones, those little gray ones. She turned them into rabbits. She said, "Now go hide in the tall weeds." So they did. She turned herself into one and hid too. She also ran and hid. By that time the enemy closed in, but they were not there. So they started looking for them. They just laid still in the weeds someplace. So they stayed hiding for a long time.

One of them said, "I don't think there's anybody out there. Let's run home."

The older one said, "Lay still, I'll go up and look around." In the form of a rabbit, she went to the top of the hill. She looked around and didn't see anything and said, "Come on! There's nobody around." And they came running as rabbits.

And she turned them back to girls again. "Just leave the turnips so we could catch up." When they moved camp, they used them poles, you know, to drag their belongings.[8] They left a trail so they would know where they go.

So they followed the trail. My sister, Grace, was sitting here, and I was telling that story. She was sitting like this: "And then what?" And then she's so anxious to hear: ... "And then what?" I kept on telling that story.

Those girls were running, following the marks on the ground. They ran until they found the camp. The people found a place and they were pulling out their thípis. They were setting up their thípis.

And then Grace said, "And then what?" she said.

Ya, they got back and then they were gonna tell the chief. He came from someplace. They told the chief what they seen. They saw a war party. "Stay alert. They might attack." That was their message.

And then Grace said, "... and then what.'"

The chief came out from his tent and then they told him about it. The chief went in; he was bringing out his loudspeakers and was putting up his loudspeakers.

By that time Grace got mad. She said, "You're just lying to me."

It wasn't like that, but I just said that, you know. But that's how it was. That's what they said. They took all the women and they put them in the middle of the camp. Some climbed trees. The men were ready for them. They had their bows and arrows. On the tip of the arrows they put poison medicine. They said when you hit somebody, they died right away.

Grandma told me those stories. Them are true stories.[9] She always told those stories.

There was one. A man, he went buffalo hunting way up in them big mountains.

He was laying there on one of them hills looking down. He seen a cloud of dirt and, here, that was a herd of buffalo. They were running along the river. There was one. Long time ago there used to be one like that. They called them crazy buffaloes. You gotta run away from them. They were no good. They're just skinny and they got no hair. They ran in a circle and liked to holler. They called them crazy buffaloes. They're buffaloes, but they're like that. They give the other ones a hard time.

There was one of those in that bunch. That man was laying on the hill looking down. He thought to himself, "if he smells me he will charge after me. I think I'll take off back to camp." They said it was out in the flats [prairie], so that man started to run.

He got so far and he had a feeling it might come after him. He looked back. That crazy buffalo was following him. It would make that noise. This is the sound it makes. . . . "Whoo whoo whoo whoo," my Grandma said.

That thing was chasing him. It was running in circles, coming after him. That thing got close so he took off one of his moccasins and threw it backwards. Where that moccasin landed, that thing started fighting that moccasin. He started to throw that moccasin around. That man had a chance to get a little farther away from him.

When that thing got tired of the moccasin, he started after him again. When that thing got closer, he took off the other moccasin. He stopped again and attacked the moccasin again, and gave him a chance to get away again.

When he got through with that, he started after him again. When the runner looked back, it was getting closer, so he took off his sleeveless buckskin jacket. He threw it backwards. He came there and he fought that a little bit longer.

The man got a distance away.

He looked ahead and saw a big black thing in his path. He said, "It must be one of those things [crazy buffaloes]." He got scared of it. He just kept on running. That buffalo got finished attacking the jacket and started after him again. His breechcloth is all he had left on.

When that thing got closer again, he threw his breechcloth

backwards. They said he continued running. He ran in the direction of the black thing. When he got there, that black thing was a big, huge black rock.

That was a big rock, a really big rock. A man could fit in there. It was open like that in the middle of that rock. When he got there, he slid in. By that time, that thing got there. They said that thing attacked and fought that rock for half a day. He fought that rock. That man stayed there that long. The man got tired and worked his way to the top. He sat on top. He thought to himself, maybe somebody would come after me. And that's the way he was thinking.

By that time Grace came back again. I told her a big lie again.

The man was looking west. A bunch of horseback riders were coming, you know, they were coming after him. The way I told it, I said a whole bunch of motorcycle riders came rumbling after him [laughs].

She was really mad at me.

But they said they came after him on horseback. Horses. Long time ago, way back, the horses were small. That's what grandma said. They called them Indian [Dakhóta] horses. That's what they were. They were small. They were really fast. Everybody had one. They had to, I guess. They all had one of those when they took their man home.

When I said they were motorcycles, Grace got mad.

I have a lot of stories like that, that grandma told.

When I was down at St. Jude's,[10] two white men came to see me with some big notebooks. They called me outside. So I went out there. They asked for old stories, Indian stories. I didn't want to tell too much, because they're going to make a lot of money.

When they hear Indian stories, they tell it different.[11]

There's one like that over here. His name is Louie Garcia. He came here and wanted stories, way back stories. I was sitting here with Grace. That's when he came. He even showed us some pictures. Way back pictures, a whole bunch of them. I wonder where he got them. He said, "There's a picture I have. In Tokio I took this around and nobody knows who that guy is." He said, "I'll bring it over," and he brought it over.

As soon as I saw that picture, I knew who he was. I said, "That's Joe Merrick. That's the way he dresses when he's gonna dance." He wrote his name down right away. He said, "I took it around in Tokio. Nobody knows who he is there." He never wears a whole outfit. He only wore a shirt over his pants. He tied a fur thing around here and his breechcloth. That's all he wore when he danced.

Joe Merrick, I used to see him dance a lot of times. Louie Merrick also danced.

There was a big, big dance hall at Wood Lake. You know where Rosalie Bear is living? There used to be a big round dance hall. Gee, they used to dance good there. A lot of people danced there. Old White Horse and old . . . what's his name? And there's Chaske, old man Chaske. He danced, too. Crazy Dog also danced there.

There's one. I can't remember his name. When he danced he takes his cane and rides it like a horse and whipped it [laughs]. Yup.

JC: On this reservation, how many different tribes?

LC: Isáŋyathi [They Live on Knives or Santee, who are the four eastern Dakhóta thióšpaye]. The Santees came here first. They came from South Dakota and settled here first. A man named Ignatius Court was, he was like a chairman.[12] Like what Belgarde is. That was Ignatius Court. He was an old man, but he was a smart man. He was always going to Washington, D.C. He kept bringing money back for the people. Ignatius Court.

And then from over here, Fort Yates, the Iháŋkthuŋwaŋ [Yankton] came.[13] They had no place to go, because Waánataŋ (Charger) was the chief, I think. The white people brought some liquor and got him drunk till he passed out. His tribe was pitiful, but he did that. Then the white people made him put his thumbmark on different documents while he was passed out. He didn't know. They did that to him, then they left.

After he came to, the papers were gone. His tribe [thióšpaye] felt bad. Some cried, but he couldn't do anything about it. He told his people not to worry about it. "The white people are going to take care of us and feed us from a white dish," he told his people. But there was nothing. They were from Fort Yates, but they're here now. That is Alvina and her family and the ones from Crow Hill. When they all moved here the (Bureau of Indian Affairs) superintendent was already here and . . . he was passing out land to the Indians. He gave them land to live on, too.

The Waánataŋ man and Ignatius Court, they never got along. Waánataŋ was always after Ignatius Court. They didn't get along. Ignatius Court didn't pay any attention to the other guy. He would travel to Washington, D.C., and bring money back. I remember. I must've been around seven years old, eight years old.

That was when my sister Grace was born; May 2, maybe, 1909. That's when they gave money away here.

On the hill up there, do you remember where the store burned up [by the CSAP building]? Right next to it there was a little house. Alphone McKay used to live there a long time. That was the office. They blocked off half the door.

Then Ignatius Court and the superintendent passed out money. At that time there was a bunch of white tents in the trees and all over. It looked white all over. The people were standing in a big long line. I was just a little girl sitting there watching. They were giving out checks. I don't know how much they gave out. I was small, so my mother took my check. So I don't know how much they gave out.

And then in the twenties, it must've been somewhere in there, they gave land, I mean money, out again. We got, I think, $55 apiece. From there it goes on to 1930. In the thirties, I think, they gave out money. That was the payment for Sullys Hill.[14] We all got $4 apiece [laughs]. Louis Good House sold it, they said.

They tried to hit him and gave him a hard time because of that. They even drug him out of the office. At that time below there there was a house. . . . That house that's standing by the road [the courthouse]. That was the office at that time. He was sitting in there. There was four women. They went in there and just drug him out. They got him by the legs and drug him out. They kicked him and pulled his hair and scratched up his face and everything.

And here he crawled back in there. They tried to throw him out again, but they didn't.

And then these guys, what do you call them guys that dance? There were two Chippewas who were running that. They used to call them something. A whole bunch came.

Over by Mary Salome's [Hill] they had a dance. Somebody

shot at them from the hills. And, here, Roger Yankton was a policeman that time. He grabbed a gun and ran up that hill. When he got to the top of the hill, they all ran into the woods. He chased after them, but the woods were too thick. He let them go. And the ones that were dancing, some kind of outfit . . . they have a name . . . what was their name? There's a name for it, but I can't remember. Remember that new jail? They all moved in there so nobody couldn't go near the jail. All the prisoners that were in there; they let them all go. Then they locked all the doors inside. Nobody couldn't go near the jail, because all the ammunition is in there, they said. They were scared to go near the jail. Florence Adams was one!

JC: Was it the AIM [American Indian Movement]? Do you remember that?

LC: No, I wasn't around here. . . . Oh, Florence Adams was one. Her and who? And then there was Israel Gourd. Uncle Israel was in it. He and Pete, they almost got into a fight.

And then Florence Adams' outfit, they had a protest right across the road.

They had a real big pile of tires. I don't know where they got them from. They started them on fire. So this way . . . the smoke was really coming this direction. So they were doing bad things. And the next day they all went into that jail and locked it up from the inside. So everybody was scared to go there, because they had all the police ammunition inside, they said. They were scared to go near that jail. They let all the jailbirds go. They sent them all away and then they all went in and took over.

Then there was a guy. . . . That guy that went there and made them open the door, was, ah, Sylvester DeMarce, they said. They said he just walked right to the door and knocked on the door easy. . . . And he talked to them just good so they opened the door for him. For a little while they were doing the wrong things. And over at the office here, there was a bunch of them up there . . . and the superintendent was up there, but they were after him, so he locked himself up in a room. We went over there that time. We was watching.

JC: How did Crow Hill get its name, do you know?

LC: Let's see [phone rings] . . . a long time ago a crow made a nest. So that's why they call it Crow Hill [goes to answer phone].

Ya, there's a lot of things. . . . But my mind is getting bad.
Well, I'm ninety years old and so my mind is getting bad. When
I want something, I go in the other room to get it and I forget
what I went in there for.

I was in St. Jude's for a long time, too. I almost died from
loneliness, so I moved back out here. I sold all my furniture, too,
so I didn't have anything when I came back. These things were
given to me.

JC: So, is that all then?

[film cut]

LC: In October or September, there were a lot of tents. Remember
that big high hill where you barely crawl up there (Sullys Hill)?
Right there someplace, they used to camp there. They piled up
wood. They called it Woodpile. They cut wood and stacked it
up like hills, all over. And then before the snow flies they hauled
it toward Crow Hill. So in winter they used it, all through the
winter. They used that for the winter.

That (Sullys Hill National Game Preserve) used to be Indian
land [Dakhóta makhočhe]. I remember my dad, they used
to live in there, mama. They made their own tent. There was
something they called Woodpile. They stacked the wood on top
of each other [makes gesture with hands, one over the other].
The last thing they did was hauled it home over here in hay-
racks, so you could carry lots, you know. They hauled wood.
Every fall they do that. That used to all be Indian land [Dakhóta
makhóčhe], but they gave it all to the white people.

They took all the good things from us and forced us into a
small ground. I don't like this at all, they way we're living now.
They put us in a bad way, the white people. All the good land,
from Minnewaukan and this way, Dakhótas used to live there
[points west]. And from Oberon this way, a lot of Dakhótas
used to live along there [points east]. And then this way towards
Sheyenne [points south], I know Frank DeMarce and them used
to live there. There never used to be anything around here; no
wood, no trees, nothing, just grass. Over that way, too [north].
They planted trees all over and now we live in the weeds.

A bunch of old guys, my papa, Rufus, was one of them. He
did his work sitting on the ground. They made them plant all
those Christmas trees over there. They planted them too close

so they can't grow out. Instead they grow straight up [chuckles]. There were no trees at all. Nothing. Yup. No one lived here at all.

When the school was running, there were only young men and it was very good. They had a carpenter shop, and every day they had the young men do something. They had a band too. When they had the band on Sunday evenings, they would clean up the Square Center really nice. Then they would all sit up there and play. And all the young girls would sit around and listen. It was really good then. It's not like that anymore. It's bad now. It seems like you have to look out all the time.

Someone came here one time and I said, "When you look out like that, somebody is looking at you already," I said.

Pasu (Percy Cavanaugh)—Louie Goodhouse used to live over here, somewhere. Pasu, he was living in a shack right below Grace, right below there someplace.

He had binoculars. He adjusted them. He was gonna look in there [toward Louie Goodhouse's] to see what they were doing. He was looking that way. Just then Louie Goodhouse's wife was looking at him [laughs].

Ya . . . this whole lake used to be ours at one time, they said.[15] One time I heard Belgarde was going to get a lawyer and fight for it, they said. I don't know if he did or not. They claim the lake now, those white people. They don't have any business.

And there's another thing I'm going to tell. Camp Grafton, where those soldiers are, that's only in lease.[16] They're there on lease, that's all. They leased that from Ignatius Court, they said. So he loaned it to them. A long time ago they had Fourth of July there, . . . the Indians. Three times they had Fourth of July that I went to. I was just a young kid. It was really pretty. Charlie White and Walt Cavanaugh used to take care of it. Then Ignatius Court leased that land out to the soldiers. Then he died away. They didn't pay their lease. Just then Ignatius died, so they took it. We should look for that, you know. It all belongs to Dakhótas. Nobody looked into it so . . . it's bad.

And then this school. The school used to be a fort. It was full of soldiers. When they were going to move out, they gave it all to the Dakhótas. Dakhótas only had thípis. Nobody had a house like this. They all lived in log houses. Then they gave them that.

Then the white men took that. I said, "If they fix those up, a lot of these couples that have no place to go could stay there." But they said Louie Goodhouse sold all those good tubs in Belcourt.

There's a lot of things that aren't right, but nobody pays attention to them. In the future, if we don't pay rent they'll kick us out, and where are we going to go?

JC: Is that it?

LC: Haŋ [yes].

Conclusion

Gathering the People

Translated Nation has examined how Dakhóta writers interrogated exclusions from and involuntary incorporations into U.S. political and domestic life, citizenship, and belonging, theorizing forms of collective identity and agency as being embodied in ethics of the thióšpaye and through their performance in oral traditions and histories, ceremony, and land tenure. In ways that safeguarded Dakhóta meanings from settler view, these writers depicted the Oyáte as originating in and continuing through thióšpaye relations, representing in veiled ways how thióšpaye ethics governed not just (human) interpersonal relations and politics but also kinship relations between human and other-than-human beings. The latter category includes animals, spirits, and other persons usually thought of as inanimate, such as rocks, stones, and lightning, who nonetheless embody capacities for volition, response, and relation, albeit in other registers of vibrancy than we human beings might.

The Oyáte thus emerges from the ways in which the diverse texts and genres I presented here—oral histories, autobiographies, autoethnographies, eháŋna woyákapi, treaties—depicted living in homelands richly inhabited by these relatives as the foundation for Dakhóta political theory and action. Following Kim TallBear's usage, I have called this theory and action a form of caretaking visible in thióšpaye ethics of sufficiency and generosity. These I glossed as friendship in my introduction, but with crucial differences from secular articulations of friendship as fraternity, owing to the fact that thióšpaye laws received their charter in origin stories. I discussed these origin stories in Charles Alexander Eastman's adaptations of the Dakhóta storytelling genre of hitȟúŋkaŋkaŋpi, or what Wazíyatawiŋ describes as "stories from the elders that teach about the past and often involve things of a mysterious nature, not easily explainable."[1] These laws provided the means with which Dakhóta engaged not only with one another, maintaining bonds of solidarity intensively—within the local band or community of close relatives—but also extensively—as part of the confederacy of Dakhóta and Lakȟóta comprising the Oyáte.

Thióšpaye ethics also crucially formed a means of engaging with U.S. national demands for incorporation through citizenship, as Dakȟóta filtered through ethical norms of being a good relative those liberal ideals of equality, citizenship, and self-determination, as well as the subjectivies of autonomous individual freedom, that were most significantly expressed in legal form first in the U.S. treaty-making period, and later in allotment policy. However, because one could be a good Dakhóta to one's relatives while at the same time being a good, or least a nominal, American citizen, I have also sought to show that kinship entailed ambivalent obligations. In highlighting deep and constitutive ambivalences as being at the heart of Dakhóta literary performances, I demonstrated how Dakhóta intellectuals leveraged this ambivalence to reclaim traditional ways of knowing in order to critically engage with settler liberalism. Thióšpaye ethics imparted to Dakota a unique capacity for multiplicity and an inclusive, nondomesticating stance toward difference. This is the upshot of the peace that Dakhóta negotiated in treaties—a peace that is not just construed negatively as the absence of conflict but that has historically been imagined positively, as being like the "loyal and disinterested friendship" that Charles Alexander Eastman invoked as the moral grounds for Indian citizenship. It is the solidarity emergent from Dakhóta practices of making relatives, literalized through the huŋkádowaŋpi or adoption ceremony.

Both the chapters and Interludes in this book highlight the rewriting across nearly a century and a half of Dakhóta as a people, as the Očhéti Šakówiŋ Oyáte, through my focus on shared frameworks of ethical meaning. I have done so at the peril of being charged with essentialism. Against that charge I would like to make a few remarks about how the ethical continuities I examined in this book challenge notions of essentialism, especially in relation to Dakhóta peoplehood. My hope is to reframe Dakhóta and other Indigenous articulations of peoplehood as inclusive, adaptive, and relational rather than exclusive, fundamentalist, and hierarchical, and to suggest how oral histories and traditions have played an integral role in remaking the Oyáte.

Wazíyatawiŋ describes how okíčiyaka uŋyáŋpi (oral tradition, but literally "to tell something in benefit of somebody" and "we go there") is not simply a repository for cultural knowledge but also "an interpretation of the past that becomes active only when a relationship has been developed between a storyteller and a listener." This relational quality of Dakhóta history, she argues, "distinguishes it markedly from the Western academic historical interpretations of the Dakota past, which rely largely on documents written within the framework of the Western-European worldview."[2] Wazíyatawiŋ's privileging of oral tradition as a location for Dakhóta cultural survival underscores how the relationship between storyteller and listener provides the formal setting for enacting thióšpaye obligations, and also how the content of stories enables cultural transmission and survival, even in cases of attempted genocide and traumatic removal from homelands. While the various bands of Dakhóta have occupied relatively the same territories for thousands of years, many other tribal peoples have not. Rather, as novelist and literary scholar Louis Owens (Choctaw and Cherokee) has asserted, the bands, through dispossession and relocation, "move and in doing so, carry with them whole cultures within memory and story."[3]

I have characterized some of these radical transformations, their embodied and written locations for ethical and political engagement, through the figure of translation, a term I have used in several senses: first, to evoke the antiessentialist aspects of citing thióšpaye relational discourses; second, to highlight acts of withholding knowledge from settler audiences; and third, to describe movement across boundaries of difference in ways that preserve rather than annul difference. The translations that Dakhóta performed under U.S. settler-colonialism, some of which took the form of actual textual translation (as with treaties and missionary's Bibles) and others that involved negotiating the subjectivities promoted by the U.S. government, underscored and maintained the distinctiveness and validity of Dakhóta truth systems.

Rewriting Sovereignty

The peoplehood that emerges from assimilation's ambivalences as the rearticulated ethical norms of kinship suggests a categorical reframing of other key terms that derive from the Euro-American nation form. As Robert Warrior puts it, the project of developing a theory of Native American literatures that is responsive to categories like sovereignty and self-determination ought to "recognize that these words are problematic in spite of continuing to carry a certain political, emotional, and critical force." He continues: "This is perhaps most true of sovereignty, a term from European theological and political discourse that finally does little to describe the visions and goals of American Indian communities that seek to retain a discrete identity. To simply abandon such terms, though, risks abandoning their abiding force and utility."[4] I take the "abiding force and utility" of the term of sovereignty to be evident from its continuing centrality in deciding Indigenous peoples' legal claims of various kinds. That is, while statist-inflected terms like "sovereignty" and "nation" may continue to be unavoidably used both for and against Indigenous peoples' struggles for self-determination in the present-day United States, their "abiding force and utility" need not foreclose other constructions of sovereignty and politics, Indigenous or otherwise, including ones based in tribal peoplehood and its constitutive ethicopolitics.

In order to evoke these alternative theories and practices of political power, I have argued that Dakhóta notions of gifting contain within them a temporality distinct from the nation-state's capitalistic "empty homogenous time." This temporality is grounded, first of all, in a ceremonial calendar that corresponds to traditional seasonal movements of Dakhóta bands in pursuit of game. But it is also importantly grounded in what I have called the pause, a marking off of narrative and economic sufficiency, seen literally in the telling of tales over many winter nights and figuratively in their interrupting the "progressive" temporality of U.S. capital and settler-colonial expansion.

This book's Interludes have formally enacted this pausing, demonstrating that a Dakhóta peoplehood based in thióšpaye ethics unfolds in time and across the many reservations and nonreservation locales where relatives have made homes. Temporally and geopolitically expansive, thióšpaye ethics are also conceptually and categorically anarchic, placing a premium on sharing power rather than on maintaining ontological distinctions and hierarchies, and doing so in ways that do not necessitate violence—not even the implicit violence of a broadly inclusive view of kinship, which says "become one of us . . . or else!" As I showed in my reading of Black Elk's transcribed interviews, the ritual sharing of a ceremony like the horse dance is an inclusive reactivation of peoplehood through which individuals do not dissolve their roots at home but rather, by becoming more rooted in the moral truths of Dakhóta communities, may extend relation nonviolently to others.

Transnational critics of peoplehood, however, might chafe at the idealized Oyáte I have drawn out from the writings of assimilation-era Dakhóta. Arjun Appadurai, for instance, places such questions of nation, blood, and kinship into the intimate context of his own family. While the purpose of his chapter is not to rehearse all the arguments that discredit what he calls "primordialist" approaches, or those approaches that tend "to account for newer and larger attachments by reference to older, smaller, more intimate ones, usually conceived in terms of blood and kinship," Appadurai's linking of narratives of purity, kinship, and the nation is typical of a transnational critique of nationalism.[5] This critique, which highlights the violent tendencies of such linkages, is also distinct enough from my own sense of how kinship and peoplehood have appeared in late nineteenth- and early twentieth-century Dakhóta contexts that it deserves further reading and reply.

At the heart of a transnational critique of nationalism is the tight linking of the nation with a sense of peoplehood, and peoplehood, writes Appadurai, "whatever the mix of *volkisch* elements involved in any particular case, depends on some sense of kind that is bounded and distinct."[6] These boundaries of "some sense of kind," or senses of difference, are nearly always racialized. Indeed, he asserts, "since this sense of distinction has to cover large and complex spaces, it cannot avoid some racialized elements, and these racialized elements can and do become, under various conditions, mobilized as racism."[7] Where Appadurai is concerned with reminding us that the ties between nation, ethnicity, and race are violently exclusive before they manifest in more overt forms of violence, other scholars, like Scott Lyons in *X-Marks* (2010), have pointed out that race, or a logic of blood, is just one logic of purity among many, including linguistic and cultural ones, and that "culture cops" exist within Indigenous communities as surely as they do outside of them. For this reason, Lyons quips that the notion of cultural purity stems from the "problematic peoplehood paradigm" that is troubling for the fictions of purity that it holds to as being anything but fictive.[8]

It is not my intent to question such critiques on the whole because the fact of nationalistic violence as a function of purity narratives is indisputable, including the violence of wašíču or settler-colonial civilizational rhetoric, so powerfully mobilized during the late nineteenth-century United States, that conflated a racialized whiteness with Christian morality, property ownership, and the nuclear family. But the implication that there is a necessary link between violence and notions of kinship, or that there is something like a universal form of kinship that is necessarily accompanied by violence, needs to be doubted. As Appadurai narrates his father's story, he describes in compelling but also problematic ways the "inner affinity between nation, ethnos, and race" that emerges during times of social stress, and as an imagined extension of the (biological) family:

> This inner affinity returns us to the question of blood, sacrifice, and war, by invoking the idiom of the shedding of blood, modeled as sacrifice, in just wars, usually in preparation for real or imagined defense of the national body and national soil, modern states are able to rewrite the family as a site of consanguinity and blood becomes the site both of purity and of connectivity. The strength of the metaphorical power of blood, so far as the nation is concerned, is that it connects the idea of the ethnos to the idea of the people and the soil, through the many languages of purity. It is thus no accident that in the era of globalization, we have witnessed a new concern with ethnic cleansing or purification, since the idea of blood allows an endlessly varied repertoire of ways to connect family and sacrifice with the fear of a contaminated national ethnos.[9]

Here what Appadurai calls the turn toward ethnic violence "in the era of globalization" is an unsurprising nomination for retrograde forms of community making, in part because of the ease and speed with which digital images of "a contaminated national ethnos" now circulate but also because the movements across borders of various kinds, and particularly those literal border crossings of migratory laborers, awakens recidivist urges to assert boundaries of supposed ontological difference. Appadurai's fixing on the family as both source and target domain for narratives of blood purity—a purity that he insightfully observes may be a powerful source of exclusion and connection, or perhaps most commonly, of a "connectivity" that is exclusive in fundamentalist ways—is in stark contrast to the inclusive theory and practices of kinship represented by the Dakhóta authors I examined here.

By turning to Dakhóta literary productions as performances of what we might call an ethics-based sovereignty of impurity, in which being and power emerge from nonhierarchical relations transacted among human and other-than-human relatives, I have aimed to provide more than just a Dakhóta rung to the ladder of Native American literary nationalism. I have certainly drawn inspiration from the critical approach that emerged in the 1990s among writers like Elizabeth Cook-Lynn, Jace Weaver, Robert Warrior, and Craig Womack, whose work positioned Indigenous intellectual and philosophical traditions as the crucial basis for reading Indigenous literatures and demanded an orientation toward what Cook-Lynn calls "the defense of tribal sovereignty and indigenousness."[10] In part, this first wave of Indigenous literary nationalism aimed at reclaiming Indigenous lifeways via literary texts and relied on a notion of nationalism as deriving from more or less clearly bounded conceptions of peoplehood. As a supplement to and continuation of that first wave and its innovative work, I have sought here to evoke the open-ended and relational nature of Dakhóta concepts and practices of peoplehood, underscoring the provisional and always challenging job of reclaiming and remaking Indigenous knowledges and peoples. How one writes the Oyáte, for whom one writes, and the ratio of signal to noise in the message that is received—all these things matter for how we carry ourselves forward. In 2016–17 the Oyáte returned as Black Snake Killers and protectors of the water. My hope is to have shown how that prophetic role and responsibility are nothing new but were given to us by ancestors who kept Dakhóta ways of knowing, relating, and caretaking ciphered but alive in their lives and works, even when the settler nation made it nearly impossible to do so.

Acknowledgments

This book, which orbits ideas and practices of relatedness, grew from my great fortune in having and making many relatives over the course of my life. My parents, Donna and Dennis, have always been supportive of the scholarly work that has grown from these relationships, though they have been somewhat puzzled by how long it has taken to finish this "paper." Wóphida tháŋka to you both for the rich life and love you have given to me and to my family, and to all my living relatives, on the reservation and off. Thanks especially to my uncle and aunt, Vernon and Velma Lambert, and their children, as well as to my friends and relatives who welcomed my family so good-heartedly and totally to Mní Sóta, especially Delta, Denise, and Adelle Nelson and Ethan Neerdaels.

Thanks to my editor, Jason Weidemann, at the University of Minnesota Press, and to his colleague Gabriel Levin, whose guidance and encouragement in revising this book have been indispensable, and to Matthew Fletcher (Grand Traverse Band of Ottowa and Chippewa) for his incisive criticism of an early draft.

Heartfelt gratitude also goes to Dana Nelson, Colin Dayan, Vera Kutzinski, Daniel Usner, Robert Barsky, and Scott Stevens. Thanks also to the members of my book reading and writing group at Vanderbilt University, Elizabeth Barnett, Matthew Duques, and Donika Ross, for their careful attention to early versions of some of these chapters.

Without support from the Ford Foundation, which granted me necessary funds and time to research and write, this book may have never been finished. I am deeply obliged to the foundation and to the brilliant, necessary work done by scholars within its ever-growing network.

While at Cornell I had the great privilege of getting feedback and support from members of the Andrew W. Mellon Diversity seminar, including Gerard Aching, Judith Byfield, Eric Cheyfitz, Naminata Diabate, Magnus Fiskesjö, Nicole Gianelli, Murad Idris, Michael Jones-Correa, Oiyan Liu, Kya Mangrum, Richard Miller, Sarah Murray,

Thomas Patton, Lorenzo Perillo, Rafael Santana, Suman Seth, and Kavita Singh. My greatest thanks and eternal regard go out to Leslie Adelson for her brilliant mentorship and friendship, and to Mary Pat Brady, who not only gave me invaluable mentoring but, along with Kate McCullough and their family, made me and mine feel at home for a time in Ithaca. I'm extremely grateful to the American studies department at Cornell University for sponsoring a review, and to Mary Pat Brady, Jolene Rickard, and Mark Rifkin for having read and offered suggestions for revision.

Shout-outs to all my friends and colleagues at Oklahoma State University, and thanks to Katherine Hallemaier, Jeff Menne, and Graig Uhlin, who read a version of my chapter on Eastman and didn't disparage it for its awkward Orson Welles pun.

Special gratitude goes to mithákhoda, Scott Manning Stevens, who braved a tour of Andrew Jackson's Hermitage with me and my daughter, and who gave me helpful advice about this book early in its genesis.

This project benefited greatly from my involvement in the National Consortium in American Indian Studies, in which I participated in a summer seminar at the Newberry Library and in a spring workshop at Harvard's Peabody Museum. The Newberry's resources, and the seminar's conversations, led me to write my first chapter on conversions of Dakhóta prisoners in the concentration camps at Fort Snelling, Minnesota, and at Camp Davenport, Iowa.

Many thanks to graduate students and colleagues in the American Indian and Indigenous Studies Workshop at the University of Minnesota for their camaraderie during my first year in the Twin Cities, and for their readings of a version of my first chapter. My work as faculty affiliated with American Indian studies has been and continues to be nothing less than inspiring, and I have been humbled and honored to learn from graduate students and colleagues whose work is not only field defining but also crucially rooted in the needs of real people, peoples, and communities. Special thanks to Agléška Cohen-Rencountre for her comments on my chapter on Ella Cara Deloria. My time at the University of Minnesota has also been greatly enriched by my study of the Dakhóta language, and I would be remiss not to say phidámayaye do to my teachers, Šišóka Dúta (Joe Bendickson) and Čhaŋté Máza (Neil McKay), and to all my fellow language learners.

I owe much of my critical temperament to my late friend and mentor Kenneth Morrison. I remain inspired by Ken's conviction—one that came from his reading as a young man of Martin Buber's *I and*

Thou—that all real living is meeting. The premium he placed on dialogue as a form of ethical engagement was everywhere apparent in Ken's life, friendships, and intellectual work. I have carried that commitment with me everywhere.

Wóphida to the school board of Taté Tópa Tribal School in Fort Totten for permission to view and transcribe the video recordings that hold some of these oral histories, with special gratitude to Pat Walking Eagle and Perry Kopp for their help, and to former tribal chairperson Leander McDonald for believing in the regenerative power of the Dakhóta language.

Finally, great love and gratitude go to my wife, Melissa, and to my children, Wren and Leo, who have taught me what it means to be a good father, husband, and relative, and with whom I am enfolded always.

Appendix

Dakhóta Pronunciation Guide

Letter	Sound	Dakhóta Example	Translation
a	ah (as in father)	até	father
aŋ	nasalized ah	áŋpao	dawn
b	b in boat	baksá	to cut
č	between ch in chair and j in jump	čístiŋna	small
čh	ch in chair	čháŋ	tree, wood
č'	ch with a pause after*	ič'íba	to feel remorse
d	d in dare	Dakhóta	
e	eh as in they	etáŋhaŋ	from
ǧ	*	ǧí	brown
h	h in hit	haŋyétu	night
ȟ	*	ȟóta	gray
i	ee in need	ištá	eye
iŋ	nasalized ee	íŋyaŋka	to run
k	between k in kiss and g in go	káǧa	to make
kh	k in kiss	kháta	hot

*These sounds are not found in English.

Letter	Sound	Dakhóta Example	Translation
k'	k with a pause after *	k'íŋ	to carry
m	m in mouse	mathó	bear
n	n in noise	núŋpa	two
o	oh as in go	ókiya	to help
p	between p in pat and b in ball	pápa	jerky
ph	p in pat	pháhiŋ	hair
p'	p with a pause after*	p'op'ó	foggy
s	s in sit	sápa	black
s'	s with a pause after*	s'amná	to smell bad
š	sh in shoot	šá	red
š'	sh with a pause after*	š'á	to shout
t	between t in toe and d in door	tókhed	how
th	t in toe	thó	blue
t'	t with a pause after*	t'at'á	to be numb
u	ooh as in rule	úma	nuts
uŋ	nasalized ooh	uŋktómi	spider
w	w in wish	wáta	boat
y	y in yell	yúte	to eat
z	z in zebra	zí	yellow
ž	s in pleasure	wóžapi	berry pudding

*These sounds are not found in English.

Notes

Preface

1. LaDonna Brave Bull Allard, "Why the Founder of Standing Rock Sioux Camp Can't Forget the Whitestone Massacre," *YES! Magazine*, September 3, 2016. http://www.yesmagazine.org.
2. Throughout this book I sometimes notate Dakhóta/Lakȟóta/Nakhóta with a slash to suggest that while there are linguistic and cultural differences among the different bands of the Očhéti Šakówiŋ Oyáte, or people of the Seven Council Fires, and while there is incessant teasing over those differences, we are all related through language, land, and kinship. More frequently, then, I refer to all three groups as either the Oyáte or simply as Dakhóta.
3. Leanne Simpson, *Dancing on Our Turtle's Back: Stories of Nishnaabeg Re-creation, Resurgence, and a New Emergence* (Winnipeg: ARP Books, 2011), 17.
4. "400 Protesters Standoff with Officers on Backwater Bridge," Morton County Sheriff's Department, news release, November 20, 2016. https://archive.org/stream/morton-county/MCSD_11-20_Riot_on_Backwater_Bridge_%282%29_djvu.txt.
5. Daniel Heath Justice, *Our Fire Survives the Storm: A Cherokee Literary History* (Minneapolis: University of Minnesota Press, 2006), 25.

Introduction

1. Here and throughout the book I use the names of thióšpaye in preference to language groups (i.e., Dakhóta, Lakhóta, or Nakhóta) as their linguistic specificities encode territorial, historical, and philosophical meanings; for instance, Sisíthuŋwaŋ or Sisseton are Dwellers of the Fishing Ground, where *sisí* abbreviates from "síŋ," the grease or fat of an animal.
2. A growing body of work by Indigenous studies scholars examines how allotment and assimilation policies specifically targeted Indigenous forms of kinship and land tenure, seeking to break down Indigenous forms of sociality in order to facilitate white settlement

249

and consequent displacement and targeted elimination of Indigenous peoples. Beth Piatote explains that these policies extended the U.S. military's Indian wars by seeking to destroy "Indian economies, lands, kinship systems, languages, cultural practices, and family relations—in short, all that constituted the Indian home." Piatote, *Domestic Subjects: Gender, Citizenship, and Law in Native American Literature* (New Haven, Conn.: Yale University Press, 2013), 2. Similarly, Mark Rifkin views U.S. allotment policies in their imposition of heteronormativity as a queering of Indigenous peoples' forms of extended family and kinship forms beyond a gender binary. Rifkin, *When Did Indians Become Straight? Kinship, the History of Sexuality, and Native Sovereignty* (New York: Oxford University Press, 2011). K. Tsianina Lomawaima observes how the militaristic boarding schools used bodily forms of discipline such as drills, uniforms, and surveillance to create compliant national subjects. Lomawaima, "Domesticity in the Federal Indian Schools: The Power of Authority over Mind and Body." *American Ethnologist* 20, no. 2 (1993): 227–40.

3. Charles Eastman, "Recollections of the Wild Life," *St. Nicholas: An Illustrated Magazine for Young Folks* 21 (December 1893–May 1894): 129–31, 226–28, 306–8, 437–40, 513–15, 607–11.

4. "Constitution and Laws of the Society of American Indians," *Quarterly Journal of the Society of American Indians* (Washington, D.C.: Society of American Indians, 1914), 2:324.

5. Robert Allen Warrior, *Tribal Secrets: Recovering American Indian Intellectual Traditions* (Minneapolis: University of Minnesota Press, 1995), 7.

6. Siobhan Senier, *Voices of American Indian Assimilation and Resistance: Helen Hunt Jackson, Sarah Winnemuca, and Victoria Howard* (Norman: University of Oklahoma Press, 2001), 18.

7. Philip Deloria, "Four Thousand Invitations," *American Indian Quarterly* 37, no. 3 (2013): 26.

8. Deloria, "Four Thousand Invitations," 26.

9. Kiara Vigil, *Indigenous Intellectuals: Sovereignty, Citizenship, and the American Imagination, 1880–1930* (New York: Cambridge University Press, 2015), 3.

10. Drawing on the work of Homi Bhabha, others have described these mixings and multiplicities in terms of a "third space" politics and hybridity, a term I find at once useful and limiting. Kevin Bruyneel defines the third space as "a location inassimilable to the liberal democratic settler-state, and as such it problematizes the boundaries of colonial rule but does not seek to capture or erase these boundaries." Its vision "is a supplementary strategy, because it refuses to

conform to the binaries and boundaries that frame dualistic choices for indigenous politics" (21). What's key in Bruyneel's reformulation of Bhabha is a greater emphasis on the explicitness of the supplement. By privileging refusal and equating the third space with "post-colonial resistance," however, modes of political life and agency that rely on—indeed exist within—the withheld and the nuanced are obscured. This privileging of the active and the explicit in political performances shows up in other theorizings of minority subjects' agency. In developing his term of "disidentification," for instance, José Muñoz notes how "minority subjects . . . must work with/resist the conditions of (im)possibility that dominant culture generates" (6). Where Muñoz looks at identity as emerging from "the point of collision of perspectives . . . when hybrid, racially predicated, and deviantly gendered identities arrive at representation" and thus "jolt" the social order, I have found among these assimilation-era writers that their political negotiations rarely announce themselves as such—that is, as political. I want to excavate and carry into the future here the absence of the jolt, the downplaying of difference, as a way of (re)making identity under exterminatory conditions. Bruyneel, *The Third Space of Sovereignty: The Postcolonial Politics of U.S.–Indigenous Relations* (Minneapolis: University of Minnesota Press, 2007); Muñoz, *Disidentifications: Queers of Color and the Performance of Politics* (Minneapolis: University of Minnesota Press, 1999).

11. Ella Cara Deloria, *Speaking of Indians* (1944; reprint, Pickle Partners Publishing, 2015, electronic edition).

12. Leslie Marmon Silko, *Ceremony* (1977; reprint, New York: Penguin 2006), 236.

13. "Dec. 26, 1862: 38 Dakota Men Executed in Mankato," (Minneapolis) *Star Tribune.* http://www.startribune.com.

14. "Dec. 26, 1862: 38 Dakota Men Executed in Mankato."

15. "Dec. 26, 1862: 38 Dakota Men Executed in Mankato."

16. Gwen Westerman and Bruce White, *Mni Sota Makoce: The Land of the Dakota* (St. Paul: Minnesota Historical Society Press, 2012).

17. Clifford Canku, "U.S.–Dakota War of 1862 Oral History Project: Interview with Clifford Canku," Minnesota Historical Society. http://www.mnhs.org/research/.

18. "Treaty with the Sioux, Sisseton and Wahpeton Bands, 1851," *Indian Affairs: Laws and Treaties*, ed. Charles J. Kappler (Washington, D.C.: Government Printing Office, 1904), 2:588–90.

19. Thomas Williamson to Selah Treat, June 13, 1855, MSS 244, no. 430, American Board of Commissioners for Foreign Missions Papers, Houghton Library, Harvard University.

NOTES TO INTRODUCTION

20. "Dec. 26, 1862: 38 Dakota Men Executed in Mankato."
21. "Dec. 26, 1862: 38 Dakota Men Executed in Mankato."
22. "Dec. 26, 1862: 38 Dakota Men Executed in Mankato."
23. "The Constitution of the State of Minnesota, Democratic Version," article 7, section 1, August 29, 1857. http://www.mnhs.org/library/constitution/pdf/democraticversion.pdf.
24. "Case 1: Godfrey (O-ta-kle)," *Famous Trials*, by Professor Douglas O. Linder. http://famous-trials.com/.
25. "Case 1: Godfrey (O-ta-kle)."
26. "Case 1: Godfrey (O-ta-kle)."
27. "Case 1: Godfrey (O-ta-kle)."
28. Carol Chomsky, "The United States–Dakota War Trials: A Study in Military Injustice," *Stanford Law Review* 43, no. 1 (1990): 32n119.
29. John Peacock, afterword to *The Dakota Prisoner of War Letters: Dakota Kaskapi Okicize Wowapi*, trans. and ed. Clifford Canku and Michael Simon (St. Paul: Minnesota Historical Society Press, 2013), 214.
30. Peacock, afterword to *Dakota Prisoner of War Letters*, 214.
31. Wazíyatawiŋ, *Remember This! Dakota Decolonization and the Eli Taylor Narratives* (Lincoln: University of Nebraska Press, 2005), 63.
32. Eric Cheyfitz, *The Poetics of Imperialism: Translation and Colonization from the Tempest to Tarzan* (Philadelphia: University of Pennsylvania Press, 1997).
33. Rifkin, *When Did Indians Become Straight?*, 8.
34. Although I owe an enormous intellectual debt to the work of Native American literary nationalists like Robert Warrior, Jace Weaver, and Craig Womack, I am less interested in (re)constructing a separate tribal nation than I am in exploring how entanglements with the settler state were themselves productive of a resurgent tribal peoplehood.
35. See especially Jennifer Nez Denetdale's "Chairmen, Presidents, and Princesses: The Navajo Nation, Gender, and the Politics of Tradition," *Wicazō Ṡa Review* 21, no. 1 (2006): 9–28; Brendan Hokowhitu, "Producing Elite Indigenous Masculinities" *Settler Colonial Studies* 2, no. 2 (2012): 23–48.
36. Elizabeth Povinelli, *The Cunning of Recognition: Indigenous Alterities and the Making of Australian Multiculturalism* (Durham, N.C.: Duke University Press, 2003); Audra Simpson, *Mohawk Interruptus: Political Life across the Borders of Settler States* (Durham, N.C.: Duke University Press, 2014), 105.
37. Audra Simpson, "On Ethnographic Refusal: Indigeneity, 'Voice,' and Colonial Citizenship," *Junctures* 9 (2007): 72.
38. Simpson, "On Ethnographic Refusal," 78.
39. Simpson, *Mohawk Interruptus*, 105.

NOTES TO INTRODUCTION 253

40. Lawrence Venuti, *The Translator's Invisibility: A History of Translation* (New York: Routledge, 2012), 1.
41. Venuti, *Translator's Invisibility*, 14.
42. Philip Deloria, *Playing Indian* (New Haven, Conn.: Yale University Press, 1998), 148.
43. Here I follow Naoki Sakai's work on the emergence of modern national languages as a practice of translational border making in *Translation and Subjectivity: "Japan" and Cultural Nationalism* (Minneapolis: University of Minnesota Press, 1997).
44. Chris Andersen, "Critical Indigenous Studies: From Difference to Density," *Cultural Studies Review* 15, no. 2 (2009): 94.
45. John P. Williamson, *An English–Dakota Dictionary* (St. Paul: Minnesota Historical Society Press, 1902).
46. Wazíyatawiŋ, *Remember This!*, 65.
47. In this respect I draw on and extend the historical scope of the recent development of a resurgent politics of indigeneity that refuses settler-colonial state frameworks of recognition and reconciliation, especially in the work of Glen Coulthard, Roxanne Dunbar-Ortiz et al., and Audra Simpson, among others. This politics' challenges to settler state sovereignty have in turn drawn on the development of Indigenous peoplehood as a key decolonizing term and set of discourses. This emergence follows the circulation of peoplehood discourses in other contexts, as with the creation in 1975 of the first international nongovernmental organization of Indigenous peoples, the World Council of Indigenous Peoples, which opened space for Indigenous self-representation without the mediation of government officials. The Working Group on Indigenous Peoples, established in 1982 as a subsidiary body of the UN Sub-Commission on the Prevention of Discrimination and Protection of Minorities, then began drafting what would, twenty-five years later, become the 2007 United Nations Declaration on the Rights of Indigenous Peoples. See Glen Coulthard, *Red Skin, White Masks: Rejecting the Colonial Politics of Recognition* (Minneapolis: University of Minnesota Press, 2014); Roxanne Dunbar-Ortiz, Dalee Sambo Dorough, Gudmundur Alfredsson, Lee Swepston, and Petter Wille, eds., *Indigenous Peoples' Rights in International Law: Emergence and Application* (Copenhagen: International Work Group for Indigenous Affairs [IWGIA], 2015), 13–14; Simpson, *Mohawk Interruptus*.
48. Scott Richard Lyons, *X-Marks: Native Signatures of Assent* (Minneapolis: University of Minnesota Press, 2010), 139.
49. Lyons, *X-Marks*, 120–31.
50. Lyons, *X-Marks*, 131.

NOTES TO INTRODUCTION

51. Lyons, *X-Marks*, 131.
52. Homi Bhabha, "The Third Space: Interview with Homi Bhabha," conducted by Jonathan Rutherford, in *Identity: Community, Culture, Difference* (London: Lawrence & Wishart, 1990), 220.
53. Bhabha, "Third Space," 32.
54. Gerald Vizenor, *Fugitive Poses: Native American Indian Scenes of Absence and Presence* (Lincoln: University of Nebraska Press, 2000), 165.
55. Thomas Biolsi, "The Birth of the Reservation: Making the Modern Indian among the Lakota," *American Ethnologist* 22, no. 1 (1995): 28–29.
56. Biolsi, "Birth of the Reservation," 28–29.
57. Povinelli, *Cunning of Recognition*, 13.
58. Povinelli, *Cunning of Recognition*, 17.
59. Povinelli, *Cunning of Recognition*, 3.
60. "U.S.–Dakota War of 1862," Minnesota Historical Society. http://www.usdakotawar.org/.
61. Colin Dayan, review of *Entangled Empathy: An Alternative Ethic for Our Relationships with Animals*, by Lori Gruen, *Boston Review*, September 28, 2015. http://bostonreview.net/.
62. Dayan, review of Gruen, *Entangled Empathy*.
63. Saba Mahmood, *Politics of Piety: The Islamic Revival and the Feminist Subject* (Princeton, N.J.: Princeton University Press, 2005), 120.
64. See Dian Million, *Therapeutic Nations: Healing in an Age of Indigenous Human Rights* (Tucson: University of Arizona Press, 2013); Rifkin, *When Did Indians Become Straight?*; Ann Laura Stoler, "Tense and Tender Ties: The Politics of Comparison in North American History and (Post) Colonial Studies," *Journal of American History* 88, no. 3 (2001): 829–65.
65. Rifkin, *When Did Indians Become Straight?*, 6.
66. Jeff Corntassel and Mick Scow, "Everyday Acts of Resurgence: Indigenous Approaches to Everydayness in Fatherhood," *New Diversities* 19, no. 2 (2017): 55–68.
67. Lauren Berlant, "Slow Death (Sovereignty, Obesity, Lateral Agency)," *Critical Inquiry* 33 (2007): 756.
68. Berlant, "Slow Death," 757.
69. Berlant, "Slow Death," 758–59.
70. Beth Piatote, *Domestic Subjects: Gender, Citizenship, and Law in Native American Literature* (New Haven, Conn.: Yale University Press, 2013), 173.
71. Piatote, *Domestic Subjects*, 4.
72. Coulthard, *Red Skin, White Masks*, 61.

NOTES TO INTRODUCTION   **255**

73. Kim TallBear, "Disrupting Settlement, Sex, and Nature: An Indigenous Logic of Relationality," lecture delivered as part of Concordia University's Future Imaginary Lecture Series, Montreal, October 13, 2016.
74. TallBear, "Disrupting Settlement."
75. My use of other-than-human persons follows from the work of TallBear but also from David Shorter's *We Will Dance Our Truths: Yaqui History in Yoeme Performances* (Lincoln: University of Nebraska Press, 2009); Kenneth Morrison's "The Cosmos as Inter-Subjective: Native American Other-than-Human Persons," in *Indigenous Religions: A Companion*, ed. Harvey Graham (London: Cassell, 2000); and the term's creator, Irving Hallowell, "Ojibwa Ontology, Behavior, and Worldview," in *Teachings from the American Earth: Indian Religion and Philosophy*, ed. Dennis Tedlock and Barbara Tedlock (New York: Liveright, 1975).
76. My sense of pausing here refers to Dakhóta storytelling, but I am grateful to Mary Pat Brady for suggesting its use to describe a temporal orientation that is distinct from capitalism's logic of limitless accumulation as an activity that need not—or cannot—be suspended.
77. Charles Alexander Eastman (Ohyesa), *Indian Heroes and Great Chieftains* (Boston: Little, Brown, 1918), available at Project Gutenberg (http://www.gutenberg.org/).
78. "N.W. Indians," in *Niles' Register*, vol. 28, ed. H. Niles, July 2, 1825.
79. "Treaty of Traverse des Sioux," in *Mni Sota Makoce: The Land of the Dakota*, ed. Gwen Westerman and Bruce White (St. Paul: Minnesota Historical Society Press, 2012), 176.
80. "Treaty of Traverse des Sioux."
81. Wazíyatawiŋ, *Remember This!*, 38.
82. Wazíyatawiŋ, *Remember This!*, 37–38.
83. Ella Cara Deloria, "Alpha. Huka Ceremony," Ella Deloria Archive, American Indian Studies Research Institute, Indiana University. http://zia.aisri.indiana.edu/deloria_archive, 60.
84. Deloria, "Alpha. Huka Ceremony," 61.
85. Kenneth Morrison, *The Solidarity of Kin: Ethnohistory, Religious Studies, and the Algonkian–French Religious Encounter* (Albany: SUNY Press, 2012), 160–61.
86. Stephen R. Riggs gives an etymology of "the terms for 'white man' in Siouan languages": "The author's [Riggs's] supposition as to the eastern origin of wašíćuŋ as 'nearly synonymous with wakaŋ' [mysterious] in the opinion of some persons. He appends the following Thíthuŋwaŋ meanings: 'A familiar spirit; some mysterious forces or

beings which are supposed to communicate with men; mitawaśíćuŋ he omakiyaka, my familiar spirit told me that." This phrase he gives as referring to the Takuśkanśkan, the Something-that-moves or the Wind powers." Riggs, *Dakota Grammar, Texts, and Ethnography* (Washington, D.C.: Government Printing Office, 1893), xxx.

87. Wazíyatawiŋ, *Remember This!*, 16.

88. Leslie Marmon Silko, "Language and Literature from a Pueblo Indian Perspective," in *Nothing but the Truth: An Anthology of Native American Literature*, ed. John L. Purdy and James Ruppert (1996; reprint, Upper Saddle River, N.J.: Prentice Hall, 2001), 161.

89. Silko, "Language and Literature," 161.

90. Wazíyatawiŋ, *Remember This!*, 41–42.

91. Audra Simpson, *Mohawk Interruptus: Political Life Across the Borders of Settler States* (Durham, NC: Duke University Press, 2014), 176.

92. Lakȟóta speakers use an added guttural "ȟ" sound in many words, including the word *Lakȟóta* itself, but also *wakȟáŋ*, where Dakȟóta speakers do not. When discussing Lakȟóta texts or persons, I follow this usage, but in Dakȟóta-language cases I use the nonguttural "h" (*wakȟáŋ*). Similarly, in Dakȟóta there is frequently an added "t" sound where there is not in Lakȟóta, as with the word *wičášta*.

93. Rifkin, *When Did Indians Become Straight?*, 277.

1. Transgressive Adoptions

1. Michel-Rolph Trouillot, *Silencing the Past: Power and the Production of History* (Boston: Beacon Press, 1995), 96–97.

2. I use the term "U.S.–Dakota War" in preference to other presentations, such as the Dakota Conflict, Dakota Uprising, or Little Crow's War. Historians writing in the early 1900s referred to the event as the Great Sioux Massacre or the Great Sioux War. Clearly many of these usages sensationalize Dakȟóta violence. My choice refuses such labels as being ideological and racist. Instead I aim to avoid trivializing, by subsuming within U.S. national narratives of dominance, Dakȟóta armed resistance to Minnesotan and federal militias. An "uprising" or "conflict" is the action of upstarts, not of peoples or nations; "war" suggests a nation-to-nation engagement. Because the war began over what Dakȟóta perceived as the failure of the federal government to uphold its treaty obligations, this seems the most apt term.

3. Wazíyatawiŋ Angela Wilson, "Time to Level," (Minneapolis) *Star Tribune*, December 2, 2007. https://web.archive.org/web/20080206084249/ http://www.startribune.com/opinion/commentary/11980331.html.

NOTES TO CHAPTER 1   257

4. "U.S.–Dakota War of 1862," Minnesota Historical Society.
5. Wazíyatawiŋ Angela Wilson, "Time to Level."
6. See generally Paul N. Beck, *Columns of Vengeance: Soldiers, Sioux, and the Punitive Expeditions, 1863–1864* (Norman: University of Oklahoma Press, 2013).
7. Here the "fires" are the Seven Council Fires, or Očhéti Šakówiŋ Oyáte.
8. Dean Blue, "We Made a Pact, and You're Not Paying It," "U.S.–Dakota War of 1862," Minnesota Historical Society.
9. To call the stockades at Mankato and Fort Snelling concentration camps is, of course, a kind of provocation, but it is one shared by Wazíyatawiŋ, who reassesses the 1862 war and its aftermath in light of the United Nations Convention on the Prevention and Punishment of the Crime of Genocide and the 2007 Declaration of the Rights of Indigenous Peoples. Wazíyatawiŋ, "Colonial Calibrations," *William Mitchell Law Review* 39, no. 2 (2013): 450–85. At the time of this writing, the term "concentration camp" is used only reluctantly by the Minnesota Historical Society, whose website states that the "civilian internment camp" outside of Fort Snelling is "sometimes referred to as a concentration camp." Yet what is at stake in this label is precisely the denaturalizing of state power wielded and abused in the service of "cleansing" the fledgling state of Minnesota of its indigenous peoples. See "The U.S.–Dakota War of 1862," Historic Fort Snelling, Minnesota Historical Society. http://www.historicfortsnelling.org/.
10. The camp is so named because it is the site where Dakhóta released 269 white captives to the military forces commanded by General Henry Sibley.
11. These include David Martínez's recent account of the trials and mass execution, "Remembering the Thirty-Eight: Abraham Lincoln, the Dakota, and the U.S. War on Barbarism," *Wicazō Ša Review* 28, no. 2 (2013): 5–29. Maybe the fullest treatment of the camps themselves is Corinne Monjeau-Marz's history, *The Dakota Indian Internment at Fort Snelling, 1862–1864*, rev. ed. (St. Paul, Minn.: Prairie Smoke Press, 2006), which is a raw assemblage of excerpted primary documents, and which fails to place the camps in their settler-colonial context as sites of "concentrating" Dakhóta people. Gary Anderson and Paul Woolworth's collection, *Through Dakota Eyes: Narrative Accounts of the Minnesota War of 1862* (St. Paul: Minnesota Historical Society Press, 1988), is a valuable starting point for considering Dakhóta points of view about state power abuses, as it culls transcriptions of oral histories from survivors of the war, camps, and relocations. Wazíyatawiŋ's *In the Footsteps of Our Ancestors: The Dakota Commemorative Marches of the 21st Century* (St. Paul, Minn.: Living

Justice Press, 2006) likewise is an anthology, but of contemporary Indigenous authors, scholars, and community members, who recount stories about the Dakhóta death march of November 1862 from Camp Release to Fort Snelling. Other scholars have focused on how legal framings of the war served as a crucial means for its remembering or forgetting, such as Marouf Hasian Jr.'s "Cultural Amnesias and Legal Recollections: Forgetting and Remembering in the 1862 U.S.–Dakota War Tribunals," chap. 3 of *In the Name of Necessity* (Tuscaloosa: University of Alabama Press, 2005), 54–78. See also Carol Chomsky's legal analysis of the tribunals, which situates them in the context of Civil War law and dominant culture notions of warfare: "The United States–Dakota War Trials: A Study in Military Injustice," *Stanford Law Review* 43, no. 1 (1990): 13–98. For further comparisons of U.S. treatment of First Nations as genocide, and the comparison of anti-Semitism to anti-Indianism, see Elizabeth Cook-Lynn's *Anti-Indianism in Modern America: A Voice from Tatekeya's Earth* (Urbana: University of Illinois Press, 2001).

12. Wazíyatawiŋ, "Grandmother to Granddaughter: Generations of Oral History," *American Indian Quarterly* 20, no. 1 (1996): 7.

13. Deloria, *Speaking of Indians*.

14. Stephen R. Riggs, *Mary and I: Forty Years with the Sioux* (Boston, Mass.: Congregational Sunday-School and Publishing Society, 1887), 334.

15. See Neal Salisbury, *Manitou and Providence: Indians, Europeans, and the Making of New England, 1500–1643* (New York: Oxford University Press, 1984); Richard White, *The Middle Ground: Indians, Empires, and Republics in the Great Lakes Region, 1650–1815* (New York: Cambridge University Press, 1991).

16. Dipesh Chakrabarty, *Provincializing Europe: Postcolonial Thought and Historical Difference* (Princeton, N.J.: Princeton University Press, 2000), 87.

17. Chakrabarty, *Provincializing Europe*, 83.

18. George Tinker, *Missionary Conquest: The Gospel and Native American Cultural Genocide* (Minneapolis, Minn.: Fortress Press, 1993), xiii.

19. Chomsky, "United States–Dakota War Trials," 75.

20. Martínez, "Remembering the Thirty-Eight," 5.

21. Chomsky, "United States–Dakota War Trials," 74–75.

22. "The Court Proceedings in the Trial of Dakota Indians Following the Massacre in Minnesota in August 1862" (Minneapolis, Minn.: Satterlee Print Company, 1927).

23. Monjeau-Marz, *Dakota Indian Internment*, 67.

NOTES TO CHAPTER 1

24. "Lincoln's Order of December 6, 1862, Authorizing the Execution of Thirty-Eight Dakota," Famous Trials, by Professor Douglas O. Linder. http://famous-trials.com/.
25. Anderson and Woolworth, "Samuel J. Brown's Recollections," *Through Dakota Eyes*, 227.
26. Mark Diedrich, *Old Betsey: The Life and Times of a Famous Dakota Woman* (Rochester, Minn.: Coyote Books, 1995), 80.
27. The Minnesota Historical Society bibliographic entry for a similar spoon to the one pictured in Figure 3 notes that "the engraved scene of the hanging was taken from a drawing by W. H. Childs commonly used for other commemorative products of this event." The fifty-year anniversary of the event, in 1902, apparently spawned a minor industry in spoons of this sort. See Minnesota Historical Society Collections Online, "U.S.–Dakota War of 1862 Commemorative Souvenir Spoon in Case," http://www.mnhs.org/research/.
28. Povinelli, *Cunning of Recognition*, 3.
29. Unsurprisingly, the term "Dakota diaspora" is not only little known but also difficult even to track down in a common Internet search. When I searched for the term "Dakota diaspora," the first entire page of results was for a memoir of Jewish homesteaders in North Dakota. However, the term "diaspora" in a Dakhóta context describes a lived and remembered experience of forced exile that began with the expulsion of Dakhóta from Minnesota in 1862 and 1863 (enforced through state bounties on scalps), then continued with the imprisonments at Fort Snelling and Mankato, as well as their removal to reservations at Crow Creek, South Dakota, and Camp Davenport, Iowa; and left Dakhóta strewn across the West as far afield as British Columbia.
30. *Mni Wakáŋ Oyate* (Greenlawn, N.Y.: Pine Woods Recording, 2007).
31. Anderson and Woolworth, "Gabriel Renville's Memoir," *Through Dakota Eyes*, 233.
32. Anderson and Woolworth, "Gabriel Renville's Memoir," *Through Dakota Eyes*, 234.
33. Anderson and Woolworth, "Gabriel Renville's Memoir," *Through Dakota Eyes*, 234.
34. Eastman, *Indian Heroes*, 49.
35. Eastman, *Indian Heroes*, 50.
36. Thaóyate Dúta (His Scarlet People, or Little Crow) was what non-Dakhóta commonly call a chief, or spokesman, among the Bdewákhaŋthuŋwaŋ (Spirit Lake Dwellers). Little Crow led the war against settlers in 1862, and after their defeat at Wood Lake, he fled west to Dakota Territory to rally the support of other Dakhóta bands.

See Gary C. Anderson, *Little Crow, Spokesman for the Sioux* (St. Paul: Minnesota Historical Society Press, 1986).

37. "Good Star Woman's Recollections," in Anderson and Woolworth, *Through Dakota Eyes*, 263.

38. Gary Clayton Anderson, *Kinsmen of Another Kind: Dakota–White Relations in the Upper Mississippi Valley, 1650–1862* (St. Paul: Minnesota Historical Society Press, 1997), 260.

39. Other Christian denominations were also represented in the camps. For instance, the Catholic priest Augustin Ravoux, from the diocese of St. Paul, ministered to Dakhóta prisoners.

40. For a historical overview of the Dakota Mission's early years, see *The First 50 Years: Dakota Presbytery to 1890* (1886; reprint, Freeman, S.D.: Pine Hill Press/Dakota Presbytery Council, 1984); *Dakota Mission Past and Present* (1886; reprint, Freeman, S.D.: Pine Hill Press/Dakota Presbytery Council, 1984).

41. Riggs, *Mary and I*, 216.

42. S. R. Riggs to S. B. Treat, March 26, 1863, A.B.C.F.M. MSS 310, no. 29—A.L.S., 3–4, MS 16, Ayer Collection, Newberry Library, Chicago, Illinois.

43. S. R. Riggs to S. B. Treat, March 26, 1863, MSS 310, no. 29, MS 16, Ayer Collection, Newberry Library.

44. S. R. Riggs to S. B. Treat, March 26, 1863, MSS 310, no. 29, MS 16, Ayer Collection, Newberry Library.

45. "Four Lightning/David Faribault, Jr., May 18, 1863," in Canku and Simon, *Dakota Prisoner of War Letters*, 11.

46. "Ruban His Sacred Nest, April [22], 1864," letter, Ruban Tahoȟpi Wakan to S. R. Riggs, in Canku and Simon, *Dakota Prisoner of War Letters*, 39.

47. John Peacock, "Introducing the Dakota Letters," in Canku and Simon, *Dakota Prisoner of War Letters*, xxvii.

48. Peacock, "Introducing the Dakota Letters," in Canku and Simon, *Dakota Prisoner of War Letters*, xxvi.

49. "James the Sacred Second Son, May 17, 1864," letter, James Hepan Wakan to S. R. Riggs, in Canku and Simon, *Dakota Prisoner of War Letters*, 44–45. Here and in all subsequent quotations of Dakhóta prisoners I include both English and Dakhóta, where the Dakhóta uses the orthography devised by Samuel and Gideon Pond, and later modified by Riggs.

50. "Mr. Uses a Cane, June 2, 1865," letter, Sagyekitun to S. R. Riggs, in Canku and Simon, *Dakota Prisoner of War Letters*, 162–63.

51. "Mr. Uses a Cane, June 2, 1865," in Canku and Simon, *Dakota Prisoner of War Letters*, 162.

NOTES TO CHAPTER 1   261

52. "Mr. Uses a Cane, June 2, 1865," in Canku and Simon, *Dakota Prisoner of War Letters*, 165.
53. "Mr. Uses a Cane, June 2, 1865," in Canku and Simon, *Dakota Prisoner of War Letters*, 167.
54. "Mr. Uses a Cane, June 2, 1865," in Canku and Simon, *Dakota Prisoner of War Letters*, 167.
55. "Mr. Uses a Cane, June 2, 1865," in Canku and Simon, *Dakota Prisoner of War Letters*, 168–69.
56. "Ruban His Sacred Nest, April [22], 1864," in Canku and Simon, *Dakota Prisoner of War Letters*, 34–35.
57. "Ruban His Sacred Nest, April [22], 1864," in Canku and Simon, *Dakota Prisoner of War Letters*, 34–35.
58. See Joseph Renville and sons, and the missionaries of the American Board of Commissioners for Foreign Missions, *Dakota Dowanpi Kin: Hymns in the Dakota or Sioux Language* (Boston, Mass.: Printed for the American Board of Commissioners for Foreign Missions by Crocker & Brewster, 1842); Rev. Samuel W. Pond, *Wowai Inonpa: Wowapi Wakan Etanhan Taju Wanjikji Oyakapi Kin He Dee: The Second Dakota Reading Book: Consisting of Bible Stories from the Old Testament* (Boston, Mass.: Printed for the American Board of Commissioners for Foreign Missions by Crocker & Brewster, 1842).
59. Stephen R. Riggs, "The Theogony of the Sioux," in *The American Antiquarian*, ed. Stephen Denison Peet (Chicago: Jameson & Morse, 1879–80), 2:255.
60. Stephen R. Riggs, *A Dakota–English Dictionary* (1890; reprint, St. Paul: Minnesota Historical Society Press, 1992), 507–8.
61. S. R. Riggs to D. Greene, February 8, 1846, MSS 244, no. 220, MS 16, Ayer Collection, Newberry Library.
62. S. R. Riggs to D. Greene, February 8, 1846, MSS 244, no. 220, MS 16, Ayer Collection, Newberry Library.
63. Raymond DeMallie, *The Sixth Grandfather: Black Elk's Teaching Given to John G. Neihardt* (Lincoln: University of Nebraska Press, 1985), 81.
64. DeMallie, *Sixth Grandfather*, 81.
65. Stephen R. Riggs, *Tah-koo wah-kan, or The Gospel among the Dakotas* (Boston, Mass.: Congregational Sabbath-School and Publishing Society, 1869), 266.
66. Monica L. Siems, "How Do You Say 'God' in Dakota? Epistemological Problems in the Christianization of Native Americans," *Numen* 45, no. 2 (1998): 163–82.
67. James R. Walker, *Lakota Belief and Ritual*, ed. Raymond DeMallie (Lincoln: University of Nebraska Press, 1991), 98–99.

68. Charles Alexander Eastman, "The Sioux Mythology," *Popular Science Monthly* 46 (November 1894): 88.
69. See *Rules Governing Court of Indian Offenses* (Washington, D.C.: U.S. Office of Indian Affairs, 1883), CIS U.S. Executive Branch Documents, 1789–1909, no. I2012-17.
70. "Robert Hopkins/First Born Son, May 3, 1864," letter, Robert Hopkins/ Chaske to S. R. Riggs, in Canku and Simon, *Dakota Prisoner of War Letters*, 38–39.
71. Riggs, *Dakota–English Dictionary*, 524.
72. New Lakota Dictionary, s.v., "úŋšikA," https://www.lakotadictionary. org.
73. Riggs, *Dakota–English Dictionary*, 378–79.
74. William K. Powers, *Oglala Religion* (Lincoln: University of Nebraska Press, 1982), 133.
75. Powers, *Oglala Religion*, 133–34.
76. Powers, *Oglala Religion*, 134.
77. T. S. Williamson to S. B. Treat, MSS 310, no. 256, MS 16, Ayer Collection, Newberry Library.
78. T. S. Williamson to S. B. Treat, MSS 310, no. 256, MS 16, Ayer Collection, Newberry Library.
79. See Anderson, *Kinsmen of Another Kind*.
80. T. S. Williamson to S. B. Treat, MSS 310, no. 227, MS 16, Ayer Collection, Newberry Library.
81. *Iápi Oáye* (The word-carrier) 2, no. 3 (1872): 36. John P. Williamson, who accompanied the Dakhóta who were moved to Santee Agency, started the newspaper in May 1871.
82. Riggs, *Dakota–English Dictionary*, 371.
83. Riggs, *Dakota–English Dictionary*, 54.

First Interlude

1. Wazíyatawiŋ, *Remember This!*, 28.
2. The story of the thunder beings that killed my grandmother's paternal grandmother, Išnáwiŋ (Lone Woman), comes right after uŋčí Grace's story about obedience and seems to have a similar point made in an inverse way: "When they tell you not to do something, that's just when you go and do it. And sometimes you get yourself in some terrible trouble, too." In the case of the thunder beings, it was not the doing of an action but rather the failure to act (to sacrifice something for the Wakíŋyaŋ) that caused "some terrible trouble."
3. My uŋčí, Rachel Charboneau, often told the story that she found her grandma (Išnáwiŋ or Lone Woman) on the day before the storm

NOTES TO CHAPTER 2

crying on the hill above their log house. She was facing west, toward the thunders, and was pleading and wailing for the thunders to take her life instead of her child's.

4. This entire exchange between my grandmas remains wonderfully rich and complicated to me even twenty years later. After all, uŋčí Rachel seems to distance herself from her younger self and relatives here by saying, "They believed in that" (in the powerful being of Wakíŋyaŋ), while uŋčí Grace nests the story of her grandma within a biblical story of Abraham and Isaac. I heard this story many times from them when I was growing up, and in those tellings—as well as in uŋčí Rachel's lifelong respect for lightning—it became clear to me that not only the Wakíŋyaŋ but also the logic of sacrifice or exchange that they embodied lived on well beyond the moments when my grandmothers became Catholics.

5. Another account by Waŋbdíthaŋka (Big Eagle) has the number at four young men, including Suŋǧíhidaŋ (Brown Wing), Kaómdeiyeyedaŋ (Breaking Up), Naǧíwičhakte (Killing Ghost), and Pazóiyopa (Runs Against Something When Crawling). I give a portion of this account in my first chapter in order to narrate Dakota starvation as a primary cause of the war. See "The Acton Incident," "U.S.–Dakota War of 1862," Minnesota Historical Society.

6. The Seven Council Fires, or Očhéti Šakówiŋ.

7. Šákpe (Shakopee), or "Six."

2. (Il)legible, (Il)liberal Subjects

1. "Dr. Charles Alexander Eastman," Redpath Chautauqua Collection, University of Iowa Digital Library. http://sdrc.lib.uiowa.edu/traveling -culture/inventory/msc150.html.

2. Tsianina Lomawaima, "The Mutuality of *Citizenship* and *Sovereignty*: The Society of American Indians and the Battle to Inherit America," *Sail* 25, no. 2 / *AIQ* 37, no. 3 (2013): 334.

3. Kiara Vigil, *Indigenous Intellectuals: Sovereignty, Citizenship, and the American Imagination* (Cambridge: Cambridge University Press, 2015), 44.

4. Vigil, *Indigenous Intellectuals*, 51.

5. Penelope Myrtle Kelsey, *Tribal Theory in Native American Literature: Dakota and Haudenosaunee Writing and Indigenous Worldviews* (Lincoln: University of Nebraska Press, 2008), 55.

6. Warrior, *Tribal Secrets*, 8.

7. James Scott, *Seeing Like a State: How Certain Schemes to Improve the Human Condition Have Failed* (New Haven, Conn.: Yale University Press, 1998), 2.

NOTES TO CHAPTER 2

8. The 1906 Burke Act modified the 1887 Dawes Act's provision for individuals to sell allotted land after a twenty-five-year holding period by introducing the notion of "competence," which was measured by "Indian blood" quantum of greater than a quarter degree. This administrative label delineated which individuals were "competent and capable of managing his or her own affairs" by virtue of performing the "habits of civilized life," which effectively meant proving oneself as a successful homesteader.

9. Kevin Bruyneel, "Challenging American Boundaries: Indigenous People and the 'Gift' of U.S. Citizenship," *Studies in American Political Development* 18 (2004): 30–43.

10. Lucy Maddox, *Citizen Indians: Native American Intellectuals, Race, and Reform* (Ithaca, N.Y.: Cornell University Press, 2005), 131.

11. Eve Kosofsky Sedgwick, *Epistemology of the Closet* (Berkeley: University of California Press, 1990), 3.

12. Charles Eastman, *The Indian To-day: The Past and Future of the First American* (Garden City, N.Y.: Doubleday, Page, 1915), 27.

13. Mark Rifkin, "Remapping the Family of Nations: The Geopolitics of Kinship in Hendrick Aupaumut's 'A Short Narration,'" *Studies in American Indian Literatures* 22, no. 4 (2010): 1.

14. My use of opacity follows Édouard Glissant's in *Poetics of Relation* (Ann Arbor: University of Michigan Press, 1997), 189–94.

15. "Ruse," *Oxford English Dictionary*. http://www.oed.com/.

16. Henry Louis Gates Jr., *The Signifying Monkey: A Theory of African-American Literary Criticism* (New York: Oxford University Press, 1988), 50.

17. Diana Taylor, *The Archive and the Repertoire: Performing Cultural Memory in the Americas* (Durham, N.C.: Duke University Press, 2003), 24.

18. Elizabeth A. Povinelli, "The Governance of the Prior," *Interventions* 13, no. 1 (2011): 28.

19. I use the term "philosophy" to describe Dakhóta thióšpaye understandings as a way of distinguishing it from the religious or the spiritual. My usage follows that of Vine Deloria Jr. in *God Is Red: A Native View of Religion* (Golden, Colo.: Fulcrum, 1994), where he describes the inadequacy of the category of religion for capturing tribal philosophies of interrelatedness.

20. Tony Dykema-Vanderark, "'Playing Indian' in Print: Charles A. Eastman's Autobiographical Writing for Children," *MELUS* 27, no. 2 (2002): 27.

21. Venuti, *Translator's Invisibility*, 5.

22. Mahmood, *Politics of Piety*, 120.

23. Deloria, *Speaking of Indians*, 40.

NOTES TO CHAPTER 2 **265**

24. Deloria, *Speaking of Indians*, 43.
25. For an account of a similar paradigm of human and other-than-human reciprocity in Australia, see Irene Watson, "Sovereign Spaces, Caring for Country, and the Homeless Position of Aboriginal People," *South Atlantic Quarterly* 108, no. 1 (2009): 27–51.]
26. Lyons, *X-Marks*, 13.
27. See especially Simon Ortiz, "Towards a National Indian Literature: Cultural Authenticity in Nationalism," *MELUS* 8, no. 2 (1981): 7–12; Warrior, *Tribal Secrets*; Jace Weaver, *That the People Might Live: Native American Literatures and Native American Community* (New York: Oxford University Press, 1997); Jace Weaver, Craig Womack, and Robert Warrior, *American Indian Literary Nationalism* (Albuquerque: University of New Mexico Press, 2006); Craig Womack, *Red on Red: Native American Literary Separatism* (Minneapolis: University of Minnesota Press, 1999).
28. Kelsey, *Tribal Theory*, 55.
29. Joanne Barker, "Recognition," *American Studies* 46, no. 3/4 (2005): 155.
30. The legal doctrine of Native wardship was based on the construal of Indigenous peoples in the United States as "domestic dependent nations" rather than independent sovereigns and as being subject to congressional power (*Cherokee Nation v. Georgia*).
31. Eastman's *Red Hunters* tales differ from posthumanist concerns for dethroning human sovereignty in that they emphasize ethical meanings that emerge at the crossroads of place (as land historically and ontologically born from), time (as occupation of and care for a place), and peoplehood (the existential basis for and way of mediating power). In his tale "The Gray Chieftain" from that collection, Eastman glosses peoplehood simply as "knowledge."
32. Piatote, *Domestic Subjects*, 49.
33. Transcript of Dawes Act (1887). https://www.ourdocuments.gov/doc .php?flash=false&doc=50&page=transcript.
34. Joel Pfister reads part of the "ideological violence" of assimilation discourses in their being "packaged as regeneration through individuality." Pfister, *Individuality Incorporated: Indians and the Multicultural Modern* (Durham, N.C.: Duke University Press, 2004), 45.
35. Maddox, *Citizen Indians*, 80.
36. Biolsi, "Birth of the Reservation," 28–53.
37. See *First 50 Years* and *Dakota Mission Past and Present*.
38. Mark Rifkin, *The Erotics of Sovereignty: Queer Native Writing in the Era of Self-Determination* (Minneapolis: University of Minnesota Press, 2012), 83–84.

NOTES TO CHAPTER 2

39. See especially Robert Alexander Innes, *Elder Brother and the Law of the People: Contemporary Kinship and Cowessess First Nation* (Winnipeg: University of Manitoba Press, 2013); Daniel Heath Justice, *Our Fire Survives the Storm: A Cherokee Literary History* (Minneapolis: University of Minnesota Press, 2006); Aileen Moreton-Robinson, "Towards an Australian Indigenous Women's Standpoint Theory: A Methodological Tool," *Australian Feminist Studies* 28, no. 78 (2013): 331–47; Rose Stremlau, *Sustaining the Cherokee Family: Kinship and the Allotment of an Indigenous Nation* (Chapel Hill: University of North Carolina Press, 2011).
40. Jodi Byrd, *The Transit of Empire: Indigenous Critiques of Colonialism* (Minneapolis: University of Minnesota Press, 2011), xv.
41. Alan Trachtenberg, *Shades of Hiawatha: Staging Indians, Making Americans, 1880–1930* (New York: Hill & Wang, 2004), 282.
42. Deloria, "Dakota Ceremonies," Ethnographic Notes Manuscript, box 1, Dakota Ethnography, Ella Deloria Archive, 4.
43. Deloria, "Dakota Ceremonies," 4.
44. Watson gives an account of a similar paradigm in Australia of Indigenous forms of caretaking land in "Sovereign Spaces."
45. Deloria. *Speaking of Indians*, 25.
46. Deloria, *Speaking of Indians*, 24.
47. "Charles Eastman," *Book Review Digest* (Minneapolis: Wilson, 1905), 1:109–10.
48. Bruyneel, *Third Space of Sovereignty*, 217.
49. Bruyneel, *Third Space of Sovereignty*, 2.
50. Wazíyatawiŋ, "Grandmother to Granddaughter," 9.
51. David Martinez, *Dakota Philosopher: Charles Eastman and American Indian Thought* (St. Paul: Minnesota Historical Society Press, 2009), 42.
52. Wazíyatawiŋ, *Remember This!*, 64.
53. Wazíyatawiŋ, *Remember This!*, 64.
54. *Wigwam Evenings: Sioux Folk Tales Retold* (Boston: Little, Brown, 1909).
55. Charles Alexander Eastman (Ohiyesa), *From the Deep Woods to Civilization* (Boston: Little, Brown, 1916), 165.
56. Eastman, *From the Deep Woods*, 141.
57. Eastman, *From the Deep Woods*, 141.
58. Partha Chatterjee, "Anderson's Utopia," *Diacritics* 29, no. 4 (1999): 131.
59. Chatterjee, "Anderson's Utopia," 132.
60. Wazíyatawiŋ, "Grandmother to Granddaughter," 12.
61. Wazíyatawiŋ, *Remember This!*, 65.

NOTES TO CHAPTER 2

62. Deloria, *God Is Red*, 66.
63. Eastman, "Sioux Mythology," 88.
64. DeMallie, *Sixth Grandfather*, 81.
65. Charles Alexander Eastman (Ohiyesa), *Red Hunters and the Animal People* (New York: Harper & Brothers, 1904, 24.
66. "Treaty with the Sioux—Sisseton and Wahpeton Bands, 1851," Indian Affairs: Laws and Treaties, digital collection at Oklahoma State Library. https://dc.library.okstate.edu/.
67. "Timeline," "U.S.–Dakota War of 1862," Minnesota Historical Society.
68. Karl Marx and Frederick Engels, "Economic Dependence of the State on the Bourgeoisie," in *The Collected Works of Marx and Engels* (Moscow: Progress Publishers, 1976), 5:372.
69. Charles Alexander Eastman (Ohiyesa), *The Soul of the Indian: An Interpretation* (New York: Houghton Mifflin, 1911), 123.
70. Robert Williams Jr., *Linking Arms Together: American Indian Treaty Visions of Law and Peace, 1600–1800* (New York: Oxford University Press, 1997), 84–85.
71. Morrison, *Solidarity of Kin*, 160–61.
72. Unilaterally conferring U.S. citizenship on Native people, and despite allowing for dual citizenship (tribal and U.S.), the ICA formally incorporated Native Americans of federally recognized tribes into a national regulatory system of laws and governance. The conferral of citizenship thus implied the presumptive greater sovereignty of the United States and reinforced the notion, articulated in *U.S. v. Kagama* (1886), of tribal "quasi-sovereignty." Finally, the ICA further reified U.S. notions of territory and territoriality, so that Indigenous identity appeared to be contained or containable by the borders of the United States. See Bruyneel, "Challenging American Boundaries"; Lomawaima, "Mutuality of *Citizenship* and *Sovereignty*."
73. Charles Alexander Eastman (Ohiyesa), "The North American Indian," in *Papers on Inter-Racial Problems, Communicated to the First Universal Races Congress, Held at the University of London, July 26–29, 1911*, ed. Gustav Spiller (Boston, Mass.: World's Peace Foundation, 1911), 369.
74. For instance, the 1851 Treaty of Traverse des Sioux, which ceded large areas of Dakhóta territory in Mní Sóta, prescribes a kind of ethic where "people of the United States and the Wahpeton and Sisseton Dakota . . . help each other and are allied with each other . . . [and] resolved and concluded forever from this time to hold each other's hearts." See "Treaty with the Sioux—Sisseton and Wahpeton Bands, 1851," Indian Affairs: Laws and Treaties, digital collection at Oklahoma State Library. https://dc.library.okstate.edu/.

NOTES TO CHAPTER 2

75. I use "Indian citizenship" as a shorthand for "U.S. citizenship for Native Americans," which is of course separate and distinct from tribal citizenship.

76. Raymond Wilson, *Ohiyesa: Charles Eastman, Santee Sioux* (Champaign: University of Illinois Press, 1999), 151.

77. See especially Judith Butler, "Performativity, Precarity, and Sexual Politics," lecture, Universidad Complutense de Madrid, 2009, in *Antropólogos Iberoamericanos en Red* 4, no. 3 (2009): i–xiii; Sasha Roseneil, ed., *Beyond Citizenship: Feminism and the Transformation of Belonging* (London: Palgrave Macmillan, 2013).

78. Rifkin, *Erotics of Sovereignty*, 80, 35.

79. Rifkin, *Erotics of Sovereignty*, 80.

80. Eastman, *Indian To-day*, 3.

81. Eastman, *Indian To-day*, 3.

82. Eastman, *Indian To-day*, 3.

83. Martinez, *Dakota Philosopher*, 35.

84. Vigil, *Indigenous Intellectuals*, 143.

85. Eastman, "North American Indian," 369.

86. Wilson, *Ohiyesa,* 83–85.

87. Eastman, *From the Deep Woods*, 150.

88. Eastman, *From the Deep Woods*, 148–49.

89. See especially Frederick Hoxie, "Exploring a Cultural Borderland: Native American Journeys of Discovery in the Early Twentieth Century," in "Discovering America," ed. Frederick Hoxie, special issue, *Journal of American History* 79, no. 3 (1992): 969–95; Wilson, *Ohiyesa.*

90. Eastman, "Sioux Mythology," 89.

91. Charles Alexander Eastman (Ohiyesa), "What Can the Out-of-Doors Do for Our Children?," *Education* 41 (1920–21): 602.

92. Eastman, "What Can the Out-of-Doors Do," 602.

93. Eastman, "What Can the Out-of-Doors Do," 603.

94. Eastman, "What Can the Out-of-Doors Do," 599.

95. Eastman, "What Can the Out-of-Doors Do," 599.

96. Eastman, *Indian To-day*, 178.

97. Eastman, *Indian To-day*, 178.

98. Eastman, *Indian To-day*, 177–78.

99. Eastman, *Indian To-day*, 178.

100. Charles Alexander Eastman (Ohiyesa), *Indian Scout Talks: A Guide for Boy Scouts and Camp Fire Girls* (1914; Boston: Little, Brown, 1915), 2.

101. Eastman, *Indian Scout Talks*, 6.

102. Deloria, *Speaking of Indians*, 30, 31.

NOTES TO SECOND INTERLUDE 269

103. Deloria, *Speaking of Indians*, 30.
104. Wilson, *Ohiyesa*, 151. Just a year after *Indian Scout Talks* was published, Eastman and his wife, Elaine, opened their own summer camp with a notably more demure name: School of the Woods.
105. Eastman, *Indian Scout Talks*, 188.
106. Eastman, *Indian Scout Talks*, 188–89.
107. Eastman, *Indian Scout Talks*, 189.
108. Eastman, *Indian Scout Talks*, 10.
109. Eastman, *Soul of the Indian*, 80.
110. Eastman, *Soul of the Indian*, 81.
111. Eastman, *Indian To-day*, 6.
112. Lillian Chase interview, February 26, 1993, in *Dakhóta Wóunspe Program* (Fort Totten, N.D.: Tate Topa Tribal School, 1998).
113. Eastman, *Indian Scout Talks*, 9.
114. Walker, *Lakota Belief and Ritual*, 51.
115. Personal interview with Grace Lambert, August 10, 1998.
116. Eastman, *Indian To-day*, 107.
117. See Melissa Meyer, *The White Earth Tragedy: Ethnicity and Dispossession at a Minnesota Anishinaabe Reservation, 1889–1920* (Lincoln: University of Nebraska Press, 1994).
118. Eastman, *Indian To-day*, 109.
119. Eastman, *Indian To-day*, 109.
120. Eastman, *Indian To-day*, 114.
121. Eastman, *Indian To-day*, 114.
122. Eastman, *Indian To-day*, 114–15.
123. Eastman, *Indian Scout Talks*, 116.
124. Eastman, *Indian To-day*, 115.
125. Linda Tuhiwai Smith, *Decolonizing Methodologies: Research and Indigenous Peoples* (London: Zed Books, 1999), 51.
126. Barker, "Recognition," 154.
127. Barker, "Recognition," 154.
128. Barker, "Recognition," 154.

Second Interlude

1. The Devils Lake reservation was established in 1867 by a treaty between the Sisseton–Wahpeton bands and the U.S. government, and like the Lake Traverse treaty of the same year, it provided for permanent reservations for members of those bands (as well as Cut Heads from the Iháŋkthuŋwaŋna) who had not been sent to the Crow Creek reservation. Here Grace probably refers to Article 5 of the 1867 treaty, which apportioned 160-acre tracts of land to each head of family or

single person aged twenty-one or older. See North Dakota Department of Public Instruction, *The History and Culture of the Mni Wakan Oyate (Spirit Lake Nation)* (Bismarck: North Dakota Department of Public Instruction, 1997). See also "Treaty with the Sioux—Sisseton and Wahpeton Bands, 1867," Indian Affairs: Laws and Treaties, digital collection at Oklahoma State Library. https://dc.library.okstate.edu/.

2. Like Grace's recollection of the ant who stores up food for winter, these sayings and teachings reflected to an extent the challenges faced by Dakhóta people in the harsh environment of their transplanted home of the Devils Lake reservation. They are also a kind of training of good habits in body and mind and part of what Wazíyatawiŋ calls in *Remember This!* "the Dakota gift of memory" (3).

3. In chapter 3 I examine Nicholas Black Elk's performances of this ceremony for tourists in Ȟé Sápa (the Black Hills).

4. Here Grace describes as "clans" the four thióšpaye of the Isáŋyati (Santee) Dakhóta. One of these, the Sisíthuŋwaŋ, can be translated as a combination of *siŋsíŋ*, or "greasy" (as from fish oil) and *othúŋwe*, "village." She also alludes to the seven "fireplaces," or council fires, of the Thíthuŋwaŋ (Teton): the Húŋkpapȟa (End Village), Itázipčho (No Bows), Mnikȟówožu (Those Who Plant Near Water), Oglála (To Scatter Or Sprinkle One's Own Into), Oóhenuŋpa (Two Kettles), Sičháŋǧu (Burned Thighs), and Sihásapa (Black Feet).

5. According to Mary Louis Defender Wilson (Wagmúhawiŋ or Gourd Woman), another name for Spirit Lake (Bdé Wakȟáŋ or Mní Wakȟáŋ) is Bdé Wáȟ'aŋksiča (Black Bear Lake).

6. The "thing" described here is probably an Uŋktéȟi or water spirit, described in the First Interlude as a "water god" and in the Third Interlude as a creature with shining eyes and bad breath.

7. In the Third Interlude, my grandmother, Lillian Chase, gives an account of this rock, saying that it is a woman who turned herself into stone to protect herself from a man chasing her.

3. Territoriality, Ethics, and Travel in the Black Elk Transcripts

1. Much of the literature on relationality that I draw on here is either anthropological or ethnohistorical and traces back to Irving Hallowell's work with Ojibwe language and categorizations for animacy and personhood. For instance, according to anthropologist Nurit Bird-David, relationality is what constitutes persons or relatives. I find that persons, rather than subjects, are the main agents in Black Elk's visionary account and in his ceremonial reenactments, and that through their orientation toward persons as ethical agents they critique

NOTES TO CHAPTER 3   271

settler-colonial distinctions between subjects and nonsubjects, human and other-than-human. Citing Kenneth Morrison's work on early relations between Algonkians and Europeans, anthropologist Graham Harvey also observes that a Cartesian nature–culture split (which gets repackaged via settler-colonialism as savage–civilized) prohibits seeing personhood as being constituted through one's actions. Harvey suggests that rather than asking "the typical European ('first contact' and anthropological) question 'Are they human?' . . . [a non-Cartesian approach would ask] 'Are they persons?'" and that "it is . . . the way in which someone (of whatever species) acts that indicates their personhood." See Bird-David, "Animism: Scales of Practice and Imagination," paper presented at the American Anthropological Association meeting, Denver, Colorado, 2015; Hallowell, "Ojibwa Ontology, Behavior, and World View," in *Culture in History: Essays in Honor of Paul Radin*, ed. Stanley Diamond (New York: Columbia University Press, 1960), 19–52; Harvey, "If Not All Stones Are Alive . . . : Radical Relationality in Animism Studies," *Journal for the Study of Religion, Nature, and Culture* 11, no. 4 (2017): 481–97; Morrison, "Animism and a Proposal for a Post-Cartesian Anthropology," in *The Handbook of Contemporary Animism*, ed. Graham Harvey (New York: Routledge, 2013); Morrison, *Solidarity of Kin*.

2. Judith Butler, *The Psychic Life of Power: Theories in Subjection* (Stanford, Calif.: Stanford University Press, 1997), 59.

3. Here and throughout this chapter I use Lakhóta dialect spellings that include guttural h's and other minor orthographic differences from Dakhóta dialects.

4. Butler, *Psychic Life of Power*, 59.

5. On settler affect attaching to territoriality, see Mark Rifkin, *Settler Common Sense: Queerness and Everyday Colonialism in the American Renaissance* (Minneapolis: University of Minnesota Press, 2014); for analyses of U.S. settler-colonialism as an assault on indigenous extended family structures through the imposition of a heteronormative nuclear family model, see Piatote, *Domestic Subjects*, and Rifkin, *When Did Indians Become Straight?*; on the co-construction of heterosexual monogamous marriage and U.S. nationalism during the nineteenth century, see Nancy Cott, *Public Vows: A History of Marriage and the Nation* (Cambridge, Mass.: Harvard University Press, 2000).

6. Qwo-Li Driskill, Chris Finley, Brian Joseph Gilley, and Scott Lauria Morgensen, "The Revolution Is for Everyone: Imagining an Emancipatory Future through Queer Indigenous Critical Theories," in *Queer Indigenous Studies: Critical Interventions in Theory, Politics, and*

Literature, ed. Brian Joseph Gilley, Chris Finley, Scott Lauria Morgensen, and Qwo-Li Driskill (Tucson: University of Arizona Press, 2011), 217.

7. Driskill et al., "The Revolution Is for Everyone," 217.

8. Kim TallBear, "Making Love and Relations beyond Settler Sexuality," lecture, Social Justice Institute Noted Scholars Lecture Series, University of British Columbia, Vancouver, February 24, 2016.

9. TallBear, "Making Love and Relations."

10. My use of DeMallie's *Sixth Grandfather* instead of John G. Neihardt's version of Black Elk's story in *Black Elk Speaks* (Lincoln: University of Nebraska Press, 2014) is not meant to signal that I view the former as being somehow purer, more authentic, or free from settler-colonial taint. After all, as an edition from a settler anthropologist published by a university press, it could at the very least be said to participate in the fetishizing of Lakȟóta life and philosophy. Yet it also provides the most complete and minimally annotated (or least colonially intrusive) version available of Black Elk's translated and transcribed interviews with Neihardt, for which the original Lakȟóta version was never written down.

11. Black Elk's own Oglála band is one of seven thióšpaye or bands that made up the Thíthuŋwaŋ. Beyond this formation, the Great Sioux Nation emerged as a discursive object after the federal creation of the Great Sioux reservation in 1868, with the Treaty of Fort Laramie. This treaty set lands apart for the Lakȟóta bands and included nearly all of what is now the western half of South Dakota. In cordoning off as U.S. national space those lands east of Pierre, however, the reservation effectively attempted to disrupt a region that was contiguous in terms of kinship affiliation and movement, and that had historically belonged to eastern Dakhóta thióšpaye.

12. Mishuana Goeman, *Mark My Words: Native Women Mapping Our Nations* (Minneapolis: University of Minnesota Press, 2013), 206.

13. George Catlin, *North American Indians*, ed. Peter Matthiessen (ca. 1841; reprint, New York: Penguin, 2004), 410.

14. Louis S. Warren, "Cody's Last Stand: Masculine Anxiety, the Custer Myth, and the Frontier of Domesticity in Buffalo Bill's Wild West," *Western Historical Quarterly* 34, no. 1 (2003): 54.

15. Here I draw on Hokowhitu's work on elite Indigenous masculinities in a Maori context and on his reading of these as all too often reproducing settler heteropatriarchy. See Hokowhitu, "Producing Elite Indigenous Masculinities," 23.

16. Black Elk, *Black Elk Speaks*, ed. Neihardt, 218.

NOTES TO CHAPTER 3   **273**

17. Ruth Underhill, review of *The Sacred Pipe*, by Black Elk. *Western Folklore* 13, no. 2/3 (1954): 146.
18. Michael Steltenkamp, *Black Elk: Holy Man of the Oglala* (Norman: University of Oklahoma Press, 1997), xv.
19. John Carlos Rowe, "The View from Rock Writing Bluff: The Nick Black Elk Narratives and U.S. Cultural Imperialism," *Literary Culture and U.S. Imperialism: From the Revolution to World War II* (New York: Oxford University Press, 2000), 217–52. In addition to Vine Deloria Jr., for work on Black Elk by Indigenous scholars, see Marie Therese Archambault (Húŋkpapȟa Lakȟóta), Mark G. Thiel, and Christopher Vecsey, eds., *The Crossing of Two Roads: Being Native and Catholic Indian in the United States* (Maryknoll, N.Y.: Orbis Books, 2000); "St. Francis Mission Records Medicine Men and Clergy Dialogue," St. Francis Mission Records, Jesuit Papers and Recordings, Marquette University, Milwaukee, Wisconsin; R. Todd Wise (Muscogee), "*Black Elk Speaks* as Testimonial Literature," in *The Black Elk Reader*, ed. Clyde Holler (Syracuse, N.Y.: Syracuse University Press, 2000), 19–38.
20. Wheeler–Howard Act, June 18, 1934 (The Indian Reorganization Act), 25 U.S. Code § 479, June 18, 1934, ch. 576, § 19, 48, Stat. 984. http://aghca.org/wp-content/uploads/2012/07/indianreorganizationact.pdf.
21. Lawrence Kelly, "The Indian Reorganization Act: The Dream and the Reality," *Pacific Historical Review* 44, no. 3 (1975): 291.
22. Lyons, *X-Marks*, 180.
23. James Calhoun in Brian Dippie, "It's Equal I Have Never Seen: Custer Explores the Black Hills in 1874," Friends of the Little Bighorn Battlefield. http://www.friendslittlebighorn.com/.
24. Ostler, *The Lakota and the Black Hills*, 68–70.
25. DeMallie, *Sixth Grandfather*, 157.
26. DeMallie, *Sixth Grandfather*, 157.
27. The quotation is from Iron Hawk, a friend of Black Elk, whose account of the 1875 Black Hills treaty council appears in DeMallie, *Sixth Grandfather*, 171.
28. DeMallie, *Sixth Grandfather*, 157.
29. Chief Arvol Looking Horse, "Sioux Spiritual Leader Speaks Out on Land Sale at Sacred Site," interview by Jason Coppola, Truthout, August 21, 2012. https://truthout.org/.
30. Chief Arvol Looking Horse, "Sioux Spiritual Leader Speaks Out."
31. Paul M. Liffman, *Huichol Territory and the Mexican Nation: Indigenous Ritual, Land Conflict, and Sovereignty Claims* (Tucson: University of Arizona Press, 2011), 5.

NOTES TO CHAPTER 3

32. Henry Lewis Morgan, *The League of the Ho-de-no-sau-nee, or Iroquois* (Rochester, N.Y.: Sage, 1851); *Ancient Society, or Researches in the Lines of Human Progress from Savagery through Barbarism to Civilization* (Cleveland, Ohio: World Publishing, 1877); H. S. Maine, *Ancient Law: Its Connection with the Early History of Society and Its Relation to Modern Ideas* (London: Murray, 1861).

33. Dmitri Bondarenko gives a useful genealogy of the categories of the social and the civil in "Kinship, Territoriality, and the Early State Lower Limit," *Social Evolution and History* 7, no. 1 (2008): 19–53.

34. Anne L. Clunan and Harold A. Trinkunas, "Conceptualizing Ungoverned Spaces: Territorial Statehood, Contested Authority, and Softened Sovereignty," in *Ungoverned Spaces: Alternatives to State Authority in an Era of Softened Sovereignty*, ed. Anne L. Clunan and Harold A. Trinkunas (Stanford, Calif.: Stanford Security Studies, 2010), 17–19.

35. Loren B. Landau and Tamlyn Monson, "Immigration and Subterranean Sovereignty in South African Cities," in Clunan and Trinkunas, *Ungoverned Spaces*, 168.

36. Bishop Henry Benjamin Whipple in Ulysses S. Grant, *The Papers of Ulysses S. Grant: January 1–October 31, 1876* (Carbondale: Southern Illinois University Press, 2005), 181.

37. Whipple in Grant, *Papers*, 181.

38. Whipple in Grant, *Papers*, 182.

39. Uday Singh Mehta, *Liberalism and Empire: A Study in Nineteenth-Century British Liberal Thought* (1999; reprint, Chicago: University of Chicago Press, 2018), 119.

40. Mehta, *Liberalism and Empire*, 119.

41. "Treaty with the Sioux-Brule, Oglala, Miniconjou, Yanktonai, Hunkpapa, Blackfeet, Cuthead, Two Kettle, San Arcs, and Santee-and Arapaho," April 29, 1868, General Records of the United States Government, Record Group 11, National Archives, Washington, D.C.

42. Powers, *Oglala Religion*, 133–34.

43. Powers, *Oglala Religion*, 134.

44. Powers, *Oglala Religion*, 134.

45. Kim TallBear, "Looking for Love in Too Many Languages . . . Polyamory? Relationship Anarchy? Dyke Ethics? Significant Otherness? All My Relations?," Critical Polyamorist (blog), March 25, 2016. http://www.criticalpolyamorist.com/.

46. DeMallie, *Sixth Grandfather*, 307.

47. DeMallie, *Sixth Grandfather*, 308.

48. TallBear, "Making Love and Relations."

49. TallBear, "Making Love and Relations."

NOTES TO CHAPTER 3   275

50. See Rauna Kuokkanen, *Reshaping the University: Responsibility, Indigenous Epistemes, and the Logic of the Gift* (Vancouver: University of British Columbia Press, 2007), 38.
51. Rowe, "View from Rock Writing Bluff," 236.
52. Frantz Fanon, *A Dying Colonialism* (New York City: Grove Press, 1967), 128.
53. Fanon, *Dying Colonialism*, 128.
54. DeMallie, *Sixth Grandfather*, 132.
55. A full account of White Buffalo Calf Woman appears in Black Elk's interviews with Joseph Epes Brown in *The Sacred Pipe: Black Elk's Account of the Oglala Sioux* (Norman: University of Oklahoma Press, 1989).
56. DeMallie, *Sixth Grandfather*, 133.
57. DeMallie, *Sixth Grandfather*, 133.
58. Morrison, *Solidarity of Kin*, 160–61.
59. Georges Bataille, "The Notion of Expenditure," in *Visions of Excess: Selected Writings, 1927–1939* (Manchester: Manchester University Press, 1985), 121.
60. Bataille, "Notion of Expenditure," 120.
61. Bataille, "Notion of Expenditure," 120.
62. Bataille, "Notion of Expenditure," 121.
63. Bataille, "Notion of Expenditure," 122.
64. Julian Rice, *Black Elk's Story: Distinguishing Its Lakota Purpose* (Albuquerque: University of New Mexico Press, 1991), 115.
65. Frances Densmore, *Teton Sioux Music* (1918; reprint, New York: Da Capo, 1972), 159, cited in Rice, *Black Elk's Story*, 115.
66. Rice, *Black Elk's Story*, 116.
67. Rice, *Black Elk's Story*, 121.
68. DeMallie, *Sixth Grandfather*, 136.
69. DeMallie, *Sixth Grandfather*, 136.
70. DeMallie, *Sixth Grandfather*, 137.
71. Rice, *Black Elk's Story*, 116.
72. Rice, *Black Elk's Story*, 69.
73. While I use the terms "directions" and "powers" interchangeably here, they are different things. Directions are cosmological orientations toward powers, which are other-than-human beings who primordially occupy those locations. In Walker's account of Lakhóta creation, the Thaté Tópa (Four Winds), who are the sons of Tháte (the Wind), found the directions out of chaos. See Walker, *Lakota Belief and Ritual*, 81.
74. DeMallie, *Sixth Grandfather*, 222.
75. Kuokkanen, *Reshaping the University*, 38–39.

76. Kuokkanen, *Reshaping the University*, 225.
77. Deloria, "Chapter 12: Relatives of Social Kinship," 283–84.
78. Deloria, "Chapter 12: Relatives of Social Kinship," 284.
79. Deloria, "Chapter 12: Relatives of Social Kinship," 284.
80. DeMallie, introduction to *Sixth Grandfather*, 63.
81. Hilda Neihardt and Lori Utecht, eds., *Black Elk Lives: Conversations with the Black Elk Family* (Lincoln: University of Nebraska Press, 2000), 134.
82. David O. Born, "Black Elk and the Duhamel Sioux Pageant," *North Dakota History* 61, no. 1 (1994): 25–26.
83. Neihardt and Utecht, *Black Elk Lives*, 134–35.
84. "Catholic Sioux Congress," *New York Times*, July 6, 1892. https://timesmachine.nytimes.com/timesmachine/1892/07/06/104139831.pdf
85. "Catholic Sioux Congress."
86. Louis J. Goll, SJ, *Jesuit Missions among the Sioux* (Saint Francis, S.D.: St. Francis Mission, 1940), 40, cited in Powers, *Oglala Religion*, 126.
87. Powers, *Oglala Religion*, 126.
88. A contemporary Dakhóta event commemorates the hanging of the thirty-eight plus two (Šákpe and Phežútaožaŋžaŋ, or "Six" and "Medicine Bottle") Dakhóta warriors after the 1862 U.S.–Dakhóta War, and involves horse riders traveling from Pine Ridge to Mankato, Minnesota. Along the way various riders add themselves to what becomes a fairly large procession. Like the Catholic congresses, their movement between not just reservations but also states draws back together Dakhóta space into a continuous whole. See Levi Rickert, "Dakota 38 + 2 Wokiksuye Ride Ends with Ceremony at Mankato," Native News Online, December 26, 2017. https://nativenewsonline.net/currents/2017-dakota-38-2-wokiksuye-ride-ends-ceremony-mankato.
89. "Duhamel Sioux Indian Pageant and Sitting Bull Crystal Cavern" (Rapid City, S.D.: Black Hill Novelty, n.d.).
90. "Duhamel Sioux Indian Pageant."
91. DeMallie, *Sixth Grandfather*, 64.
92. DeMallie, *Sixth Grandfather*, 66.
93. Born, "Black Elk and the Duhamel Sioux Pageant," 26.
94. In addition to Charlotte and Olivia Black Elk, firsthand accounts of the pageants appear in Born, "Black Elk and the Duhamel Sioux Pageant," which excerpts 1991 and 1992 interviews with Francis "Bud" Duhamel, and in DeMallie's introduction to *Sixth Grandfather*.
95. Neihardt and Utecht, *Black Elk Lives*, 135.
96. Glissant, *Poetics of Relation*, 190.
97. Glissant, *Poetics of Relation*, 133.
98. DeMallie, *Sixth Grandfather*, 65.

NOTES TO CHAPTER 4 277

99. Nicholas Black Elk, letter to Claude and Frances Hansen, May 15, 1947, Black Elk Collection, M570, Western History Collection, Denver Public Library, Denver, Colorado.
100. Benjamin Black Elk, letter to Curly Bear and White Buffalo Calf Woman, March 21, 1948, Black Elk Collection, M570, Western History Collection, Denver Public Library.
101. Joseph Epes Brown, introduction to Black Elk, *Sacred Pipe*, xx.
102. Nicholas Black Elk, letter to Curly Bear and White Buffalo Calf Woman, February 24, 1948, Black Elk Collection, M570, Western History Collection, Denver Public Library.
103. Nicholas Black Elk, letter to Curly Bear and White Buffalo Calf Woman, February 24, 1948, Black Elk Collection, M570, Western History Collection, Denver Public Library.

4. Peoplehood Proclaimed

1. Dian Million, "There Is a River in Me: Theory from Life," in *Theorizing Native Studies*, ed. Audra Simpson and Andrea Smith (Durham, N.C.: Duke University Press, 2014), 33.
2. Million, "There Is a River in Me," 35.
3. Million, "There Is a River in Me," 40.
4. Judith Butler, *Gender Trouble: Feminism and the Subversion of Identity* (1990; reprint, New York: Routledge, 2002), xiii.
5. Deloria, *Speaking of Indians*.
6. Deloria, *Speaking of Indians*.
7. Deloria, *Speaking of Indians*.
8. Deloria, *Speaking of Indians*.
9. Ella Cara Deloria, *Waterlily* (Lincoln: University of Nebraska Press, 1988), 10–11.
10. Maria Eugenia Cotera, "'All My Relatives Are Noble': Recovering the Feminine in Ella Cara Deloria's *Waterlily*," *American Indian Quarterly* 28, no. 1/2 (2004): 53.
11. For a comparative account of allotment's epistemological assumptions, see Adrea Lawrence and Brec Cooke, "Law, Language, and Land: A Multimethod Analysis of the General Allotment Act and Its Discourses," *Qualitative Inquiry* 16, no. 217 (2010): 217–29.
12. John Collier, "Minutes of the Plains Congress, Rapid City, South Dakota" (1934), in *The Indian Reorganization Act: Congresses and Bills*, ed. Vine Deloria Jr. (Norman: University of Oklahoma Press, 2002), 38.
13. Rifkin, *When Did Indians Become Straight?*, 226.
14. Rifkin, *When Did Indians Become Straight?*, 227.

NOTES TO CHAPTER 4

15. Rifkin, *When Did Indians Become Straight?, 22–23.*
16. Susan Gardner, preface to Deloria, *Waterlily*, xxiv.
17. Cotera, "All My Relatives Are Noble," 60.
18. Simpson, "On Ethnographic Refusal," 69; Denise Ferreira da Silva, *Toward a Global Idea of Race* (Minneapolis: University of Minnesota Press, 2007); Andrea Smith, "Queer Theory and Native Studies: The Heteronormativity of Settler Colonialism" *GLQ* 16, no. 1/2 (2010): 41–68.
19. Andrea Smith, "Native Studies at the Horizon of Death: Theorizing Ethnographic Entrapment and Settler Self-Reflexivity," in Simpson and Smith, *Theorizing Native Studies*, 213.
20. Collier, "Minutes of the Plains Congress," 39.
21. Collier, "Minutes of the Plains Congress," 25.
22. Riggs, *Dakota–English Dictionary*, 106.
23. Deloria, *Speaking of Indians*, 24.
24. Gloria Valencia-Weber, "Racial Equality: Old and New Strains and American Indians," *Notre Dame Law Review* 80, no. 1 (2004): 335.
25. Amalia Sa'ar, "Postcolonial Feminism, the Politics of Identification, and the Liberal Bargain," *Gender and Society* 19, no. 5 (2005): 681.
26. Sa'ar, "Postcolonial Feminism," 681.
27. Sa'ar, "Postcolonial Feminism," 681.
28. Wheeler–Howard Act, June 18, 1934 (The Indian Reorganization Act).
29. Frederick E. Hoxie, "The Goals of the Indian Reorganization Act," n.d. https://www.indian.senate.gov/sites/default/files/upload/files/Frederick-Hoxie-testimony.pdf.
30. Collier, "Minutes of the Plains Congress," 38.
31. Laurence M. Hauptman, "The American Indian Federation and the Indian New Deal: A Reinterpretation," *Pacific Historical Review* 52, no. 4 (1983): 390.
32. Paul Spruhan gives a valuable overview of the development of the use of blood quantum, arguing that blood quantum was not widely used in federal law until the twentieth century. Spruhan, "A Legal History of Blood Quantum in Federal Indian Law to 1935," *South Dakota Law Review* 51, no. 1 (2006): 1–50.
33. Hauptman, "American Indian Federation," 395.
34. Hauptman, "American Indian Federation," 392.
35. In a Dakhóta/Lakhóta context, Ben Reifel (Brulé) recalled in a 1967 interview how intratribal factions coalesced after the IRA legislation. Calling one group the "so-called old dealers" (as opposed to the supporters of the IRA, or the "Indian New Deal"), Reifel describes

that these were the "old generation of leadership . . . the older people [who] were largely full-bloods," who opposed the IRA in large part because it invested in the handful of tribal council members what had been a more diffuse power of consensus making. These "older people, those who were opposed, said, 'Well, here's a group of people that are governing our people. They are a small group; they aren't representing all the people. And the older people didn't think they were being represented adequately.'" Reifel goes on to elaborate how the issue of land ownership was complicated by the governance of a tribal council generally but also more specifically by the federal charter of the corporation, which "authorized the tribe to accept gifts and property, and also to hypothecate tribal property for any loans that they may get from the Federal Government." By turning tribes into corporate entities, and so also into debtors whose primary collateral was land, the U.S. government could continue to erode the tribal land base, effectively continuing the spirit, if not the letter, of allotment law: "And if they borrowed the money, the Federal Government would come along later on, and if they want to claim this would be an offset against the claim. There are many things like that—every kind of ghost was raised against it [adopting the IRA] that they could imagine. And some of it had just enough fact to give it a color of truth. And I could understand their apprehensiveness on this regard." Reifel, *To Be an Indian* (St. Paul: Minnesota Historical Society Press, 1971), 124–25.

36. This excerpt from Valandry's interview, and all other quotations from it, appear in Julian Rice, "'It Was Their Own Fault for Being Intractable': Internalized Racism and Wounded Knee," *American Indian Quarterly* 22, no. 1/2 (1998): 63–82. Valandry's interview, as well as others collected by Deloria, are in the Franz Boas Papers, American Philosophical Society, Philadelphia, Pennsylvania, under "Dakota Autobiographies," MS.X 8a.4. https://search.amphilsoc.org/collections/view?docId=ead/Mss.B.B61-ead.xml.

37. Valandry interview.

38. Deloria, "I Am Admitted to the Hunka," 1937, MS X 8a.4, 29, Franz Boas Papers, American Philosophical Society.

39. Deloria, *Waterlily*, 180.

40. Rifkin, *Erotics of Sovereignty*, 159.

41. Rifkin, *Erotics of Sovereignty*, 159.

42. Rifkin, *Erotics of Sovereignty*, 165.

43. Deloria, *Waterlily*, 6.

44. Deloria, *Waterlily*, 6.

45. Deloria, *Waterlily*, 6.
46. Frantz Fanon, *Black Skin, White Masks* (1952; reprint, New York: Grove Press, 2008), xiii.
47. Deloria, *Waterlily*, 213–14.
48. Deloria, *Waterlily*, 214.
49. Deloria, *Waterlily*, 214.
50. Deloria, *Waterlily*, 214.
51. Deloria, *Waterlily*, 214.
52. Deloria, *Waterlily*, 214.
53. Deloria, *Waterlily*, 214.
54. Ella Cara Deloria, *Dakota Texts* (1932; reprint, Lincoln: University of Nebraska Press, 2006), 175.
55. Deloria, *Dakota Texts*, 177.
56. Deloria, *Dakota Texts*, 178.
57. Deloria, *Dakota Texts*, 162.
58. Deloria, *Dakota Texts*, 215.
59. Deloria, *Dakota Texts*, 215.
60. Deloria, *Dakota Texts*, 216.
61. Deloria, *Dakota Texts*, 216.
62. Deloria, *Dakota Texts*, 58.
63. Deloria, *Waterlily*, 60.
64. Butler, *Gender Trouble*, 32.
65. Wheeler–Howard Act, June 18, 1934 (The Indian Reorganization Act), Section 14.
66. Eastman, *Soul of the Indian*, 41.
67. Eastman, *Soul of the Indian*, 41.
68. Joyzelle Godfrey, "Speaking of Ella Deloria: Conversations with Joyzelle Gingway Godfrey, 1998–2000, Lower Brule Community College, South Dakota," by Susan Gardner, *American Indian Quarterly* 24, no. 3 (2000): 461.
69. Godfrey, "Speaking of Ella Deloria," 461.
70. Wazíyatawiŋ, *Remember This!*, 132.
71. Deloria, *Waterlily*, 4.
72. Ella Cara Deloria, "Relatives of Marriage," *The Dakota Way of Life*, Ella Deloria Archive, 204.
73. Deloria, "Relatives of Marriage," 204.
74. Deloria, "Relatives of Marriage," 200.
75. Deloria, "Relatives of Marriage," 202.
76. Deloria, "Relatives of Marriage," 202.
77. Deloria, "Relatives of Marriage," 202.
78. Deloria, "Relatives of Marriage," 202.
79. Deloria, "Relatives of Marriage," 202.

NOTES TO CHAPTER 4　　281

80. Deloria, *Waterlily*, 5.
81. Deloria, "Birth and Infancy," *Dakota Way of Life*, 306.
82. Deloria, "Eta. About Children," Ethnographic Notes Manuscript, box 2, Dakota Ethnography, Ella Deloria Archive, 9.
83. Deloria, "Eta. About Children," 9.
84. Deloria, "Eta. About Children," 9.
85. Deloria, *Waterlily*, 122.
86. Deloria, *Waterlily*, 122.
87. Deloria, *Waterlily*, 127.
88. Deloria, *Waterlily*, 127.
89. Deloria, *Waterlily*, 127.
90. Deloria, *Waterlily*, 12.
91. Deloria, "The Family," *Dakota Way of Life*, 60.
92. Deloria, "The Family," 62.
93. Deloria, "The Family," 60.
94. Deloria, "The Family," 61.
95. Deloria, *Waterlily*, 62.
96. Deloria, *Dakota Way of Life*, 369.
97. Raymond DeMallie, "Male and Female in Traditional Lakota Culture," in *The Hidden Half: Studies of Plains Indian Women*, ed. Patricia Albers and Beatrice Medicine (Lanham, Md.: University Press of America, 1983), 249.
98. Deloria, *Waterlily*, 88.
99. Deloria, *Waterlily*, 97.
100. Rifkin, *When Did Indians Become Straight?*, 226.
101. Sue-Ellen Jacobs, "Berdache: A Brief Review of the Literature," *Colorado Anthropologist* 1 (1968): 25–40; Beatrice Medicine, "'Warrior Women'—Sex Role Alternatives for Plains Indian Women," in *The Hidden Half: Studies of Plains Indian Women*, ed. Patricia Albers and Beatrice Medicine (Lanham, Md.: University Press of America, 1983), 268–69.
102. Beatrice Medicine, *How to Be an Anthropologist and Remain "Native": Selected Writings* (Urbana: University of Illinois Press, 2001), 122.
103. Deloria, *Waterlily*, 137. Deloria also describes in *Dakota Way of Life* both male and female ceremonies through which young men or women could be declared as being exempt from marriage. See Deloria, "Beta. The Virgin's Fire [and Other Women's Rites]," Ella Deloria Archive.
104. Riggs, *Dakota–English Dictionary*, 484.
105. Wazíyatawiŋ, *Remember This!*, 63–64.
106. Wazíyatawiŋ, *Remember This!*, 64.

107. Susan Gardner has two articles on Deloria's pageants that provide a more comprehensive historicizing than I give here: "'Weaving an Epic Story': Ella Cara Deloria's Pageant for the Indians of Robeson County, North Carolina, 1940–1941," *Mississippi Quarterly* 60, no. 1 (2006–7): 33–57; "Piety, Pageantry, and Politics on the Northern Great Plains: An American Indian Woman Restages Her People's Conquest," *Forum on Public Policy*, spring 2007. http://www.forumonpublicpolicy.com/.

108. Deloria, *Waterlily*, 50.

109. Wazíyatawiŋ, *Remember This!*, 22.

110. Gardner, "Piety, Pageantry, and Politics," 10.

111. The pageant appears in Deloria's unpublished manuscripts under the title "Pageant of the Robeson County Indians, Pembroke, North Carolina," Ella Deloria Archive.

112. Deloria, "Pageant of the Robeson County Indians, Pembroke, North Carolina."

113. Deloria, "Pageant: The Wohpe Festival," Ella Deloria Archive.

114. Deloria, "Pageant: The Wohpe Festival."

115. Walker, *Lakota Belief and Ritual*, 35.

116. Carol A. Markstrom gives an account of Wohpe and Ptesáŋwiŋ, drawing on a nonscholarly "as told to" account by a non-Lakȟóta, Mark St. Pierre, *Walking in the Sacred Manner: Healers, Dreamers, and Pipe Carriers—Medicine Women of the Plains Indians* (New York: Touchstone Press, 1995): "The Lakota term Whope [sic] refers to the embodiment of feminine ideals and is the most descriptive term of White Buffalo Calf Woman according to St. Pierre and Long Soldier (1995). These authors state that the puberty ceremony is 'so strongly related to Whope' that it is also known as the White Buffalo Calf Ceremony.' In the Lakota creation story, Whope was actually the daughter of the male Sun and the female Moon, and she is regarded as the precursor to White Buffalo Calf Woman. Hence, the identification of the female pubescent with White Buffalo Calf Woman is consistent with the theme of the centrality of a female supernatural being in the puberty ceremony and the goal of transformation of the initiate into this personage." Markstrom, *Empowerment of North American Indian Girls: Ritual Expressions at Puberty* (Lincoln: University of Nebraska Press, 2008), 321.

117. Ptésaŋwiŋ appears among other Indigenous peoples too, including the Mandan and Hidatsa, who have historically had White Buffalo Calf Woman societies. German explorer Prince Maximillian of Wied-Neuwied observed such societies in 1834, noting that they were composed of postmenopausal women. See Tom McHugh and

NOTES TO THIRD INTERLUDE **283**

Victoria Hobson, *The Time of the Buffalo* (Lincoln: University of Nebraska Press, 1979), and David C. Hunt, ed., *Karl Bodmer's America* (Omaha: Joslyn Art Museum, 1984).

118. Walker, *Lakota Belief and Ritual*, 109.
119. Walker, *Lakota Belief and Ritual*, 110.
120. Walker, *Lakota Belief and Ritual*, 111.
121. Deloria, "Pageant: The Wohpe Festival," 2.
122. Deloria, "Pageant: The Wohpe Festival," 3.
123. Deloria, introduction to "Pageant: The Wohpe Festival."

Third Interlude

1. This "creature" is an Uŋktéȟi or water spirit.
2. Lillian's grandmother was Makhá Iná Mániwiŋ, or Walks Mother Earth Woman.
3. Uŋčí Lillian's mild exasperation here with wašíču or settler names for places echoes that of uŋčí Grace Lambert in the Second Interlude. It's probably no accident that these names map different parts of the devil's body onto the reservation (heart, backbone, tooth). Her giving the Dakhóta term of Íŋyaŋ Watháŋka instead of Devils Tooth is a decolonial translation back to the relational reality of these places—a reality that is still unfolding through stories. For instance, one might assume that the íŋyaŋ or stone that she describes as coming to be one Fourth of July night is many thousands of years old. But from her story it seems to have come into being—from the sacrifice of the Dakhóta woman who turned herself into stone—in the early years after the reservation was made.
4. The "thunders" here are the Wakíŋyaŋ, or thunder beings, who return every summer. Another account of them appears in my interview with uŋčí Grace Lambert in the First Interlude of this book, as well as in Black Elk's account of the horse dance ceremony in chapter 3.
5. A water being, or Uŋktehi, again.
6. If the horse-dance ceremony is in part about reclaiming a masculine warrior identity that had been outlawed by the United States, then it is maybe not surprising in this moment to hear uŋčí Lillian say that a woman should not have been riding in the ceremony. But I love the way she undercuts or at least complicates that prohibition by saying "and still she rode that horse," as well as her admiring tone in describing the beauty of Mázakhaŋ, the rider.
7. The wild turnips described here are thíŋpsiŋna, which are dug up, braided, and dried in summertime. In Lakhótiyapi, the month of June is Thíŋpsiŋna Itkáȟča Wi, "moon when turnip seeds mature."

8. The poles here are probably those of a travois.
9. In this story of the young women who transform into rabbits in order not to be sexually violated or killed by enemy warriors, I hear reverberations of the female solidarity and survival that are so strongly present in my grandmother's telling of the story of Íŋyaŋ Watháŋka.
10. This is most likely St. Jude's Catholic Church in Thompson, North Dakota.
11. Uŋčí Lillian's account here of the "two white men" who solicit her for "old Indian stories"—who deserve to be avoided because they "tell it different" and stand to profit from those stories—underscores the constant threat of co-optation and exploitation of Indigenous knowledge. This is the kind of extractive and colonizing research that Indigenous scholars like Wazíyatawiŋ and Linda Tuhiwai Smith (Maori) argue must be refused and replaced with protocols of respect and reciprocity, through which researchers may forge long-term relationships with communities, disseminate their research back to communities, and center Indigenous values, attitudes, and practices, among other things. In a way, uŋčí's peppering of modern elements—motorcycles and loudspeakers, for instance—into her long-ago stories or hithúŋkaŋkaŋpi is not only an example of how she teased her little sister, Grace but also perhaps a way of making these stories less palatable to wašíču audiences and culture collectors. As such, it illustrates the dynamic of withholding or protecting knowledge at the heart of this book. For recommended best practices for decolonizing research methods, see Smith, *Decolonizing Methodologies*.
12. In October 1901, Ignatius Court was one of ten Dakhóta men appointed to serve as a tribal committee to speak with Inspector James McLaughlin, who had come to broker an agreement by which Dakhóta people would cede their 100,000 "surplus" acres to the federal government. Court served as a kind of tribal delegate to Washington for the next several decades, and after Spirit Lake Dakhóta rejected the 1934 Indian Reorganization Act, he was elected the first president of a "tribal business committee" that was to handle matters related to the tribe's economic development. See Mark Diedrich, *Mni Wakan Oyate (Spirit Lake Nation): A History of the Sisitunwan, Wahpeton, Pabaksa, and Other Dakota That Settled at Spirit Lake, North Dakota* (Fort Totten, N.D.: Cankdeska Cikana Community College, 2007), 130, 165.
13. North Dakota Department of Public Instruction, *History and Culture of the Mni Wakan Oyate*, gives an account of the arrival of Waánataŋ: "Waanatan was born in 1828 to a Sisseton mother who was related to Chief Standing Buffalo. His father was the famous Yanktonai, Chief

Waanatan I (1795–1840) of the Cuthead Band. His father claimed more than eleven million acres of land from Granite Falls to the Missouri River. Their main village was on the west side of Lake Traverse. The Cutheads traveled to all points in their territory hunting buffalo which brought them into direct conflict with the Ojibwa, and the riverine tribes, the Arikara, Mandan and Hidatsa along the Missouri River. Many Yanktonais were lost to the smallpox epidemic of 1837. At age 12 his father was killed by a rival in the year 1840. The Cutheads split into three groups. Waanatan's older brothers, Red Thunder and Catfish, took the majority of the band and remained near the Missouri River. Waanatan and his mother left the group and settled with her people, the Sissetons, at Lake Traverse. Eventually Waanatan II became chief and hunted mainly between Devils Lake and Lake Traverse. In fall 1862, Waanatan and his Sissetons were hunting buffalo near present day Hamar, North Dakota, when news came of the Dakota Conflict. Together with Chief Standing Buffalo, Waanatan forbade Little Crow to flee across their territory. Anticipating the army would follow, Standing Buffalo and Waanatan declined to give them aid. In spite of their efforts to remain neutral, Waanatan and Standing Buffalo were drawn into the war. After the Battle of Big Mound in 1863 Waanatan remained in the Mouse River Loop area, his band traveled back and forth across the Canadian Border. Because of the dwindling numbers of buffalo, and the need to survive, he returned to Devils Lake and surrendered in 1867 at Fort Totten with only 62 people" (54).

14. Sullys Hill is now a national game preserve that was established as a national park on April 27, 1904 and is named after General Alfred Sully, who led the largest contingent of soldiers (4,000) ever assembled against Indigenous people in the United States. The first Dakhóta deaths (and atrocities) of the 1863 campaign occurred on September 3, 1863, when Sully's men massacred 150 encamped warriors and nearly 200 other men, women, and children at Whitestone Hill near what is now Kulm, North Dakota. A year later, on a second "punitive expedition," Sully distinguished himself further as a war criminal when he ordered that three Dakhóta warriors be decapitated and their heads impaled on poles on a hill near Medicine Rock, in what is now called North Dakota, as a warning to other Dakhóta. Here, uŋčí Lily describes a cash payment made to tribal members when Sullys Hill was converted by the U.S. Congress from a national park into a wildlife preserve on March 3, 1931. See Louis Pfaller, *The Sully Expedition of 1864 Featuring the Killdeer Mountain and Badlands Battles* (Bismarck, N.D.: State Historical Society of North Dakota, 1964);

Brad Tennant, "The 1864 Sully Expedition and the Death of Captain John Feilner," *American Nineteenth Century History* 9, no. 2 (2008): 183–90.

15. The boundaries of the Devils Lake reservation were established by treaty in 1867 in its fourth article: "Beginning at the most easterly point of Devil's Lake; thence along the waters of said Lake to the most westerly point of the same." In a series of legal actions going back to 1951, the tribe has contended that Devils Lake is within the reservation's territory because the treaty established the northern shore of Devils Lake as the boundary, but also that the treaty's language is ambiguous. As a 2001 U.S. 8th Circuit Court appeal by the tribe states, both the original wording of the treaty and the fact of its ambiguity are important because "courts traditionally resolve ambiguities in favor of Indian tribes," and in both cases, "the Tribe asserts entitlement to Devils Lake." The federal government claims, however, that the lake was not included in the 1867 treaty, asserting "that it continued to hold title to Devils Lake until 1889, when it conveyed the lake to the State of North Dakota at its statehood." See *Spirit Lake Tribe v. State of North Dakota*, 262 F.3d 732 (8th Cir. 2001) WL 936299.

16. Camp Grafton, at the northern end of Devils Lake, was created in 1904 when the federal government ceded land to the state of North Dakota in order to use as a permanent military reservation. Here, uŋčí Lily asserts that the land was never owned by the federal government but instead was allotted to Ignatius Court and leased out by him for military use. As with her remembering that the reservation used to extend from the lake's northern shore (where the town of Devils Lake now is), to its western shore (where Oberon is), to the town of Sheyenne south of the lake, this statement about Camp Grafton materializes memory to reterritorialize places and spaces now occupied and only presumptively owned by settlers.

Conclusion

1. Wazíyatawiŋ, *Remember This!*, 63.
2. Wazíyatawiŋ, *Remember This!*, 23.
3. Louis Owens, quoted in Daniel Heath Justice, "'Go Away, Water!' Kinship Criticism and the Decolonization Imperative," in *Reasoning Together: The Native Critics Collective*, ed. Craig S. Womack, Daniel Heath Justice, and Christopher B. Teuton (Norman: University of Oklahoma Press, 2008), 163.
4. Warrior, *Tribal Secrets*, xxi.

5. Arjun Appadurai, *The Future as Cultural Fact: Essays on the Global Condition* (London: Verso, 2013), 104.
6. Appadurai, *Future as Cultural Fact*, 104.
7. Appadurai, *Future as Cultural Fact*, 104.
8. Lyons, *X-Marks*, 143–44.
9. Appadurai, *Future as Cultural Fact*, 104.
10. See, e.g., Womack, *Red on Red*; Weaver, Womack, and Warrior, *American Indian Literary Nationalism*; Womack, Justice, and Teuton, *Reasoning Together*; Elizabeth Cook-Lynn, *Anti-Indianism in Modern America*, 25.

Index

Abbott, Lyman, 101
academic content vs. tribal interviews, 28
accumulation, 20, 22, 27, 109, 170–71
Adams, Florence, 230
Alfred, Taiaiake, 14
allotment: Dawes Act, 31, 101, 152, 191; era, 1; and gender, 195–96, 202, 208, 213; and heterosexuality, 20, 185; and identity, 195; and Indian Reorganization Act, 190–91; and kinship, 192; and land theft, 131–33, 152, 191; vs. matrilineality, 202; policy, 31, 152, 190, 195, 249n2, 264n8; and subjectivity, 236
ambivalence, 3; of Black Elk, 181; as crisis of relationality, 56–57; as Dakhóta predicament, 7–8; of Deloria, 185, 187; and ethnographic refusal, 11; and kinship, 236; and racism, 193; radical, 17; and withholding, 91
American Indian Federation, 191–92
American Indian Movement, 230
Amiotte, Emma, 179
anarchic responsibility, 18, 148, 185, 220, 238
Andersen, Chris, 13
Anderson, Benedict, 106
Anderson, Gary Clayton, 47

animacy/inanimacy, 149
animals: Eastman's stories about, 94, 97–100, 102, 104–5, 107, 115, 189, 214; and human beings, 98, 100, 109, 113–15, 125; and medicine men, 143; and names, 133; and thióšpaye, 99, 102; wild, 98, 125, 127; wolves, 111–12
anthropology. *See* ethnography
anticapitalist: ethic of sufficiency, 30; gift, 161; pause as, 106
Appadurai, Arjun, 238–40
assimilation: critical responses to, 1–2; as detribalizing Indigenous peoples, 20–21; and Eastman, 90–91; and Indian Reorganization Act, 191–92; and Indian writers, 2; policy of, 249n2; resurgence in wake of, 184; transgression under guise of, 40
authenticity: consumable, 12; Indigenous, 91, 96; savage, xiii; of "tradition," 17

Barker, Joanne, 99, 134–35
Bataille, Georges, 164–66, 169, 171
belonging: and citizenship, 134, 235; and gender violence, 19–20; and kinship, 104; and nation, 10, 39; and relationality, 21, 37, 159, 172; and territoriality, 30

289

Benedict, Ruth, 187
Berlant, Lauren, 20
Bhabha, Homi, 15, 92
Bible, 51, 54, 58, 68, 74, 110, 237
Biolsi, Thomas, 16, 101
Blackbird, Charlie, 73
Black Elk (Nicholas), 1, 18–19,
  149–55, 161–81, 214; *Black Elk
  Speaks,* 30, 151, 272n10; and
  decolonization, 22, 150–51;
  and gender, 151; great vision of,
  161; and horse dance, 161–63,
  166, 168–71, 238; iconicity
  of, 151–52, 180; and Indian
  pageants, 150, 174–77, 179–81;
  on Lakȟóta ceremonialism,
  154–55, 157; on Lakȟóta land
  tenure practices, 154; on
  origins of the Oyáte, 159; and
  performance, 150, 162, 173–74;
  and politics, 152; *The Sixth
  Grandfather,* 30, 149, 272n10;
  travels of, 150, 173–77, 181
Black Elk, Benjamin, 180
Black Elk DeSersa, Esther, 179
Black Elk Pourier, Olivia, 174–75
Black Snake Killers, 241
blood, 7–8, 26, 39, 135, 265n8;
  blood quantum, 4, 91, 101,
  147–48, 152, 192, 195, 264n8,
  278n32; interfusion of, 123; and
  nation, 240; and racism, 152,
  192, 195, 239–40
Blue, Dean, 37
Blueshield, Martin, 62
Boas, Franz, 183–84, 192
bodies: and animacy hierarchy,
  149; in Eastman, 95; embodied experience, 117–18; and
  kinship, 148; and out-of-doors,
  121; and performance, 148; and
  relationality, 22; and thióśpaye,

19; time as embodied encoun-
  ter with specific places, 106. *See
  also* performance
Bordeaux, Mary Sully (Deloria's
  mother), 184
Born, David O., 174
Boy Scouts of America, 1, 12, 117
*Boy Scouts of America Official
  Handbook,* 123
Bradley, George, 33, 39, 48
Brown, Joseph Epes, *The Sacred
  Pipe,* 151, 180–81
Bruyneel, Kevin, 92, 104
Buffalo Bill's Wild West, 150–51, 176
Bureau of Indian Affairs, ix, 92,
  152, 191, 228
Burke Act, 131, 264n8
Butler, Judith, 148, 185; *Gender
  Trouble,* 202
Byrd, Jodi, 102

Calhoun, James, 153
Calhoun, John, 92
Camp Fire Girls, 12, 117, 215
Canku, Clifford, xiv, 6, 40, 50, 56
capitalism: accumulation, 20, 22,
  27, 109, 170–71; anticapitalist
  opportunities, 30, 106, 161;
  corruption of, 105; ethic of
  sufficiency disturbs, 22–23;
  and land, 153; pausing as relief
  from, 27; and potlatch, 165; and
  time, 106, 115, 153
caretaking, 21–23, 26, 159, 235;
  and children, 203, 206–7; to
  hold each other's hearts, 24–26,
  267n74; and other-than-human
  persons, 195; and the Oyáte, 21,
  159, 213, 241; and women, 187,
  196, 203, 208, 220
Carlisle Indian School, 1, 89–90
Catholic Congresses, 175–77

Catlin, George, 150
Cavanaugh, Cap, 83–84
Cavanaugh, Percy, 232
Cavanaugh, Walt, 232
Cavender, Naomi, 214
ceremonialism, 154–55, 157–58,
  161; and gift, 171–72; memorial feast giveaway outlawed,
  158; potlatch, 165; vs. settler-
  colonialism, 172, 180. *See also*
  ethics; gift; performance
Ceremony (Silko), 4
Chakrabarty, Dipesh, 39
Charboneau, Rachel (née Young,
  author's grandmother), xiii, 35,
  137, 166, 221; interview with,
  61–87; multiple ways of belonging of, 26; picture of, x
Chase, Lillian (author's grandmother), 27–29, 36, 71–73, 80,
  86, 158–59, 183; interview with,
  221–33; Ínyaŋ Watháŋka (rock/
  woman story), 128–30; picture
  of, x
Chaske, John, 66
Chatterjee, Partha, 106
Chavis, Ben, 14
Cheyfitz, Eric, 10
children: care for, 203, 206–7;
  Indian Child and Welfare Act,
  25; "What Can the Out-of-
  Doors Do for Our Children?"
  (Eastman), 117, 120–22, 124
Chomsky, Carol, 42
Christianity, 7; Catholic Congresses, 175–77; conversion to,
  34, 38, 40, 56, 60; Dakhóta imprisoned by vocabulary of, 54;
  and Eastman, 119–20, 126, 128;
  and heterosexual individualism, 101; and inequality, 115;
  in letters from concentration

camps, 51–52; and settler-
  colonialism, 41; skepticism
  for, 57; small results of, 105;
  time after, 142; time before,
  141, 143; YMCA, 105, 119, 121,
  127–28. *See also* concentration
  camps; missionaries; religious
  conversion
Citizen Kane (Welles), 133–34
citizen kin, 133–34
citizenship: and civilization, 7,
  101; vs. critical relationality,
  22; Eastman on, 91, 97, 102,
  116, 120–21, 123, 126–27, 133,
  236; and heteronormative
  notions of biological legitimacy, 195; Indian Citizenship
  Act, 90, 267n72; and Indian
  Reorganization Act, 191–92;
  and Indians, 116–19, 133, 236,
  267n72, 268n75; as melodrama
  of monadic self, 20; in Minnesota, 7; missionaries preach
  ideals of, 47; reframing of, 124;
  and sovereignty, 267n72; and
  thióšpaye, 236; and tribal belonging, 134; and whiteness, 7
civilization: and citizenship, 7,
  101; to be civilized, 3, 185; in
  concentration camps, 38–39,
  47–49, 51, 59–60; Eastman
  on, 89, 105–6; and ethics, 189;
  and extermination, 41, 113; of
  Indians, 33, 47–48, 101, 175, 193,
  216; and the pause, 105; and
  savage, 39, 104, 120, 126, 201,
  271n1; warfare of, 105
Clark, William, 24
Clunan, Anne L., 155
Collier, John, 186, 191
colonialism. *See* decolonization;
  settler-colonialism

concentration camps, 33–49, 59–60; civilizational conversion in, 38–39, 47–49, 51, 59–60; countertranslations in, 39; critical responses to, 257n11; description of, 38, 41; experience of, 37–40, 48; extralegal status of, 42–43; and land theft, 45; letters from, 47–57; memorabilia of, 43–45; missionaries in, 47–48; picture of, 44; thióšpaye in, 39; transgressive adoptions in, 40; tribunals for, 42, 44–45; use of term, 257n9. *See also* ethnic cleansing; extermination; reservations

Congressional Record, 122

Cook-Lynn, Elizabeth, 240–41

Coolidge, Sherman, 2

Corntassel, Jeff, 14, 20

cosmology: and other-than-human, 53, 162; and peoplehood, xii; and politics, 103, 160; and relationality, 55, 99, 110; and spirits, 54–55

Cotera, Maria, 186

Coulthard, Glen, 21

countertranslation: in concentration camps, 39; conditions for, 44; decolonial, 44; and density, 12–13; and Eastman, 92–93; and opacity, 12–13, 94, 188; and power, 34, 39; of settler-colonial vocabularies, 34. *See also* ruse; translation; withholding

courage, 211–12; decolonial, 103, 151, 169–70, 173–74, 181, 207. *See also* decolonization

Court, Ignatius, 228–29, 232, 284n12

cover art (of this book), 16

critical relationality, 21–22, 30, 103, 135, 148–49; as mode of place-making, 108–9, 111–13; as ontology, 56, 96–97, 102, 107–8, 126–31; as temporality, 22, 100, 107, 153, 238. *See also* relationality; thióšpaye; wakhán

Crow Hill, 61, 63, 66–67, 77, 128, 141, 145, 228, 230–31

culture/nature distinction, 103, 190

Curly Bear, 179–81

Curtis, Edward, 16

Custer, George A., 4, 150, 153, 156

Cycles of Conquest (Spicer), 14

Dakhóta culture, opacity of, 12–13, 94, 188

Dakhóta language. *See* language

Dakota Access Pipeline, ix

Dakota Prisoner of War Letters, The (Canku & Simon), 40

Dakota Texts (Deloria), 185–86, 194, 199

Dakota Way of Life, The (Deloria), 187, 204, 206, 209

Dawes Act, 31, 101, 152, 191, 264n8

Dayan, Colin, 18

decolonization: and animal stories, 99–100; and Black Elk, 150–51; and countertranslation, 44; and Deloria, 213; in encounters with oppressive others, 162; and ethics, 18; and gender and sexuality, 19; and gift, 115, 164, 173; and horse dance, 161, 171, 221; Indigenous questioning of heteronormativity, 149; #NoDAPL, ix; and peoplehood, 14; radical decolonial relationality, 18; radical indigenism, 11; in *Red*

Hunters, 111; relationality as restructuration of tradition for, 22; resurgence at Standing Rock reservation, ix–x; and settler-colonialism, 173; and thióšpaye, 159; and translation, xii–xiii, 9, 188; unheroic decolonizer, 4, 16, 21, 92, 147–51, 181; water is life, ix–x, 21; in *Waterlily,* 197. *See also* resurgence; settler-colonialism

Deloria, Ella Cara, 1, 19, 183–220; on adoption obligations, 25; on avoidance, 204–6; background of, 184–85; on being unrelated, 172; "Dakota Autobiographies," 192–97; *Dakota Texts,* 185–86, 194, 199; *The Dakota Way of Life,* 187, 204, 206, 209; and decolonization, 213; and Eastman, 189–90; ethnographic work, 187–88, 192, 202, 204; on female independence, 203–5; first language of, 184; on gender roles, 185, 187, 197–213, 220; "Incest" in *Dakota Texts,* 199–201; and Indian Reorganization Act, 190; on kinship, 103, 185, 202, 209–10; "The Life-Story of a People, for the Indians of Robeson County and Adjacent Areas" (pageant), 215–16; on matrilineality, 202–3; and pageants, 186, 215–20; and relational decolonization, 22; "The Rock-Cave Dweller," 112; *Speaking of Indians,* 3, 37–38, 97, 125–26, 183, 185, 189; on thióšpaye, 18, 37–38, 102; on Valandry's story, 193–94; *Waterlily,* 31, 183–213, 216,

220; "The Wohpe Festival" (pageant), 186, 216; "A Woman Kills Her Daughter," 194–96; and women, 186–87, 216–17

Deloria, Philip (historian), 2, 12, 93; *Playing Indian,* 93

Deloria, Philip Joseph (Ella Cara's father), 184

Deloria, Vine, Jr. (historian, Ella Cara's nephew), 108, 151

DeMallie, Raymond, 30, 53, 110, 149, 177, 211

DeMarce, Frank, 231

DeMarce, Sylvester, 230

density, 12–13

Densmore, Frances, 166

devil, 141–42, 222, 283n3

Devils Heart, 66–67, 222

Devils Lake, 29, 33, 63, 77, 137, 141, 269nn1–2, 285nn13–15

Devils Tooth, 68, 129–30, 142, 221–22, 224; naming of, 222, 283n3

diaspora, 44, 259n29

difference: and indigeneity, 187; and liberalism, 17; vs. settler-colonialism, 197; and translation, 12–13

domestic dependent nations, 10, 15, 42, 265n30

Driskill, Qwo-Li, 148–49

Du Bois, W. E. B., "The Modern Conscience in Relation to Racial Questions (The Negro and the American Indian)," 116

Duhamel, Alex, 174

Duhamel, Bud, 174, 179

Duhamel Indian Pageant, 150, 173–81; and gift, 177; opacity of, 179; representation of, 176–78, 180

Dykema-Vanderark, Tony, 96

INDEX

Eastman, Charles Alexander, 1, 15, 18, 89–135; animal stories, 94, 97–100, 102, 104–5, 107, 115, 189, 214; and assimilation, 90–91; autobiographical sketches of, 2; childhood and conversion of, 89; and Christianity, 119–20, 126, 128; on citizenship, 91, 97, 102, 116, 120–21, 123, 126–27, 133, 236; on citizenship, Indian, 116–19; on civilization, 89, 106; as Dakhóta philosopher, 3, 96; and Deloria, 189–90; *From the Deep Woods to Civilization,* 30, 89–90, 100, 105, 115, 120, 128; *Indian Scout Talks,* 12, 90, 95, 117, 123–26, 132; *The Indian To-day,* 117–19, 123–24, 127, 131, 135; on land, 46, 111, 135; liberalism in, 118; on matrilineality, 202–3; name of, 132; on nation, 106, 115; "The North American Indian" (talk), 115–16, 119, 125; on physical education, 121, 124, 126–27, 202; racist vocabulary in, 118; *Red Hunters and the Animal People,* 30, 97, 100, 103–6, 109–11; and relational decolonization, 22; on relationality, 94, 99; ruses in, 95; "The Sioux Mythology," 55, 110; *The Soul of the Indian,* 100, 113, 127, 202; and storytelling, 235; thióšpaye in, 97, 99–100, 102, 119, 122; and translation of names for allotment, 131–32; as translator, 91, 131; treaty language in, 116, 125; "Wechah the Provider," 22–23; "What Can the Out-of-Doors Do for Our Children?," 117, 120–22, 124; white reception of, 90–91,

94–96, 103–4, 127; and withholding, 92–96; on world's first treaty, 113–14
Eastman, Jacob, 89
Education (journal), 121
egg story, 35–36, 79
Emancipation Proclamation, 43
Engels, Friedrich, 113
equality, 105
essentialism, 11, 15; and Dakhóta language, 13; vs. ethics, 236; and Indian Reorganization Act, 152
ethics, 18–19; and avoidance, 204–6, 209; of careful listening, 104; and civilization, 189; of countertranslation in concentration camps, 34, 59–60; and decolonization, 18; in Eastman, 95, 100; vs. essentialism, 236; at forefront of Dakhóta endeavors, 25; of friendship, 125; and gender, 217–18; generosity, 30, 58, 105, 128, 220; and gift, 114–15, 158, 160, 162, 170–71; to hold each other's hearts, 24–26, 267n74; hospitality, 176, 198–99, 201, 219; and Indians, 97; and personhood, 18, 149; and politics, 238; potlatch, 165; and relationality, 102–3; and resurgence, 184; of sufficiency, 22–23, 30, 60, 99, 103, 108–9, 147, 149, 181, 235, 238; and territory, 173; training for white people in Indian ethics, 124–26; and *wištélkiya* (to be bashful towards), 204. *See also* relationality; thióšpaye
ethnic cleansing, 33–34, 96, 157; embodied Dakhóta pasts

recoverable despite, 121; and governance, 157; Minnesota founded on, 34; Religious Crimes Code, 56, 148; and reservations, 33, 91, 156–57; thióšpaye continues despite, 159; United Nations Convention on the Prevention and Punishment of the Crime of Genocide, 257n9. *See also* allotment; assimilation; execution of Dakhótas at Mankato; extermination; reservations

ethnography: Deloria's, 187–88, 192, 202, 204; and entrapment, 188; and refusal, 11; and tradition, 11

execution of Dakhóta at Mankato, 5–7; ephemera of, 43–45; and land theft, 46; largest mass execution in United States, 42; tribunals before, 7–8, 42, 44–45; Whipple's protest against, 156

extermination: and civilization, 41, 113; and concentration camp ephemera, 43; cultural camouflage aids response to, 1; embodied Dakhóta pasts recoverable despite, 121; as engine of rusing, 17; vs. ethics, 161; Governor Ramsey calls for, 17, 34–35; literary depictions of the Oyáte after violence of, 2; and pronouncement of the Oyáte, 4; and storytelling, 237; United Nations Convention on the Prevention and Punishment of the Crime of Genocide, 257n9; of wolves, 112–13. *See also* allotment; assimilation; ethnic cleansing; execution; reservations

Fanon, Frantz, 162, 197
Faribault, David, Jr., 48
feasting, 56, 58–59
feminist theory, 19–20
Finley, Chris, 148
Foucault, Michel, 202
friendship, 116, 125, 189, 200, 235–36
From the Deep Woods to Civilization (Eastman), 30, 89–90, 100, 105, 115, 120, 128

Garcia, Louie, 227
Gardner, Susan, 188
Gates, Henry Louis, Jr., *The Signifying Monkey,* 94–95
Gates, Merrill, 101
gender and sexuality: and allotment, 195–96, 202, 208, 213; and Black Elk, 151; in Deloria, 185, 187, 197–213, 220; and ethics, 217–18; feminist theory, 19–20; gender binary, 10, 148, 185, 187, 197, 203, 210–11, 213, 220; gender violence hinders Indigenous relationality, 19–20, 200–201; "Incest" in *Dakota Texts,* 199–201; and kinship, 201–2; matrilineality, 202–3; paternalism, 116–17; perpetual virgin, 186–87, 213; polygamy, 208–9; and settler colonialism, 11, 19, 22; and thióšpaye, 199–202, 220; third gender, 186, 210, 216; in *Waterlily,* 197–98, 200–201, 210–12; wíŋkte, 212–13. *See also* heteronormativity; heterosexuality; marriage; masculinity; women
Gender Trouble (Butler), 202
General Allotment Act. *See* Dawes Act

generosity, 30, 58, 105, 128, 220
genocide. *See* ethnic cleansing
ghost dance, 192–93
gift, 103, 106, 114–15, 128, 130, 132, 147, 149; anthropology on, 164–65; and ceremonialism, 171–72; and decolonization, 115, 164, 173; and ethics, 114–15, 158, 160, 162, 170–71; generosity, 30, 58, 105, 128, 220; giveaway, 57, 158–59; and horse dance, 166, 170; hospitality, 176, 198–99, 201, 219; and Indian pageant, 177; memorial feast outlawed, 158; potlatch, 165; and power, 114–15; and religion, 114, 164; and temporality, 238; and thióšpaye, 164; and únšika (pitiful), 57, 158, 170. *See also* caretaking; ethics; peoplehood
Gift, The (Mauss), 165
Gilley, Brian Joseph, 148
Glissant, Édouard, 179
Godfrey, Joseph, 7–8
Godfrey, Joyzelle, 188, 203
Goeman, Mishuana, 150
Going Native (Huhndorf), 93
Goll, Louis J., 176
Goodhouse, Louie, 82, 229, 232–33
good relative, 25, 37–39, 51, 97, 102, 110, 114, 154, 185, 189, 236
Gourd, Israel, 230
governance, 156–57; and ethnic cleansing, 157; and Indian Reorganization Act, 191; and Indigenous territoriality, 155; and liberalism, 17; Native Americans incorporated into national system of, 267n72; and nonstate actors, 155–56; and peoplehood, 99, 115. *See*

also nation(s); peoplehood; politics; self-determination; sovereignty
Grant, Ulysses, 156–57
Great Mystery, 53–56, 109–10, 119–20, 216. *See also* Wakháŋ Tháŋka
Green, Marianne, 84

habitus, 118
Hale, Eugene, 28, 86, 137, 221
hanging. *See* execution of Dakhótas at Mankato
Hansen, Claude, 179–81
Hansen, Frances, 179–81
Hauptman, Laurence M., 192
Hazelwood Republic, 7
hearts, to hold each other's, 24–26, 267n74
Ȟé Sápa (Black Hills), 23, 140, 150, 153–58, 174–75, 180
heteronormativity: decolonial questioning of, 149; and Indian Reorganization Act, 152; institutionalization of, 148; and notions of biological legitimacy, 195; and translation, 10. *See also* gender and sexuality
heterosexuality: and allotment, 185; and citizenship, 101; compulsory, 20; vs. kinship, 190. *See also* gender and sexuality
Holm, Tom, 14
homestead law, 64
honoring, 102
Hopkins, Robert, 48, 56–57
horse dance, 76, 161–63, 166, 168–71, 177, 221–23, 238, 283n6; and decolonization, 161, 171; and gift, 166, 170; and thióšpaye, 162
hospitality, 176, 198–99, 201, 219

INDEX

Hoxie, Frederick, 191
Huhndorf, Shari, *Going Native,* 93
human beings: and animals, 98, 100, 109, 113–15, 125; and kinship, 189; and other-than-human, 107, 110; and wolves, 111–12. *See also* Indians; Indigenous peoples; medicine men; missionaries; white people
huŋkádowaŋpi, 25

identity: and allotment, 195; and definition of Indians, 152–53; and embodied experience, 117–18; and gender, 195–96; of Native peoples, 14; and oral histories, 107; and race, 194–95; and storytelling, 215. *See also* gender and sexuality; masculinity; subjects/subjectivity; women
imprisonment. *See* concentration camps
"Incest" (in *Dakota Texts*), 199–201
Indian Child and Welfare Act, 25
Indian Citizenship Act, 90, 267n72
Indian Reorganization Act (IRA), 1, 21, 31, 152–53; and assimilation, 191–92; and citizenship, 191–92; and definition of Indians, 152–53; and Deloria, 190; and ethnographic entrapment, 188; goals of, 191; Indian reorganization policy, 17; and self-determination, 186, 188; and tribal survival, 186
Indians, 152–53; and citizenship, 116–19, 133, 236, 267n72, 268n75; civilization of, 33, 47–48, 101, 175, 193, 216; and

ethics, 97; "the Indian," 97, 119, 123–24, 152–53; Indianness, 12, 60, 99, 117, 122, 153, 176, 191–92; and intermarriage, 8, 80; "The North American Indian" (Eastman), 115–16, 119, 125; playing Indian, xiii, 19, 93–94, 97, 126, 134, 174; and white people, 78, 123; wild Indians, 92, 94, 124–25, 128, 173. *See also* Indigenous peoples; Native Americans; playing Indian
Indian Scout Talks (Eastman), 12, 90, 95, 117, 123–26, 132
Indians Playing Indian (Siebert), 93
Indian To-day, The (Eastman), 117–19, 123–24, 127, 131, 135
Indigenous literatures, 237, 241
Indigenous peoples: communitism of, 2; decolonial questioning of heteronormativity, 149; and density, 12–13; as domestic dependent nations, 10, 15, 42, 265n30; and gift, 114–15; and governance, 156–57; humanization of, through performance, 178; radical indigenism, 11; resisting multicultural incorporation through performance, 94; and sovereignty, 11, 14, 20, 39, 240–41; United Nations Declaration on the Rights of Indigenous Peoples, 253n47; World Council of Indigenous People, 253n47. *See also* peoplehood
Indigenous studies, xi, 10–11, 13–14, 20, 101, 249n2
Indigenous theory, 183
individualism: and allotment policy, 20; and American Indian

298 INDEX

writers, 2; and Bataille, 165; and citizenship, 101; Indian Reorganization Act aims to halt, 191; institutionalization of, 148; vs. kinship, 103, 190; kinship ensures against isolation, 189; and land as abstract category, 119; and language, 13–14; and liberal bargain, 192; missionaries preach ideals of, 47; and religion, 180; and sovereignty, 189; state constructed, 101

inequality, 105, 128; and Christianity, 115

inípi, 127

Interludes (in this book), 27–29, 137, 183, 221, 236, 238

Íŋyaŋ, 129–30, 155, 195; and power, 129–30

Íŋyaŋ Watháŋka, 128–30, 183–84, 221–22, 283n3, 284n9

Išnáwiŋ (Lone Woman, author's great-great-grandmother), 71–74

Jacobs, Sue-Ellen, 212

Jefferson, Thomas, 47

Jungle Book (Kipling), 30, 98

Justice, Daniel Heath, xii

Kane, Charles Foster, 134

Kellogg, Laura Cornelius, 2

Kelsey, Penelope Myrtle, 90, 99

kettle dance, 139, 179

kinship: as aim of Dakhóta life, 185; and allotment, 192; and ambivalence, 236; avoidance, 204–6; and bodies, 148; citizen kin, 133–34; and Dakhóta language, 9; Deloria on, 103, 185, 202, 209–10; extended beyond heterosexuality, 148; extended

beyond human beings, 18, 160; extended to tourists, 173–74; and female independence, 203–5; and gender, 201–2; and gift, 158; and land, 133; letters on, 48–49; and liberalism, 103, 189–90; and oral histories, 104; and other-than-human, 128; and peoplehood, 239; and polygamy, 209; as protection against isolation, 189; vs. racism, 190, 193–94, 197; and relationality, 110, 115, 172, 189; rules of, 37–38, 201–2, 204–6; U.S. failure to uphold, 111; and violence, 239; widening of, 103. *See also* thióšpaye

Kipling, Rudyard, *Jungle Book,* 30, 98

Kuokkanen, Rauna, 170–71

Lakȟóta: ceremonialism, 154–55, 157; land tenure practices, 154; and settler-colonialism, 16–17

Lakota Belief and Ritual (Walker), 41

Lambert, Grace (author's grandmother), xiii, 26–28, 130, 135, 166–68, 225, 227, 229, 232; interview with, 61–87, 137–45; picture of, x; on U.S.–Dakhóta War, 35–36

land: as abstract category in liberalism, xii, 119, 153, 157; allotment policy and theft of, 131, 152, 191; animal stories and, 99; concentration camps and, 45; Dakhóta exiled from homeland by treaty, 6, 23, 111, 231; Dakhóta never say "this is my land," 140–41; Dawes Act replaces communal holdings of,

101; definition of territory fuels intertribal warfare, 93; Eastman on, 46, 111, 135; embodied Dakhóta pasts recoverable despite theft of, 121; execution of Dakhóta for, 46; farms/farming, 63–65, 138; and gift, 130; and heterosexuality, 20, 148; and Indian Reorganization Act, 191–92; and kinship, 133; Lake Traverse Treaty, 269n1; and matrilineality, 202–3; missionaries break up community holdings of, 47; and nonstate actors, 155–56; no record of lease to Indians, 77; as other-than-human relative, 21, 97, 102; ownership of, 63–64; and politics, xii, 116, 157; and racism, 152; and relationality, 134; and religion, 108; right of soil, 152–53; and settler-colonialism, 133; and thióšpaye, 102–3, 111, 160; and training in Indian ethics, 124–25; as way of knowing, 21. *See also* nature; reservations; territory

Landau, Loren B., 156

language: and animals, 98; archive of Dakhóta language, 137; Christian vocabulary imprisons Dakhóta, 54; and citational practices, 9; and concentration camp experience, 39–40; Dakhóta language, 9, 12–13; Dakhóta language teaching program, 27, 137, 221; Dakhóta letter "h" (nonguttural), 256n91; Dakhóta terms, 9, xii, xiv, 9, 247; and definition of Indian, 152–53; double voicedness, 94–95; and

individualism, 13–14; instrumental, 122; Lakȟóta letter "ȟ" (guttural), 256n91; and performance, 13; problematic translation of Treaty of Traverse des Sioux, 24–26; and storytelling, 215; and treaties, 116, 125; Wazíyatawiŋ on, 9, 13. *See also* legibility; letters; names; oral histories; representation; storytelling; translation

Laubin, Gladys, 177

Laubin, Reginald, 177

laughter, 130

Lea, Luke, 23

legibility, 3, 10, 60, 91–92, 94, 96, 101, 121, 131, 147, 188, 195; community remaking illegible to settler-colonialism, 8–9; of future-oriented Oyáte, 188; Scott on, 91, 133; and settler-colonialism, 17, 39; and sovereignty, 31; and translational withholding, 34; and translation of names for allotment, 131. *See also* letters; names; representation; translation

letters, 34, 37, 39–40; from concentration camps, 47–57; *The Dakota Prisoner of War Letters,* 40; extermination as backdrop for, 43; on kinship, 48–49; and thióšpaye, 40, 50–51, 60; translation of, 48, 50–51, 53

liberalism: and citizenship, 101; and Dakhóta peoplehood discourse, 3; and difference, 17; in Eastman, 118; and kinship, 103, 189–90; and land as abstract category, 119, 153, 157; liberal bargain, 190, 192; other-than-human relations exceed, 22; people-hood challenges atomized family of, 100; and property, 115; and representation, 18; and self-determination, 236; and thióšpaye, 102; and understanding of Dakhóta experience of concentration camps, 39

Liffman, Paul M., 155

lightning, xii–xiii, 13, 28, 71, 74–75, 77, 142, 169, 200, 235

Lincoln, Abraham, 8, 42–43

Lippincott's Magazine, 98

literacy training, 34, 39–40; by missionaries, 47–48

literature: Indigenous, 241; Native American, 2, 237, 240; and remaking of the Oyáte, 16

Little Crow (Thaóyate Dúta), 5–6, 33, 35, 46, 259n36

Lomawaima, K. Tsianina, 90, 250n2

Longie, Francis, 84

Longie, Louie, 83

Looking Horse, Arvol, 154–55

Lyons, Scott, 99; on definition of Indian, 152–53; on Indigenous peoplehood, 10, 14; on nation form, 15; on purity, 239; on translation from *ethnie* to nation, 15; *X-Marks,* 239

Maddox, Lucy, 92, 101

Mahmood, Saba, 16, 18, 20, 97

Maine, Henry Sumner, 155

Makhá Iná Mániwiŋ (Walks the Earth Woman), 83, 166–67, 283n2

Mankato, 5–7

marriage, 8, 80; and animacy hierarchy, 149; and matrilineality, 203; polygamy, 208–9

Martínez, David, 42, 96, 119

Marx, Karl, 113

masculinity, 19; and courage, 211–12; of Dakhóta/Lakhóta warriors, 6–7, 19, 30, 43, 150; and gender binary, 220; and horse dance, 283n6; and hospitality, 198; hypervisibility of Dakhóta warrior, 43; Indigenous vs. white, 150–51; and matrilineality, 203; paternalism, 116–17

matrilineality, 202–3

Mauss, Marcel, 164–65; *The Gift,* 165

McCay, Luke, 80

McDowell, Tony, 85

McKay, Alphone, 229

Medicine, Beatrice, 213, 217

medicine men, 139, 143–44, 154; banning of, 56

Mehta, Uday Singh, 157

Merrick, Joe, 227–28

Merrick, Louie, 228

Million, Dian, 19, 183

Minnesota, founded on genocide, 34

missionaries, 47–48; impressions of Dakhóta religion, 55, 58–59; impressions of relationality, 58; imprison Dakhóta with Christian vocabulary, 54; indigenization of, 59; and thióšpaye, 101

modernity: nation as hallmark of, 15; on nature, 124; and temporality, 106

Monson, Tamlyn, 156

Montezuma, Carlos, 2

Morgan, Henry Lewis, 155

Morgan, Terry, 45

Morgenson, Scott Lauria, 148

Morrison, Kenneth, 26, 114–15, 164
Morton, Gary Saul, 94–95
Myrick, Andrew, 36

names/naming: and allotment, 131–33; before Christianity, 143; Crow Hill, 145; Devils Tooth, 283n3; Lakȟóta, 16; and places, 283n3; Sullys Hill, 285n14; and thióšpaye, 160; of tribes, 140; in *Waterlily*, 196–97
nation(s): and animal stories, 100; and belonging, 10, 39; and blood, 240; critique of, 239; domestic dependent, 10, 15, 42, 265n30; Eastman on, 106, 115–17; as hallmark of modernity, 15; Indigenous peoples as, 10, 15; nationhood, 10, 15, 106, 115; Native thought lives in, 123, 134; and peoplehood, 10, 103, 237, 239; and politics, 115, 238; and settler-colonialism, 10–11; and sovereignty, 10; and temporality, 106; tribal, 99, 134
nationalism: and Indigenous literatures, 241; transnational critique of, 239
Native Americans: and citizenship, 267n72; and Indigenous studies, xi, 10–11, 13–14, 20, 101, 249n2; literature, 2, 237, 240; "The North American Indian" (Eastman), 115–16, 119, 125; and politics, 116
nature: and culture, 103, 190; location of, 119; out-of-doors, 117, 120–22, 124, 126; and thióšpaye, 124
Neihardt, John, 30, 151, 159, 161
New York Times, 5–7, 175
#NoDAPL, ix

normalcy, 148, 187
nuclear family, 10, 31, 101, 148, 187

obedience, 70–71
Očhéti Šakówiŋ Oyáte, ix–x, 212, 214, 236; use of term, 249n2
Office of Indian Affairs, 17, 215
oneness, 110
ontology of earth, 96–97, 102
opacity, 12–13, 94, 188. *See also* ruse; withholding
oral histories, 13, 46–47, 95, 235–37; archive of Dakhóta language, 137; and collective identity, 107; in Eastman, 97–98, 104; and ethic of careful listening, 104; and the Oyáte, 236; and peoplehood, 236–37; and thióšpaye, 235–36; Wazí yatawiŋ on, 104, 107, 236–37. *See also* Interludes; storytelling
Ostler, Jeffrey, 154
other-than-human: as bodies, 22; and caretaking, 195; and cosmology, 53, 162; in Eastman, 95, 99–100; and ethics, 23; and gift, 128; and human beings, 107, 110; kinship extended to, 18, 133; and land, 21, 97, 102; and names, 133; and performance, 137; as relatives, 21; and territory, 151; and thióšpaye, 97, 102, 114, 160, 199–200; use of term, 255n75
out-of-doors, 117, 120–22, 124, 126
Owens, Louis, 237
Oyáte: coded representation of, 17, 150; conditions for survival of, 44; constitution of, 219–20; earliest literary representations of, 2; and horse dance, 161; and legibility, 188; literary remaking

of, 16; Očhéti Šakówiŋ, ix, 236, 249n2; and oral histories, 236; origins of, 159; and politics, 235; pronouncement of, 4; relations of care make and remake, 21, 159, 213, 241; and representation, 181; and resurgence, 184, 241; rupture of, 4–5, 33; and storytelling, 61; and territory, 119; and thióšpaye, 102, 235; and transnational critiques of peoplehood, 238; unassimilability of, 134; use of term, 249n2; and women, 187

pageants. *See* performance
Parker, Arthur, 2
paternalism, 116–17
pause/pausing, 22, 27, 238; as embodied encounter with specific places, 106; and storytelling, 105; use of term, 255n76
Peacock, John, 8, 48
Pearson, Diane, 14
Pearson, Myra, 45
peoplehood, xii, 14–16; and animals, 98–99; and atomized family in liberal nation-state, 100; and cosmology, xii; Dakhóta discourse of, 3; and definition of Indian, 153; and Deloria, 220; and Eastman, 92; emergence of, 16, 241; and gift, 115; and governance, 99, 115; and kinship, 239; and nation, 10, 103, 237, 239; and nationhood, 115; and oral histories, 236–37; and politics, 9, 16, 238, 253n47; and power, 30, 60, 115; production of discourse of, 3; and purity, 14, 239; question of, 9; and relationality, 103, 236–37; and

resurgence, xi; and sovereignty, 14, 253n47; and subjectivity, 117; and thióšpaye, xiii, 3–4, 37–38, 97, 101–3, 238; transnational critiques of, 238–39; widening web of, 160, 179; and withholding, 148. *See also* caretaking; gift; governance; nation(s); other-than-human; politics; sovereignty
performance: and Black Elk, 150, 162, 173–74; and bodies, 148; Deloria and pageants, 186, 215–20; Duhamel Indian Pageant, 150, 173–81; Lakȟóta ceremonialism, 154–55, 157; and other-than-human, 137; and settler-colonialism, 236; and territory, 149; and travel, 150; Wild West show, 150–51, 176. *See also* bodies; ceremonialism; ethics; ghost dance; gift; horse dance; kettle dance; oral histories; storytelling; sun dance
personhood: and ethics, 18, 149; and neoliberal subjectivity, 20; and relationality, 270n1
Pexa, Donna (author's mother), 35, 61
Piatote, Beth, 19–21, 100, 250n2
Pike, Zebulon, 23
Pine Ridge reservation, 63, 66, 85, 172, 174, 177, 181, 216, 221
pity, 57; únšika (pitiful), 57, 158, 170. *See also* ethics
playing Indian, xiii, 19, 93–94, 97, 126, 134, 174, 219
Playing Indian (P. Deloria), 93
politics: and Black Elk, 152; and cosmology, 103, 160; in Eastman, 99–100, 102; and ethics, 238; and land, xii, 116,

157; and nation, 115, 238; and Native Americans, 116; and other-than-human relations, 114; and the Oyáte, 235; and peoplehood, 9, 16, 238, 253n47; as playing Indian, 174; of recognition, 17; right of soil, 152–53. *See also* governance; nation; peoplehood; self-determination; sovereignty

polygamy, 208–9

Pond, Gideon, 38–39, 53

potlatch, 165

Pourier, Olivia Black Elk, 174–75

Povinelli, Elizabeth, 11, 17, 44, 96

power: in *Citizen Kane,* 134; in concentration camps, 37–38, 49; and countertranslation, 34, 39; and critical relationality, 22; decolonial, 161, 168–69, 181; and emplaced living, 23; and gift, 114–15; and Íŋyaŋ, 129–30; and kinship, 197; and other-than-human, 135, 137, 144, 154–55, 162, 164, 199–200, 216–17, 240, 275n73; and peoplehood, 30, 60, 115; and remaking the Oyáte, 16; and resurgence, 20; and settler-colonialism, 161; sharing of, 54–57, 60, 99, 103, 114–15, 156, 160, 163, 170, 179, 220, 238; and translation, 56; and treaties, 24; and Wakháŋ Tháŋka, 54–55; and women, 187–88, 198, 208, 212–16, 218, 220

Powers, William K., 57, 158

proliferation, 148; and withholding, 12–13

property ownership: and allotment name translation, 131–33; Dawes Act replaces communal landholdings, 101; and gender, 196; and gift, 132; and heterosexuality, 148; and Indian Reorganization Act, 191; and liberalism, 115; lifelessness of, 22, 97, 190; and matrilineality, 203; missionaries preach ideals of, 47; nature instrumentalized by, 103; right of soil, 152–53

Provençalle, Antoine, 48

purity, 11, 239–40; and peoplehood, 14, 239. *See also* blood; race/racism

race/racism: and allotment, 192; animal stories as analog to, 98; and blood, 152, 192, 195, 239–40; Eastman as spokesman of his race, 90; in Eastman's vocabulary, 118; ethnographic entrapment, 188; and identity, 194–95; vs. kinship, 190, 193–94, 197; and land, 152; as liberal bargain, 190, 192; "The Modern Conscience in Relation to Racial Questions" (Du Bois), 116; and nation, 239; racial uplift for Indians, 2; and settler-colonialism, 194–96. *See also* Indians; whiteness; white people

Races Congress: Du Bois's talk at, 116; Eastman's talk at, 115–16, 119, 125

radical indigenism, 11

Ramsey, Alexander, 17, 23, 34–35

Red Hunters and the Animal People (Eastman), 30, 97, 100, 103–6, 109–11; and Dakhóta storytelling, 104; decolonization in, 111; and relationality, 110

relationality: ambivalence as crisis of, 56–57; and animal stories, 102; and bodies, 22; and caretaking, 203, 206–7; and cosmology, 55, 99, 110; Eastman on, 94, 99; and ethics, 102–3; good relative, 25, 37–39, 51, 97, 102, 110, 114, 154, 185, 189, 236; to hold each other's hearts, 24–26, 267n74; intergenerational, 121–22, 138, 206; and kinship, 110, 115, 172, 189; and land, 134; literature on, 270n1; missionaries on, 58; and peoplehood, 103, 236–37; and personhood, 270n1; radical decolonial, 18; as restructuration of tradition for decolonization, 22; and resurgence, 21; settler-colonialism as lack of, 161, 164; and social non-existence, 172; and territory, 157; and thióšpaye, 97, 102, 148, 160, 173. *See also* critical relationality; ethics; kinship; peoplehood; thióšpaye

religion: as definition of "the people," 14; and gift, 114, 164; and hospitality, 176; and individualism, 180; and land, 108; Religious Crimes Code, 56, 148, 208; theistic view of, 52–55; translation of, 41, 120; of white people, 105. *See also* Christianity; missionaries

religious conversion, 34, 38, 40, 51, 53; and concentration camps, 59; and missionaries, 47–48, 60. *See also* Christianity; concentration camps; missionaries

Remember This! (Waziyatawiŋ), 214

Renville, Gabriel, 45

representation: of Black Elk, 151–52; coding of, 17; concentration camp memorabilia, 43; critical Indigenous theorizing of, 92; of Indian pageants, 176–78, 180; liberal vs. Dakhóta, 19; and the Oyáte, 181; and peoplehood, 14; and performance of indigeneities, 15; refusing totalizing forms of, 11; and resurgence, 20; and settler-colonialism, 148

reservations, 63–65, 81–82; and Black Elk's traveling performances, 173–77, 181; confinement on, 37, 148, 153, 156–57, 161; Deloria born on, 184; Eastman's tours of, 119–20; and ethnic cleansing, 33, 91, 156–57; Great Sioux Nation, 149, 157; horse dance as decolonizing ceremony on, 161, 171, 221; and "Indian" defined, 152; life before, 2, 99–100, 117, 124, 130, 134, 139, 185, 203; Pine Ridge, 63, 66, 85, 172, 174, 177, 181, 216, 221; Standing Rock, ix–x, 184; survival of Lakhóta thióšpaye on, 149; tribes present on, 140, 228; unfit for individualizing citizenship, 101; Whipple's solution to the "Indian problem," 156–57; and white people, 62–65. *See also* concentration camps

resurgence, 17; Eastman and covert, 92, 134; everyday acts of, 20; letters provide evidence of, 34; and nation form, 15; and the Oyáte, 184, 241; and peoplehood, xi; and power,

INDEX 305

20; and relationality, 21; and
representation, 20; and ruse/
rusing, 4; at Standing Rock reservation, ix–x; and tourism, 181;
in wake of U.S.–Dakhóta War,
184. *See also* decolonization
Rice, Julian, 166, 168–69
Rifkin, Mark, 10, 19–20, 31, 93,
101, 117, 186–88, 195, 202, 213,
220, 250n2; *When Did Indians
Become Straight?*, 212
Riggs, Stephen R., 24, 38, 41,
47–54, 56–57; indigenization
of, 59; religiosity misunder-
stood by, 53; translation difficulties of, 53–54, 57, 59–60
right of soil, 152–53
Roosevelt, Theodore, 131
Rosebud Agency, 66, 140, 158;
census of 1885, 16
Rowe, John Carlos, 152
ruse/rusing, 4, 94; in Deloria, 187;
in Eastman, 95; and with-
holding, 124–25, 187. *See also*
countertranslation; opacity;
translation; withholding

Sa'ar, Amalia, 190
sacred, 141, 144–45, 164. *See also*
critical relationality; wakháŋ
Sacred Lake, 140–42
Sacred Pipe, The (Brown), 151,
180–81
sacrifice, 164–65, 167–68, 200
Sagyékituŋ, Mr., 49–51
Salome, Mary, 229
Santees, 89, 139–40, 228
savage, 6, 47, 92–93, 98, 176; and
civilization, 39, 104, 120, 126,
201, 271n1; savagely authentic,
xiii
Scott, James C., 34, 91, 133

Scow, Mick, 20
Sedgwick, Eve Kosofsky, 89, 92
self-determination, 236–38; and
embodied experience, 117; and
Indian Reorganization Act, 186,
188, 190; as liberal ideal, 236;
problematic of, 237–38
Senier, Siobhan, 2
Seton, Ernest Thompson, 1
settler-colonialism: animal stories
as critiques of, 99–100; and
authenticity, 91; vs. ceremonialism, 172, 180; and Christianity,
41; civilizing Indians by imprisonment, 33–34; community
remaking illegible to, 8–9; and
concentration camps, 39; criticism of, 3; and decolonization,
173; vs. difference, 197; and
Eastman, 92, 98–99; vs. ethics,
102, 161; and ethnographic
entrapment, 188; execution of
Dakhóta, 5–7; Fanon on, 162;
and gender and sexuality, 11,
19, 22; vs. gift, 115, 164; and
Indigenous density, 13; as lack
of relationality, 161, 164; and
Lakhóta, 16–17; and land, 133;
and legibility of colonized,
17, 39; letters as response to,
40; and modern subjects, 101;
and nation form, 10–11; and
overconsumptive capitalistic
relations, 22–23; pausing as relief from, 27; and performance,
236; and politics, 116; and
pronouncement of the Oyáte,
4; and racism, 194–96; and
representation, 148; resistance
to, 160; at root of heteronormativity, 148; and rupture of the
Oyáte, 4–5; transforms family

via Dawes Act, 101; and translation, 10, 237; and U.S.–Dakhóta War, 37, 93, 153

Seven Council Fires. *See* Očhéti Šakówiŋ Oyáte

sexuality. *See* gender and sexuality

shaming, 113–15; shame histories, 195

Sibley, Henry Hastings, 35, 41, 43

Siebert, Monika, *Indians Playing Indian,* 93–94

Siems, Monica, 54–55

Signifying Monkey, The (Gates), 94–95

Silko, Leslie Marmon, 28; *Ceremony,* 4

Silva, Denise Ferreira da, 188

Simon, Michael, 40, 50, 56

Simpson, Audra, 11, 29, 188

Sixth Grandfather, The (Black Elk), 30, 149, 272n10

Slow Buffalo, 159–60, 173, 181

Smith, Andrea, 188

Smith, Linda Tuhiwai, 133

Society of American Indians (SAI), 90, 119, 131; and racial uplift, 2

Soul of the Indian, The (Eastman), 100, 113, 127, 202

sovereignty, 148–49; and citizenship, 267n72; and critical relationality, 149; in Eastman, 99, 115–18, 120–21; and Indigenous peoples, 11, 14, 20, 39, 240–41; and individualism, 189; and nation form, 10; nonstate articulations of, 156; and peoplehood, 14, 253n47; problematic of, 30, 237–38; and subjectivity, 20, 117; tribal, 31, 92–93, 134, 241; and unheroic

decolonizer, 92. *See also* governance; nation(s); peoplehood; politics; self-determination

Speaking of Indians (Deloria), 3, 37–38, 125–26, 183, 185, 189; on thióšpaye, 3, 97

Spicer, Edward, *Cycles of Conquest,* 14

spirits, 54–55; and *Waterlily,* 196

Standing Bear, Luther, 102, 112; *Stories of the Sioux,* 112

Standing Rock reservation: decolonial resurgence at, ix–x; Deloria born on, 184

starvation, 5–6, 35–37, 41, 46–47, 78–79, 111

Steltenkamp, Michael, 152

St. Nicholas: An Illustrated Magazine for Young Adults, 2

Stoler, Ann, 19

Stories of the Sioux (Standing Bear), 112

storytelling: academic vs. tribal, 28; and Eastman, 235; Eastman's animal stories, 94, 97–100, 102, 104–5, 107, 115, 189, 214; egg story, 35–36, 79; and extermination, 237; family stories, 26–28; hithúŋkaŋkaŋpi (long-ago stories), 95, 100, 104–5, 107, 214–15, 235; and identity, 215; as Indigenous theory, 183; Interludes (in this book), 27–29, 137, 183, 221, 236, 238; Íŋyaŋ Watháŋka (rock/woman story), 128–30, 142, 184, 222, 224, 283n3; and the Oyáte, 184; and pause, 105; ram/spoonhorn story, 106–8; in *Red Hunters,* 104; Slow Buffalo story, 159–60, 173, 181; and

thióšpaye, 220; Wazíyatawiŋ on, 61, 105, 214–15, 235–37; and white people, 227, 284n11; and women, 61, 213–15, 220. *See also* oral histories; performance
Straight, Nancy, 80
subjects/subjectivity: as constitutive of Dakhóta interiority, 125; and ethnographic entrapment, 188; and peoplehood, 117; vs. persons, 270n1; and sovereignty, 20, 117; state constructed individual, 101, 148, 236
sufficiency, 22, 30, 60, 99, 103, 108–9, 147, 149, 181, 235, 238
Sully, Alfred, 35
Sullys Hill, 229, 231, 285n14
sun dance, 66, 136–37, 139, 155, 175–76, 179, 207
Sword, George, 54–55
syncretism, 39

TallBear, Kim, 22, 147, 149; on caretaking, 159, 235; on thióšpaye as migratory social form, 160
Taté Tópa Tribal School, 137, 221
Taylor, Diana, 95
Taylor, Eli, 27
tease/teasing, 16–17. *See also* ruse; withholding
temporality. *See* time/temporality
territory, 21; and ethics, 173; as fueling intertribal warfare, 93; Indigenous vs. settler territoriality, 155; Lakȟóta, 149–51, 153; and other-than-human, 151; and the Oyáte, 119; and performance, 149; and relationality, 157; right of soil, 152–53; thióšpaye as basic unit

of, 160; and time, 149; and travel, 176; and treaty violations, 156; U.S. Supreme Court rules illegal seizure of, 157–58. *See also* land
thióšpaye, 3, 147–51; and animal stories, 99, 102; as being a good relative, 38; and Black Elk, 151; and bodily practices, 19; bridging cosmology and politics, 160; and citizenship, 236; in concentration camps, 39; continual remaking of, 103; at core of peoplehood, 37–38; and critical relationality, 21, 103; and decolonization, 159; defined, 3, 37, 102; Deloria on, 18, 37–38, 102; despite ethnic cleansing, 159; in Eastman, 97, 99–100, 102, 119, 122; and gender and sexuality, 199–202, 220; and gift, 164; and horse dance, 162; and land, 102–3, 111, 160; and letters, 40, 48, 50–51, 60; as migratory social form, 160; missionaries aim to supplant ties of, 47–48; and nature, 124; beyond nuclear family, 21; and oral histories, 104, 235–36; and other-than-human, 97, 102, 114, 160, 199–200; and the Oyáte, 102, 235; and peoplehood, xiii, 3–4, 37–38, 97, 101–3, 238; and polygamy, 208–9; and relationality, 97, 102, 148, 160, 173; resurgence of, 4, 181; and storytelling, 220; and territory, 150; threatened by concentration camps, 59; and treaties, 23; and unheroic decolonialism, 147–51; use

of term, 249n1; *Waterlily* on, 186–87, 197–98, 207, 209; and women, 203–4

third gender, 186, 210, 216

Thomas, Robert, 14

Thunder Beings, 166, 168, 170

time/temporality: and capitalism, 106, 115, 153; and critical relationality, 22, 100, 107, 153, 238; in Eastman, 99, 104–5; as embodied encounter with specific places, 106; and gift, 238; and modernity, 106; and nation, 106; pause/pausing, 22, 27, 105–6, 238; and sovereignty, 20; and territory, 149

Tinker, George, 41

Tokaheya, 52–53

Tokio (North Dakota), 61–63, 65, 227–28

tourism: and Black Elk's performances, 162, 173; and ceremonial performances, 155; and consumable authenticity, 12; as humanizing of Indigenous peoples, 178; kinship extended to, 173–74; and pronouncement of the Oyáte, 4; thióšpaye resurgence in, 181. *See also* white people

Trachtenberg, Alan, 102

translation, 237; of "church," 59; in concentration camps, 39; of Dakhóta names for allotment, 131–33; of Dakhóta terms, 9, xii, xiv, 9, 247; decolonial, xii–xiii, 9, 188; Eastman as translator, 91–93, 131–32; from *ethnie* to nation, 15, 34; fluency of, 12, 96; of "God," 51, 54–55, 121–22, 216; and heteronormativity,

10; inadequacy of English-- language equivalents, 9; of kúŋši, 213; of Lakȟóta names, 16; of letters, 48, 50–51, 53; and power, 56; and religion, 41, 120; Riggs's difficulty with, 53–54, 57, 59–60; of "Savior" concept, 56–57; and settler-colonialism, 10; of "sorry," 13; of Treaty of Traverse des Sioux, 24–26; two forms of, 12–13; of unčí, 213; of wakȟáŋ, 51–55; of Whakȟáŋ Tȟáŋka, 51, 53–55; of wíŋkte, 212–13; of Wohpe, 216, 218–19, 282n116. *See also* countertranslation

travel: annual caravan to Duhamel Indian pageant, 174, 178; Black Elk's traveling performances, 173–77, 181; Catholic Congresses, 175–77; and performance, 150; and territory, 176; thióšpaye as migratory social form, 160

treaties: and annuities withheld, 6, 37, 46, 111; Dakhóta exiled from homeland by, 6, 23, 111; failure to deliver on promises of, 46–47, 150; and Indigenous peoples as nations, 10, 15; and language, 116, 125; and pause of activity, 22; and power, 24; and rations withheld, 35; and subjectivity, 236; and thióšpaye, 23; violations of, 156–58; world's first, 113–14

Treaty of Fort Laramie, 149, 153, 157–58

Treaty of Lake Traverse, 269n1

Treaty of Traverse des Sioux, 6, 23–24, 111, 267n74

Trinkunas, Harold A., 155
Trouillot, Michel, 33, 41
Tuck, Eve, 93

Underhill, Ruth, 151
unheroic decolonizer, 4, 10, 16, 21, 92, 147–51, 181
United Nations, 14; Convention on the Prevention and Punishment of the Crime of Genocide, 257n9; Declaration on the Rights of Indigenous Peoples, 253n47
Uŋktéȟi, 26, 75–76, 221–22, 270n6, 283n1 283n5
únšika (pitiful), 57, 158, 170
Upton, Benjamin F., 42
U.S.–Dakhóta War: ambivalence of Dakhóta in, 7–8; causes of, 5–6, 23, 34, 36, 47, 93, 111, 114, 256n2; historiographical erasure surrounds, 33; human costs of, 34; Lambert on, 35–36; legal proceedings nonexistent, 42; name of, 256n2; resurgence in wake of, 184; and settler-colonialism, 37, 93, 153; and treaty violations, 156; use of term, 256n2. *See also* concentration camps
U.S. government: concentration camps as spectacles for, 43; drafting of soldiers, 212; kinship failure of, 111; permissible indigeneity in, 17; treaties ignored by, 23
U.S. Supreme Court: on illegal seizure of Dakhóta territory, 157–58; on Indigenous peoples as domestic dependent nations,

15; *U.S. v. Sioux Nation of Indians,* 157
utopianism, 106, 113, 124, 134

Valandry, Emmy, 192–97; renunciation of kinship by, 193–94
Valencia-Weber, Gloria, 189
Venuti, Lawrence, 12, 96
Vigil, Kiara, 2, 90, 119
Vizenor, Gerald, 16

Wakan, James Hepan, 49
Wakantanka, 51, 54
wakháŋ, 9–10, 51–55, 75. *See also* critical relationality; ethics; gift
Wakháŋ Tháŋka, 51, 53–55, 109–10
Wakíŋyaŋ, 74, 166, 168, 170
Walker, James R., 129–30, 158, 216; *Lakota Belief and Ritual,* 41, 54
Warrior, Robert, 2, 91, 237, 240, 252n34
wašíču (fat-takers), 26, 134, 255n86, 283n3, 284n11
water: Mní Wičhóni, ix; as other-than-human relative, 21; water protectors, x, 241
Waterlily (Deloria), 31, 183–213, 216, 220; accomplishment of, 220; decolonization in, 197; gender in, 197–98, 210–12; newborn baby linked with water-lilies, 196–97; summary of, 185–86; on thióšpaye, 186–87, 197–98, 207, 209; on women and storytelling, 213, 220
Wazíyatawiŋ, 37–38; on academic vs. tribal goals, 28; on concentration camps, 257n9; on Dakhóta terms, 9, 13; on family stories, 27; on female independence, 203–4; on Minnesota's

founding, 34; on oral histories, 104, 107, 236–37; *Remember This!*, 214; on storytelling, 61, 105, 214–15, 235–37; on translation of treaties, 24–25
wealth, and inequality, 105, 128
Weaver, Jace, 2, 240, 252n34
Welles, Orson, *Citizen Kane*, 133–34
Westerman, Gwen, 24
Wheeler-Howard Act. *See* Indian Reorganization Act
When Did Indians Become Straight? (Rifkin), 212
Whipple, Henry, 156–57
White, Bruce, 24
White, Charlie, 78, 232
White Buffalo Calf Woman, 53, 110, 155, 163, 180–81, 188, 216, 275n55, 282nn116–17
whiteness: and allotment policy, 20; and citizenship, 7; and purity, 239; transgressive adoption of, 40
white people: and accumulation, 171; acting as if they have no relatives, 111; civilizational superiority claims of, 41; claiming Minnesota as fruit of genocide, 34; as concentration camp tutors, 39; in Dakhóta letters, 49; Dakhóta peoplehood discourse unintelligible to, 3, 176; Dakhóta term for, 26; Eastman on, 115; Eastman's reception by, 90–91, 94–96, 103–4, 127; failure to share wealth, 105; hate speech of, 92, 120; Indian ethics training for, 124–26; and Indians, 78, 123; and Indigenous performance, 178; intermarriage with Dakhóta, 8,

80; and land theft, 134, 231–33; living like, 63–64; and out-of-doors, 121; playing Indian, 97; print fetishized by, 51; religion of, 105; and reservations, 62–65; and storytelling, 227, 284n11; thióšpaye distinguishes Dakhóta from, 59; transgressive adoptions from, 40; unlawful violence of, 43, 46–47, 57, 60; whiteman complex, 194; and wolves, 112–13. *See also* race/racism; tourism
Wilcox, Dwayne, 16
wild animals, 98, 125, 127
wild Indians, 92, 94, 124–25, 128, 173
wildness, 118, 124–25, 128
Wild West Show, 150–51, 176
Williams, Robert A., 114
Williamson, Thomas, 41, 50, 53, 58–59
Wilson, Raymond, 215
wíŋkte, 212–13
Wissler, Clark, 216
withholding, 124–25, 127–28; and ambivalence, 91; Eastman and poetics of, 92–96; gender and sex in Deloria, 187; and peoplehood, 148; and proliferation, 12–13. *See also* countertranslation; opacity; ruse
Wohpe, 186, 216–19, 282n116
wolves, 111–12; and white people, 112–13
Womack, Craig, 240, 252n34
women: and caretaking, 187, 196, 203, 208, 220; and Deloria, 186–87, 216–17; female independence, 203–5; feminist theory, 19–20; Íŋyaŋ Watháŋka (rock/woman story), 128–30;

matrilineality, 202–3; and mourning, 71; nonreproductive female sexuality, 199–200; polygamy, 208–9; and power, 187–88, 198, 208, 212–16, 218, 220; and soldiers, 78; and storytelling, 61, 213–15, 220; and thióšpaye, 203–4; wíŋkte, 212–13. *See also* gender and sexuality

World Council of Indigenous People, 253n47

Wounded Knee, 2, 91, 131, 152, 173, 192–93

X-Marks (Lyons), 239

Yang, K. Wayne, 93

Yankton, Alex, 223

Yankton, Roger, 230

YMCA, 105, 119, 121, 127–28

Young, Adele (author's great-grandmother), 83

Young, Gabe (author's uncle), 62

Young, Lydia (author's grandmother), 71, 74, 167; picture of, x

Christopher Pexa (Spirit Lake Dakhóta) is assistant professor of English at the University of Minnesota, where he is also affiliated with American Indian studies.